Leadership

Leaders, Followers, and Context

A Volume in Research in Human Resource Management

Series Editors

Dianna L. Stone
Universities of New Mexico, Albany, and Virginia Tech
James H. Dulebohn
Michigan State University

Research in Human Resource Management

Dianna L. Stone and James H. Dulebohn, Series Editors

Founding Editor Rodger Griffeth, *Ohio University*

Leadership: Leaders, Followers, and Context (2022)
edited by James H. Dulebohn, Brian Murray, and Dianna L. Stone

Research Methods in Human Resource Management: Toward Valid Research-Based Inferences (2020)
edited by Eugene F. Stone-Romero and Patrick J. Rosopa

Diversity and Inclusion in Organizations (2020)
edited by Dianna L. Stone, James H. Dulebohn, and Kimberly M. Lukaszewski

The Only Constant in HRM Today is Change (2019)
edited by Dianna L. Stone and James H. Dulebohn

The Brave New World of eHRM 2.0 (2019)
edited by James H. Dulebohn and Dianna L. Stone

Human Resource Management Theory and Research on New Employment Relationships (2016)
edited by Dianna L. Stone and James H. Dulebohn

Human Resource Strategies for the High Growth Entrepreneurial Firm (2016)
edited by Robert L. Heneman and Judith Tansky

IT Workers Human Capital Issues in a Knowledge Based Environment (2006)
edited by Tom Ferratt and Fred Niederman

Human Resource Management in Virtual Organizations (2002)
edited by Robert L. Heneman and David B. Greenberger

Innovative Theory and Empirical Research on Employee Turnover (2002)
edited by Rodger Griffeth and Peter Hom

Leadership

Leaders, Followers, and Context

Edited by

James H. Dulebohn
Michigan State University

Brian Murray
University of Dallas

Dianna L. Stone
Universities of New Mexico, Albany, and Virginia Tech

IAP

INFORMATION AGE PUBLISHING, INC.
Charlotte, NC • www.infoagepub.com

Library of Congress Cataloging-in-Publication Data

CIP record for this book is available from the Library of Congress
http://www.loc.gov

ISBNs: 978-1-64802-664-5 (Paperback)

978-1-64802-665-2 (Hardcover)

978-1-64802-666-9 (ebook)

Printed in the United States of America

CONTENTS

CHAPTER 1

LEADERSHIP RESEARCH AT THE CROSSROADS OF LEADERS, FOLLOWERS, AND CONTEXT

Brian Murray, James H. Dulebohn, and Dianna L. Stone

ABSTRACT

As we enter the third decade of the 21st century, we are seeing a renaissance of context in studies of leadership, leader-follower relations, and leader effectiveness as well as a recognition of the tripartite nature of leadership. To fully understand and appreciate leadership, one must see the multiple parts of it as well as the connections among them. In this introductory chapter, we review the chapters included in the present volume of the *Research in Human Resource Management* series, which is dedicated to a contemporary examination of leadership theory and research. In the volume, an outstanding roster of established and emerging leadership authors tackle questions of leadership at the intersections of leaders, followers, and context. Among the issues addressed are emerging trends in leadership research, theory development and integration for leadership and diversity, inclusion, and identity, perspectives on leader-member relations, theory refinements and applications of authentic leadership, and systems of leadership exploring the toxic triangle, a microprocess model of power's role, and configurational study of leadership elements and substitutes. The volume also includes an essay recommending improvements to the conduct of management and leadership research.

Leadership:
Leaders, Followers, and Context, pp. 1–13

> *Leaders don't exist in a void, nor can they lead without followers. As someone has noted, if a man runs down the street yelling that he's going to save the world, and someone follows him, then he's a charismatic leader. If no one pays any attention, he's a lunatic.* (Padilla, 2012, p. 3)

The study of leadership has employed multiple perspectives across several decades of research. A large body of literature has focused on the leader, the patterns of leader behavior, and the leader's traits and other characteristics (Dinh et al., 2014; Lord et al., 2017; Zhao & Li, 2019). A growing body of literature has emerged regarding the follower and the follower's characteristics and behavioral responses to the leader (e.g., Leroy et al., 2012; Owens et al., 2015). At various points in time, the context, environment, or situation has taken a central role in explaining leader and follower decisions, behaviors, or effectiveness (e.g., Baker et al., 2011; Gardner et al., 2019). Connections among leader, follower, and environment have long been examined in studies of pairings between leader and environment or follower, such as leader member exchange (Graen & Cashman, 1975; Graen & Scandura, 1987; Liden & Maslyn, 1998). Finally, there is a cadre of leadership scholars who have developed a systems perspective of how leader, follower, and environment interact simultaneously to drive leadership outcomes (e.g., Kellerman, 2016; Padilla et al., 2007; Whittington et al., 2013).

This volume in the *Research in Human Resource Management* series adopts the interactional lens in its chapters by examining connections among leaders, followers, and context as well as the dynamics of the leadership system as a whole. The authors for this volume present leadership questions, derive understanding from the literature, and propose models and implications that integrate leaders, followers, and environment. Figure 1.1 illustrates a conceptual map of our positioning of this volume's authors on a leader-follower-context triangle. While the specific applications of leadership theories vary among authors, they share in common the contemporary focus on the connections among the leadership triangle's components either bilaterally or as a tripartite system. Together the collected body of work in this volume addresses the question of what current and future leadership theory and research looks like at the crossroads of leaders, followers, and context.

How We Arrived at the Crossroads and Where We Are Headed

Whether by traditional methods of literature review or innovative application of artificial intelligence and mapping, leadership researchers

Figure 1.1

Mapping of Articles on the Leadership Research Triangle

have identified consistent trends in topics and informed our understanding of the underlying conceptual structure of the field (e.g., Dinh et al., 2014; Lord et al., 2017; Zhao & Li, 2019). In this volume, Bommer, Milevoj, and Biggane (Chapter 3) joined this conversation in their review of 21st century leadership trends. From an action-oriented perspective, they examined the patterns in research production for who was doing the research, where or with what samples was the research being conducting, and what methods were being applied. They found trends of a growing diversity of scholar origin with a significant increase in Chinese scholars, a transition from neo-charismatic leadership research to a broader base of theoretical perspectives, and an increase in multilevel analysis. Among the growing areas of research interest, they identified abusive leadership, ethical or moral approaches, and social exchange and relationship frameworks with particular attention to leader-member exchange (LMX) theory.

Bommer and colleagues' observations about the trends in leadership topics complements their predecessors' conclusions. Zhao and Li (2019) reported a comprehensive review of the leadership literature from 1990 to 2017 and demonstrated that the most frequently studied leadership topics included transformational leadership, LMX, and charismatic leadership; however, they pointed out a recent decline in the study and publication of charismatic and transactional leadership. They also identified a growth in trends for ethical, authentic, and abusive leadership. Dinh and colleagues (Dinh et al., 2014) in a review of the leadership literature between 2000 and 2012 identified the dominance of neo-charismatic leadership as well as emphases on information processing and social exchange and relational approaches dominated by LMX. Lord and colleagues (Lord et al., 2017) in a review of influential leadership studies published in the *Journal of Applied Psychology* identified what they termed "The Third Wave" as a focus of recent research on transformational and charismatic research, LMX, gender, and team leadership. Together these reviews point to a dominant emphasis across the last 30 years on research about neo-charismatic leader style or approaches to leading and the relationship between the leader and the follower. Over this time period, though, the emphasis on transformational and charismatic leadership has waned, and the reviews highlighted the growing diversity of emerging perspectives.

Consistent with the over-arching theme of the present volume, leadership research may be heading down a path where leader style and behaviors and leader-follower relationships are incorporated with research that is particularly sensitive to context. Looking to the future, Bommer and colleagues (Chapter 3) speculated that we may be entering a time for a reemergence of situational perspectives in leadership research. Prior comprehensive reviews support Bommer and colleagues' expectations. In their review, Dinh and colleagues (Dinh et al., 2014) observed a rise in research emphasizing context in the century's first decade, but claimed it to be "an under-researched topic, given the central importance of context to the emergence and manifestation of leadership processes" (p. 41). Among many directions future leadership research may take, Lord and colleagues (Lord et al., 2017) pointed out its potential to be responsive to contextual elements such as multigenerational workforces, shared leadership structures, and the changing nature of work due to technology, virtual interactions, and working at a distance. They also considered dark leadership concerns that may arise due to sociopolitical, demographic, and crisis-driven change and competition, and observed that "a great deal needs to be learned about what instigates the emergence of abusive or destructive forms of leadership focusing on the leader, followers, and context, which is relatively under-researched in this journal" (p. 446). In their discussion of future leadership research, Zhao and Li (2019) suggested that leadership research would be well served by studies of the contextual boundaries to existing theories.

The authors in the present volume contribute to the conversation on leadership as intersections among leaders, followers, and context from several perspectives. We present the chapters first with a look at diversity and inclusion to answer the questions of who the leaders are, how might the diversity of potential leader voices be nurtured and supported, what contributes to the quality of the relationship between the leader and follower, and under what conditions are relationships among leaders and followers fostered that allow for expression of individual voice while supporting a shared commitment to overall goals. Second, we turn our attention to a set of chapters that focus on the leader-follower relationship relative to context. The questions addressed by these authors include how leader-member exchange might exist in a team context to improve performance, what are contextual barriers to authentic leader-follower relationships, and how does authentic leadership influence follower behaviors and responses to affect the harassment climate in organizations. The third set of chapters considers phenomena incorporating the full system of leaders, followers, and context. They address questions of how power is manifest in leadership as a process, how organizations enable and do or do not learn from destructive leadership, and how multiple configurations of leader, follower, and context may similarly affect important outcomes or differentially affect the outcomes at high versus low levels. The volume opens with an invited essay on doing meaningful research to establish a context for future leadership research.

Diversity and Inclusion at the Crossroads of Leader, Follower, and Context

Leadership is slowly beginning to reflect the broader realties of demographic representation in the workforce. New voices are being heard by leaders and as leaders in organizations. Leadership research is informing who those voices are, what is being heard, how they are being regarded, and what they mean for leader-follower relationships in the future. In this volume, Cheng, Bilotta, Lu, and King (Chapter 4) lay out an examination of diversity theories in juxtaposition to established theories of leadership. They explain how stereotype and context both feed and reinforce within self-decisions and perceptions about being a leader as well as interpersonal interactions and resources that influence opportunity and development.

Cheng and colleagues' discussion has the potential to augment recent findings and conclusions in leadership review research about opportunities for future research. In their network assessment of leadership topics, Zhao and Li (2019) identified leadership emergence and development as an identifiable cluster and found that among its components were studies of gender, diversity, and age. By the connections present or absent in the network, they reported that there were a substantial number of links among these constructs and all other constructs on their leadership network map. They suggested that where there are more links, a topic is broadly studied within the network, and where there are fewer links, there is an opportunity to generate new knowledge. Cheng and colleagues' presentation suggests that some of the links in and extending from the leader emergence and development cluster may need to be reexamined in light of diversity theory and social identity. Likewise, contextual research connections may need to be formed or strengthened by examination of organizational processes as systematic oppression in the development and evaluation of potential leaders.

Cox (Chapter 5) complements the work of Cheng and colleagues by extending the question of representation and diversity to the question of inclusion. Cox develops a theoretical perspective for the alignment of diverse individuals toward a common goal while advancing individuals' unique identities and perspectives, sense of belongingness, and respectful relational practices. Cox further proposes an interaction between diversity and inclusion to explain organizational outcomes. Cox's development of inclusive leadership as a leadership theory is grounded in correlations with both trait and behavioral aspects of the leader. He also shows its relationship to LMX and authentic leadership. He closes his discussion with a consideration of culture as a potential contextual boundary for his theory of inclusive leadership.

While Cheng and colleagues raised the question of social identity and Cox considered relational aspects of inclusive leadership, Sharif and Scandura (Chapter 6) round out the volume's examination with a deep-dive assessment of immigrant ethnic identity and its implications for leader-member relationships. Their theory development illuminates how followers' prioritization and compartmentalization of immigrant ethnic identity affects the resultant LMX as well as how cultural intelligence on the part of both the leader and follower interacts in determining LMX. In their discussion Sharif and Scandura firmly ground their propositions in issues of context. They assert that "the extent to which there is a climate of diversity in an organization is important for the moderating effects of cultural intelligence. Being in an organization that is tolerant and supportive of diversity is very different than being in one that is discriminatory" (Chapter 6). Taken together, the work of Cheng and colleagues, Cox, and Sharif and Scandura set a path for future studies of leadership, diversity, inclusion, and leader-member relationships that incorporate contextual questions of organizational processes, climate, and cultural influence.

Leader-Follower Relationships in Context

The connection between the leader and follower has been an enduring topic in leadership study. Leader-member exchange and the quality of relationship had its origins over 40 years ago in studies of vertical dyad linkages (Dansereau et al., 1975; Graen & Scandura, 1987; Graen & Uhl-Bien, 1995) that have evolved to today's ongoing trends in contemporary leadership research (Bommer et al., Chapter 3; Zhao & Li, 2019). Leader-follower relationships are facing new work structures, such as teams, and work environments and technology, such as virtual teams and distanced teammates. They also are being managed within an environment of growing emphasis on authentic leadership which extends beyond the neo-charismatic styles of the most recent era. This changing environment evokes new research questions about how the leader-follower relationship may be more effectively managed and under what conditions leadership styles or behaviors influence the quality of the relationship.

Graen, Canedo, Johnson, and Grace (Chapter 7) introduce an extension of LMX that applies to the team context and the management of team member relations. As an example of Bommer and colleagues' (Chapter 3) observation that leadership research is increasingly incorporating multi-level questions and research methods, Graen and colleagues explore the question of leaders' relations not only with a subordinate but with a team of followers and as the leader of relationships among the team members. Their model considers subordinate, lateral, and superordinate relationships as drivers of organizational outcomes. Applying an alliance model for LMX, they introduce a set of factors organized as an *enhance-act-perform* process. An important contribution of their chapter is the discussion of the mechanism by which LMX-alliance can be managed to realize potential individual and organizational outcomes.

Undoubtedly LMX has been one of the most important conceptualizations of leader-follower relationships, and its intersection with authentic leadership is well represented in Gardner, Carlson, Gullifor, Cogliser, and Williams' (Chapter 8) examination of contextual barriers to authentic leader-follower relationships. Both Bommer and colleagues (Chapter 3) and Zhao and Li (2019) identified the emergence of authentic leadership as an important area of study within the last two decades, and other chapters within this volume adopt it as a basis of discussion within their studies (Cox, Chapter 5; Schmidtke & Walumbwa, Chapter 9). Gardner and colleagues contribute to the discussion of authentic leader-follower relationships by examining them relative to LMX theory and developing propositions about the contextual characteristics that limit the formation of authentic relationships. By identifying the contextual limits to the application of authentic leadership, the authors strengthen it as a theoretical perspective and improve its potential for future study and explanation of leader-follower-context dynamics.

While the largest portion of the interactional studies of leaders focus on the leader-follower side of the leadership triangle, Schmidtke and Walumbwa (Chapter 9) demonstrate the efficacy of studying the leadership triangle's leader-context side for developing leadership theory. They articulate a mechanism by which an authentic leader's modeling of behavior influences the followers' perceptions of the organization's climate relative to harassment and their consequent behaviors within that climate. They also propose a connection between authentic leadership style and the role the leader may play in facilitating and transforming the process for managing a harassment claim.

The chapters in this volume signal a path forward for leadership research that remains strongly grounded in studying the social exchange between leaders and followers; however, the next step in that research is to strengthen it by articulating its contextual boundaries and influence. As Gardner and colleagues (Chapter 8) demonstrated, the emerging leadership theories are more useful and hold greater promise for future research when we can fully articulate them by considering their contextual elements. For human resource researchers there is a lesson to be learned from Schmidtke and Walumbwa's (Chapter 9) study that they can play a significant part in advancing leadership research by coming at leader-follower relationships from the leader-context side of the triangle.

The Confluence of Leader, Follower, and Context

When elements of the leader, follower, and context converge, their outcomes may be different than those driven by any bilateral interactions among them. Conversely, various combinations of the three may each lead to the same outcome. Three chapters in this volume provide insight specifically to how the three elements of leadership combine and are necessary to one another in producing outcomes. Among the perspectives presented are the toxic triangle, a microprocess model of power and leadership, and a configurational approach to systems and leadership substitutes.

The present volume is led in this discussion by a team of authors respected for their development and articulation of the toxic leadership triangle and the joint necessity of destructive leaders, susceptible followers, and conducive environments to drive organizational outcomes. Lunsford, Padilla, and Mulvey (Chapter 10) build on past theory and research of the toxic triangle to both better explain negative episodes in organizations and to propose managerial implications for limiting or mitigating their occurrence. Beginning with an understanding that all three elements must be present in forms that foster destructive leadership, the authors examine the influence of two contextual elements, time and whistleblower protections, and the influence of LMX. Applying close examination of three destructive episodes at universities, Lunsford and colleagues show the necessity of the three elements, how leader-follower relations must be supported by or balanced against systems such as whistleblower processes in order to break the triangle's influence, the potential ambiguity of whether an actor is the leader or the follower, and how the triangle may develop over a long period of time.

Like Lunsford and colleagues (Chapter 10), Bastardoz and Day (Chapter 11) anchor their discussion of leadership in episodes. Bastardoz and Day present a process model of leadership that integrates the study of leaders with theory regarding power. They argue that successful goal directed leadership is a function of the interaction among power bases and context, leader characteristics and behaviors, and follower characteristics. They observe that leadership and its outcomes are not a singular interaction between leaders acting from positions power and their followers' response but are a series of episodes that commence with the activation of a power base leading to an influence attempt toward a goal that may or may not excite cooperation. The outcomes of the leader's influence attempts provide feedback to affect the power base and the leader's characteristics. They proposed several moderators encompassing leader motives, beliefs, personality, reputation, and credibility, contextual characteristics including whether it is beneficial to lead, and leadership is needed, and follower characteristics including openness to influence, belongingness needs, and identification. Fundamental to Bastardoz and Day's model is the incorporation of time. Leadership is a series of influence episodes that impact the leader's ability to influence in the future. Leadership is a microprocess that unfolds and develops over time as additional episodes occur, relies on characteristics of not only the leader but also the follower and context, and changes the leader's characteristics and effectiveness with each subsequent episode.

Whittington, Murray, and Bell (Chapter 12) complement Lunsford and colleagues' examination of the toxic triangle as a system of leadership relying on a specific configuration of elements. Whittington and colleagues expand the idea of leadership triangle configurations by considering their equifinality. Configurations with different levels and types of the leader, follower, and context elements may lead to the same outcome. They also challenge the prevailing linear, symmetric notion that elements relate to both the high and low levels of outcomes equivalently. They propose an asymmetry of effect such that different configurations of leader, follower, and contextual elements are related to high levels of outcomes than are related to low levels of outcomes. They further propose that configurations and their effects develop over time and may have different effects at different points in time. They support the utility of a configurational perspective relative to linear regression with a comparative examination of relationships among transformational leadership, LMX, trust, and job design configurations with follower outcomes including job performance, organizational citizenship behavior (OCB), and affective commitment.

In addition to exploring and demonstrating the leader-follower-context system, these three chapters, along with Gardner and colleagues' chapter (Chapter 8), introduce and advocate an additional contextual construct that will influence future leadership research: time. Time is not entirely new to leadership research and is gaining in the recognition of its importance (Dinh et al., 2014; McClean et al., 2019; Porter & McLaughlin, 2006; Thoroughgood et al., 2018). The chapters in this volume demonstrate that there is opportunity to further explore time's role in leadership, particularly in how it determines or interacts with the leader-follower-context system and the system's influence on individual and organizational outcomes.

Putting Leadership Research in Context

The volume opens with an essay by Locke and Latham (Chapter 2). The authors deliver a stern rebuke to management researchers and business schools for generating and rewarding scholarship that is disconnected from practical context. They advocate inductive theory development over deductive theory testing and lament the stunting of research streams when a single study reports a supportive finding. They offer several recommendations for improving the state of management research and incorporating relevance. Among them are calls for more emphasis on theory building, greater clarity, grounding, and succinctness in construct definitions, introductions, and discussions, and less emphasis on statistical sophistication and results creation and more emphasis on well designed, focused studies, practical significance, and replication.

There is a lesson in Locke and Latham's concerns for leadership scholars. In their reviews, Bommer and colleagues (Chapter 2), Lord et al. (2017), and Dinh et al. (2014) each pointed to forms of complex statistical analysis as a basis or enabler for trends and advances in particular streams of leadership research. Locke and Latham's admonitions remind leadership researchers not to let the statistical methods drive the research focus and not to let statistical ability to produce results supplant the practical relevance of the results for leadership in the real world as the measure of productivity and advancement of the field. The field of leadership research is influenced by the concerns raised by Locke and Latham as evidenced by all major leadership reviews' focus on elite journals, citations, and article production by a limited set of researchers.

While there is an undeniable grounding among the present volume's chapters in scholarship and theory indicative of the *Research in Human Resource Management* series, we believe they err toward the more favorable aspects of research discussed by Locke and Latham. They are a mix of perspectives ranging from those a practicing manager is less likely to read, understand, or find direct relevance in to those that speak directly to practice and have immediate implications such as Graen et al.'s (Chapter 7) discussion of implementing LMX-alliance in team based organizations, Schmidtke and Walumbwa's (Chapter 9) demonstration of authentic leadership's potential for managing harassment, and Lunsford et al.'s (Chapter 10) deconstruction and diagnosis of destructive leadership episodes in universities and their recurrence across institutions. The topics covered in this volume's chapters definitely are not trivial and speak directly to contemporary organizational issues such as diversity and inclusion (Cheng et al., Chapter 4; Cox, Chapter 5) and immigrant ethnic identity in the workplace (Sharif & Scandura, Chapter 6). Central to the theme of this volume, we believe the focus on situation or context predicted as a potential future trend by Bommer et al. (Chapter 3) and applied to theory and analysis by Gardner et al. (Chapter 8), Bastardoz and Day (Chapter 11), and Whittington et al. (Chapter 12) speaks well for where leadership research is going in the future. When leadership research is grounded in the context in which leaders encounter followers, it remains grounded in its historical roots as a practical and relevant field of study.

REFERENCES

Baker, S. D., Mathis, C. J., & Sites-Doe, S. (2011). An exploratory study investigating leader and follower characteristics at U.S. healthcare organizations. *Journal of Managerial Issues, 23*(3), 341–363. https://www.jstor.org/stable/23209120

Dansereau, F., Graen, G., & Haga, W. J. (1975). A vertical dyad linkage approach to leadership within formal organizations: A longitudinal investigation of the role making process. *Organizational Behavior and Human Performance, 13*(1), 46–78. https://doi.org/10.1016/0030-5073(75)90005-7

Dinh, J. E., Lord, R. G., Gardner, W. L., Meuser, J. D., Liden, R. C., & Hu, J. (2014). Leadership theory and research in the new millennium: Current theoretical trends and changing perspectives. *The Leadership Quarterly, 25*, 36–62. https://doi.org/10.1016/j.leaqua.2013.11.005

Gardner, W. L., Karam, E. P., Tribble, L. L., & Cogliser, C. C. (2019). The missing link? Implications of internal, external, and relational attribution combinations for leader-member exchange, relationship work, self-work, and conflict. *Journal of Organizational Behavior, 40*, 554–569. https://doi.org/10.1002/job.2349

Graen, G., & Cashman, J. (1975). A role-making model of leadership in formal organization: A development approach. In J. G. Hunt & L. L. Larson (Eds.), *Leadership frontiers* (pp. 143–165). Kent State University Press.

Graen, G. B., & Scandura, T. A. (1987). Toward a psychology of dyadic organizing. *Research in Organizational Behavior, 9*, 175–208.

Graen, G. B., & Uhl-Bien, M. (1995). Relationship-based approach to leadership: Development of leader-member exchange (LMX) theory of leadership over 25 years: Applying a multi-level multi-domain perspective. *Leadership Quarterly, 6*(2), 219–247. https://doi.org/10.1016/1048-9843(95)90036-5

Kellerman, B. (2016). Leadership—It's a system, not a person! *Daedalus, 145*, 83–94. https://doi.org/10.1162/DAED_a_00399

Leroy, H., Palanski, M. E., & Simons, T. (2012) Authentic leadership and behavioral integrity as drivers of follower commitment and performance. *Journal of Business Ethics, 107*, 255–264. http://dx.doi.org/10.1007/s10551-011-1036-1

Liden, R. C., & Maslyn, J. (1998). Multidimensionality of leader-member exchange: An empirical assessment through scale development. *Journal of Management, 24*(1), 43–72. https://doi.org/10.1016/S0149-2063(99)80053-1

Lord, R. G., Day, D. V., Zaccaro, S. J., Avolio, B. J., & Eagly, A. H. (2017). Leadership in applied psychology: Three waves of theory and research. *Journal of Applied Psychology, 102*, 434–451. https://doi.org/10.1037/apl0000089

McClean, S. T., Barnes, C. M., Courtright, S. H., & Johnson, R. E. (2019). Resetting the clock on dynamic leader behaviors: A conceptual integration and agenda for future research. *Academy of Management Annals, 13*, 479–508. https://doi.org/10.5465/annals.2017.0081

Owens, B., Wallace, A. S., & Waldman, D. A. (2015). Leader narcissism and follower outcomes: The counterbalancing effect of leader humility. *Journal of Applied Psychology, 100*, 1203–1213. https://doi.org/10.1037/a0038698

Padilla, A. (2012). *Leadership: Leaders, followers, and environments*. Wiley.

Padilla, A., Hogan, R., & Kaiser, R. B. (2007). The toxic triangle: Destructive leaders, susceptible followers, and conducive environments. *The Leadership Quarterly, 18*, 176–194. https://doi.org/10.1016/j.leaqua.2007.03.001

Porter, L. W., & McLaughlin, G. B. (2006). Leadership and the organizational context: Like the weather? *The Leadership Quarterly, 17*, 559–576. https://10.1016/j.leaqua.2006.10.002

Thoroughgood, C. N., Sawyer, K. B., Padilla, A., & Lunsford, L. (2018). Destructive leadership: A critique of leader-centric perspectives and toward a more holistic definition. *Journal of Business Ethics, 151*, 627–649. https://doi.org/10.1007/s10551-016-3257-9

Whittington, J. L., McKee, V., Goodwin, V. L., & Bell, R. G. (2013). Applying fuzzy set methodology to evaluate substitutes for leadership. In P. C. Fiss, B. Cambré, & A. Marx (Eds.), *Research in sociology of organizations (RSO): Configurational theory and methods in organizational research, 38* (pp. 279–302). https://doi.org/10.1007/s10551-016-3257-9

Zhao, H., & Li, C. (2019). A computerized approach to understanding leadership research. *The Leadership Quarterly, 30,* 396–416. https://doi.org/10.1016/j.leaqua.2019.06.001

CHAPTER 2

HOW CAN WE DO MANAGEMENT RESEARCH THAT IS VALID AND USEFUL?

Edwin A. Locke and Gary P. Latham

ABSTRACT

In this chapter, we question the usefulness of management research including the existing promotion and tenure (P&T) system in business schools. Ways of improving both are provided. We critique the current domination of the deductive method in developing theory, the focus on statistically focused articles that managers will not understand, the publication of articles that are written just for other scholars, and a reward system for research paperts that managers will never use. We suggest ways of changing business school policies to promote useful research and practical theory building, especially the method of induction. We identify numerous problems with the quality of published research and give suggestions for improvement.

The *Academy of Management Learning and Education* (AMLE) June 2012, and February, 2020 Special Section on Academic Research raised issues regarding the lack of actionable management research that have concerned us for years (e.g., Latham, 2001a, 2001b, 2011; Locke & Latham, 2020).

Leadership:
Leaders, Followers, and Context, pp. 15–27

The same issue was visited again in the June 2020 issue of AMLE. However, we believe that recommendations to rate management research as "actionable" is not useful (Bartunek & Egri, 2012; Pearce & Huang, 2012) because ratings by academics indicate nothing about whether managers would really use our research. Others have made similar critiques and argued that there is too much emphasis on theory (Tourish, 2020a, 2020b). Underlying this is a problem of what standards should be used to conduct and evaluate research.

Some years ago, the editor of the *Academy of Management Journal* (AOM) ended his presentation to an AOM doctoral consortium with the following advice: "Do good research that will help managers to manage better." After he left, Locke, who was to discuss how to do research, began his talk with the comment: "I'm sorry to tell you that managers do not read our journals. Your published research will only be read by management professors and their doctoral students." Why is this the case?

First, management articles in today's scholarly journals are too complex for managers (and sometimes for academics) to understand. For example, consider an article that focuses on many correlates of variable X. What is the likelihood a manager can find useful takeaways in such a study, over and above the issue of causal inference.? If an article includes advanced statistical analyses, most managers would not understand the results, especially if the results include complex regression methods that involve multi-level moderation, mediation, and moderated-mediation analyses. Most managers (and even many academics) would find such articles to be the norm in scholarly journals. It is likely that the results would be impossible to hold in mind and even incomprehensible. Meta-analyses do not necessarily help because they too are likely to involve many variables, and statistical results alone do not prove causality and knowing this is critical for application.

Second, let's say that a manager ignored the empirical studies and just looked at our theory articles. Our academic journals are presently committed to deductive rather than inductive studies even though the latter are a critical method for advancing science (Locke, 2007; Locke & Latham, 2020). Once deductions in a study are verified, often by just one study, the theory building process is often considered done.[1] A study's findings almost never accumulate based on additional studies because most journal editors want research on "new/hot" topics. Consequently, replications of studies today are difficult, if not impossible, to publish and hence are rarely conducted. Thus, the results of a given study, even if understood by managers, do not provide a solid scientific base that can be used confidently in application.

Inductively based theories are far more likely than one-shot deductive studies to be useful for managers, if they are written in a style that is understandable by them. Our support for induction is based on the philosophy of Aristotle. He believed that the senses are valid sources of knowledge of the world. Concepts and conceptual conclusions should be induced based on integrations of perceptual knowledge (experience). Aristotle was the first biologist to begin his work by systematically observing and dissecting numerous animals and plants. He formed conclusions based on these observations. In contrast, Plato considered the senses to be invalid and argued that knowledge was deduced from innate or intuitively derived ideas (e.g., the forms)—from reason divorced from the senses (Peikoff, 2012). The "ivory tower" metaphor, consistent with Plato's philosophy, represents a version of the deductive approach in that abstractions are put on a separate and allegedly "higher" plane and then attached to one another rather than concrete practices and results and thus are disconnected from reality. Papers of this ilk are, in practice, treated as ends in themselves rather than as useful guides to action—professors trying to impress each other with "theory."

Third, we believe that the most effective CEOs emphasize simplification through basic principles based on their integrations of myriad factual observations (Locke, 2008, 2009). Such principles would be based on observations about the real world of business that would have implications for the future (e.g., online sales seem to be growing fast) but could also be bets on the future (e.g., here is something that could be far more useful to customers or decision makers than what they have or do now).

So in relation a typical management article, we can ask:

- Are managers likely to see it?
- If they see it, will they understand it?
- If they understand it, will they see it as potentially useful for them?
- If yes, do they use it?

At the present time, the answers to each of these questions is likely to be "No."

Most managers find useful, innovative ideas elsewhere. Martin (2012), the former Dean of the Rotman School of Management at the University of Toronto, observed that very few of the 50 "top management thinkers" publish in academic journals. Moreover, many of these individuals are not even management professors. Leaders and managers get their ideas mainly from four sources in addition to their own personal discoveries:

- Business periodicals, such as articles in the *Harvard Business Review* (HBR) and *Organizational Dynamics,* to take two examples, are explicitly written for managers. The content has high credibility among businesspeople. There are no inferential statistics in those articles. Each article only makes a few key points. The articles are inductively based. They describe experiences in, or case studies of, an actual organization. In these respects, articles in business periodicals are radically different from those published in academic journals.

- Selected management books. These books are typically written by other managers based on their own experiences, academics with extensive consulting experience and by full-time consultants. These books tend to be free of jargon and complex statistical processes. Most such books are written in meaningful, memorable ways (e.g., see those written by Ram Charan, Peter Drucker, Roger Martin, Tom Peters, and Jack Welch).
- Scholar-practitioners. Only a handful of academics in business schools are scholar-practitioners whose writing influences the practice of management (e.g., Michael Beer, Ed Lawler, Jeffrey Pfeffer, Michael Porter)

The problem of pervasive "non-useful," non-actionable research on management is a systems issue. To paraphrase Mason Haire, "that which gets measured gets done." To be more accurate, that which gets measured in relation to the goals that are set gets done (Locke & Latham, 1990). Goals reflect the values of those who set them.

Many applied university departments, including business schools, have been viewed by academics as lacking in status relative to liberal arts faculties (e.g., psychology, sociology, economics, mathematics). This has resulted in business school departments (e.g., organizational behavior, organizational theory, strategy) being viewed as suspect by academicians outside the business school. (This is also partly because they find business research to be to "materialistic," i.e., to concerned with money rather than "ideas.") To increase their academic status, most business school deans urge their faculty to do "scholarly" research. This goal includes publishing in scholarly management journals. To become "pure" as organizational scientists, business school faculty have been rewarded for building theories deductively either as ends in themselves (pure theory) or through testing them through esoteric, quantitative analyses. This has led to the goal of separating ourselves from the world of business enterprise. For example, Martin (2012) quoted a member of his faculty who boasted that he has never even visited a business. Moreover, this faculty member views this fact as indicative of his identity as a "pure" scholar in the sense advocated by Plato. Studying business, presumably, would be, by implication, "impure."

Deans of business schools are typically hired in large part to take steps to ensure their respective business schools attain and maintain a "good scholarly reputation," not just within the university, but in the eyes of other business school Deans, as well as the media who rank business schools (e.g., *Business Week, The Financial Times*). This usually requires the hiring of outstanding academic scholars. Outstanding scholars are generally viewed as people who publish articles that are cited by other scholars in scholarly journals. Currently, pursuing the goal of becoming an outstanding scholar does not include influencing the behavior of managers.

Most Deans ensure that both the P&T and the pay systems reward scholarship defined primarily, if not solely, as publishing in highly-ranked, scholarly journals, and being cited in articles written by other scholars. Based on the frequency that a journal is cited in scholarly articles, a journal itself is ranked as top tier, second tier, third tier etc. In short, just about everyone in academia is "preaching to the choir."

Contributing to this systems problem is the obvious fact that the vast majority of academics have bought into this system. The goal or goals for becoming a "successful" academic are specific and challenging: (1) publish in top tier academic journals where the rejection rate approximates 90% or higher. For some schools this is all that is needed, given that a scholar's teaching ratings and service are adequate. Other schools demand more: (2) high teaching ratings from students and/or (3) outstanding service on committees that increase the business school/university's effectiveness or visibility. Actionable research findings for managers is not an articulated goal for the overwhelming majority of business school faculty. Consulting services for managers are allowed by Deans, but only to a limited extent (e.g., often 1-day per week). Consulting services for managers is not rewarded by most Deans. Publishing articles and books written explicitly for managers rarely influence a tenure and promotion decision favorably. Worse, business schools (and peers) may view doing so as negative: too far from the ivory tower.

These "two solitudes," namely the world of business versus the scholarly schools of business, have gradually become institutionalized. They now exist in parallel universes. Deans who might want to change the present system can readily be gotten rid of by disgruntled senior faculty who do not appreciate a Dean's attempts to change the current system—a system which has given so many them prestige and tangible rewards. Currently there is an imbalance of power in many business schools: Deans can be pushed out by tenured faculty, but we tenured faculty can rarely be pushed out by Deans unless we engage in egregious behavior (e.g., hateful speech, crimes, sexual misconduct, plagiarism). What can be done to change this institutionalized system? We will discuss how to do better quantitative research later, but here we ask: what can be done to create business schools populated by at least a decent number of scholar-practitioners?

We believe the keys for change are at least twofold, one at the macro level and one at the individual level. Both changes could lead to a population of scholar-practitioners and good scholars inhabiting, if not dominating, tomorrow's business schools.[2]

CONNECTING SCHOLARS WITH BUSINESS

Macro

At the macro level, business schools need to, insofar as possible, move away from their universities, geographically, financially, and administratively. The Harvard Business School (HBS), for example, is across the Charles River away from the main campus. The physical distance from the main campus puts HBS outside the mainstream academic culture. HBS is self-financed. It does its own P&T. Tenure often requires a book or two written specifically for managers, rather than articles solely published in academic journals. Of the top 50 "management thinkers," only 21 are professors of which 14 are either at HBS or are HBS trained (Martin, 2012). Recently, the UCLA school of business, like Harvard, became administratively independent of the rest of the university

Second, hire Deans similar to Martin, who are willing to initiate a new system. Ensure that the Dean has the support of and funding from the business community. This would give Deans more power. The P&T system should reward scholar-practitioners as well as "pure" scholars (but see below). Faculty should be rewarded for consulting for business and writing up what they learned and achieved and teaching in the school's executive programs. The P&T system should reward writing books for managers equally with writing scholarly articles. Scholarly articles should not automatically be given higher status than publications in high status business periodicals. Even the issue of status should be questioned. We believe that many articles in high status publications are of very poor quality. (We will discuss the issue of standards in the following sections).

Third, we academics should teach MBA students general principles that are practically useful, that are generalizable across industries. The students should be assigned applied books, articles, and chapters. *Neither of us have ever assigned a scholarly journal article when teaching MBA students*. One especially useful method is teaching inductively based "general principles" which can be applied to many specific situations (e.g., Latham, 2018; Locke, 2009). Case studies can be useful, but they only deal with a concrete situation in a specific company; this minimizes generalizability, but a series of cases could be used to inductively derive actionable principles. Our impression is that this is not the way the case study method is used; each case is routinely treated as an end in itself.

Fourth, the AOM should develop strategies for becoming the source for evidence-based management, that is, evidence derived from inductively validated theories which are tied to the real world based on induction and which could actually be used. This may sound easy but it can be very difficult to decide what theories or principles have been validated. (see following section)

Fifth, the AOM should reframe the *Academy of Management Perspectives* so that it is a journal published explicitly for managers' consumption. Business schools should reward faculty for publishing in this journal.

Sixth, the AOM should set up a link that informs managers of significant research programs (not just single articles) published in scholarly journals that can be used by them using a language that managers can understand.

Micro

The credo of the second author throughout his academic years is one expressed more than a half century ago by Kurt Lewin (1945): no research without action, no action without research. Actionable research is that which *influences* and is influenced by practice in organizational settings. Locke and Latham (2020) and Latham's (2001a, 2001b) research on goal setting is one such example. As argued elsewhere (Latham, 2011), it is worse than useless for us as management scholars to restrict the findings, assuming the findings are useful, of our research to readers of scholarly journals. It is arguably unethical to withhold our knowledge from managers when we may have answers to so many issues troubling organizations (e.g., creating high performing teams; performance management). How can we remain sanguine knowing that most organizations continue to use an unstructured interview to select people? If the medical profession remained silent regarding their knowledge of action steps to be taken for preventing cholera, measles, mumps, or polio they would suffer the wrath of the public. If economists, with no lowering of the bar for scholarship, can gain the ear of the public, so can we. To do so, we need to support a scholar-practitioner model. And to do that we need to turn out not only MBAs who learn something in the classroom they can use, but also doctoral students who:

1. Become bilingual. Many, if not most of us, in the AOM have used the language of obfuscation when addressing a management audience. We are masterful at making straightforward explanations sound complex (Tourish, 2020a). Tomorrow's doctoral students

need to learn the art of speaking to, and writing clearly for, the public in addition to scholars.

2. Actively seek venues for educating managers (e.g., as noted: teaching in executive MBA courses as well as executive education courses).
3. Conduct research that cumulatively leads to a theory of diffusion. As Lewin (1951) once said, and most of us today agree, there is nothing so practical as a good theory. But the theory has to be validated. We need to find ways of transferring management research into management practice. An initial step would be to follow the advice of both Argyris (1991) and Bandura (2005), namely, for us as scholars to include operational validity as an essential criterion for evaluating research and theory.
4. Publish in practitioner journals such as *Harvard Business Review, Human Resource Management,* and *Organizational Dynamics.* Perhaps new sophisticated practitioner journals could be founded.
5. Spend time in private or public sector organizations, or if employed by an academic institution, spend part of a sabbatical in one or both settings. As noted elsewhere (Latham, 2007), there is no better place to become familiar with the questions and concerns of managers, understand the contextual conditions, offer research-based suggestions, and subsequently receive an offer to join teams formed to solve problems important to an organization.

The above suggestions are not a panacea for the above issues, and undoubtedly need further development. Nevertheless, we hope we have made it clear that reconnecting the business school universe to the business universe can and should be done.

Suggested Standards for Quality Research

None of the above suggestions deny the potential value of high quality, basic research. Valid, nontrivial findings from inductive, basic research can usually be applied somewhere, sometime. To do so they must involve replicable main effects—something a manager can readily understand, depend on, and use. Making a theory "work" also requires identifying relevant moderating conditions (Locke & Latham, 2020). As noted earlier, complex statistical models can be baffling, are rarely replicated and can be almost impossible to use.

We believe published research, whether basic or not, today is often poorly done. As noted above, the typical standard for evaluating basic research is publication in "A" journals. Aguinis et al. (2020) have made clear the pros and cons of this practice. On the pro side for faculty, the route to promotion is clear if this standard is used. On the con side, *this standard is only a proxy for good research, not an objective measure of it.* The question is: what does objectively good research consist of? What should be the core standards?

Having each been in the field for 50 or so years and each of us having reviewed thousands of submissions and hundreds that have been published, we have observed 13 problems that occur over and over.

1. **Stress theory building, not theory stating**. Deduction is the core method required by journal editors. Researchers create a theory then collect data. If a prediction is verified, the process typically stops. There are no accumulated data from which to put together facts that can be used to build a relatively enduring theory. Deduction, as the sole method for developing a theory, constitutes a fallacious approach to science, namely, science in reverse. Using deduction to develop a theory is arguably more responsible for "harking" than any other factor. This is because the results of a study "must" be consistent with the predictions, predictions made after the data were collected. However, the core method of theory building in the behavioral sciences should accumulate data and integrate the findings into theory. In short, induction should precede deduction (Locke, 2007; Locke & Latham, 2020). There is nothing wrong with a single hypothesis based on a previous finding. A hypothesis, however, is not a theory. Induction allows exploration, testing hunches, and taking into account failures to support a hypothesis. If something is discovered by "chance," research is conducted to see if the finding can be replicated.
2. **Avoid long introductions**. The introductions to a deductive study are often tedious because of authors' desperation to search for ways to justify the study. Supporting "theories" are grabbed from every direction, often straining credulity. In many cases a single hypothesis, even based on minimal data (e.g., from a previous study) should suffice, or even an exploratory question.
3. **Have thorough knowledge of the domain of interest to you**. Not knowing what has already been published can lead to wasted effort. This issue is compounded by the use of reviewers (often junior faculty) who do not know the subject matter domain. Junior faculty may substitute their lack of subject matter expertise with their knowledge of complex statistics. Adding to this issue is reliance on recent references and obliviousness to seminal ones. An example is self-efficacy (Bandura, 1997) among the most well researched motivational concepts in the history of psychology. We see study after study where self-efficacy is relevant as a predictor or independent

variable yet ignored (e.g., stress, resilience, performance). In cases where task performance is the dependent variable, useful studies would document factors that add to the variance accounted for by the most well-established causes of performance (e.g., self-efficacy, goal setting, training, conscientiousness, intellectual ability). To warrant publication, a new study should demonstrate that a "new" variable adds incremental variance.

4. **Clearly define key concepts**. When definitions are used, they are often chosen arbitrarily by researchers without much forethought. For example, there are hundreds of definitions of leadership. Which one do you choose and how do you justify it? The best place to start is to pose the question: what facts of reality gave rise to this concept? Start with the observation that some people are able to induce others to pursue a goal.
5. **Tie measurements logically to definitions** (this is often called construct validity). Many researchers, by default, rely on existing scales that have been developed by other researchers. Scales developed by others seem to be accepted by reviewers while developing one's own scales is seen as suspect. This is potentially a huge mistake. Many scales in psychology have been sloppily constructed. Either they are not connected to the concept of interest or they include a variety of different concepts, some relevant and some not. This confounding maybe be "covered up" by factor analysis which does not substitute for identifying logical inconsistencies and irrelevancies in a scale's item content.
6. **Do not take low correlations seriously**. More and more common in the literature are predictors that "account for" a very small percentage of variance in the dependent criterion. Witness the correlations in the literature that account for 1% or even only 0.5%. of the variance Such correlations lack practical significance. Some researchers choose a variable only because it is "timely." Fads come and go. Fads do not make a concept important, especially if the data yield results that are virtually nil.
7. **Beware of control variables**. Control variables may account for much more variance that the IV or predictor. In fact, this is a common occurrence, yet ignored. For example, an r-squared of 25% is potentially much more practically important than one of 0.05%.
8. **Don't attempt to save a study through statistical "expertise."** The literature is full of correlations that are not statistically significant at any level, yet are subsequently made significant using a multitude of control variables and/or other sophisticated techniques. The finding is rarely if ever replicated, let alone justified logically. How useful is

a variable that is so weak that it can only be salvaged by statistical "mumbo-jumbo?"

9. **Do not rely on concurrent correlations to make causal inferences**. Conducting causal experiments are often shunned by researchers because they are harder to conduct and typically take more time than a correlational study. This is especially dangerous when, as often happens, the respondent is required to rate both the predictor and the criterion.
10. **Present essentials**. Resist using 5, 10, 20, or 30 or more concurrent measures analyzed in all sorts of combinations. We call this: "playing with scales." Often, reviewers fall for this nonsense because they think: "wow, look at all the data; this must be important!" But the human mind cannot integrate that much data (30 x 30 = 900 correlations). Cognitive overload can cause the mind to go blank unless most of the data are ignored. A lasting contribution to the literature can be made by presenting a few essentials. Do not attempt to hide results you did not expect.
11. **Pick an important topic**. Avoid triviality. Many times we have read articles and asked ourselves: Why would anyone, least of all a manager, be interested in an issue so trivial or esoteric? Graduate students often have a difficult time determining what is more and what is less important to advance the field. Discuss a topic of interest with colleagues before conducting your study. Stay abreast of published research and focus on articles that conclude with suggestions for future studies.
12. **Write a Discussion that is based on your data**. In writing the Discussion, stick to what was found. Refrain from making grandiose generalizations, especially from a single study. Conclusions are often inappropriately drawn on the ways the results are useful in organizations based mainly on the author's imagination. Instead, lay the groundwork for a programmatic agenda.

DISCUSSION

The above problems are avoidable if journal editors agree to "universal" standards for submissions. Journal rankings or status should be less important, if not often irrelevant. Many journal editors are not concerned with the above list of issues. They do not support induction and programmatic research (Locke & Latham, 2020). Many of them demand studies on new topics and in doing so do not allow the building process through induction to proceed. Instead editors are concerned primarily with increasing the number of articles in their journal that are cited. A more fruitful procedure for the development of our field would be to only accept articles that meet high standards, as suggested above.

CONCLUSION

Simply urging faculty in psychology departments and business schools to do useful research is unlikely to change behavior. Why should we? What benefit would we get from doing so? If we are going to do research that society will find useful, the present system of P&T must change. Business schools need to become self-sufficient and relatively independent of the university. We have to abandon the view that because the world of business is messy, we should stand above the fray, safe in our "ivory tower." The time has come to respect publishing in outlets that practitioners read. The time has also come to reward scholar-practitioners and researchers who do well designed, useful basic studies and write the results in memorable, meaningful ways for our business school's primary stakeholders—managers. And the time has come to upgrade the quality of quantitative research if it is to be useful.

REFERENCES

Aguinis, H., Cummings, C., Ramani, R. S., & Cummings, T. G. (2020). "An A Is An A" The new bottom line for valuing academic research. *Academy of Management Perspectives, 34(1)*, 135–154. https://doi.org/10.5465/amp.2017.0193

Aldag, R. (2012). Bump it with a trumpet: On the value of our research to management education. *Academy of Management Learning and Education, 11*, 285–292. https://doi.org/10.5465/amle.2012.0087

Argyris, C. (1991). The use of knowledge as a test for theory: The case of public administration. *Journal of Public Administration, 3*, 337–354. https://www.jstor.org/stable/1181917

Bandura, A. (1997). *Self-efficacy: The exercise of control*. Freeman.

Bandura, A. (2005). Evolution of social cognitive theory. In K. G. Smith & M. A. Hitt (Eds.), *Great minds in management* (pp. 9–35). Oxford University Press.

Bartunek, J. M., & Egri, C. P. (2012). Introduction: Can academic research be managerially actionable? What are the requirements for determining this? *Academy of Management Learning and Education, 11*, 244–246. https://doi.org/10.5465/amle.2012.0134

Latham, G. P. (2001a). The reciprocal effects of science on practice: Insights for the practice and science of goal setting. *Canadian Psychology, 41*, 1–11. https://doi.org/10.1037/h0086875

Latham, G. P. (2001b). The reciprocal transfer of learning from journals to practice. *Applied Psychology: An International Review, 50,* 201–211. https://doi.org/10.1111/1464-0597.00054

Latham, G. P. (2007). A speculative perspective on the transfer of behavioral science to the workplace: "The times they are a changin." *Academy of Management Journal, 50,* 1027–1032. https://doi.org/10.5465/AMJ.2007.27153899

Latham, G. P. (2018). *Becoming the evidence-based manager.* Nicholas Brealey/Society for Human Resource Management.

Latham, G.P. (2011). Observations concerning pathways for doing "useful research". In E. Lawler (Ed.), *Doing research that is useful for theory and practice* (pp. 309–318). Barrett-Koehler.

Lewin, K. (1945). The Research Center for Group Dynamics at Massachusetts Institute for Technology. *Sociometry, 8,* 126–136. https://doi.org/10.2307/2785233

Lewin, K. (1951). *Field theory and social science.* Harper & Row.

Locke, E. A. (2007). The case for inductive theory building. *Journal of Management, 33,* 867–980. https://doi.org/10.1177/0149206307307636

Locke, E. A. (2008). *The prime movers: Traits of the great wealth creators.* Ayn Rand Bookstore.

Locke, E. A. (2009). *Handbook of principles of organizational behavior.* (2nd ed.). Wiley.

Locke, E. A., & Latham, G.P. (1990). *A theory of goal setting and task performance.* Prentice Hall.

Locke, E. A. & Latham, G. P. (2020). Building a theory by induction: The example of goal setting theory. *Organizational Psychology Review, 10*(3–4), 223–239. https://doi.org/10.1177/2041386620921931

Martin, R. (2012). The price of actionability. *Academy of Management Learning and Education,11,* 293–299. https://doi.org/10.5465/amle.2012.0064

Pearce, J. L. & Huang, L. (2012). The decreasing value of our research to management education. *Academy of Management Learning and Education, 11,* 247–262. https://doi.org/10.5465/amle.2011.0554

Peikoff, L. (2012). *The DIM hypothesis.* New American Library.

Tourish, D. (2020a). The triumph of nonsense in management studies. *Academy of Management Learning & Education, 19*(1), 99–109. https://doi.org/10.5465/amle.2019.0255

Tourish, D. (2020b). On crisis, genuine imposters, and complacency in management studies. *Academy of Management Learning & Education, 19*(2), 247–251. https://doi.org/10.5465/amle.2020.0133

NOTES

1. We have much anecdotal evidence that in recent years many allegedly deductive theories were deduced after, rather than before, the data were collected so as to appease journal editors who routinely insist on deductively-based articles.
2. The Academy of Management gives the prestigious scholarly-practitioner award annually to one individual. Our goal is for thousands of business school professors to be deserving of this award.

CHAPTER 3

21ST CENTURY LEADERSHIP RESEARCH IN ELITE GENERAL MANAGEMENT JOURNALS

Where the First 20 Years Have Taken Us and Where We May Be Going

William H. Bommer, Emil Milevoj, and Jonathan Biggane

ABSTRACT

The last two decades have witnessed important changes in the type of leadership research being undertaken, who is leading the research, and how it is being conducted. We review these changes by examining leadership research from 2000 to 2019 published in 10 premier outlets. We first describe notable trends in the focus of the research and show how major paradigms that dominated leadership research 20 years ago are being displaced by emerging theoretical perspectives. We then discuss where the research is coming from by analyzing author affiliation and other key metrics. We subsequently shift our focus to describe how the research is being conducted, reviewing changes in the frequency of multilevel research analyses. We conclude with a discussion of highly impactful scholarship during this time

Leadership:
Leaders, Followers, and Context, pp. 29–61

period and provide some insight regarding future directions in leadership theory and research.

A new millennium provides a clear demarcation and a touchstone for new challenges. Taking stock of the leadership research is hardly a unique endeavor. Numerous excellent reviews have been done over the past 70 years. For example, Stogdill (1948) reviewed the personal factors associated with leadership, reflecting the leadership trait literature of the early 1900s. The predominantly behavioral era (i.e., the 1950s and 1960s) was reviewed succinctly by Yukl (1971) and others (e.g., Schriesheim & Bird, 1979). The situational approaches which prevailed throughout the 1970s were reviewed in both general terms (e.g., Bass & Stogdill, 1990) and for specific approaches including path-goal (House, 1996), Fielder's LPC (Strube & Garcia, 1981), and situational leadership theory (Graeff, 1983). In the late 20th century, charismatic and transformational leadership (now more referred to under the umbrella of neo-charismatic approaches) became the most researched area in the field and has been reviewed numerous times (e.g., Judge & Piccolo, 2004). It is with an appreciation for where leadership research has been in the past that the current review is conducted.

While there have been excellent reviews of specific leadership theories (cf. Badura et al., 2018; Grijalva et al., 2015) and even a few overarching reviews of the leadership literature (cf. Dinh et al., 2014; Lord et al., 2017; Zhao & Li, 2019) in recent years, there has not been an examination of leadership with an applied focus in mind for the non-leadership researcher or for researchers in areas that often overlap with leadership research (e.g., human resources researchers and practitioners). As a result, this review simultaneously fills a few overlooked niches.

The current review's first goal is to examine the *content* of what has been studied in the first 20 years of the 21st century and to identify trends across this period. To accomplish this, a few questions will be addressed. More specifically, we explore what leadership approaches have been used over the past 20 years. As a follow up, we will also examine the relative growth or decline of different leadership paradigms, some of which were dominant as the 21st century began, and others that were not developed in any meaningful way 20 years ago.

Second, but closely related to the first goal, the current review seeks to provide *context*. Beyond the content of what has been published, we also explore *who* is publishing this research, and *how* the research has been conducted. There have been many recent technological and global changes and we examine whether leadership research is keeping up with these changes.

Third, we look at a number of external trends to determine whether the trajectory of the leadership literature is keeping pace with external forces. This has implications for the utility of leadership research and may also provide some prescription for where leadership research should go to make sure that it reflects and drives practices in the field.

It is with these three goals in mind that we set out to review the last 20 years of research published in premier general management journals. These premier general management journals were chosen based on their broad impact on the field, their reliability in selection and publication practices, and their demonstrated quality over time. As a result, the findings outlined in the following sections provide an empirically driven perspective of the current state of leadership research, where it came from, and where it is going.

In the following sections, we first define leadership as it operationalized in this review, and offer a more detailed look at the quantitative and qualitative strategies we employed to answer our central questions. We then provide specific criteria for the inclusion of studies in this paper. Subsequently, we present the sample and the coding procedures that were followed. Next, we examine trends in what is being published, where the research is coming from, and how it is being conducted. Finally, we review the most highly cited papers of the last two decades and explore future directions for leadership research.

How Is Leadership Defined for the Purposes of This Chapter?

Bass and Stogdill's *Handbook of Leadership* (Bass & Stogdill, 1990) described leadership as an "interaction between two or more members of a group that often involves a structuring of the situation and the perceptions and expectations of the members… Leadership occurs when one group member modifies the motivation or competencies of others in the group" (pp. 19–20). For our review, we start with the definition from the *Handbook of Leadership* but then put some restrictions on it to make the review most relevant for people doing research in human resources and applied fields related to leadership. As a result, we have taken a decidedly action-oriented focus on leadership in our review.

In other words, for this review we are focusing on actions taken by a person (or a group of people) intended to modify the behaviors, attitudes, or other organizationally-relevant outcomes associated with individuals, groups, teams, or organizations. To further refine our analyses, we did not include research that was not explicitly focused on leadership as its primary content area. Some specific examples of areas that include leadership, but are not primarily research focus is the research on teams. For example, some excellent research in the team area overlaps significantly with leadership (e.g., Lanaj et al., 2018). For this review, however, these papers were excluded because they were focused more on teams than on leadership.

Other examples of excluded studies are the numerous papers that include a leadership approach (e.g., empowering leadership or transformational leadership), but do so as moderators of the paper's primary variables of interest. For instance, Klein et al. (2011) is primarily focused upon team members' values but uses leadership as a moderator. Similarly, van Dijke et al. (2012) examine the relationship between fairness and organizational behavior, with leadership playing a moderating role. While these studies are relevant to the field, they do not fit the relatively narrow guidelines that we utilize for the current review.

Lastly, an examination of the themes presented by Dinh et al. (2014) provided our third set of inclusion criteria. Dinh et al. used 17 themes under which they classified leadership research conducted between 2000 and 2012. We did not wish to simply redo and update Dinh et al.'s exhaustive review. Instead, we selected those themes which imply an action by a leader that fits the Bass and Stogdill (1990) definition presented at the beginning of this section. As a result, we intentionally decided to exclude multiple approaches and to use neo-charismatic, social exchange/relational, dispositional/trait, behavioral, contingency, contextual, leader emergence, ethical/moral leadership, and abusive leadership theories. Table 3.1 contains a list of themes, the most common theories classified under each theme, and an example or two of articles that fit each theory.

By selecting the themes described above, we explicitly left out other approaches. These were omitted for a variety of different reasons depending on the specific theoretical approach, but in general, these approaches were not directly action-oriented in terms of what actions people in organizations engage in to impact goal attainment in an organization. Examples of these approaches are information processing approaches (including implicit leadership theories and attribution approaches), follower-centric models (i.e., romance of leadership), power and influence approaches, strategic leadership, team leadership, leadership development, identity-based leadership theories, or theories specific to creativity, innovation, and change. It is important to note that there is not a value judgment being made whether these approaches are important to leadership research.

Much in the same way as we do not wish to redo the work of Dinh et al. (2014), we also wish to distinguish the current review from the recent work of Zhao and Li (2019). Zhao and Li's review utilized an artificial-intelligence approach to categorize all leadership-related work between 1990 and 2017. Their analysis reported popular topics by journal, identified a series of topical or theoretical clusters of research areas, identified

Table 3.1

Common Examples of Leadership Theories Associated With Each Category and Example Articles

Neo-Charismatic Theories

- Transformational leadership (Piccolo & Colquitt, 2006; Kang et al., 2015)
- Charismatic leadership (LePine et al., 2016)
- Transactional leadership (Kark et al., 2015)
- Self-sacrificing leadership (De Cremer et al., 2009)
- Inspirational leadership (Molenberghs et al., 2017)

Social Exchange/Relational Leadership Theories

- Leader-member exchange (LMX) (Kauppila, 2016; Sparrowe & Liden, 2005)
- Relational leadership (Wellman, 2017)

Dispositional/Trait Theories

- Trait theories (Owens et al., 2015; Hu & Judge, 2017)

Behavioral Theories

- Participative leadership (Chen & Tjosvold, 2006; Lam et al., 2015)
- Empowering leadership (Wong & Giessner, 2018)
- Behavioral approaches (OSU/LBDQ) (DeRue et al., 2012)
- Leadership reward and punishment behavior (Podsakoff et al., 2006; Han et al., 2015)

Contingency Theories

- Path-goal theory (Perry et al., 2010)
- Leadership substitute theory (Keller, 2006)

Contextual Complexity and Systems Perspectives

- Social networks theories of leadership (Venkataramani et al., 2014)
- Complexity theories of leadership (Hannah et al., 2013)

Ethical/Moral leadership Theories

- Authentic leadership theory (Leroy et al., 2015)
- Ethical leadership theory (Fehr et al., 2015)
- Servant leadership theory (Gill & Caza, 2018; Peterson et al., 2012)

Abusive Leadership

- Destructive Leadership (Mackey et al., 2019)
- Abusive supervision (Yu et al., 2018; Yam et al., 2016)
- Leader mistreatment (Mayer et al., 2012)

author research productivity clusters at the individual level of analysis, and then constructed network maps to show the interconnections between these researchers and the topical clusters. As described above, our review takes a narrower action-oriented leadership focus designed to inform human resource researchers and practitioners about the current state of leadership research in the general management journals and focuses on more macro author information (e.g., country of affiliation, number of authors per article, and academic field of their affiliation). As a result, we consider our review to be complementary to these other reviews, and not as an update, or a critical analysis of them.

It is with the caveats described above that we now present the sample and the coding procedures for the leadership studies conducted over the past 20 years.

METHOD

Sample

We sought to include a wide representation of the leadership literature from top-ranked, generalist, management, and applied psychology journals. As a result of this focus, we purposely did not include *The Leadership Quarterly* for two specific reasons. First, *The Leadership Quarterly* is a premier leadership journal, but is a journal directed toward generalists in the field. In addition, the sheer volume of leadership-focused articles published in *The Leadership Quarterly* would significantly skew the results of our analyses.

To determine the specific journals for inclusion in our analyses, we sought out the social science impact factors for journals in management and applied psychology over the past 20 years. We then looked at the reviews conducted by Dinh et al. (2014) and Zhao and Li (2019) to determine if they had included distinct journals that could be helpful additions for our review.

In determining our list of journals to include we were cognizant of a few decision criteria. First, all journals had to be in existence before 2000, and were of generalist appeal with high impact factors; second, we wanted to make sure that both micro- and macro-focused journals were included, and third, we wanted to ensure that journals containing both empirical and theoretical articles were included. Importantly, we were not specifically concerned with the likely prevalence of leadership research appearing in a specific journal as we did not wish to bias the sample towards journals with more voluminous leadership research. Lastly, our journal sample was not explicitly concerned with an applied focus for the human resources practitioner. To the contrary, we explicitly attempted to analyze research from top-tier journals that may not be frequently consumed by human resources professionals so that we could provide a broad review and present more meaningful trends in the leadership literature which would likely not be readily available to this audience. In the end, we settled upon a list of 10 journals for our analyses. These journals are identified in Table 3.2 along with the journals that were used in other reviews mentioned above. As it can be seen in Table 3.2, the current list largely reflects journals common to other recent reviews, but takes a more macro-oriented approach with the inclusion of the *Journal of Management Studies* and *Strategic Management Journal*.

The search began by conducting an EBSCO database search using the journals' ISSN number and leadership as a keyword. This search was conducted at the end of 2019 for articles published between 2000 and 2019, representing a 20-year period. This initial search yielded 922 total hits. We

Table 3.2

List of Journals Included in the Review

Current Study	Dinh et al. (2014)	Zhao and Li (2019)
Academy of Management Journal	*Academy of Management Journal*	*Academy of Management Journal*
Academy of Management Review	*Academy of Management Review*	*Academy of Management Review*
Administrative Science Quarterly	*Administrative Science Quarterly*	*Administrative Science Quarterly*
Journal of Applied Psychology	***American Psychologist***	***European Journal of Work and Organizational Psychology***
Journal of Management	*Journal of Applied Psychology*	*Journal of Applied Psychology*
Journal of Management Studies	*Journal of Management*	*Journal of Management*
Organization Science	*Organizational Behavior and Human Decision Processes*	***Journal of Organizational Behavior***
Organizational Behavior and Human Decision Processes	*Organization Science*	*Organizational Behavior and Human Decision Processes*
Personnel Psychology	*Personnel Psychology*	*Personnel Psychology*
Strategic Management Journal	*The Leadership Quarterly*	*The Leadership Quarterly*

Note: Unique journal selections are listed in bold.

first read the abstracts to check whether the article was primarily leadership focused. We then narrowed our list to studies that included an action-oriented approach we described earlier. We further removed any articles which were not considered "original research." In other words, letters, book reviews, or statistical clarifications were removed. Lastly, we also removed papers that were primarily psychometric or methodological in nature. In all, this process retained 299 articles for subsequent analyses (articles available upon request).

To provide a structured approach through the research, we answer a series of questions to address the research's content and context. More specifically, we first focus on the *what* question. In other words, we look for trends to identify the research's content and to examine whether there are notable content trends. Second, we seek to better understand *who* conducted this research. To answer the *who* question, we examine the affiliations of the authors and show trends in their country of affiliation. We also examine the number of authors per article, and the mix of academic disciplines that have been responsible for the extant leadership research. Third, we shift our attention to present data addressing the *where* question. We show where the articles are appearing (in which journals), and where the samples being studied were located. Lastly, we seek to better understand *how* the research has been conducted. To do this, we present findings regarding the prevalence of theoretical and empirical articles, the utilization of third-party samples (e.g., MTurk, Qualtrics Online Sample), the number of studies included in each article, and the prevalence of multilevel statistical methods in the article's analysis. Before we present these analyses, we provide a detailed explanation of the study's coding procedures.

Study Coding Procedure

To explore the research questions presented above (i.e., the what, who, where, and how questions) relating to the *content* and the *context* of the leadership research conducted since the year 2000, we engaged in a series of steps. First, the full citation for each study was put into a Microsoft Excel workbook. For each article, our coding included: the journal name, the publication year, the full citation, the number of authors, the country of each author's affiliation, the department/college of each author, the leadership approach(es) predominantly used in the article, whether the paper was empirical or theoretical, the number of studies contained in the paper, the country where the study's sample was located, whether the study used a third-party (i.e., purchased) sample, and whether the study used multilevel statistical analyses or not.

To present our data, we found it beneficial to divide the 20-year period into time periods, rather than analyzing the data year-by-year. Consequently, the results will be presented using the time periods of 2000–2004, 2005–2009, 2010–2014, and 2015–2019. This decision was made so that the data was put into meaningful blocks of time, could be clearly presented in graphical form, and left enough studies in each period so that a few studies would not materially impact our conclusions. In addition, similarly to the study conducted by Zhao and Li (2019) our results are presented over four 5-year intervals while their study had four 7-year intervals.

In the presentation of our findings, we also made the decision to present our analyses as percentages rather than absolute numbers. This was done to provide a proportional view of the literature (e.g., the percentage of articles utilizing a specific theoretical framework, or the percentage of articles associated with authors from a specific country) where the absolute numbers are unable to communicate this relative aspect.

RESULTS: THE *WHAT, WHO, WHERE,* AND *HOW* OF LEADERSHIP RESEARCH

Answering the *What* Question

To address the question of what has been studied in the past 20 years, we used the categories identified by Dinh et al. (2014) in their thoroughly conducted review. In some cases, however, more than one category of theory was used in a single study. A clear example of such a study can be seen in Keller (2006). Keller's paper uses transformational leadership, initiating structure, and substitutes for leadership in a single study. Bono and Judge's (2004) meta-analysis uses both leader personality and transformational leadership. In these and other similar cases, we made the decision to assign an equal fraction of a study for each distinct category of leadership theory represented. In specific terms, in a case where two categories were represented (see, e.g., Bono & Judge, 2004), one-half of an article was assigned, and if three were included (see, e.g., Keller, 2006), then one-third of an article was assigned to each category. It should be pointed out that when multiple theories from the same category were present in one study (see, e.g., Hoch et al., 2018), no fractional assignment was needed or conducted.

As can be clearly seen in Figure 3.1, studies using neo-charismatic theories (e.g., transformational, charismatic, and visionary leadership approaches) began the 21st century in the dominant position, and finished the 20-year period as the most common theoretical approach, but by a much smaller margin. More specifically, neo-charismatic studies accounted for 57.1% of the studies during 2000–2004, 44.8% of the studies in 2005–2009, 23.9%

of the studies in 2010–2014, and 18.7% of the studies in the 2015–2019 time period. Thus, neo-charismatic studies have gone from representing almost three of every five studies published to less than one in five. This is a large drop and the trend shown in Figure 3.1 is clear and consistent.

The steep decline in the prevalence of neo-charismatic research (in percentage terms) had to be picked up by another approach or multiple approaches. Somewhat surprisingly, the replacements came from a diverse set of approaches, and not primarily from a single approach that experienced large growth. Theories consistent with abusive leadership (e.g., abusive supervision, leader mistreatment, etc.) saw immense growth with virtually no studies published between 2000–2004, but more than 12% of the total studies in the 2014–2019 period. These studies were primarily associated with Tepper's abusive supervision (e.g., Tepper et al., 2006) work that has received a great deal of attention from multiple researchers in multiple journals over a relatively short period of time (e.g., Liu et al., 2012; Yam et al., 2016).

Another approach that has shown an increase against the decreases associated with the neo-charismatic approach has been research using ethical/moral theories of leadership. The ethical/moral approach includes authentic leadership, ethical leadership, and servant leadership theories. Of these three, only servant leadership (Greenleaf, 1970, 1977) existed in

Figure 3.1

Analysis of the Leadership Themes by Time Period

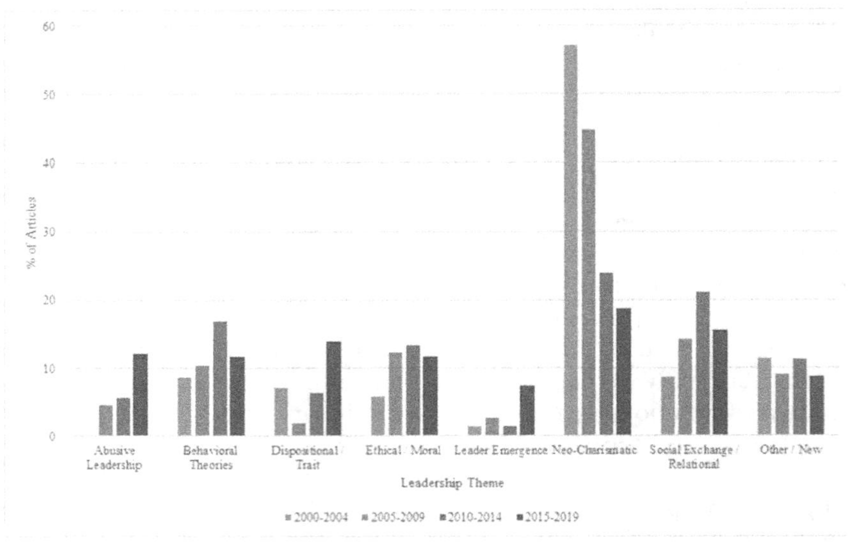

any meaningful way before the year 2000 and the empirical literature on servant leadership before 2000 was extremely limited (e.g., Hoch et al., 2018). These studies, likely driven by well-publicized ethical violations of the early 2000s (e.g., Enron, WorldCom, etc.), more than doubled their share of leadership research over the 20 years of our review.

Lastly, studies using a social/exchange/relationship framework (i.e., primarily LMX) have also gained a significant portion of the leadership research over the past 20 years. While LMX and its related approach have been popular throughout the last 20 years, the last 10 years have seen significant growth (e.g., Liu et al., 2014).

When taken as a whole, the shift in the content of the research has been a consistent one and has led to a much "busier" theoretical mix than existed 20 years ago. A useful way of thinking about this, is that during 2015–2019 it took the top four themes (neo-charismatic, social exchange/relational, dispositional/trait, and abusive leadership) to represent a roughly equivalent portion of the leadership research as neo-charismatic alone occupied during 2000–2004. Clearly, the diversity of theoretical themes has been significant. With the content issue of what is being published having been addressed, we now shift our attention to answering the *who* question.

Answering the *Who* Question

Rather than looking at individual names that have been publishing leadership research in the top general management outlets, we looked at the frequency with which different countries appeared as the primary affiliation for an author. We also coded the academic unit with which the author(s) was affiliated, as well as how many authors were associated with each article.

In those cases where an author was associated with multiple universities in different countries, we used the affiliation listed first. Since multiple authors on an article are the rule rather than the exception, we decided to assign fractional authorship to each country without a consideration of author order. For instance, if an article was co-authored by two researchers from the United States and two researchers from China (see, e.g., Zhang et al., 2014), each country was assigned one-half of an article. In a similar manner, if three countries were each represented each country received one-third (e.g., Schaubroeck et al., 2007).

Because the United States has been responsible for a large portion of the overall research, we broke the country analysis into two separate figures. As can be seen in Figure 3.2, the share of leadership research conducted by U.S.-based researchers has been high over the past 20 years. The 2015–2019 represented the low during the past 20 years, but even the low value was 64%, which means that almost two of every three articles can be attributed to research conducted by a U.S.-affiliated researcher. While the United States has accounted for most of the research, we also set out to determine whether there were notable trends associated with researchers in other parts of the world. These results are presented in Figure 3.3. It should be pointed out that the journals selected for our analyses could have the effect of increasing the percentage of U.S.-affiliated researchers. This is because some other journals may be rated higher in Europe and elsewhere than they are in a global sense. This impact, however, should not impact trends across time, but only the absolute share of U.S.-based affiliations.

Figure 3.3 demonstrates a strong pattern that requires specific comment. China has moved from having no articles during 2000–2004 to almost 10% of the research output in 2015–2019. In addition, a further analysis reveals that authors from China have been accounting for a higher percentage of the total authors on their recent articles. More specifically, in 2010–2014, an article involving an author with a China-based affiliation had a share of 35.2% of the article being associated with an author from China. During 2015–2019, however, the comparable author representation on an article was 44.1%. This means that in more recent years, more than 2 in 5 authors had Chinese affiliations when any Chinese-affiliated authors were present.

Figure 3.2

Articles Published by Researchers from U.S.-Affiliated Institutions

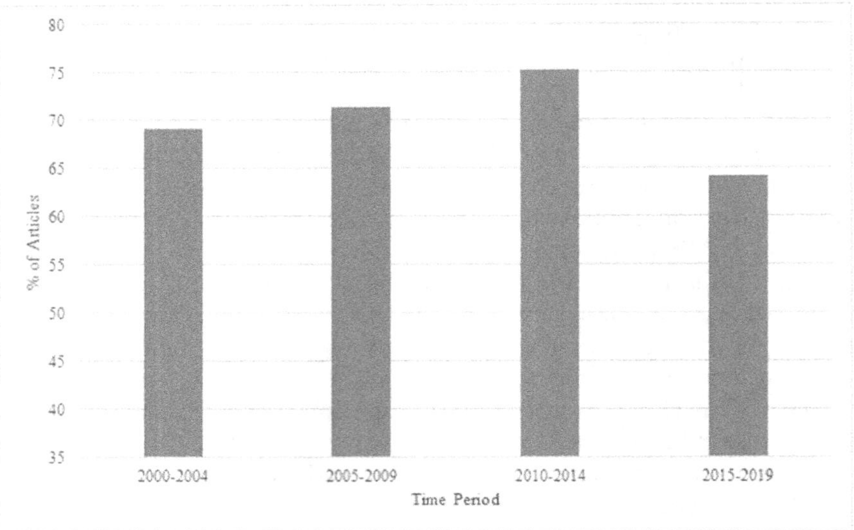

Figure 3.3

Authorship by Location Excluding the United States

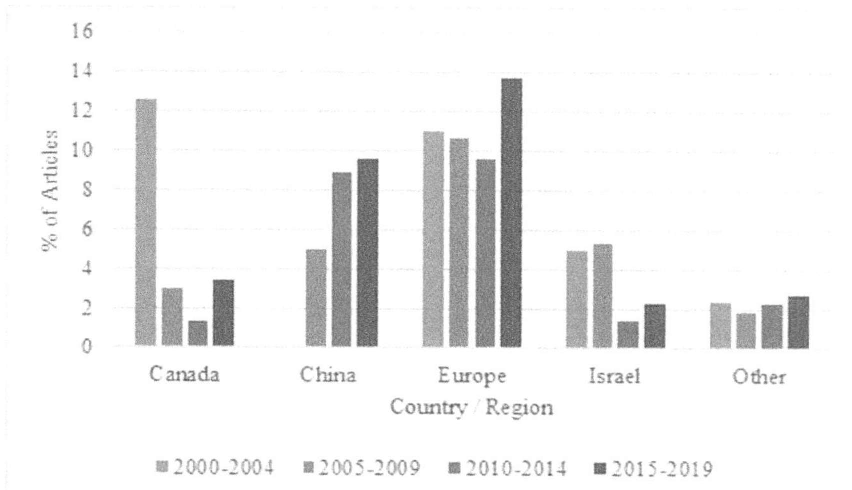

This pattern shows not only more research coming from Chinese-affiliated authors, but more authors with Chinese affiliations were involved in these research teams as well.

In addition to the country of origin for the authors, we also wanted to examine the authors' academic unit. For this analysis, we coded whether an article was written by teams of authors from multiple disciplines. After identifying the affiliations of each author in the paper, the authors were coded as either business, psychology, mixed (business and psychology), or other. The category "other" included other disciplines such as health, sociology, anthropology, and nonacademic affiliations. We did not weight the discipline affiliations, rather we just counted if the cross-discipline relationship was present or not. The results are presented in Figure 3.4.

Interestingly, the results show that the collaboration across disciplines is on the decline. During the 2000–2004 period the cross-discipline collaboration was at its highest with 'mixed' teams of authors representing 25.7% or leadership articles. It is also worth noting that the number of authors affiliated with psychology and other disciplines has diminished in their contribution of studying leadership, whereas business schools have been on the rise. This may be partially due to business schools hiring away well-published authors from psychology in recent years, but it is doubtful that this alone could account for the patterns seen in Figure 3.4.

Figure 3.4

Authors' Academic Discipline and Collaboration Across Disciplines

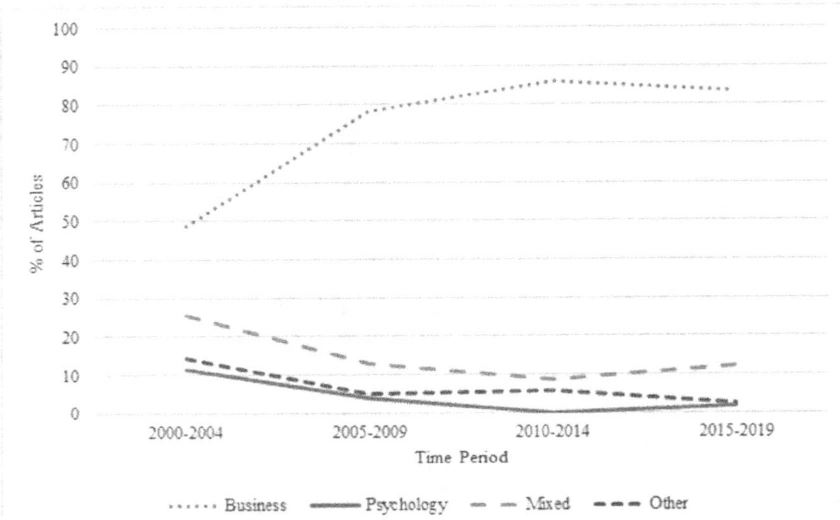

The third examination we conducted addressing the issue of *who* is publishing focused on the number of authors per article. More specifically, we coded the number of authors for each of the articles across the time periods examined. The results of this analysis are shown in Figure 3.5.

Figure 3.5 shows a few clear patterns related to the number of authors per article. First, the frequency with which five or more authors publish a single article has increased markedly in the past 20 years. The relative portions with three or four authors has increased somewhat as well, as the combination of these larger author "teams" has been associated with a commensurate reduction in the proportion of articles with one or two authors.

Taken together, Figures 3.3, 3.4, and 3.5 reveal that the typical article has a larger research team, most likely consisting of researchers from business schools, with affiliations in the United States. The trend, however, toward more authors coming from China and Europe (with some reduction in the prevalence of authors with a U.S. affiliation), has been fairly strong. Having addressed the *who* question, the review now shifts towards the issue of *where*.

Answering the *Where* Question

Addressing the issue of *where* takes us in two distinct directions. First, we were interested in determining where the subjects were located. Second, we

Figure 3.5

Number of Authors Per Article

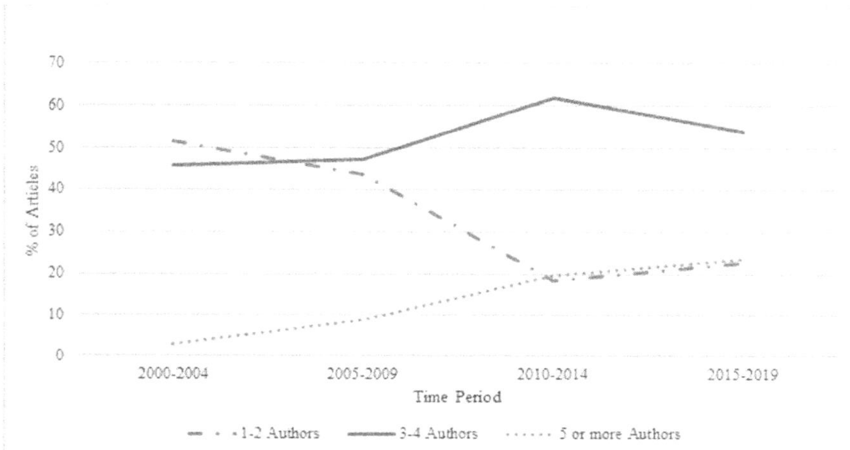

were interested to see where articles were actually published (i.e., in which of the journals we examined).

To further explore the context of the published articles, we examined the location of samples for each paper and from which countries the samples were collected. Studies with samples coming from numerous countries were coded as multinational, while the others included the specific names of countries or regions. In cases when an article had three or more studies with samples being utilized from two countries (e.g., one sample from the United States and two samples from China), the article was coded as having a multinational sample location.

We decided to not assign weights to each sample location in a multi-sample study, but instead to just determine if samples in the article come from more than one location. Some studies used a sample from one multinational organization, but the study was global in its reach (e.g., Hill & Bartol, 2016) and was therefore coded as multinational. Lastly, once all the countries were identified and analyzed, the decision was made to group certain countries into their respective regions. For example, the countries in the European Union were coded as Europe while countries in Africa, Oceania and Asia (excluding China) were coded as "other."

As shown in Figure 3.6, the analysis of the locations of samples, shows the increase in research samples using subjects from China and the relatively sharp-decline in the samples using subjects from the United States.

It is likely that this shift is responsible for the higher proportion of Chinese authors shown in Figure 3.3. When we dove a little deeper into the data, we also discovered, as one would expect, articles with three or more studies were more likely to also have samples that spanned multiple countries, than were articles containing one or two studies.

Figure 3.6

Location of Sample for Included Articles

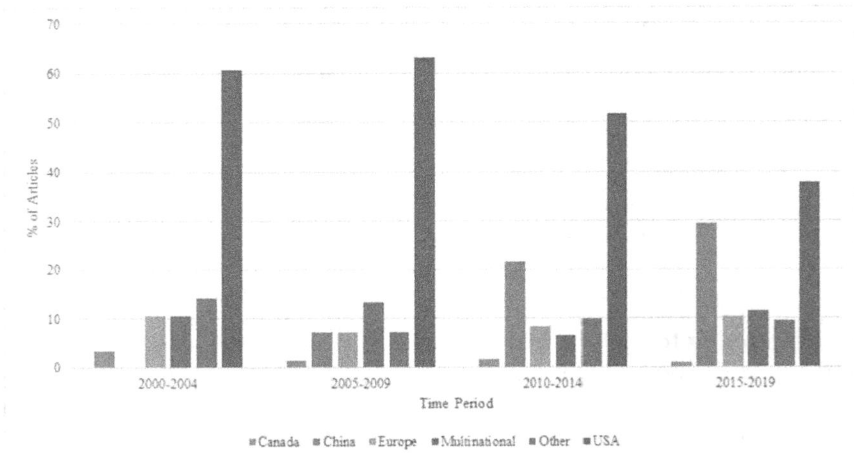

In addition to addressing the issue of the location of the research sample used, we also explored where the leadership research was published. As a result, we analyzed the representation of leadership articles in our sample journals across the 20-year time period. We took the number of leadership articles and divided it by the total number of articles each journal published for the specific time period. The results are presented in Figure 3.7.

Overall, it was clear from the analysis presented in Figure 3.7 that there was significant variance in the degree to which the journals published the type of leadership research we examined. The *Journal of Applied Psychology*, *Journal of Management*, *Personnel Psychology*, and the *Academy of Management Journal* had a higher percentage of their articles dedicated to leadership than the other journals. The *Academy of Management Review* has included more leadership articles recently and importantly has the highest representation of articles among the more theoretical journals. On the other end of the spectrum, *Organization Science*, *Strategic Management Journal*, and *Organizational Behavior and Human Decision Processes*, publish relatively few leadership articles relative to their overall publication volumes.

Figure 3.7

Percentage of Leadership Articles in the Included Journals

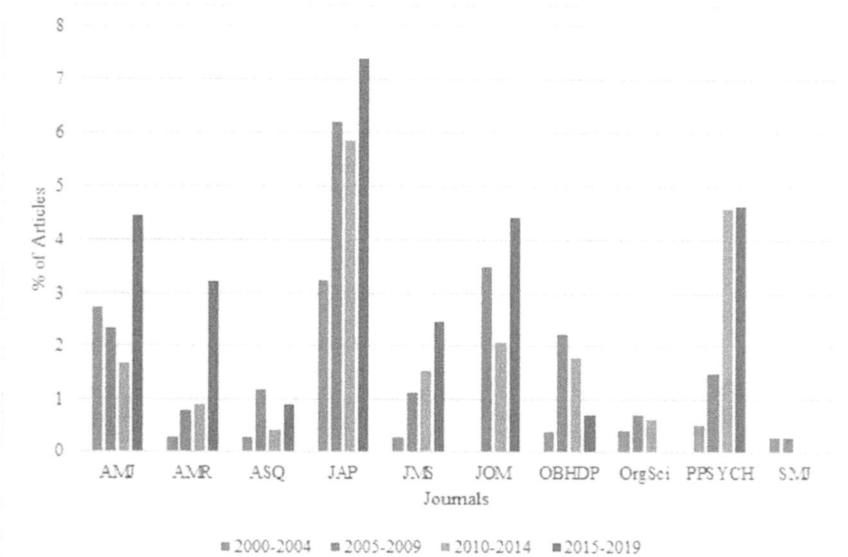

With the analysis of the journals and the proportion of leadership articles each journal published, our analyses regarding the *where* question is concluded. At this point, our attention shifts to the final area we addressed, the issue of *how* the leadership research has been conducted.

Answering the *How* Question

Our final area of exploration examined issues relating to how the leadership research has been conducted and analyzed over the past 20 years. Specifically, we wanted to assess the proportion of research that has been primarily theoretical in nature and to measure the prevalence of third-party samples that have been used, how many studies per article are included, and whether or not the article uses multilevel analytical tools in their analyses.

As a first step in exploring issues relating to *how* leadership research has been conducted, we coded for whether the study article was empirical or theoretical. The results of this analysis can be seen in Figure 3.8, and the percentage of theoretical articles has gone up significantly from 5.7% in 2000–2004 to 9.7% in 2015–2019. This growth came mainly from an increased percentage of theoretical articles relating to leadership appearing in the *Academy of Management Review* and a few other theoretical articles being distributed across a number of other journals.

Figure 3.8

Percentage of Theoretical Articles

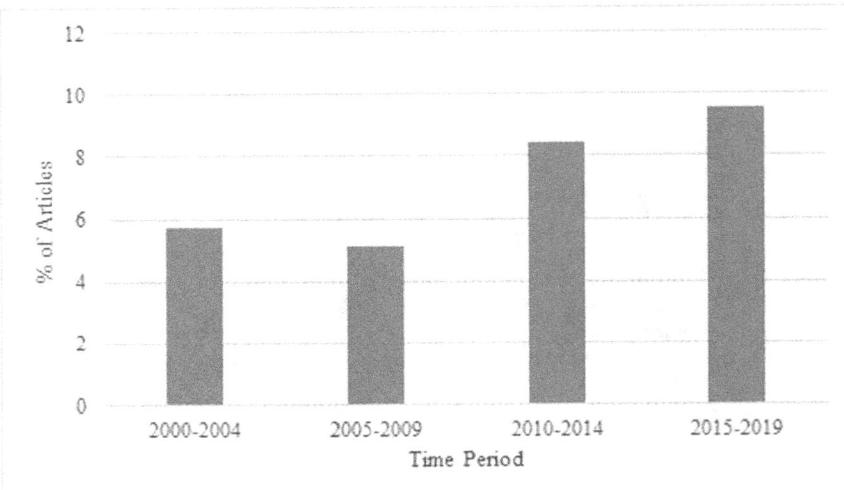

Even though the percentage of articles was still less than 10% in the most recent time period, it should be remembered that the nature of our inclusion rules tends to exclude a number of articles that are more theoretical in nature (i.e., because they may be less likely to fit the categories of leadership theories that were included). Since our analysis is holding the journals constant, to see a rise from less than 6% in 2000–2004 and 2005–2009 to almost 10% in 2015–2019 suggests that there has been a trend toward relatively more theoretical leadership work being published in the premier general management outlets in recent years.

Even though the relative frequency of theoretical articles has been increasing, empirical articles still garner most of the journal space in the set of journals we examined. As such, we sought to determine if these empirical articles were becoming more likely to use third-party samples to test their research questions. When we discuss third-party subjects, we are referring to subjects recruited by outside firms including Amazon's MTurk, Qualtrics Online Panels, and Survey Monkey Audience, among others. To track the use of these services, we coded any study using subjects recruited by third-party sources as using purchased third-party subjects, even if there were other samples collected by the researchers (e.g., Lin et al., 2016).

Figure 3.9 shows a recent growth in the use of third-party subjects. This finding shows that 17.8%, or more than one-in-six, of studies during 2015–2019 utilized data collected from third-party subjects as part of the empirical tests. Clearly, third-party samples have become more common and have gained acceptance from journal reviewers and editors in recent years.

Figure 3.9

Use of Purchased Third-Party Subjects Over Time

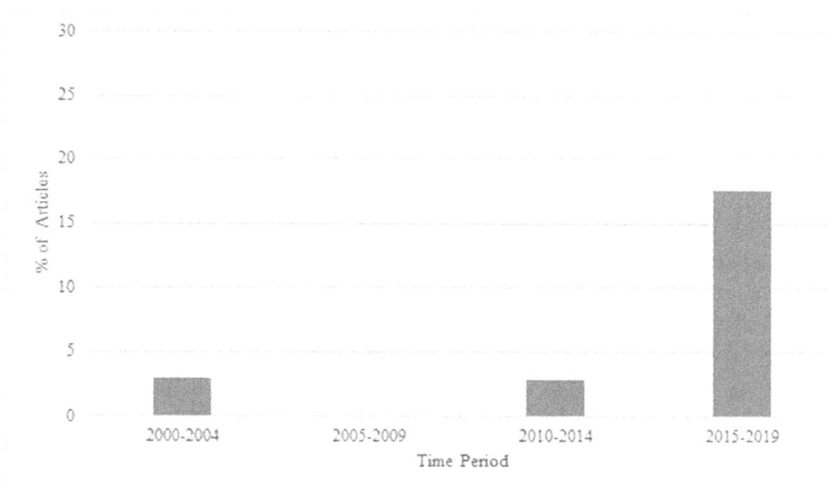

Despite this recent uptick, it is important to note the limitations of utilizing such third-party samples. For example, although MTurk samples represent over 190 countries, 57% of respondents come from the U.S. and 32% come from India (Ross et al., 2010). MTurk respondents from the U.S. tend to be younger, educated, and have a lower salary than the general population (Paolacci & Chandler, 2014; Ross et al., 2010). Only 43% work full-time for an organization and many are students (21%), homemakers (8%), out of work (18%), or retired (3%) (Stritch et al., 2017). There is also some evidence to suggest that MTurk respondents may be likely to lie about their work status (Ipeirotis, 2010), indicating that the unemployed respondents may be even higher.

A related issue is that respondents from third-party surveys typically get paid for completion of the survey rather than for providing accurate data. This presents several problems including the potential for "spammers" to fill out as many surveys as possible without regard to instructions (Mason & Suri, 2012). It also opens the door for more sophisticated participants to choose socially acceptable answers so as to fly beneath the radar and not be revealed as a "faker" (Landers et al., 2011). These more covert examples may be more difficult to identify, increasing the likelihood that any findings will not be valid.

Another complication arises regarding the amount of control one relinquishes when relying on third party data. For instance, it is not possible to calculate response rates since respondents do not come from a predetermined population. Furthermore, since only one follower per leader is included, cross-level effects cannot be investigated. This not only limits the researchers' ability to investigate leader differences, but it also prohibits any multilevel designs.

Due to these factors, the validity and generalizability of findings based on third-party data may be suspect in some cases. As a result, scholars relying on this type of sample may benefit from asking questions relevant to the selective subpopulations being surveyed and limiting the extent to which they generalize their findings across organizational settings.

Continuing with the issue of *how* leadership research is conducted and potentially tied to the use of third-party subjects, we also measured the number of studies per article. To code this, we relied upon the text and the number of studies described. In other words, to be counted as a multiple-study article, the authors had to label and describe "Study 1," "Study 2," and so forth. In almost all cases, these multiple study articles also had multiple sample descriptions, measures utilized, and statistical analyses, and their own results sections as well (e.g., Kark et al., 2015).

An examination of Figure 3.10 clearly shows that after a relative stable relationship from 2000–2014, that the frequency of multiple-study articles increased notably during 2015–2019. More specifically, 44% of articles published during 2014–2019 contained more than one study, where that number had varied between 18–24% over the previous three 5-year periods. It is quite possible that this finding may be one of the reasons why the number of third-party subjects has also increased. As authors are encouraged to include more studies (and more data samples) into a single article, third-party subjects can be expedient, cost-effective means of either establishing, validating, or extending the findings from other studies in an article.

The final issue we explored concerning *how* leadership was conducted was an examination of the use of multilevel statistical methods. At the close of the 1990s, the need for multilevel statistical testing methods was being acknowledged but their use was still rare in publications (see, e.g., Klein & Kozlowski, 2000). To test if these methods have become more common, we coded the empirical studies to determine whether they used multiple-level methods or not. It is important to note that not every study should use multilevel methods and that these methods are only recommended when

Figure 3.10

Number of Studies Per Article

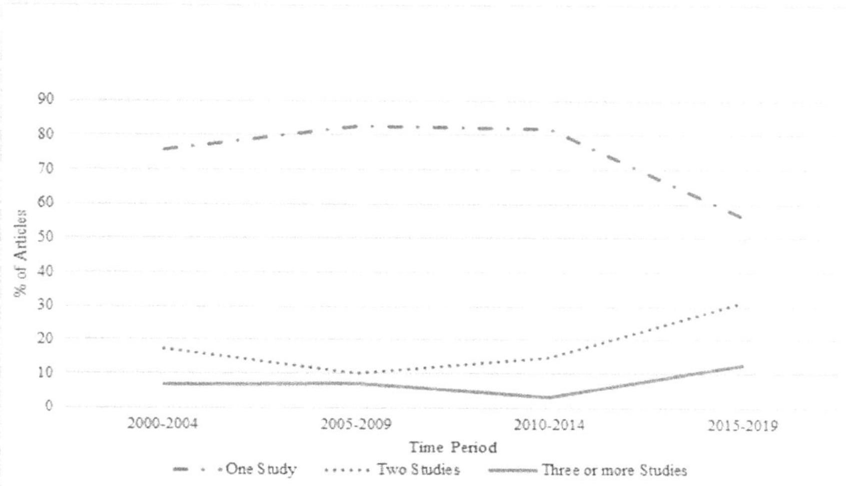

data is nested with variance being explained by some type of nested group membership. Keeping this qualifier in mind, Figure 3.11 shows the results.

As can be seen in Figure 3.11, the relative use of multilevel analyses being conducted in empirical research has been steadily increasing and approached half of all published leadership research in 2015–2019. This is in contrast to less than one-in-20 studies using multilevel methods during 2000–2004. It is likely that a combination of significantly more researchers being trained in multilevel methods, improvements in the usability of the software programs, and the demands of leadership reviewers associated with these top journals has brought about a relatively rapid adoption of multilevel methods. This is a positive development that has also allowed for the study of topics that were often deemed too complex to study by many people.

What Articles From Each Time Period Have Been Cited the Most?

In addition to addressing the *what, who, where,* and *how* questions, we also examined the impact of the articles in our journal list based on their Google Scholar citations. Obviously, older articles have more time with which to be cited, and this holds true across the 20-year time period as well as within each 5-year time period which our analysis used. As a result, our

Figure 3.11

Percentage of Studies Using Multilevel Analysis

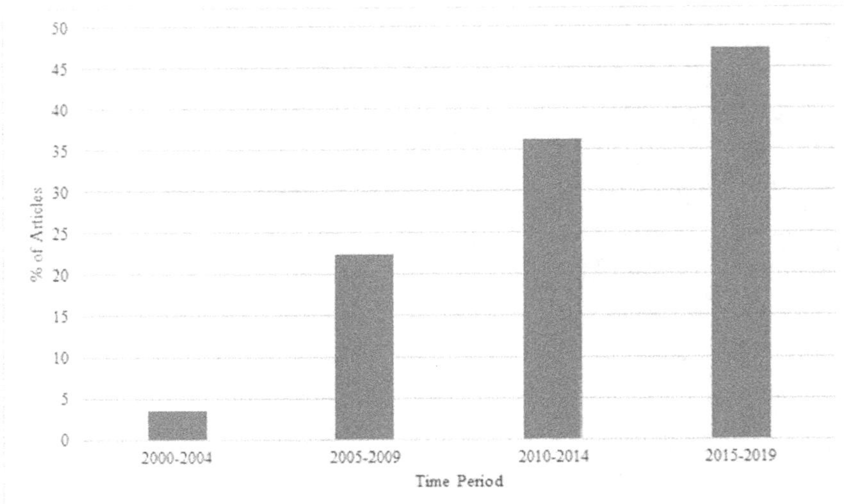

analysis should not be taken as "the most influential articles in leadership research," but we believe that the following list does provide a useful representation of articles that have been highly impactful during the last 20 years. To keep this analysis brief, in Table 3.3 we provided the three most cited articles from each period based on results from the end of December 2019.

Table 3.3 shows a few patterns that should not be considered to be too surprising. First, a number of the most cited articles are reviews. Reviews are typically cited frequently as they fill a summary role for authors doing subsequent work. In addition to reviews, a few of the most cited articles are seminal pieces for a specific theoretical approach where the approach is described and possibly a scale is provided. Again, these articles serve functional roles for subsequent researchers doing work in a specific content area. Finally, it should be pointed out that some of the most common leadership themes (e.g., neo-charismatic, ethical/moral, and dispositional/trait) are the most represented articles in terms of their volume of citations.

DISCUSSION

At the turn of the century, scholarship on leadership was already very well established. Certain paradigms had taken hold, such as neo-charismatic

Table 3.3

Article Citations by Time Period

Article Reference	Category	Citations
2000–2004		
Judge, T. A., & Piccolo, R. F. (2004). Transformational and transactional leadership: A meta-analytic test of their relative validity. *Journal of Applied Psychology, 89*(5), 755–768.	Neo-charismatic	4,778
Bass, B. M., Avolio, B. J., Jung, D. I., & Berson, Y. (2003). Predicting unit performance by assessing transformational and transactional leadership. *Journal of Applied Psychology, 88*(2), 207–218.	Neo-charismatic	4,079
Judge, T. A., Bono, J. E., Ilies, R., & Gerhardt, M. W. (2002). Personality and leadership: A qualitative and quantitative review. *Journal of Applied Psychology, 87*(4), 765–780.	Dispositional/ Trait and Leader Emergence	3,767
2005–2009		
Brown, M. E., Treviño, L. K., & Harrison, D. A. (2005). Ethical leadership: A social learning perspective for construct development and testing. *Organizational Behavior and Human Decision Processes, 97*(2), 117–134.	Ethical/Moral	3,903
Walumbwa, F. O., Avolio, B. J., Gardner, W. L., Wernsing, T. S., & Peterson, S. J. (2008). Authentic leadership: Development and validation of a theory-based measure. *Journal of Management, 34*(1), 89–126.	Ethical/Moral	3,043
Piccolo, R. F., & Colquitt, J. A. (2006). Transformational leadership and job behaviors: The mediating role of core job characteristics. *Academy of Management Journal, 49*(2), 327–340.	Neo-charismatic	1,904
2010–2014		
DeRue, D. S., Nahrgang, J. D., Wellman, N. E. D., & Humphrey, S. E. (2011). Trait and behavioral theories of leadership: An integration and meta-analytic test of their relative validity. *Personnel Psychology, 64*(1), 7–52.	Dispositional/ Trait and Behavioral Theories	1,389
Morgeson, F. P., DeRue, D. S., & Karam, E. P. (2010). Leadership in teams: A functional approach to understanding leadership structures and processes. *Journal of Management, 36*(1), 5–39.	Behavioral Theories	1,042

(Table continued on next page)

Table 3.3 (Continued)

Article Citations by Time Period

Article Reference	Category	Citations
2010–2014		
Walumbwa, F. O., Hartnell, C. A., & Oke, A. (2010). Servant leadership, procedural justice climate, service climate, employee attitudes, and organizational citizenship behavior: a cross-level investigation. *Journal of Applied Psychology, 95*(3), 517–529.	Ethical/Moral	831
2015–2019		
Leroy, H., Anseel, F., Gardner, W. L., & Sels, L. (2015). Authentic leadership, authentic followership, basic need satisfaction, and work role performance: A cross-level study. *Journal of Management, 41*(6), 1677–1697.	Ethical/Moral	317
Hoch, J. E., Bommer, W. H., Dulebohn, J. H., & Wu, D. (2018). Do ethical, authentic, and servant leadership explain variance above and beyond transformational leadership? A meta-analysis. *Journal of Management, 44*(2), 501–529.	Ethical/Moral and Neo-charismatic	273
Grijalva, E., Harms, P. D., Newman, D. A., Gaddis, B. H., & Fraley, R. C. (2015). Narcissism and leadership: A meta-analytic review of linear and nonlinear relationships. *Personnel Psychology, 68*(1), 1–47.	Dispositional/ Trait	260

research, and it was clearly dominated by research using a few statistical methods (i.e., regression and structural equation modeling), being conducted using samples from relatively few countries by researchers from even fewer countries.

The current review has revealed several interesting changes over the past 20 years. In our investigation of the *what* aspect of leadership research, we found a steady decline in the prevalence of neo-charismatic research. In its place, a more diverse collection of theoretical perspectives including abusive leadership, ethical/moral approaches, social/exchange, and an even stronger focus on relationship frameworks (primarily LMX). Taken as a whole, this tells us that the content of the research has changed in such a way that we are now approaching leadership from more distinct viewpoints. In other words, our toolbox has been filled with more tools that may help to better understand the dynamic and ever changing nature of leading others.

In examining the *who* aspect of leadership research, we found that the U.S. continues to be the leader in leadership research with about two of every three leadership articles in premier outlets being attributed to authors affiliated with U.S. universities. Similarly, the majority of samples used come from the United States. However, taking a more in-depth look at the data paints a somewhat different picture. China has moved from producing almost no leadership research from 2000–2004 to nearly 10% of the total in 2015–2019. As a consequence, the number of Chinese samples and authors has drastically increased, providing a much needed look at leadership from an Eastern perspective. A specific example of this can be seen in the research focusing on leader humility and humbleness (see, e.g., Owens et al., 2019; Ou et al., 2014).

U.S-based samples have shown a marked decline, particularly during 2015–2019. To add to this, we are seeing an increasing trend of multi-country samples. Thus, scholarship in the field is becoming more diverse from an author and country perspective. A caveat being that the amount of cross-disciplinary research has been decreasing, suggesting that authors have been venturing out beyond their countries, but not as much outside of their own disciplines.

Other important trends include a significant uptick in theoretical articles relating to leadership, changes in the type of samples found within empirical articles, and the type of statistical methods used. Although empirical studies tend to be the norm among the journals we reviewed, we saw an increasing acceptance of leadership articles within preeminent theoretical outlets such as the *Academy of Management Review*. Furthermore, the use of third-party data is becoming much more prevalent, indicating that reviewers and editors are more accepting of data derived from third-party sources such as Amazon's MTurk. Moreover, we have seen rapid adoption of multilevel statistical methods, which was found in nearly half of all leadership research published during 2015–2019.

Another notable trend is the number of authors and studies found in recent publications. For example, the number of single author papers over the last 20 years has decreased from 5.7% during 2000–2004 to 2.6% during 2015–2019. Even more striking, the number of publications with five or more authors has increased from 2.9% in 2000–2004 to 23.5% during 2015–2019. This may be due to the factors of more studies per article and the increased use of multiple samples and more specialized statistical analysis techniques (e.g., multilevel analysis).

All in all, these findings indicate that leadership research has become increasingly complex and the ingredients of a premier journal article are quite different than they were 20 years ago. Put another way, the prototypical leadership study during 2015–2019 had three or four researchers from more than one country, using multiple and likely hierarchical methods to analyze data from more than one country. In contrast, for studies conducted during 2000–2004, the most common case was for two authors from the same country, to conduct a single study using regression or structural equation modeling based upon a single sample from one country.

FUTURE RESEARCH AND LIMITATIONS

When looking at the evolution of leadership research over time, it is important to consider the direction we are heading and, perhaps more importantly, to ask whether we are heading in the right direction. While trying to avoid the trap of being overly prescriptive, it is necessary to examine the gaps between where scholars and practitioners are spending their time. Generally speaking, the lion's share of the problems faced by leaders remain unchanged. The ability to manage change, work in ambiguous environments, retain and motivate employees, collaborate with others, and manage stakeholder expectations continue to be a challenge that leaders must contend with and leadership researchers have come to better understand. There are, however, newer issues that have outpaced scholarship. Such areas like dealing with an aging workforce, managing across generations and cultures, the gig economy, and leading in virtual settings have not yet been adequately researched. These fields are rife with opportunities for researchers to extend our understanding of how, where, and when practitioners can employ evidence-based management to increase their success.

With the diversity of theoretical and statistical approaches currently being used, and the need to address an ever-increasing number of settings, it would appear that leadership research may be approaching an era where situational approaches rise in popularity as approaches to weave together these disparate needs. If history is an indication of the future, the 1950s and 1960s saw more behaviors being studied and simultaneously saw a more robust discussion of the context in which those behaviors were happening. These forces came together to lead to a time of multiple situational approaches that attempted to better reflect the needs of people in the field. Whether the next 20 years will see an analogous period is yet to be seen, but the current diversity suggests that such a shift is at least a reasonable possibility.

Last, the trends identified herein have several implications for scholarship specifically aimed at human resource management (HRM). The traditional view of HRM scholarship aligned with many of the issues we have discussed, including the rise of perspectives related to social exchange, LMX, and to some extent abusive supervision. Specifically, the unfolding model of turnover (Lee & Mitchell, 1994) highlighted the importance of negative organizational shocks that might arise from this type of supervision and how such events might enact the intrapsychic analyses involved in quitting. However, it tended to underestimate the importance of ethical/moral leadership. Examples of such leadership failings can be found throughout organizations in the U.S. and abroad. For instance, in 2015 when Twitter laid off 336 employees, many of the terminated workers found out through a tweet. Of course, this had widespread implications for not only those who were let go, but also the survivors who had to deal with the lack of interactional fairness and moral underpinnings of such a strategy. In 2020, Tesla CEO Elon Musk made the decision to restart automotive production in the midst of a pandemic and against the state and local government officials enforcing shelter in place orders. Although it is quite possible that this move prevented further layoffs, there are apparent implications and decisions that would benefit from guidance based on strong theoretical and empirical research. In this respect, we commend HRM scholars who are crossing the boundaries of traditional management research to weave in the often difficult and hard to measure aspects of moral dilemmas that may be better suited to theoretical journals such as *Academy of Management Review* and *Human Resource Management Review*.

While the current study can be described as a relatively straightforward accounting of action-oriented leadership research that has appeared in premier general management journals, this approach is certainly not without a number of important limitations. First and foremost, the decision to focus upon only premier general management journals certainly omits important research that has appeared in outlets including the *Journal of Organizational Behavior, Human Relations, Journal of Occupational and Organizational Psychology* among others. While we attempted to include as relevant of a list as possible, it is difficult to know if these decisions led to other issues.

Beyond the journals examined, there were issues that we were not able to explore in the current review due to our focus and article length. A few points not explored in the current review included the issues of university prestige, and the previous publication record or specific identity of individual authors. Some of these issues have been previously addressed (e.g., Zhao & Li, 2019), but there are numerous areas that we did not explore in the current paper.

CONCLUSION

The state of leadership research is, in three words, *promising but unfocused*. The last two decades have given rise to many new theoretical perspectives as well as a large rise in testing and a better understanding of a host of leadership approaches that fall under the broad umbrella of ethical/moral leadership theories. As a result, scholars are able to tackle leadership issues from different vantage points and offer a more robust look at the problems faced by today's leaders. These trends are generally positive for both leadership research specialists as well as for the generalists looking for applied answers to applied questions. At the same time, however, such vast perspectives can create confusion about the leadership construct and inhibit our ability to accumulate knowledge in a way that promotes clarity and understanding. Future research may benefit from a parsimonious classification that analyzes the relationship between perspectives, looking for commonalities, with a subsequent narrowing of the approaches and their associated measures to allow for a better knowledge aggregation and subsequent field application.

The changing dynamics of who is conducting the research, such as the increasing number of scholars from China, offers unique opportunities for the future of leadership research. Combined with the increasing complexity of statistical methods being utilized and efficiency of sampling, we expect to see a great deal of progress as we move forward into the next decade. However, with new opportunities come new challenges, and it will likely require more effort and collaboration in order to meet the demands of this new environment. We look forward to what the future of leadership research will bring.

REFERENCES

Badura, K. L., Grijalva, E., Newman, D. A., Yan, T. T., & Jeon, G. (2018). Gender and leadership emergence: A meta-analysis and explanatory model. *Personnel Psychology, 71*(3), 335–367. https://doi.org/10.1111/peps.12266

Bass, B. M., & Stogdill, R. M. (1990). *Bass & Stogdill's handbook of leadership: Theory, research, and managerial applications*. Simon and Schuster.

Bass, B. M., Avolio, B. J., Jung, D. I., & Berson, Y. (2003). Predicting unit performance by assessing transformational and transactional leadership. *Journal of Applied Psychology, 88*(2), 207–218. https://doi.org/10.1037/0021-9010.88.2.207

Bono, J. E., & Judge, T. A. (2004). Personality and transformational and transactional leadership: A meta-analysis. *Journal of Applied Psychology, 89*(5), 901–910. https://doi.org/10.1037/0021-9010.89.5.901

Brown, M. E., Treviño, L. K., & Harrison, D. A. (2005). Ethical leadership: A social learning perspective for construct development and testing. *Organizational Behavior and Human Decision Processes, 97*(2), 117–134. https://doi.org/10.1016/j.obhdp.2005.03.002

Chen, Y. F., & Tjosvold, D. (2006). Participative leadership by American and Chinese managers in China: The role of relationships. *Journal of Management Studies, 43*(8), 1727–1752. https://doi.org/10.1111/j.1467-6486.2006.00657.x

De Cremer, D., Mayer, D. M., van Dijke, M., Schouten, B. C., & Bardes, M. (2009). When does self-sacrificial leadership motivate prosocial behavior? It depends on followers' prevention focus. *Journal of Applied Psychology, 94*(4), 887–899. https://doi.org/10.1037/a0014782

DeRue, D. S., Nahrgang, J. D., Wellman, N. E. D., & Humphrey, S. E. (2011). Trait and behavioral theories of leadership: An integration and meta-analytic test of their relative validity. *Personnel Psychology, 64*(1), 7–52. 10.1111/j.1744-6570.2010.01201.x

DeRue, D. S., Nahrgang, J. D., Hollenbeck, J. R., & Workman, K. (2012). A quasi-experimental study of after-event reviews and leadership development. *Journal of Applied Psychology, 97*(5), 997–1015. https://doi.org/10.1037/a0028244

Dinh, J. E., Lord, R. G., Gardner, W. L., Meuser, J. D., Liden, R. C., & Hu, J. (2014). Leadership theory and research in the new millennium: Current theoretical trends and changing perspectives. *The Leadership Quarterly, 25*(1), 36–62. https://doi.org/10.1016/j.leaqua.2013.11.005

Fehr, R., Yam, K. C., & Dang, C. (2015). Moralized leadership: The construction and consequences of ethical leader perceptions. *Academy of Management Review, 40*(2), 182–209. https://doi.org/10.5465/amr.2013.0358

Gill, C., & Caza, A. (2018). An investigation of authentic leadership's individual and group influences on follower responses. *Journal of Management, 44*(2), 530–554. https://doi.org/10.1177/0149206314566461

Graeff, C. L. (1983). The situational leadership theory: A critical view. *Academy of Management Review, 8*(2), 285–291. https://doi.org/10.5465/amr.1983.4284738

Greenleaf, R. K. (1970). *The servant as leader.* Indianapolis: Robert K. Greenleaf Center.

Greenleaf, R. K. (1977). *Servant-leadership: A journey into the nature of legitimate power and greatness*. Paulist Press.

Grijalva, E., Harms, P. D., Newman, D. A., Gaddis, B. H., & Fraley, R. C. (2015). Narcissism and leadership: A meta-analytic review of linear and nonlinear relationships. *Personnel Psychology, 68*(1), 1–47. https://doi.org/10.1111/peps.12072

Han, J. H., Bartol, K. M., & Kim, S. (2015). Tightening up the performance-pay linkage: Roles of contingent reward leadership and profit-sharing in the cross-level influence of individual pay-for-performance. *Journal of Applied Psychology, 100*(2), 417–430. https://doi.org/10.1037/a0038282

Hannah, S. T., Balthazard, P. A., Waldman, D. A., Jennings, P. L., & Thatcher, R. W. (2013). The psychological and neurological bases of leader self-complexity and effects on adaptive decision-making. *Journal of Applied Psychology, 98*(3), 393–411. https://doi.org/10.1037/a0032257

Hill, N. S., & Bartol, K. M. (2016). Empowering leadership and effective collaboration in geographically dispersed teams. *Personnel Psychology, 69*(1), 159–198. https://doi.org/10.1111/peps.12108

Hoch, J. E., Bommer, W. H., Dulebohn, J. H., & Wu, D. (2018). Do ethical, authentic, and servant leadership explain variance above and beyond transformational leadership? A meta-analysis. *Journal of Management, 44*(2), 501–529. https://doi.org/10.1177/0149206316665461

House, R. J. (1996). Path-goal theory of leadership: Lessons, legacy, and a reformulated theory. *The Leadership Quarterly*, 7(3), 323–352. https://doi.org/10.1016/S1048-9843(96)90024-7

Hu, J., & Judge, T. A. (2017). Leader–team complementarity: Exploring the interactive effects of leader personality traits and team power distance values on team processes and performance. *Journal of Applied Psychology, 102*(6), 935–955. https://doi.org/10.1037/apl0000203

Ipeirotis, P. G. (2010). Analyzing the Amazon Mechanical Turk marketplace. *XRDS: Crossroads, The ACM Magazine for Students, 17*(2), 16–21. https://doi.org/10.1145/1869086.1869094

Judge, T. A., Bono, J. E., Ilies, R., & Gerhardt, M. W. (2002). Personality and leadership: A qualitative and quantitative review. *Journal of Applied Psychology, 87*(4), 765–780. https://doi.org/10.1037/0021-9010.87.4.765

Judge, T. A., & Piccolo, R. F. (2004). Transformational and transactional leadership: A meta-analytic test of their relative validity. *Journal of Applied Psychology, 89*(5), 755–768. https://doi.org/10.1037/0021-9010.89.5.755

Kang, J. H., Solomon, G. T., & Choi, D. Y. (2015). CEOs' leadership styles and managers' innovative behaviour: Investigation of intervening effects in an entrepreneurial context. *Journal of Management Studies, 52*(4), 531–554. https://doi.org/10.1111/joms.12125

Kark, R., Katz-Navon, T., & Delegach, M. (2015). The dual effects of leading for safety: The mediating role of employee regulatory focus. *Journal of Applied Psychology, 100*(5), 1332–1348. https://doi.org/10.1037/a0038818

Kauppila, O. P. (2016). When and how does LMX differentiation influence followers' work outcomes? The interactive roles of one's own LMX status and organizational context. *Personnel Psychology, 69*(2), 357–393. https://doi.org/10.1111/peps.12110

Keller, R. T. (2006). Transformational leadership, initiating structure, and substitutes for leadership: A longitudinal study of research and development project team performance. *Journal of Applied Psychology, 91*(1), 202–210. https://doi.org/10.1037/0021-9010.91.1.202

Klein, K. J., & Kozlowski, S. W. J. (2000). From micro to meso: Critical steps in conceptualizing and conducting multilevel research. *Organizational Research Methods, 3*(3), 211–236. https://doi.org/10.1177/109442810033001

Klein, K. J., Knight, A. P., Ziegert, J. C., Lim, B. C., & Saltz, J. L. (2011). When team members' values differ: The moderating role of team leadership. *Organizational Behavior and Human Decision Processes, 114*(1), 25–36. https://doi.org/10.1016/j.obhdp.2010.08.004

Lam, C. K., Huang, X., & Chan, S. C. (2015). The threshold effect of participative leadership and the role of leader information sharing. *Academy of Management Journal, 58*(3), 836–855.

Lanaj, K., Foulk, T. A., & Hollenbeck, J. R. (2018). The benefits of not seeing eye to eye with leadership: Divergence in risk preferences impacts multiteam system behavior and performance. *Academy of Management Journal, 61*(4), 1554–1582. https://doi.org/10.5465/amj.2015.0946

Landers, R. N., Sackett, P. R., & Tuzinski, K. A. (2011). Retesting after initial failure, coaching rumors, and warnings against faking in online personality measures for selection. *Journal of Applied Psychology, 96*(1), 202. https://doi.org/10.1037/a0020375

Lee, T. W., & Mitchell, T. R. (1994). An alternative approach: The unfolding model of voluntary employee turnover. *Academy of Management Review, 19*(1), 51–89. https://doi.org/10.5465/amr.1994.9410122008

LePine, M. A., Zhang, Y., Crawford, E. R., & Rich, B. L. (2016). Turning their pain to gain: Charismatic leader influence on follower stress appraisal and job performance. *Academy of Management Journal, 59*(3), 1036–1059. https://doi.org/10.5465/amj.2013.0778

Leroy, H., Anseel, F., Gardner, W. L., & Sels, L. (2015). Authentic leadership, authentic followership, basic need satisfaction, and work role performance: A cross-level study. *Journal of Management, 41*(6), 1677–1697. https://doi.org/10.1177/0149206312457822

Lin, S.-H. (J.), Ma, J., & Johnson, R. E. (2016). When ethical leader behavior breaks bad: How ethical leader behavior can turn abusive via ego depletion and moral licensing. *Journal of Applied Psychology, 101*(6), 815–830. https://doi.org/10.1037/apl0000098

Liu, D., Liao, H., & Loi, R. (2012). The dark side of leadership: A three-level investigation of the cascading effect of abusive supervision on employee creativity. *Academy of Management Journal, 55*(5), 1187–1212. https://doi.org/10.5465/amj.2010.0400

Liu, D., Hernandez, M., & Wang, L. (2014). The role of leadership and trust in creating structural patterns of team procedural justice: A social network investigation. *Personnel Psychology, 67*(4), 801–845. https://doi.org/10.1111/peps.12062

Lord, R. G., Day, D. V., Zaccaro, S. J., Avolio, B. J., & Eagly, A. H. (2017). Leadership in applied psychology: Three waves of theory and research. *Journal of Applied Psychology, 102*(3), 434–451. https://doi.org/10.1037/apl0000089

Mackey, J. D., McAllister, C. P., Maher, L. P., & Wang, G. (2019). Leaders and followers behaving badly: A meta-analytic examination of curvilinear relationships between destructive leadership and followers' workplace behaviors. *Personnel Psychology, 72*(1), 3–47. https://doi.org/10.1111/peps.12286

Mason, W., & Suri, S. (2012). Conducting behavioral research on Amazon's Mechanical Turk. *Behavior Research Methods, 44*(1), 1–23. https://doi.org/10.3758/s13428-011-0124-6

Mayer, D. M., Thau, S., Workman, K. M., van Dijke, M., & De Cremer, D. (2012). Leader mistreatment, employee hostility, and deviant behaviors: Integrating self-uncertainty and thwarted needs perspectives on deviance. *Organizational Behavior and Human Decision Processes, 117*(1), 24–40. https://doi.org/10.1016/j.obhdp.2011.07.003

Molenberghs, P., Prochilo, G., Steffens, N. K., Zacher, H., & Haslam, S. A. (2017). The neuroscience of inspirational leadership: The importance of collective-oriented language and shared group membership. *Journal of Management, 43*(7), 2168–2194. https://doi.org/10.1177/0149206314565242

Morgeson, F. P., DeRue, D. S., & Karam, E. P. (2010). Leadership in teams: A functional approach to understanding leadership structures and processes. *Journal of Management, 36*(1), 5–39. https://doi.org/10.1177/0149206309347376

Ou, A. Y., Tsui, A. S., Kinicki, A. J., Waldman, D. A., Xiao, Z., & Song, L. J. (2014). Humble chief executive officers' connections to top management team integration and middle managers' responses. *Administrative Science Quarterly, 59*(1), 34–72. https://doi.org/10.1177/0001839213520131

Owens, B. P., Yam, K. C., Bednar, J. S., Mao, J., & Hart, D. W. (2019). The impact of leader moral humility on follower moral self-efficacy and behavior. *Journal of Applied Psychology, 104*(1), 146–163. https://doi.org/10.1037/apl0000353

Owens, B. P., Wallace, A. S., & Waldman, D. A. (2015). Leader narcissism and follower outcomes: The counterbalancing effect of leader humility. *Journal of Applied Psychology, 100*(4), 1203–1213. https://doi.org/10.1037/a0038698

Paolacci, G., & Chandler, J. (2014). Inside the Turk: Understanding Mechanical Turk as a participant pool. *Current Directions in Psychological Science, 23*(3), 184–188. https://doi.org/10.1177/0963721414531598

Perry, S. J., Witt, L. A., Penney, L. M., & Atwater, L. (2010). The downside of goal-focused leadership: The role of personality in subordinate exhaustion. *Journal of Applied Psychology, 95*(6), 1145–1153. https://doi.org/10.1037/a0020538

Peterson, S. J., Galvin, B. M., & Lange, D. (2012). CEO servant leadership: Exploring executive characteristics and firm performance. *Personnel Psychology, 65*(3), 565–596. https://doi.org/10.1111/j.1744-6570.2012.01253.x

Piccolo, R. F., & Colquitt, J. A. (2006). Transformational leadership and job behaviors: The mediating role of core job characteristics. *Academy of Management Journal, 49*(2), 327–340. https://doi.org/10.5465/amj.2006.20786079

Podsakoff, P. M., Bommer, W. H., Podsakoff, N. P., & MacKenzie, S. B. (2006). Relationships between leader reward and punishment behavior and subordinate attitudes, perceptions, and behaviors: A meta-analytic review of existing and new research. *Organizational Behavior and Human Decision Processes, 99*(2), 113–142. https://doi.org/10.1016/j.obhdp.2005.09.002

Ross, J., Irani, L., Silberman, M. S., Zaldivar, A., & Tomlinson, B. (2010). Who are the crowdworkers? Shifting demographics in Mechanical Turk. *In CHI'10 Extended Abstracts on Human Factors in Computing Systems (CHI EA '10). Association for Computing Machinery*, 2863–2872. https://doi.org/10.1145/1753846.1753873

Schaubroeck, J., Lam, S. S. K., & Cha, S. E. (2007). Embracing transformational leadership: Team values and the impact of leader behavior on team performance. *Journal of Applied Psychology, 92*(4), 1020–1030. https://doi.org/10.1037/0021-9010.92.4.1020

Schriesheim, C. A., & Bird, B. J. (1979). Contributions of the Ohio State studies to the field of leadership. *Journal of Management, 5*(2), 135–145. https://doi.org/10.1177/014920637900500204

Sparrowe, R. T., & Liden, R. C. (2005). Two routes to influence: Integrating leader-member exchange and social network perspectives. *Administrative Science Quarterly, 50*(4), 505–535. https://doi.org/10.2189/asqu.50.4.505

Stogdill, R. M. (1948). Personal factors associated with leadership: A survey of the literature. *The Journal of Psychology, 25*(1), 35–71. https://doi.org/10.1080/00223980.1948.9917362

Stritch, J. M., Pedersen, M. J., & Taggart, G. (2017). The opportunities and limitations of using Mechanical Turk (MTurk) in public administration and management scholarship. *International Public Management Journal, 20*(3), 489–511. https://doi.org/10.1080/10967494.2016.1276493

Strube, M. J., & Garcia, J. E. (1981). A meta-analytic investigation of Fiedler's contingency model of leadership effectiveness. *Psychological Bulletin, 90*(2), 307–321. https://doi.org/10.1037/0033-2909.90.2.307

Tepper, B. J., Duffy, M. K., Henle, C. A., & Lambert, L. S. (2006). Procedural injustice, victim precipitation, and abusive supervision. *Personnel Psychology, 59*(1), 101–123. https://doi.org/10.1111/j.1744-6570.2006.00725.x

van Dijke, M., De Cremer, D., Mayer, D. M., & Van Quaquebeke, N. (2012). When does procedural fairness promote organizational citizenship behavior? Integrating empowering leadership types in relational justice models. *Organizational Behavior and Human Decision Processes, 117*(2), 235–248. https://doi.org/10.1016/j.obhdp.2011.10.006

Venkataramani, V., Richter, A. W., & Clarke, R. (2014). Creative benefits from well-connected leaders: Leader social network ties as facilitators of employee radical creativity. *Journal of Applied Psychology, 99*(5), 966–975. https://doi.org/10.1037/a0037088

Walumbwa, F. O., Avolio, B. J., Gardner, W. L., Wernsing, T. S., & Peterson, S. J. (2008). Authentic leadership: Development and validation of a theory-based measure. *Journal of Management, 34*(1), 89–126. https://doi.org/10.1177/0149206307308913

Walumbwa, F. O., Hartnell, C. A., & Oke, A. (2010). Servant leadership, procedural justice climate, service climate, employee attitudes, and organizational citizenship behavior: A cross-level investigation. *Journal of Applied Psychology, 95*(3), 517–529. https://doi.org/10.1037/a0018867

Wellman, E. (2017). Authority or community? A relational models theory of group-level leadership emergence. *Academy of Management Review, 42*(4), 596–617. https://doi.org/10.5465/amr.2015.0375

Wong, S. I., & Giessner, S. R. (2018). The thin line between empowering and laissez-faire leadership: An expectancy-match perspective. *Journal of Management, 44*(2), 757–783. https://doi.org/10.1177/0149206315574597

Yam, K. C., Fehr, R., Keng-Highberger, F. T., Klotz, A. C., & Reynolds, S. J. (2016). Out of control: A self-control perspective on the link between surface acting and abusive supervision. *Journal of Applied Psychology, 101*(2), 292–301. https://doi.org/10.1037/apl0000043

Yu, L., Duffy, M. K., & Tepper, B. J. (2018). Consequences of downward envy: A model of self-esteem threat, abusive supervision, and supervisory leader self-improvement. *Academy of Management Journal, 61*(6), 2296–2318. https://doi.org/10.5465/amj.2015.0183

Yukl, G. (1971). Toward a behavioral theory of leadership. *Organizational Behavior and Human Performance, 6*(4), 414–440. https://doi.org/10.1016/0030-5073(71)90026-2

Zhang, Y., LePine, J. A., Buckman, B. R., & Wei, F. (2014). It's not fair … or is it? The role of justice and leadership in explaining work stressor–job performance relationships. *Academy of Management Journal, 57*(3), 675–697. https://doi.org/10.5465/amj.2011.1110

Zhao, H., & Li, C. (2019). A computerized approach to understanding leadership research. *The Leadership Quarterly, 30*(4), 396–416. https://doi.org/10.1016/j.leaqua.2019.06.001

CHAPTER 4

IT'S NOT JUST ABOUT REPRESENTATION

Integrating Diversity Into Leadership Research

Shannon K. Cheng, Isabel Bilotta, Brook Lu, and Eden B. King

ABSTRACT

Workplaces continue to become more diverse, and although there have been long-standing efforts to increase the number of women, racially minoritized individuals, and other historically underrepresented social identities in leadership positions, there continue to be multiple challenges in creating and sustaining diverse representation in leadership. In this paper, we build on previous theory and research to discuss how diversity can be better incorporated into leadership theories related to leader emergence, development, behavior, and evaluation. We argue that diversity theories inform the formation and persistence of socialized stereotypes, and we use both an intrapersonal and interpersonal lens to understand how these stereotypes can permeate most leadership theories and underlie all aspects of the leadership experience for individuals from underrepresented groups. In addition to highlighting leadership theories through a diversity lens, we

Leadership:
Leaders, Followers, and Context, pp. 63–98

provide theoretical and practical implications for diversity and leadership scholarship moving forward.

Workplaces around the world continue to become more diverse, with respect to gender, race/ethnicity, age, nationality, sexual orientation, religion, and disability status—and as employee demographics change, it is important that organizational leadership accurately reflects these changes. Having more diverse representation in leadership positions can lead to more inclusive and democratic practices, as well as improved employee satisfaction and organizational performance (Eagly & Chin, 2010; Hebl et al., 2012; Hunt et al., 2015). There have been strong efforts to increase representation in leadership across different industries and fields, and for the most part, awareness surrounding the issues of representation has helped improve these numbers. However, it is clear that we still have a long way to go (Catalyst, 2019; Deloitte, 2019). For example, in 2020, although the number of women CEOs in the Fortune 500 hit a record high of 37 women, only three of them were women of color—and none were Black or Latinx (Hinchliffe, 2020).

Leadership for underrepresented groups (URGs) has often been described as a "labyrinth," highlighting the multiple barriers that these individuals must negotiate, such as stereotypes and role expectations, ingroup-outgroup dynamics, status differentials, and social network limitations (Ayman & Korabik, 2010; Eagly & Carli, 2007). However, most leadership theories and research rarely integrate diversity into their work—the impact of diversity is often instead mentioned in discussion sections as a limitation or future direction. In 2010, the *American Psychologist* published a special issue on diversity and leadership, where the contributors called for better integration of diversity into leadership research (Chin, 2010). However, a more recent review on leadership theory and research by Dinh et al. (2014) still demonstrated limited improvement in the trajectory of incorporating diversity in the leadership literature. Research on diversity in leadership is growing (e.g., Rast et al., 2018), but not at the pace of diversity in actual organizations.

In addition, the lack of adequate and sustained representation highlights a larger issue than just pushing individuals from URGs into leadership positions. Society has started to become more willing to recognize talent in a select number of individuals from URGs, and as such, more are entering top leadership positions across fields, industries, and identities (e.g., Indra Nooyi of PepsiCo, President Barack Obama, Satya Nadella of Microsoft, Jason Wright of the Washington Football Team). However, systemic changes in the ways that organizations identify and develop talent have yet to occur, which will continue to make it more likely for White men to emerge and succeed as leaders. In addition, as leaders, individuals from URGs continue to be impacted by their identities; they tend to face more hurdles and biases, which can lead to higher levels of turnover (Thomas et al., 2019). In order to promote and retain more leaders from different backgrounds, we need to better incorporate diversity into how we think about leadership and its current theories. Otherwise, the systemic disadvantages that URGs face in the labyrinth will continue to be perpetuated.

In this chapter, we use the term "URG leader" to refer to leaders who hold social identities that are historically underrepresented in leadership positions, and to broadly discuss how leadership theories can be informed by diversity research. This discussion is not limited to gender or racially minoritized groups, which have been the most common social identities studied in leadership research; rather, we aim to include all marginalized identities (e.g., LGBTQ+ individuals, individuals with disabilities, underrepresented religious groups). However, we acknowledge the limitation and danger of lumping URGs together in this way, which can erase the unique histories of and challenges faced by different groups. This erasure can also dilute efforts in improving the representation and experiences of leaders from specific groups. However, the primary goal of this paper is to build off of previous research and provide an integrated perspective on how diversity influences multiple aspects of leadership, while providing space for continued examination of the unique barriers that different URGs encounter (e.g., see Roberts et al., 2019, for research and discussion on the Black leadership experience). Similarly, throughout the paper, we make comparisons between URG and dominant (or non-URG) group members in their experiences throughout the leadership process, and we primarily refer to White men as our comparison group. However, we acknowledge the other identities that these dominant group members tend to hold as well, such as being heterosexual, cisgendered, and nondisabled, and how different intersections with these identities can shape individuals' experiences. Lastly, we acknowledge that the focus of this chapter is American-centric, with the best understanding of American organizations and socialized stereotypes in American culture. However, there is incredible value in understanding how diversity and leadership plays out in different cultures, and we hope that this chapter provides a stepping stone to understanding how these processes may unfold in other cultures, comparing and contrasting these processes, and learning and adapting best practices from each other.

Previous researchers have examined possible ways to help incorporate diversity into leadership theories and research, such as how diversity applies to specific leadership theories, how specific leadership theories apply to understanding bias, or how different identities impact leadership development and effectiveness (e.g., Ayman & Korabik, 2010; Fassinger et al., 2010; Hogue & Lord, 2007; Rast et al., 2018; van Knippenberg & Hogg, 2003). In this chapter, we build on this work and argue that diversity theories inform the formation and persistence of socialized stereotypes, which can permeate most leadership theories and underlie all aspects of the leadership experience for URGs. For example, the biases that often result from these stereotypes can impact whether someone is perceived as having leadership potential, as well as how someone is perceived as a leader (e.g., how likable, competent, and effective they are).

In addition, current leadership theories not only focus on the individual leader, but also on followers, peers, supervisors, organizational setting/context, and culture. As a result, leadership is no longer conceptualized as an individual characteristic or difference, but rather is depicted in different models as dyadic, shared, relational, strategic, global, and a complex social dynamic (Avolio et al., 2009; Yukl, 2006). Taking into consideration this current direction of leadership theories, in this paper, we use both an intrapersonal and interpersonal lens in discussing how stereotypes and biases play a role in existing leadership theories (e.g., trait, social exchange, behavioral theories), and what this means for URGs as employees with leadership potential and as individuals in leadership positions (see Figure 4.1). We will start by providing a brief overview of relevant diversity theories, discuss how these diversity theories can manifest in leadership theories related to leader emergence, development, behavior, and evaluation, and then provide implications and future directions on how to better integrate diversity into leadership theory and research.

DIVERSITY THEORIES

As many leadership theories depend on how we perceive and evaluate each other, diversity theories can provide important insight into how these processes occur. At work and in our everyday lives, we are constantly being inundated with new information. In order to sort through all of this information without getting overwhelmed, we frequently use cognitive shortcuts that allow us to move throughout the world more efficiently (Shah & Oppenheimer, 2008). For example, we are often inclined to group individuals into social categories to more easily understand who they are and how we should interact with them. These social categories are based on different characteristics (e.g., race, gender, sexual orientation) and come with unique stereotypes for each category. These stereotypes are generalized beliefs about a specific group of people and are based on information that we have received throughout our early lives, such as from family and peers, education and government systems, and media (Myers, 2010). Stereotypes quickly become ingrained in how people think, behave,

Figure 4.1

An Integrated Model of Diversity and Leadership

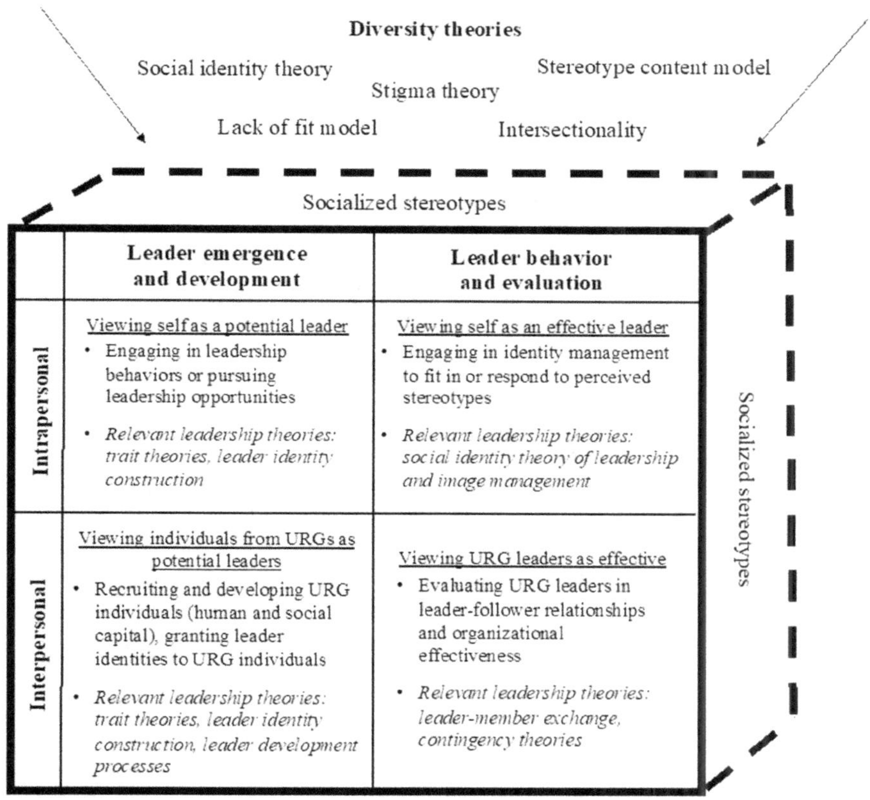

Note. Biases against URGs are manifested at the intrapersonal and interpersonal levels with respect to how URG leaders emerge and are evaluated. The underlying force behind these biases are the stereotypes and beliefs that we have been socialized to accept, as informed by a number of diversity theories.

and feel, and although they often allow for quicker information processing, they can be detrimental when overgeneralized and used to simplify perceptions of an individual to perceptions of their group identity. There are wide variations among individuals within a group, and if stereotypes are relied on too heavily in judgments and decision making, they can lead to prejudice and discrimination—whether intentional or not (Dovidio et al., 1996). For example, research has demonstrated strong evidence for discrimination against multiple different URGs in the workplace, from hiring decisions to everyday interactions, and how this biased treatment often stems from social categorization and stereotypes (e.g., Cohen & Bunker, 1975; Finkelstein & Burke, 1998; Giel et al., 2010; King et al., 2006).

There are a number of different theories from diversity scholarship that help explain both the formation and manifestation of stereotypes and other socialized beliefs. Social identity theory helps explain the natural tendency to categorize and label ourselves and others into different groups; stigma theory helps us understand why certain groups are viewed more negatively than others; the stereotype content model provides more details on how different stigmatized groups are viewed; the lack of fit model explains how stereotypes might limit perceptions of certain groups and what they can do; and lastly, intersectionality theory highlights the multiple identities an individual can hold and how these different identities can impact their experiences and others' perceptions of them.

Social Identity Theory

Within social identity theory, there are two common processes that impact how people view themselves and others: self-categorization and social comparison (Tajfel & Turner, 1985). Self-categorization occurs when individuals classify themselves and others into different social categories. These categories can be based on a wide variety of characteristics, both visible (e.g., race, gender, age) and invisible (e.g., sexual orientation, religion, some disabilities). This categorization typically results in the formation of an "in-group" (those who are in the same social category) and an "out-group" (those who are in a different social category than the in-group), and after categorization occurs, social comparison often follows. The in-group is often viewed as an extension of one's self, and in order to protect one's sense of self, there is often a tendency to view one's in-group positively. This can sometimes lead to favoritism toward in-group members, which can then lead to intentional or unintentional discrimination against out-group members (Hennessy & West, 1999; Oakes & Turner, 1980). For example, research has demonstrated that we tend to be more willing to help others when they are in our in-group (Levine et al., 2005).

Stigma Theory

Discrimination against out-group members can be exacerbated when the out-group is stigmatized. One of the most commonly used definitions of stigma comes from Goffman (1963), who claimed that marks of stigma are socially constructed attributes that deeply discredit, taint, and discount individuals. He defined three categories of stigma—abominations of the body (e.g., physical deformities, chronic diseases, physical disabilities), characterological flaws (e.g., drug addicts, criminals and convicts, sexual deviants), and tribal stigmas (e.g., race, religion, national origin; Goffman, 1963). Individuals who hold these types of identities are often denigrated as a lesser out-group, holding less power and influence than individuals without these stigmas. Link and Phelan (2001) outline the process of these negative interpersonal effects, defining stigmatization as the co-occurrence of labeling, stereotyping, separation, status loss, and discrimination. It is also important to note that stigmatization does not simply impact one's relationships with others; stigma is often internalized and impacts how individuals view themselves as well.

In addition, there are different aspects of stigmatized identities that can impact how the stigma is perceived, as well as how an individual might choose to manage their identities in their interactions with others. For example, stigmatized identities are often categorized as visible and invisible; invisible identities do not have observable attributes (e.g., sexual orientation, religious affiliation), and individuals with these identities may try to conceal and "pass" as a less stigmatized identity. Another important aspect of stigmatized identities is perceived controllability; individuals with stigmatized identities that are seen as controllable are often perceived more negatively. For example, Hebl and Kleck (2002) demonstrated that interview applicants were perceived as less favorable and hireable when the onset of their obesity or physical disability was portrayed as controllable versus uncontrollable.

Stereotype Content Model

Stereotypes are often the reason why some identities are more stigmatized than others. According to the stereotype content model, stereotypes can be thought of having two dimensions: competence and warmth (Fiske et al., 2002). The most common stereotypes are of mixed stereotype content, either low competence-high warmth or high competence-low warmth. Individuals viewed as having low competence and high warmth (e.g., pregnant women, individuals with disabilities, older adults) are seen as not likely or capable of harming others. On the other hand, individuals viewed as having high competence and low warmth (e.g., career-oriented women, Asians) are seen as capable, but their intentions are not always perceived as positive (Fiske et al., 2002). The stereotype content model suggests that status typically predicts high competence, and that threat of competition typically predicts low warmth. The stereotype content model also discusses the different types of emotions associated with the four competence-warmth combinations—individuals who are perceived as low competence-high warmth tend to be viewed with pity, high competence-low warmth with envy, high competence-high warmth with admiration, and low competence-low warmth with contempt.

Lack of Fit Model

The lack of fit model (Heilman, 1983, 1997) was initially used to explain gender inequities in the workplace, such that women were "unfit" for jobs that were considered masculine. Jobs that were high-powered and high-paying were more often categorized as men's rather than women's work (Duehr & Bono, 2006). These high-powered jobs include leadership positions, and the lack of fit model helps explain why women have historically struggled, and continue to struggle, to enter and stay in leadership roles. This lack of fit is often based on stereotypes, as stereotypes are not only descriptive (e.g., describing how men and women are) but also prescriptive (e.g., describing how men and women should be), and the latter can engender backlash when individuals act counter to their stereotypes (Eagly & Karau, 2002; Heilman, 2012).

In more recent years, the lack of fit model has also been applied to other groups. For example, Sy et al. (2010) discussed how this model applies to Asian Americans and how they do not fit typical ideas of what a leader should be, in that they are perceived as good workers but not good leaders. More broadly, other research has shown how being White (versus non-White) is perceived as more consistent with the prototypical view of a leader (Rosette et al., 2008). This perceived lack of fit results in decreased expectations of success by others, increased expectations of failure, and ultimately diminished performance as well (Heilman, 1983), which can significantly impact how both URG employees themselves and others perceive their work performance and leadership potential.

Intersectionality

The aforementioned categorization and evaluative processes are often even more complex, because every individual holds multiple identities, and the salience and stigmatization of an identity can change based on different situations. For example, if a Muslim woman is in an organization where most people are Muslim, but she is the only woman, her gender identity will be more salient than her religious identity; in contrast, if she is in an organization where most people are women, but she is the only

Muslim individual, her religious identity will be more salient than her gender identity. Intersectionality looks at the meaning and implications of simultaneous membership in multiple social identity groups (Cole, 2009; Crenshaw, 1989; Hall et al., 2019), proposing that the inequities related to one identity (e.g., gender) can interrelate with the inequities related to another identity (e.g., race). For example, women leaders may be perceived differently based on their race—Black women may be perceived as more dominant and Asian women may be perceived as more competent when compared to White women, which may impact how others respond to them as leaders (Rosette et al., 2016).

EXAMINING LEADERSHIP THEORIES THROUGH THE LENS OF DIVERSITY THEORIES

Using diversity theories and their explanation of how stereotypes are formed and manifested in attitudes and behaviors, we now have a foundation to examine leadership theories through a diversity lens. This lens is both intrapersonal and interpersonal, and helps explain how individuals from URGs are perceived and evaluated (and perceive and evaluate themselves) throughout the leadership process, elucidating why it is consistently harder for URGs to reach and stay in leadership positions in organizations. In this section, we examine leadership theories relevant to leadership emergence, development, behavior, and evaluation—including trait theories, leader identity construction, leader development, social identity theory of leadership, leader-member exchange, and contingency theories. Although these leadership theories are noncomprehensive, they can provide a foundation in discussing the important role that diversity theories play in the understanding and application of leadership theories more broadly.

How URG Leaders Emerge and Develop

According to Smith and Foti (1998), "Individuals emerge as group leaders by fitting the shared conceptions of followers. This shared conception exists as a set of expectations, concerning appropriate leader attributes and behaviors" (p. 148). Thus, leader emergence depends not only upon the traits enacted by the individual attempting to lead, but also that others notice and acknowledge these attempts (Hollander, 1992; Lord & Maher, 1991). Eagly (2018) contends that "special conditions" and "unusual competence" are often prerequisites for individuals from URGs (e.g., women, racially minoritized groups) to emerge as leaders. That is, in order to be viewed by others (and themselves) as having leadership potential, these individuals may be held to a higher standard or need to be perceived as extraordinary. In this section, we examine how URG leaders navigate both intrapersonal and interpersonal challenges to leader emergence, highlighting the role of trait theories, leader identity construction, and leader development processes.

Intrapersonal: Viewing Self as a Potential Leader

Trait Theories and Leader Identity Construction: Claiming a Leader Identity. Lord and colleagues introduced implicit leadership theory (ILT) to describe the cognitive prototypes (i.e., leadership schemas) that underlie employees' perceptions of the ideal business leader (Lord, 1985; Epitropaki & Martin, 2005). People are often regarded as leaders if they exhibit characteristics, behaviors, or traits that followers deem inherently leader-like, based on preexisting notions about and prior experiences with leadership prototypes (Forsyth, 2009). Some of the common ILT factors that have emerged include sensitivity, charisma, intelligence, dedication, dynamism, and masculinity (Offerman et al., 1994; Epitropaki & Martin, 2004). These factors represent the "typical" leadership prototype and are often positively related to followers' perceptions of leader effectiveness (Junker & van Dick, 2014).

However, in the United States, trait theories of leadership have often been applied to narrow samples of mainly White men; as such, certain leadership traits that are deemed effective (e.g., assertiveness) may be rooted in biases that keep White men in positions of power—as opposed to acknowledging "the potential for people from outside the dominant group to provide excellent leadership because of their differences" (Eagly & Chin, 2010, p. 216). Independent studies and meta-analyses have consistently shown that White employees emerge as leaders more often than racially minoritized groups (Chung-Herrera & Lankau, 2005; Rosette et al., 2008), and men emerge as leaders more often than women (Badura et al., 2018; Heilman et al., 1989; Nye & Forsyth, 1991). For decades, people have discussed the "think manager, think male" phenomenon (e.g., Koenig et al., 2011; Schein, 1973), and there is no doubt that—at least in America—the "prototypical" leader in mind is a White man (Liberman & Golom, 2015; Rosette et al., 2008). As a result, anything outside of the White man demographic can seem like a lack of fit when it comes to leadership potential. In addition, although research on URG leader emergence has traditionally examined the influence of demographic characteristics separately (e.g., the influence of gender on leader emergence, the impact of race on leader emergence; Rosette & Livingston, 2012; Sanchez-Hucles & Davis, 2010), individuals with multiple URG identities (e.g., Black women) may be perceived as having additional degrees of separation from the prototypical leader.

These socialized perceptions of who leaders "should" be can impact individuals' perception of their own ability to engage in leadership behaviors or pursue leadership opportunities. Leader identity construction theory (DeRue & Ashford, 2010) focuses on the social process through which individuals claim and grant leadership identities, and the likelihood that someone will claim or grant leader identities can depend on ILT, the risks and rewards associated with claiming and granting a leader identity, and organizational structures that may automatically impose leader and follower identities (DeRue & Ashford, 2010). Based on existing biases in ILT and lack of representation in current leadership, URG employees may internalize messages that they are not "leadership material," lowering their leader self-efficacy. Research has demonstrated that leader self-efficacy, which are evaluations of one's own ability, knowledge, and skills for leading effectively, can exert substantial influence on leader emergence by positively impacting both motivation and performance (Chan & Drasgow, 2001; Hannah et al., 2008; Machida & Schaubroeck, 2011). In addition, research has shown how, compared to men, women are less likely to apply to jobs unless they feel fully qualified (Ignatova, 2019; Mohr, 2014), and this phenomenon likely applies to other URGs as well. For example, if URG employees know they will be judged to a higher standard as nonprototypical applicants for leadership roles, they will likely make sure that they are fully ready for the job before they put themselves up for a leadership position. But if their non-URG counterparts (e.g., White men) are less likely to experience this hesitation, and if others reward them for pursuing leadership opportunities early and often (without questioning why URG individuals are not pursuing these opportunities as well), homogeneous leadership will continue to be perpetuated in organizations.

Interpersonal: Viewing Individuals from URGs as Potential Leaders

Trait Theories and Leader Identity Construction: Granting a Leader Identity. The root of diversity and inclusion issues is never simply because URG individuals are not going after what they want or because they are not "leaning in" enough. They face a multitude of barriers from others, who also hold biased beliefs about who has leadership potential and may be less likely to grant leader identities to individuals from URGs. People who are perceived as "leader-like" tend to receive higher ratings of job performance and promotability (Porath et al., 2015; Staw & Barsade, 1993; Zhang et al., 2012); however, URG employees often struggle more in demonstrating this potential to others (Blau & DeVaro, 2007). For example, if women act in an agentic manner (e.g., independent, assertive, self-confident), which is how leaders are expected to behave, they often receive backlash—from both men and other women—in the form of decreased likability and hireability (e.g., Bowles et al., 2007; Heilman & Okimoto, 2007; Rudman & Glick, 2001). However, if women act according to their stereotype (i.e., in a communal manner—friendly, unselfish, concerned for others; Eagly & Wood, 1991), they will not be seen as having leadership potential either, resulting in the double bind that many women face when trying to pursue higher-level positions (Zheng et al., 2018).

These barriers hold for other URG identities as well. For example, Black and Latinx employees are often stereotyped as less intelligent and less competent (Rosette et al., 2008); individuals with disabilities are perceived as handicapped and less capable (Colella, 1994); and individuals from underrepresented religions may be perceived as holding different values that are not aligned with the organization. Even Asian Americans, who hold the stereotype of being competent and good workers, are often seen as not having leadership potential—leading to the idea of the "bamboo ceiling" (Burris et al., 2013). The bamboo ceiling is similar to the "glass ceiling" initially coined for women (Powell & Butterfield, 1994), where these individuals can succeed to a certain extent but are less able to make it all the way to the top of an organization. These stereotypes make it more likely that a more prototypical candidate (e.g., White man) will be granted a leader identity than someone whose identity is systematically portrayed as a worse fit for leadership by education systems, media, organizations, and others.

In addition to the lack of fit with others' ILTs, another potential driving force preventing URGs from reaching leadership positions may be others' desire to maintain the status quo. For example, Rudman et al. (2012) found that backlash against agentic women was more severe when the raters held gender system-justifying beliefs and when they perceived that there was a threat to the gender hierarchy. Relatedly, McDonald et al. (2018) assessed White male managers' reactions to the appointment of a woman or racially minoritized CEO, finding that White male managers experienced decreased identification with their organization and decreased helping behavior (especially towards women or racially minoritized colleagues). These studies show how biases not only affect who is perceived as having leadership potential, but also who is desired as a leader, both of which can pose significant barriers to URG individuals pursuing leadership positions.

Leadership Development Processes. Leader and leadership development focus on both the development of human capital (i.e., building individual knowledge, skills, and abilities) and social capital (i.e., building relationships that enhance cooperation and resource exchange; Day, 2000), and interpersonal biases can prevent URG employees from developing to their full potential by impacting day-to-day opportunities and interactions. For example, research has demonstrated that, despite being equally likely to express interest in challenging experiences, women are given fewer challenging developmental experiences at work than men (Eagly & Carli, 2007; King et al., 2012). The same effect holds for men and women of color across several studies (Cianni & Romberger, 1995; Hite, 2007; Smith & Joseph, 2010), suggesting that URGs have limited access to mastery experiences (e.g., challenging or high-profile assignments, on-the-job training) that would greatly benefit their career advancement. Women are also less likely than men to receive negative feedback for their work (King et al., 2012), which may initially be seen as a positive; however, if this stems from benevolent sexism and a desire to protect women from criticism, then it may actually prevent women from receiving constructive feedback that would help them continue to improve and develop. Inaccuracies in feedback have also been demonstrated with Black individuals and individuals with disabilities, even when the person's performance was subpar (Harber, 2004; Hastorf et al., 1979).

With respect to social capital, individuals from URGs often experience general exclusion from formal and informal networks (Ibarra, 1995; Wyatt & Silvester, 2015) and a lack of mentorship and sponsorship (especially from high-status others, such as White men; Eagly & Chin, 2010; Sanchez-Hucles & Davis, 2010). Social capital theory contends that one's membership in a group confers greater opportunities (e.g., acquiring valued information and resources from colleagues; Brass, 1995), and if URG employees are continuously left out of important networks and fail to receive appropriate mentorship, they will continue to cluster in the lower levels of organizations—rather than rise to the upper echelons of leadership like their non-URG counterparts (Pedulla & Pager, 2019; Tharenou, 1999). Research has also shown that even with a network that includes influential ties, racially minoritized groups and women receive fewer job leads from their social networks (McDonald, 2011; McGuire, 2002). These findings demonstrate that access to leadership opportunities not only depends on "who you know," but also how you are perceived and integrated into the network.

In addition, due to their underrepresentation in leadership positions, it is much harder for URG employees to find an influential mentor who fully understands their experiences and can provide instrumental advice on how to navigate the workplace and pursue leadership opportunities (Hebl et al., 2012; Underhill, 2006). Unfortunately, research has also shown how, although "like" mentors for URG employees (compared to mentors who are of a different social identity group, such as a heterosexual mentor for an LGBTQ+ employee or a male mentor for a female employee) often provide psychosocial support and have benefits for job satisfaction, they can be less effective at providing instrumental support, such as increased salary or promotions (Hebl et al., 2012). This is likely due to their status as individuals from URGs; even though they are in higher positions than their mentees, they may not have as much power or influence as a non-URG mentor—emphasizing the deeply-rooted power structures within organizations and broader society.

How URG Leaders Behave and Are Evaluated

After individuals from URGs enter leadership positions, stereotypes and biases continue to influence their experiences. It impacts how they view themselves as leaders and how much they engage in identity management behaviors. For example, do they downplay their URG identities and try to fit in? Do they actively work to counteract stereotypes that others may hold about them? These stereotypes also impact how others view URG leaders and how effective they perceive these leaders to be. Ingrained biases can cause others to inappropriately attribute the successes and failures of URG leaders and continue to hold them to higher standards than their non-URG counterparts. In this section, we look at the social identity theory of leadership, leader-member exchange, and contingency theories to examine how intrapersonal and interpersonal biases impact how individuals from URGs and others respond to their status as leaders and how they are evaluated in these leadership positions.

Intrapersonal: Viewing Self as an Effective Leader

Social Identity Theory of Leadership and Leader Image Management. The social identity approach to leadership emphasizes the idea that leaders not only lead groups of people, but also are part of the groups that they lead (van Knippenberg & Hogg, 2003). When taking into consideration this group identity, the social identity theory of leadership argues that leaders who are more prototypical of the group are better supported and perceived as more effective, especially when group membership is salient and central to the group members' identities (Hogg et al., 2012). This impacts URG leaders through metastereotypes, which are beliefs about how others view us and what stereotypes they hold about us (Vorauer et al., 1998). Metastereotypes are shaped by the descriptions and prescriptions we have received about our social identities throughout our lives, and awareness of these stereotypes can impact URG leader behaviors and how they manage their identities in the workplace (Voyles et al., 2014). In general, image management is important for leaders because they need to appear credible and demonstrate legitimate authority in order for social influence processes to take place (Chemers, 2000). On top of that, URG leaders often have to work harder to establish their legitimacy as nonprototypical leaders (e.g., Vial et al., 2016).

If URG leaders perceive that others feel that they are a poorer fit for the position, they may experience stereotype threat. This is the apprehension that people feel in an interaction or situation where they know their group holds a specific stereotype (Steele & Aronson, 1995). For example, Steele and colleagues have demonstrated how stereotype threat in academic settings can negatively impact female and Black students' math and general test performance, respectively (Spencer et al., 1999; Steele & Aronson, 1995), as well as White individuals' behaviors in interracial contexts (Goff et al., 2008). In the leadership context, stereotype threat can make individuals from URGs continue to have lower self-efficacy as leaders and doubt their abilities (Chin, 2013; Hoyt & Murphy, 2016). Consequently, they may perceive themselves as less effective and often feel like they need to prove themselves (Chin, 2013), which can be exhausting to constantly think about how one's behaviors will be perceived and evaluated by others.

Indeed, a recent Catalyst report examined the "emotional tax" that many racially minoritized groups face at work, where they feel the need to be on guard to protect themselves against potential bias from their coworkers and employers (Travis & Thorpe-Moscon, 2018). Zweigenhaft and Domhoff (2006, p. 7) also discuss how racially minoritized leaders often work to demonstrate that they are "willing to join the game as it has always been played" by reducing visible signs of their racial and ethnic background (e.g., appearance, language, conversation topics), in order to fit in and not make others feel as if they are threatening the status quo. These efforts can be emotionally and physically exhausting, especially if these changes are not authentic to the individual's sense of self and identity. It is also important to note that this is an additional, significant part of image management that non-URG individuals often do not have to engage in, because their identities already fit in with the dominant workplace culture.

In addition, based on the social identity of leadership, non-URG leaders often have greater leeway to challenge norms, as their identity may be perceived as more representative of the group (i.e., more prototypical). They may be more trusted to act in the group's best interest, whereas less prototypical leaders may need to gain the group's trust by engaging in more group-oriented behaviors (van Knippenberg & Hogg, 2003). As a result, although URG leaders may want to challenge inequities in their organizations, they may feel constrained by their nonprototypical identities. In order to demonstrate that they are part of the larger group and receive more support from others, URG leaders may actually double down on traditional organizational practices and structures—even if they know that these practices and structures perpetuate inequity (Seegars & Ramarajan, 2019). The external pressures that impact URG leaders' image management and leadership behaviors clearly demonstrate that although promoting URG individuals is a critical step, more work is needed to eliminate the longstanding inequities and biases within organizations.

Interpersonal: Viewing Individuals from URGs as Effective Leaders

Leader-Member Exchange Theory. Leader-member exchange (LMX) theory postulates that the relationship between a supervisor and subordinate is dyadic and involves a unique, reciprocal exchange (Dulebohn et al., 2012). Supervisors establish different relationships with their subordinates, yielding high- or low-quality relationships. In addition, the relationships that leaders hold with their followers are an important aspect in how others perceive their effectiveness as leaders. Research has demonstrated the challenges that URG leaders face when attempting to develop successful relationships and effectively engage followers (see Scandura & Lankau, 1996 for a theoretical model of the effects of leader-member diversity in LMX). Demographic heterogeneity in the composition of the leader-follower dyad appears to impact the quality of these relationships (particularly when the leader is from a URG). Scholars have shown differences in effective communication, mentoring relationships, and development of networks for homogenous dyads compared to cross-race or cross-gender dyads (Ibarra, 1993; Ragins, 1995; Thomas, 1993). A recent study by Randolph-Seng et al. (2016) also empirically examined the theoretical framework put forth by Scandura and Lankau (1996), demonstrating that in dyads where the leader and follower were both racial majority group members, followers perceived their relationship with the leaders more positively with respect to professional respect, affect, and contribution than followers who were in dyads that were cross-race or both racially minoritized group members.

The differences in LMX relationships may be in part due to follower biases that prevent them from fully trusting or believing in their URG leaders. For example, research has shown that individuals with greater levels of social dominance orientation and patriotism for America are more likely to be biased in favor of leaders who are White and men, and biased against leaders who are from racially minoritized groups or women (Hoyt & Simon, 2016). It is possible that these followers adamantly believe that individuals from URGs cannot be as good of leaders as White men, or that they are opposed to URG leaders threatening the status quo. These biases can cause individuals to disrespect their leaders or inaccurately attribute the outcomes of their leaders' behaviors (Scandura & Lankau, 1996). Attribution errors highlight how we tend to attribute others' successes to the situation (e.g., "they just got lucky") and their failures to personal attributes (e.g., "they are a bad leader"; Pettigrew, 1979; Rosette et al., 2008). It is important to note that these errors do not only occur with people who hold explicit biases; we all have tendencies to make attribution errors when it comes to others—especially those that we may hold stronger stereotypes for. This demonstrates how leader-follower relationships can be more complicated for URG leaders and how the navigation of these dynamics heavily depends on how their followers view them, and not just their own personal behaviors as leaders.

Contingency Theories. Contingency theories attempt to unpack how situations might impact or constrain leader behaviors—emphasizing that there may not be "one best way" to approach leadership (Lord et al., 2017; Vroom & Jago, 2007). For example, Fiedler (1967) found that relationship- and task-motivated leaders performed better or worse than the other style depending on the type of situation they were in, which varied by leader-member relations, follower-task structure, and leader-position power. Similarly, House and Mitchell (1974) found that when behaviors are properly matched to the situation, based on follower and environmental characteristics, better attitudinal and behavioral outcomes occur. However, although contingency theories take into consideration that different leader behaviors and styles are appropriate for different situations, these behaviors and styles are often still examined with prototypical leaders who are White men. URG employees are often held to higher performance standards than their non-URG counterparts, such as needing higher ratings in order to be promoted (Lyness & Heilman, 2006) or being punished even when they are doing well (Berri, 2018; Carton & Rosette, 2011). As such, URG leaders may need to further adjust their behaviors and leadership style in different situations, because it may not just be the situation and behaviors that matter, but also how the individuals engaging in the behaviors are perceived.

URG leaders may also be punished more when they make a mistake. Research has demonstrated that the less a leader's identity fits with the prototypical White man, the more they may be punished (Brescoll et al., 2010). For example, Black women are evaluated more negatively as leaders than both Black men and White women when they make a mistake—likely due to the fact that Black men and White women can benefit from one dominant identity (being a man or White, respectively), while Black women are unable to benefit from either (Rosette & Livingston, 2012). Previous research has also demonstrated how URG leaders are evaluated worse when they have more URG followers (e.g., Hernandez et al., 2016) or when they engage in diversity-valuing behaviors (e.g., Hekman et al., 2017)—

contexts and behaviors that White men are not punished for, emphasizing how URG leaders are often evaluated differently, simply based on their identity. These more negative evaluations are also demonstrated in how URG leaders are often attacked more frequently and aggressively than their non-URG counterparts; for example, American political leaders like Alexandria Ocasio-Cortez, Hillary Clinton, Kamala Harris, and Lina Hidalgo have faced high levels of scrutiny and criticism, not only on their work and policies, but also their personal lives, appearance, and character (O'Rourke, 2020; Strachan et al., 2019; Wemple, 2017). As such, URG leaders often carry an additional emotional and psychological burden—not only trying to prevent and protect themselves from these attacks, but also addressing the inevitable attacks when they come.

The types of leadership positions that URG employees enter can also impact their perceived effectiveness. When leadership roles are offered to women and racially minoritized groups, they tend to be higher risk (Morgenroth et al., 2020)—a concept scholars refer to as the "glass cliff" phenomenon, where URG leaders are more likely to be promoted or selected when the organization is in crisis. For example, Jason Wright was hired as the National Football League's first Black team president in the midst of the COVID-19 pandemic, a significant racial reckoning in the United States, a recent re-branding of his team's name, the Washington Football team (formerly known as the Washington Redskins), and multiple sexual harassment and bullying allegations on the team (Doubek & Shapiro, 2020)—which not only begs the question of why it has taken so long for the National Football League to hire a Black team president, but also why the first one was hired in the midst of multiple significant crises. This phenomenon is not unique to the National Football League, and in addition to being offered riskier and potentially more challenging positions when promoted, URG leaders often cite a lack of support from their colleagues, as well as insufficient authority to address challenges (Glass & Cook, 2016). Research has also shown how, if the URG leader is unable to fix the problems, they are often quickly replaced by a White man, which is known as the "savior effect" (Cook & Glass, 2014). These examples further demonstrate how URG leaders face many challenges throughout their experiences as leaders, highlighting deeply-rooted issues in the way that URG leaders are selected, developed, supported, and evaluated.

DISCUSSION

The goals of the current chapter were to (a) discuss how leadership and diversity scholarship might be better integrated, and (b) highlight existing research and inspire new avenues of thinking on the intrapersonal and interpersonal dynamics of leader development, emergence, behavior, and evaluation. To that end, we have described the ways that socialized stereotypes and biases influence how individuals from different backgrounds view themselves and are viewed by others throughout the leadership process. Now we will explore the implications of this integration for theory, practice, and research, and provide a few prioritized future research questions.

Theoretical and Future Research Implications

A deeper integration of diversity theory and evidence into the leadership domain offers value for both leadership and diversity scholarship. From the perspective of leadership theory, it is uniquely valuable to consider how social identities and stereotypes shape the ways that leaders are developed and evaluated. This perspective demands an explicit acknowledgement that leadership is not experienced, achieved, or performed in a uniform manner. Instead, integrating the lens of diversity necessitates consideration of variety in the intrapersonal and interpersonal development and manifestation of leadership. Understanding leader development, as an example, thus requires consideration of the complex ways that individuals from different backgrounds come to understand what it means to be a good leader and how their own identity may or may not be aligned with this ideal. Understanding leader effectiveness must also take into account behavioral patterns that reflect identity-based socialization; the behaviors used to define effective leadership may look different for leaders from some backgrounds compared to others. This means that foundational leadership theories could be strengthened by considering the ways that social identities and stereotypes influence how people perceive themselves and how they are perceived by others.

It is important to note that some theories like the social identity theory of leadership (van Knippenberg & Hogg, 2003) have started to tie in concepts from diversity theories, such as how people often define group identities and categorize others as part of the group (in-group) or not (out-group). In addition, leader identity construction and other theories have started to question more traditional conceptualizations of leadership as "top-down, hierarchical, and equivalent to formal supervisory roles in organizations" (DeRue & Ashford, 2010, p. 627), opting for more sociorelational and dynamic processes. Due to the longstanding issues of representation in leadership positions, researchers often discuss how individuals from URGs might be considered less prototypical or less likely both to claim and be granted a leader identity (DeRue & Ashford, 2010; van Knippenberg & Hogg, 2003). However, we encourage researchers to also take a proactive approach to examining these phenomena—not only recognizing how socialized stereotypes impact their theories and research, but also challenging previous conceptualizations of leadership and leadership potential. Researchers do not only have to describe how intrapersonal and interpersonal biases continue to manifest in the leadership process; they can also innovate and push forward new ways of thinking. How can we broaden our perspectives of leadership and leadership potential, or redefine group identities and norms? What aspects of our current definitions and implicit theories of leadership are still rooted in society's preferences for leaders who are White men?

For example, what are the criteria used to define someone as having "leadership potential?" Throughout the past few years, there has been an increasing push to value diversity, equity, and inclusion in organizations, and these efforts are best implemented and sustained in organizations where there is leadership buy-in and support (Wentling, 2007). As a result, inclusive leadership may become more important and even integral to what is valued in our leaders. Recent theorizing on inclusive leadership suggests that inclusive leaders facilitate belongingness and value the unique contributions and experiences that their followers bring to the table (Randel et al., 2018). URG leaders may have greater potential to be inclusive leaders, as they may have a greater ability to convey a message of identity safety to other marginalized groups and a greater ability to convey a message of identity safety to other marginalized groups (Purdie-Vaughns et al., 2008; Randel et al., 2018). This leads to our first research question:

Research Question 1: How might leadership theory and research continue to re-evaluate common definitions and assumptions of leadership and leadership potential, as well as what it means to be an effective leader?

Importantly, a shift in definitions and criteria will not fix everything. Even when URG individuals engage in "effective" behaviors, they continue to be underrepresented in leadership positions. For example, women leaders have been shown to engage in more transformational leadership compared to men and have also been demonstrated to be more effective leaders in some situations (Eagly et al., 1995; Paustian-Underdahl et al., 2014; Sergent & Stajkovic, 2020). How do intrapersonal and interpersonal biases continue to hinder URG individuals throughout the leadership process, even when there is knowledge that counters these biases (e.g., that URG leaders are just as effective, if not more so)? Leadership theories may benefit from more thoroughly integrating diversity theories in how they examine leadership behaviors and contexts. Building on contingency theories, it is not only about understanding what behaviors work best in different situations, but also how an individual's social identity impacts how others perceive those behaviors. For example, an effective behavior for a White male leader in a certain situation may not always be perceived as effective for a woman and/or racially minoritized leader—or even if it is perceived as effective, individuals may still prefer the White male leader, and it is important to understand why (and how to counteract these biases). This leads to our second research question:

Research Question 2: How might leadership theory and research more actively incorporate how social identities impact intrapersonal and interpersonal dynamics throughout the leadership process? How might leadership models better reflect how diversity theories and socialized stereotypes play a role in proposed relationships?

Deepening these ideas further, a diversity lens of leadership could continue to problematize the hierarchical system of power and subjugation implicit in leader-follower dynamics. Integrating diversity into leadership theory could raise important questions about the inequitable structure of contemporary organizations and the perpetuation of inequity in society. From the perspective of diversity scholarship, better understanding leadership processes offers a deeper comprehension of how, when, why, and where social identities affect organizational life. That is, rather than focusing primarily on outcomes (e.g., how represented women and racially minoritized groups are in high-profile leadership positions) or intrapersonal and interpersonal processes, examining the complex processes involved in leadership can further highlight the importance of historical and structural barriers. Our current systems were built and sustained by existing biases, and many organizations' diversity and inclusion practices continue to leave those biased structures intact (Lowe, 2013; McCluney & Rabelo, 2019). For example, organizations may be conscious about hiring and promoting URG individuals, and even firing individuals who are discriminatory towards others; however, there is far less questioning of how organizational infrastructures continue to systematically grant more power to White men (McCluney et al., 2020).

In addition, there needs to be more discussion about the barriers and constraints that URG leaders continue to face once they are in leadership positions (Glass & Cook, 2016; McCluney & Rabelo, 2019). Ushering URG individuals into leadership roles is not a panacea for addressing the discriminatory structures and interactions that continue to operate while they are in these roles. For example, when Barack Obama was elected President of the United States in 2008, many claimed that the U.S. had moved into a "post-racial" society and no longer had issues with racism (Lum, 2009); however, recent years have clearly shown how racism in both overt and subtle forms have persisted in the U.S. and across the world (Hebl et al., 2020; López, 2010). This demonstrates how the selection of URG individuals into leadership positions are still exceptions to the rule, rather than the result of eradicated biases. However, together, diversity and leadership theories can help elucidate ways in which current structures and processes in organizations oppress certain groups of individuals, and consider paradigm shifts in how we think about these structures and processes. This leads to our third research question:

Research Question 3: How might leadership theory and research consider existing structures and processes in organizations, how certain social identity groups may be systematically oppressed, and how to potentially reimagine these structures and processes to create more equitable and fair organizations?

In order to address these questions, there are also a number of methodological considerations for leadership research. None of these considerations are necessarily new; however, they are important to emphasize due to their significance in providing needed insight for diversity and leadership. At a basic level, scholars must continue attending to the characteristics of the samples we analyze. How can we make generalizable conclusions about constructs like leader emergence or leader effectiveness when our samples are almost entirely White, cisgendered, heterosexual, nondisabled men? Theories and evidence of leadership may need to be qualified and certainly contextualized by more fully assessing the perspectives of individuals from a variety of backgrounds; we simply need to collect and analyze data from more diverse samples.

In addition, we need to expand our definition of what we mean by diversity in leadership. Most research on diversity and leadership is focused on gender and race representation, which are both very important, and although some researchers have examined intersectionality in these identities and their relationship to leadership (e.g., Rosette et al., 2016; Smith et al., 2019), future researchers should continue highlighting other social identities—including less visible identities (e.g., sexual orientation, disability status) and intersections with these as well. For example, there is now a small number of Fortune 500 Chief Executive Officers who have openly identified as LGBTQ+, such as Tim Cook at Apple, Jim Fitterling at Dow Chemical, and Beth Ford at Land O'Lakes. This is in contrast to just a few years ago, when John Browne was outed in 2007 and quickly resigned as Chief Executive Officer of BP, citing his desire to keep his sexuality a private and personal matter, as well as his awareness of the homophobia present in the world (Stewart, 2014). It is important to better understand how leaders manage invisible stigmatized identities, and what intrapersonal and interpersonal factors impact their decisions to disclose these identities to their followers and the general public. Researchers also often lose certain identities when examining group differences (e.g., nonbinary individuals when examining gender) or sample sizes may be too small for comparisons. However, researchers can still use other methods with these smaller samples, such as qualitative research (e.g., Smith et al., 2019), to generate a more in-depth understanding of these individuals' experiences, how they may have different beliefs about leaders and leadership, and how their own identities fit into those beliefs.

Integrating multiple perspectives (both individual and sociorelational) in leadership theory and research is also critical. That is, learning will be maximized to the extent that scholars investigate not only how leaders from different backgrounds are evaluated, but also how those leaders see themselves. Future research, for example, might more deeply consider the role of stereotypes in conjunction with the role of metastereotypes. For example, research on leader-member exchange and other leader-follower theories could simultaneously assess leaders' and followers' stereotypes and metastereotypes as they relate to interpersonal behaviors and dyadic and team performance. It may also be interesting to examine other perspectives of leader behavior and effectiveness, such as employees who may not interact as much with the leader, potential job applicants, board members, or other everyday individuals outside of the organization. How might the cues used to evaluate leader effectiveness differ, based on the frequency and type of interactions with the leader? These are important perspectives to also consider, because they can impact how well the organization is doing—both internally and externally.

It would also be extremely valuable for future research on diversity in leadership to take a longitudinal approach. As an example, research could consider how URG leaders' self-concept (e.g., leader self-efficacy) develops over the life course and how this is impacted by different manifestations of oppression, such as unequal access to education and stereotypical representations in the media. Biases and inequities accumulate over a lifetime and across generations, and thus longitudinal research is needed to fully understand their implications for leadership. On the other hand, this type of research can also highlight factors and experiences that have a positive impact on URG leader development (e.g., role models and mentors, allies, formative internships, community and/or professional development programs). A deeper understanding of all these effects over time may help paint a clearer picture and make a stronger argument for what types of interventions and policies we need to implement. In addition, many of the sociorelational aspects of leadership (e.g., leader identity construction, leader-member exchange) take time to develop as well. Relationships evolve and change over time, and cross-sectional research is unable to capture the dynamic nature of relationships. Particularly for URG employees and leaders, who are often engaging in much more identity management than their peers, it is important to understand how their and others' perceptions of them change over time and what different factors play a role in shaping these perceptions, interactions, and evaluations.

Practical Implications

In this paper, we emphasize that stereotypes and other socialized beliefs underlie the intrapersonal and interpersonal dynamics of leadership, which also has important practical implications. Putting individuals from URGs into leadership positions is a necessary step in addressing underrepresentation; however, it is only part of the solution. The roots of the problems are much deeper. People develop inaccurate beliefs about themselves and the people around them long before they join any particular organization or take any particular role, and these beliefs will have a profound impact on leadership experiences. It follows that solutions need not address only the prejudice and discrimination that arise from these stereotypes, but also the social and structural factors on which these biases are predicated.

For example, inside the organization, systemic and strategic initiatives that holistically create and support inclusion can shape the development and retention of URG leaders. Attention to how stereotypes and other biases can manifest across the human resource cycle—including recruitment, selection, promotion, development, and compensation—could enhance organizational diversity. Careful and cultivated attention to diversity in mentoring and sponsorship programs, leader development programs and activities, and succession planning is also critical to overcoming the impact of stereotypes on intrapersonal and interpersonal experiences. Scholars can also partner with community organizations (e.g., schools and universities, nonprofits, community centers) to influence factors outside of the organizational context, such as by facilitating educational programs focused on highlighting the historical and psychological bases of stereotypes and discrimination, or discussions aimed at highlighting the intrapersonal, interpersonal, and structural biases that perpetuate inequity within a specific organization or group.

An important part of many diversity initiatives is also building allies. The term ally was originally used to refer to individuals who are supportive of LGBTQ+ issues (but do not personally identify as being part of these groups; Evans & Wall, 1991); now, the term is readily applied to any supporter of a group to which they do not belong. Although this is not always the case, because of our socialization and current systems, allies often have more power and influence that can help get the message across that prejudice or discrimination is occurring. For example, research has demonstrated that people are sometimes more likely to listen or believe an issue is serious when a nontargeted ally (e.g., a male ally for women) confronts them about discriminatory behavior—as opposed to when the target themselves does the confronting (Cheng et al., 2019; Czopp & Monteith, 2003).

This is not to say that individuals from URGs need to be "saved" by others, rather, that we can achieve the greatest progress towards equity when everyone is engaged in the conversation and working on positive change. Since individuals from URGs continue to face discrimination in access to employment and promotions, allies who sit on decision-making committees should pay attention to when URG applicants are passed over for more prototypical applicants. Was it because the prototypical applicant was objectively better, or because they simply seemed like a "better fit?" If the decision was based on the latter, then allies should speak up and push back—engaging their colleagues in a discussion on how subtle biases can nudge people towards favoring in-group members or higher-status others without necessarily having objective evidence to support their decisions. Allies can also advocate for structural changes that can further reduce biases in hiring and promotion processes; for example, having structured (versus unstructured) interviews and clear, unbiased criterion have been shown to ameliorate discrimination in these processes (Levashina et al., 2014; Uhlmann & Cohen, 2005).

In addition, if there is not currently "room at the table" for new voices, allies can even give up their seats to make room for underrepresented perspectives; for example, in 2020, Reddit's cofounder Alexis Ohanian stepped down from Reddit's board of directors and asked that his seat be replaced with a Black person (Togoh, 2020). In recent years, there has been increased discussion on what it means to be an ally, and many criticize the label as a superficial signal of support without meaningful action (Carlson et al., 2019). Ohanian's example demonstrates active allyship, where someone who uses their privilege to take personal risks for historically oppressed groups. Those who want to engage in allyship should continuously reflect on what power and privilege they have been given by existing systems and structures, and what actions they can take to help redistribute power and give others voice and opportunity.

CONCLUSION

The ideas offered here suggest that the invisible barriers between diversity and leadership scholarship can and should be dismantled. Indeed, theories and evidence from each domain benefits the other. Diversity perspectives emphasize the importance of stereotypes and biases in the intrapersonal and interpersonal dynamics that determine leader emergence, development, behavior, and evaluation; and together, diversity and leadership scholarship can elucidate the many social and structural barriers that continue to remain in place for URG employees and leaders. It is our hope that integrating these two domains will help us better address the roots that underlie the lack of diverse representation and retention in leadership.

REFERENCES

Avolio, B. J., Walumbwa, F. O., & Weber, T. J. (2009). Leadership: Current theories, research, and future directions. *Annual Review of Psychology, 60,* 421–449. https://doi.org/10.1146/annurev.psych.60.110707.163621

Ayman, R., & Korabik, K. (2010). Leadership: Why gender and culture matter. *American Psychologist, 65*(3), 157-170. https://doi.org/10.1037/a0018806

Badura, K. L., Grijalva, E., Newman, D. A., Yan, T. T., & Jeon, G. (2018). Gender and leadership emergence: A meta-analysis and explanatory model. *Personnel Psychology, 71*(3), 335–367. https://doi.org/10.1111/peps.12266

Berri, D. (2018, January). Black NFL coaches appear much more likely to be fired with a winning record. *Forbes.* https://www.forbes.com/sites/davidberri/2018/01/02/black-head-coaches-in-the-nfl-are-much-more-likely-to-be-fired-with-a-winning-record/#53a643001cb8

Blau, F. D., & DeVaro, J. (2007). *New evidence on gender differences in promotion rates: An empirical analysis of a sample of new hires.* Cornell University, School of Industrial and Labor Relations. http://digitalcommons.ilr.cornell.edu/articles/113/

Bowles, H. R., Babcock, L., & Lai, L. (2007). Social incentives for gender differences in the propensity to initiate negotiations: Sometimes it does hurt to ask. *Organizational Behavior and Human Decision Processes, 103*(1), 84–103. https://doi.org/10.1016/j.obhdp.2006.09.001

Brass, D. (1995). A social network perspective on human resources management. *Research in Personnel and Human Resources Management, 13,* 39–79.

Brescoll, V. L., Dawson, E., & Uhlmann, E. L. (2010). Hard won and easily lost: The fragile status of leaders in gender-stereotype-incongruent occupations. *Psychological Science, 21*(11), 1640–1642. https://doi.org/10.1177/0956797610384744

Burris, K., Ayman, R., Che, Y., & Min, H. (2013). Asian Americans' and Caucasians' implicit leadership theories: Asian stereotypes, transformational, and authentic leadership. *Asian American Journal of Psychology, 4*(4), 258–266. https://doi.org/10.1037/a0035229

Carlson, J., Leek, C., Casey, E., Tolman, R., & Allen, C. (2019). What's in a name? A synthesis of "allyship" elements from academic and activist literature. *Journal of Family Violence, 35,* 1-10. https://doi.org/10.1007/s10896-019-00073-z

Carton, A. M., & Rosette, A. S. (2011). Explaining bias against black leaders: Integrating theory on information processing and goal-based stereotyping. *Academy of Management Journal, 54*(6), 1141–1158. https://doi.org/10.5465/amj.2009.0745

Catalyst. (2019, August). *Women in management: Quick take.* https://www.catalyst.org/research/women-in-management/

Chan, K. Y., & Drasgow, F. (2001). Toward a theory of individual differences and leadership: Understanding the motivation to lead. *Journal of Applied Psychology, 86*(3), 481–498. https://doi.org/10.1037/0021-9010.86.3.481

Chemers, M. M. (2000). Leadership research and theory: A functional integration. *Group Dynamics: Theory, Research, and Practice, 4*(1), 27–43. https://doi.org/10.1037/1089-2699.4.1.27

Cheng, S. K., Ng, L. C., Traylor, A. M., & King, E. B. (2019). Helping or hurting?: Understanding Women's Perceptions of Male Allies. *Personnel Assessment and Decisions, 5*(2), 44–54. https://doi.org/10.25035/pad.2019.02.006

Chin, J. L. (2010). Introduction to the special issue on diversity and leadership. *American Psychologist, 65*(3), 150–156. https://doi.org/10.1037/a0018716

Chin, J. L. (2013). Diversity leadership: Influence of ethnicity, gender, and minority status. *Open Journal of Leadership, 2*(1), 1–10. https://doi.org/10.4236/ojl.2013.21001

Chung-Herrera, B. G., & Lankau, M. J. (2005). Are we there yet? An assessment of fit between stereotypes of minority managers and the successful-manager prototype. *Journal of Applied Social Psychology, 35*(10), 2029–2056. https://doi.org/10.1111/j.1559-1816.2005.tb02208.x

Cianni, M., & Romberger, B. (1995). Perceived racial, ethnic, and gender differences in access to developmental experiences. *Group & Organization Management, 20*(4), 440–459. https://doi.org/10.1177/1059601195204004

Cohen, S. L., & Bunker, K. A. (1975). Subtle effects of sex role stereotypes on recruiters' hiring decisions. *Journal of Applied Psychology, 60*(5), 566–572. https://doi.org/10.1037/0021-9010.60.5.566

Cole, E. R. (2009). Intersectionality and research in psychology. *American Psychologist, 64*(3), 170–180. https://doi.org/10.1037/a0014564

Colella, A. (1994). Organizational socialization of employees with disabilities: Critical issues and implications for workplace interventions. *Journal of Occupational Rehabilitation, 4,* 87–106. https://doi.org/10.1007/BF02110048

Cook, A., & Glass, C. (2014). Above the glass ceiling: When are women and racial/ethnic minorities promoted to CEO?. *Strategic Management Journal, 35*(7), 1080–1089. https://doi.org/10.1002/smj.2161

Crenshaw, K. (1989). Demarginalizing the intersection of race and sex: A black feminist critique of antidiscrimination doctrine, feminist theory and antiracist politics. *University of Chicago Legal Forum, 1*(8), 139–168.

Czopp, A. M., & Monteith, M. J. (2003). Confronting prejudice (literally): Reactions to confrontations of racial and gender bias. *Personality and Social Psychology Bulletin, 29*(4), 532–544. https://doi.org/10.1177/0146167202250923

Day, D. V. (2000). Leadership development: A review in context. *The Leadership Quarterly, 11*(4), 581–613. https://doi.org/10.1016/S1048-9843(00)00061-8

Deloitte. (2019, March). *Women and minorities on Fortune 500 boards: More room to grow.* https://deloitte.wsj.com/riskandcompliance/2019/03/12/women-and-minorities-on-fortune-500-boards-more-room-to-grow/

DeRue, D. S., & Ashford, S. J. (2010). Who will lead and who will follow? A social process of leadership identity construction in organizations. *Academy of Management Review, 35*(4), 627–647. https://doi.org/10.5465/amr.35.4.zok627

Dinh, J. E., Lord, R. G., Gardner, W. L., Meuser, J. D., Liden, R. C., & Hu, J. (2014). Leadership theory and research in the new millennium: Current theoretical trends and changing perspectives. *The Leadership Quarterly, 25*(1), 36–62. https://doi.org/10.1016/j.leaqua.2013.11.005

Doubek, D., & Shapiro, A. (2020, August). *Jason Wright on leading the Washington Football Team amid multiple crises.* National Public Radio. https://www.npr.

org/2020/08/28/907055200/jason-wright-on-leading-the-washington-football-team-amid-multiple-crises

Dovidio, J. F., Brigham, J. C., Johnson, B. T., & Gaertner, S. L. (1996). Stereotyping, prejudice, and discrimination: Another look. In C. N. Macrae, C. Stangor, & M. Hewstone (Eds.), *Stereotypes and stereotyping* (pp. 276–319). The Guilford Press.

Duehr, E. E., & Bono, J. E. (2006). Men, women, and managers: Are stereotypes finally changing?. *Personnel Psychology, 59*(4), 815–846. https://doi.org/10.1111/j.1744-6570.2006.00055.x

Dulebohn, J. H., Bommer, W. H., Liden, R. C., Brouer, R. L., & Ferris, G. R. (2012). A meta-analysis of antecedents and consequences of leader-member exchange: Integrating the past with an eye toward the future. *Journal of Management, 38*(6), 1715–1759.

Eagly, A. H. (2018). Some leaders come from nowhere: Their success is uneven. *Journal of Social Issues, 74*(1), 184-196. https://doi.org/10.1111/josi.12263

Eagly, A. H., & Carli, L. L. (2007, September). Women and the labyrinth of leadership. *Harvard Business Review.* https://hbr.org/2007/09/women-and-the-labyrinth-of-leadership

Eagly, A. H., & Chin, J. L. (2010). Diversity and leadership in a changing world. *American Psychologist, 65*(3), 216–224. https://doi.org/10.1037/a0018957

Eagly, A. H., & Karau, S. J. (2002). Role congruity theory of prejudice toward female leaders. *Psychological Review, 109*(3), 573–598. https://doi.org/10.1037/0033-295X.109.3.573

Eagly, A. H., Karau, S. J., & Makhijani, M. G. (1995). Gender and the effectiveness of leaders: A meta-analysis. *Psychological Bulletin, 117*(1), 125–145. https://doi.org/10.1037/0033-2909.117.1.125

Eagly, A. H., & Wood, W. (1991). Explaining sex differences in social behavior: A meta-analytic perspective. *Personality and Social Psychology Bulletin, 17*(3), 306–315. https://doi.org/10.1177/0146167291173011

Epitropaki, O., & Martin, R. (2004). Implicit leadership theories in applied settings: Factor structure, generalizability, and stability over time. *Journal of Applied Psychology, 89*(2), 293–310. https://doi.org/10.1037/0021-9010.89.2.293

Epitropaki, O., & Martin, R. (2005). From ideal to real: A longitudinal study of the role of implicit leadership theories on leader-member exchanges and employee outcomes. *Journal of Applied Psychology, 90*(4), 659–676. https://doi.org/10.1037/0021-9010.90.4.659

Evans, N. J., & Wall, V. A. (Eds.). (1991). *Beyond tolerance: gays, lesbians, and bisexuals on campus.* American College Personnel Association.

Fassinger, R. E., Shullman, S. L., & Stevenson, M. R. (2010). Toward an affirmative lesbian, gay, bisexual, and transgender leadership paradigm. *American Psychologist, 65*(3), 201–215. https://doi.org/10.1037/a0018597

Fiedler, F. E. (1964). A contingency model of leadership effectiveness. *Advances in Experimental Social Psychology, 1,* 149–190. https://doi.org/10.1016/S0065-2601(08)60051-9

Finkelstein, L. M., & Burke, M. J. (1998). Age stereotyping at work: The role of rater and contextual factors on evaluations of job applicants. *The Journal of General Psychology, 125*(4), 317–345. https://doi.org/10.1080/00221309809595341

Fiske, S. T., Cuddy, A. J., Glick, P., & Xu, J. (2002). A model of (often mixed) stereotype content: Competence and warmth respectively follow from perceived status and competition. *Social Cognition*, 171–222. https://doi.org/10.1037/0022-3514.82.6.878

Forsyth, D. R. (2009). *Group dynamics.* Wadsworth.

Giel, K. E., Thiel, A., Teufel, M., Mayer, J., & Zipfel, S. (2010). Weight bias in work settings—A qualitative review. *Obesity Facts, 3*(1), 33–40. https://doi.org/10.1159/000276992

Glass, C., & Cook, A. (2016). Leading at the top: Understanding women's challenges above the glass ceiling. *The Leadership Quarterly, 27*(1), 51–63. https://doi.org/10.1016/j.leaqua.2015.09.003

Goff, P. A., Steele, C. M., & Davies, P. G. (2008). The space between us: stereotype threat and distance in interracial contexts. *Journal of Personality and Social Psychology, 94*(1), 91–107. https://doi.org/10.1037/0022-3514.94.1.91

Goffman, E. 1963. *Stigma: Notes on the management of a spoiled identity*. Prentice-Hall.

Hall, E. V., Hall, A. V., Galinsky, A. D., & Phillips, K. W. (2019). MOSAIC: a model of stereotyping through associated and intersectional categories. *Academy of Management Review, 44*(3), 643–672. https://doi.org/10.5465/amr.2017.0109

Hannah, S. T., Avolio, B. J., Luthans, F., & Harms, P. D. (2008). Leadership efficacy: Review and future directions. *The Leadership Quarterly, 19*(6), 669–692. https://doi.org/10.1016/j.leaqua.2008.09.007

Harber, K. D. (2004). The positive feedback bias as a response to out-group unfriendliness. *Journal of Applied Social Psychology, 34*(11), 2272–2297.https://doi.org/10.1111/j.1559-1816.2004.tb01977.x

Hastorf, A. H., Northcraft, G. B., & Picciotto, S. R. (1979). Helping the handicapped: How realistic is the performance feedback received by the physically handicapped. *Personality and Social Psychology Bulletin, 5*(3), 373–376. https://doi.org/10.1177/014616727900500321

Hebl, M., Cheng, S. K., & Ng, L. C. (2020). Modern discrimination in organizations. *Annual Review of Organizational Psychology and Organizational Behavior, 7*, 257–282. https://doi.org/10.1146/annurev-orgpsych-012119-044948

Hebl, M. R., & Kleck, R. E. (2002). Acknowledging one's stigma in the interview setting: Effective strategy or liability?. *Journal of Applied Social Psychology, 32*(2), 223–249. https://doi.org/10.1111/j.1559-1816.2002.tb00214.x

Hebl, M. R., Tonidandel, S., & Ruggs, E. N. (2012). The impact of like-mentors for gay/lesbian employees. *Human Performance, 25*(1), 52–71. https://doi.org/10.1080/08959285.2011.631645

Hekman, D. R., Johnson, S. K., Foo, M. D., & Yang, W. (2017). Does diversity-valuing behavior result in diminished performance ratings for non-white and female leaders? *Academy of Management Journal, 60*(2), 771–797. https://doi.org/10.5465/amj.2014.0538

Heilman, M.E. (1983). Sex bias in work settings: The lack of fit model. *Research in Organizational Behavior, 5*, 269–298.

Heilman, M.E. (1997). Sex discrimination and the affirmative action remedy: The role of sex stereotypes. *Journal of Business Ethics, 16*(9), 877–889. https://doi.org/10.1023/A:1017927002761

Heilman, M. E. (2012). Gender stereotypes and workplace bias. *Research in Organizational Behavior, 32,* 113–135. https://doi.org/10.1016/j.riob.2012.11.003

Heilman, M. E., Block, C. J., Martell, R. F., & Simon, M. C. (1989). Has anything changed? Current characterizations of men, women, and managers. *Journal of Applied Psychology, 74*(6), 935–942. https://doi.org/10.1037/0021-9010.74.6.935

Heilman, M. E., & Okimoto, T. G. (2007). Why are women penalized for success at male tasks?: The implied communality deficit. *Journal of Applied Psychology, 92*(1), 81–92. https://doi.org/10.1037/0021-9010.92.1.81

Hennessy, J., & West, M. A. (1999). Intergroup behavior in organizations: A field test of social identity theory. *Small Group Research, 30*(3), 361–382. https://doi.org/10.1177/104649649903000305

Hernandez, M., Avery, D. R., Tonidandel, S., Hebl, M. R., Smith, A. N., & McKay, P. F. (2016). The role of proximal social contexts: Assessing stigma-by-association effects on leader appraisals. *Journal of Applied Psychology, 101*(1), 68–85. https://doi.org/10.1037/apl0000030

Hinchliffe, E. (2020, May). The number of female CEOs in the Fortune 500 hits an all-time record. *Fortune.* https://fortune.com/2020/05/18/women-ceos-fortune-500-2020/

Hite, L. M. (2007). Hispanic women managers and professionals: Reflections on life and work. *Gender, Work & Organization, 14*(1), 20–36. https://doi.org/10.1111/j.1468-0432.2007.00330.x

Hogue, M., & Lord, R. G. (2007). A multilevel, complexity theory approach to understanding gender bias in leadership. *The Leadership Quarterly, 18*(4), 370–390. https://doi.org/10.1016/j.leaqua.2007.04.006

Hogg, M. A., van Knippenberg, D., & Rast, D. E., III. (2012). The social identity theory of leadership: Theoretical origins, research findings, and conceptual developments. *European Review of Social Psychology, 23*(1), 258–304. https://doi.org/10.1080/10463283.2012.741134

Hollander, E. P. (1992). Leadership, followership, self, and others. *The Leadership Quarterly, 3*(1), 43–54. https://doi.org/10.1016/1048-9843(92)90005-Z

House, R. J., & Mitchell, T. R. (1974). Path-goal theory of leadership. *Journal of Contemporary Business, 3,* 81–97.

Hoyt, C. L., & Murphy, S. E. (2016). Managing to clear the air: Stereotype threat, women, and leadership. *The Leadership Quarterly, 27*(3), 387–399. https://doi.org/10.1016/j.leaqua.2015.11.002

Hoyt, C. L., & Simon, S. (2016). The role of social dominance orientation and patriotism in the evaluation of racial minority and female leaders. *Journal of Applied Social Psychology, 46*(9), 518–528. https://doi.org/10.1111/jasp.12380

Hunt, V., Layton, D., & Prince, S. (2015). Diversity matters. *McKinsey & Company,* 15–29.

Ibarra, H. (1995). Race, opportunity, and diversity of social circles in managerial networks. *Academy of Management Journal, 38*(3), 673–703. https://doi.org/10.5465/256742

Ignatova, M. (2019, March). New report: Women apply to fewer jobs than men, but are more likely to get hired. *LinkedIn.* https://business.linkedin.com/talent-solutions/blog/diversity/2019/how-women-find-jobs-gender-report

Junker, N. M., & van Dick, R. (2014). Implicit theories in organizational settings: A systematic review and research agenda of implicit leadership and followership theories. *The Leadership Quarterly, 25*(6), 1154–1173. https://doi.org/10.1016/j.leaqua.2014.09.002

King, E. B., Botsford, W., Hebl, M. R., Kazama, S., Dawson, J. F., & Perkins, A. (2012). Benevolent sexism at work: Gender differences in the distribution of challenging developmental experiences. *Journal of Management, 38*(6), 1835–1866. https://doi.org/10.1177/0149206310365902

King, E. B., Mendoza, S. A., Madera, J. M., Hebl, M. R., & Knight, J. L. (2006). What's in a name? A multiracial investigation of the role of occupational stereotypes in selection decisions. *Journal of Applied Social Psychology, 36*(5), 1145–1159. https://doi.org/10.1111/j.0021-9029.2006.00035.x

Koenig, A. M., Eagly, A. H., Mitchell, A. A., & Ristikari, T. (2011). Are leader stereotypes masculine? A meta-analysis of three research paradigms. *Psychological Bulletin, 137*(4), 616–642. https://doi.org/10.1037/a0023557

Levashina, J., Hartwell, C. J., Morgeson, F. P., & Campion, M. A. (2014). The structured employment interview: Narrative and quantitative review of the research literature. *Personnel Psychology, 67*(1), 241–293. https://doi.org/10.1111/peps.12052

Levine, M., Prosser, A., Evans, D., & Reicher, S. (2005). Identity and emergency intervention: How social group membership and inclusiveness of group boundaries shape helping behavior. *Personality and Social Psychology Bulletin, 31*(4), 443–453. https://doi.org/10.1177/0146167204271651

Liberman, B. E., & Golom, F. D. (2015). Think manager, think male? Heterosexuals' stereotypes of gay and lesbian managers. *Equality, Diversity and Inclusion: An International Journal, 34*(7), 566–578. https://doi.org/10.1108/EDI-01-2015-0005

Link, B. G., & Phelan, J. C. (2001). Conceptualizing stigma. *Annual Review of Sociology, 27*(1), 363–385. https://doi.org/10.1146/annurev.soc.27.1.363

López, I. F. H. (2010). Post-racial racism: Racial stratification and mass incarceration in the age of Obama. *California Law Review, 98*(3), 1023–1074. https://www.jstor.org/stable/27896699

Lord, R. G. (1985). An information processing approach to social perceptions, leadership perceptions and behavioral measurement in organizational settings. In B. M. Staw & L. L. Cummings (Eds.), *Research in Organizational Behavior* (Vol. 7, pp. 85–128). JAI Press.

Lord, R. G., Day, D. V., Zaccaro, S. J., Avolio, B. J., & Eagly, A. H. (2017). Leadership in applied psychology: Three waves of theory and research. *Journal of Applied Psychology, 102*(3), 434–451. https://doi.org/10.1037/apl0000089

Lord, R. G., & Maher, K. J. (1991). Cognitive theory in industrial and organizational psychology. In M. D. Dunnette & L. M. Hough (Eds.), *Handbook of industrial and organizational psychology* (2nd ed., Vol. 2, pp. 1–62). Consulting Psychologist Press.

Lowe, F. (2013). Keeping leadership white: Invisible blocks to Black leadership and its denial in White organizations. *Journal of Social Work Practice, 27*(2), 149–162. https://doi.org/10.1080/02650533.2013.798151

Lum, L. (2009). The Obama era: A post-racial society?. *Diverse Issues in Higher Education, 25*(26), 14–16.

Lyness, K. S., & Heilman, M. E. (2006). When fit is fundamental: Performance evaluations and promotions of upper-level female and male managers. *Journal of Applied Psychology, 91*(4), 777–785. https://doi.org/10.1037/0021-9010.91.4.777

Machida, M., & Schaubroeck, J. (2011). The role of self-efficacy beliefs in leader development. *Journal of Leadership & Organizational Studies, 18*(4), 459–468. https://doi.org/10.1177/1548051811404419

McCluney, C. L., King, D. D., Bryant, C., & Ali, A. (2020). From "calling in Black" to "calling for antiracism resources": The need for systemic resources to address systemic racism. *Equality, Diversity, and Inclusion.*

McCluney, C. L., & Rabelo, V. C. (2019). Managing diversity, managing Blackness? In L. M. Roberts, A. J. Mayo, & D. A. Thomas (Eds.), *Race, work, and leadership: New perspectives on the black experience* (pp. 373–388). Harvard Business Press.

McDonald, S. (2011). What's in the "old boys" network? Accessing social capital in gendered and racialized networks. *Social Networks, 33*(4), 317–330. https://doi.org/10.1016/j.socnet.2011.10.002

McDonald, M. L., Keeves, G. D., & Westphal, J. D. (2018). One step forward, one step back: White male top manager organizational identification and helping behavior toward other executives following the appointment of a female or racial minority CEO. *Academy of Management Journal, 61*(2), 405–439. https://doi.org/10.5465/amj.2016.0358

McGuire, G. M. (2002). Gender, race, and the shadow structure: A study of informal networks and inequality in a work organization. *Gender & Society, 16*(3), 303–322. https://doi.org/10.1177/0891243202016003003

Mohr, T. S. (2014, August). Why women don't apply for jobs unless they're 100% qualified. *Harvard Business Review.* https://hbr.org/2014/08/why-women-dont-apply-for-jobs-unless-theyre-100-qualified

Morgenroth, T., Kirby, T. A., Ryan, M. K., & Sudkämper, A. (2020). The who, when, and why of the glass cliff phenomenon: A meta-analysis of appointments to precarious leadership positions. *Psychological Bulletin, 146*(9), 797–829. https://doi.org/10.1037/bul0000234

Myers, D. G. (2010). *Social psychology* (10th ed.). McGraw Hill.

Nye, J. L., & Forsyth, D. R. (1991). The effects of prototype-based biases on leadership appraisals: A test of leadership categorization theory. *Small Group Research, 22*(3), 360–379. https://doi.org/10.1177/1046496491223005

Oakes, P. J., & Turner, J. C. (1980). Social categorization and intergroup behaviour: Does minimal intergroup discrimination make social identity more positive? *European Journal of Social Psychology, 10*(3), 295–301 https://doi.org/10.1002/ejsp.2420100307

Offermann, L. R., Kennedy, J. K., Jr., & Wirtz, P. W. (1994). Implicit leadership theories: Content, structure and generalizability. *Leadership Quarterly, 5*, 43–58. https://doi.org/10.1016/1048-9843(94)90005-1

O'Rourke, C. (2020, September). The Latina progressive who faced down Texas Republicans. *Politico.* https://www.politico.com/news/magazine/2020/09/02/latina-progressive-texas-lina-hidalgo-407001

Paustian-Underdahl, S. C., Walker, L. S., & Woehr, D. J. (2014). Gender and perceptions of leadership effectiveness: A meta-analysis of contextual moderators. *Journal of Applied Psychology, 99*(6), 1129–1145. https://doi.org/10.1037/a0036751

Pedulla, D. S., & Pager, D. (2019). Race and networks in the job search process. *American Sociological Review, 84*(6), 983–1012. https://doi.org/10.1177/0003122419883255

Pettigrew, T. F. (1979). The ultimate attribution error: Extending Allport's cognitive analysis of prejudice. *Personality and Social Psychology Bulletin, 5*(4), 461–476. https://doi.org/10.1177/014616727900500407

Phillips, K. W., Dumas, T. L., & Rothbard, N. P. (2018). Diversity and authenticity. *Harvard Business Review, 96*(2), 122–136.

Porath, C. L., Gerbasi, A., & Schorch, S. L. (2015). The effects of civility on advice, leadership, and performance. *Journal of Applied Psychology, 100*(5), 1527–1541. https://doi.org/10.1037/apl0000016

Powell, G. N., & Butterfield, D. A. (1994). Investigating the "glass ceiling" phenomenon: An empirical study of actual promotions to top management. *Academy of Management Journal, 37*(1), 68–86. https://doi.org/10.5465/256770

Purdie-Vaughns, V., Steele, C. M., Davies, P. G., Ditlmann, R., & Crosby, J. R. (2008). Social identity contingencies: how diversity cues signal threat or safety for African Americans in mainstream institutions. *Journal of Personality and Social Psychology, 94*(4), 615–630. https://doi.org/10.1037/0022-3514.94.4.615

Ragins, B. R. (1995). Diversity, power, and mentorship in organizations: A cultural, structural, and behavioral perspective. In M. M. Chemers, S. Oskamp, & M. A. Costanzo (Eds.), *Claremont symposium on applied social psychology, Diversity in organizations: New perspectives for a changing workplace* (Vol. 8, pp. 91–132). https://doi.org/10.4135/9781452243405.n5

Randel, A. E., Galvin, B. M., Shore, L. M., Ehrhart, K. H., Chung, B. G., Dean, M. A., & Kedharnath, U. (2018). Inclusive leadership: Realizing positive outcomes through belongingness and being valued for uniqueness. *Human Resource Management Review, 28*(2), 190–203. https://doi.org/10.1016/j.hrmr.2017.07.002

Randolph-Seng, B., Cogliser, C. C., Randolph, A. F., Scandura, T. A., Miller, C. D., & Smith-Genthôs, R. (2016). Diversity in leadership: race in leader-member exchanges. *Leadership & Organization Development Journal, 37*(6), 750–773. https://doi.org/10.1108/LODJ-10-2014-0201

Rast, D. E., III, Hogg, M. A., & Randsley de Moura, G. (2018). Leadership and social transformation: The role of marginalized individuals and groups. *Journal of Social Issues, 74*(1), 8–19. https://doi.org/10.1111/josi.12253

Roberts, L. M., Mayo, A. J., & Thomas, D. A. (2019). *Race, work, and leadership: New perspectives on the black experience*. Harvard Business Press.

Rosette, A. S., Koval, C. Z., Ma, A., & Livingston, R. (2016). Race matters for women leaders: Intersectional effects on agentic deficiencies and penalties. *The Leadership Quarterly, 27*(3), 429–445. https://doi.org/10.1016/j.leaqua.2016.01.008

Rosette, A. S., & Livingston, R. W. (2012). Failure is not an option for Black women: Effects of organizational performance on leaders with single versus dual-subordinate identities. *Journal of Experimental Social Psychology, 48*(5), 1162–1167. https://doi.org/10.1016/j.jesp.2012.05.002

Rosette, A. S., Leonardelli, G. J., & Phillips, K. W. (2008). The White standard: Racial bias in leader categorization. *Journal of Applied Psychology, 93*(4), 758–777. https://doi.org/10.1037/0021-9010.93.4.758

Rudman, L. A., & Glick, P. (2001). Prescriptive gender stereotypes and backlash toward agentic women. *Journal of Social Issues, 57*(4), 743–762.https://doi.org/10.1111/0022-4537.00239

Rudman, L. A., Moss-Racusin, C. A., Phelan, J. E., & Nauts, S. (2012). Status incongruity and backlash effects: Defending the gender hierarchy motivates prejudice against female leaders. *Journal of Experimental Social Psychology, 48*(1), 165–179. https://doi.org/10.1016/j.jesp.2011.10.008

Sanchez-Hucles, J. V., & Davis, D. D. (2010). Women and women of color in leadership: Complexity, identity, and intersectionality. *American Psychologist, 65*(3), 171–181. https://doi.org/10.1037/a0017459

Scandura, T. A., & Lankau, M. J. (1996). Developing diverse leaders: A leader-member exchange approach. *The Leadership Quarterly*, 7(2), 243–263. https://doi.org/10.1016/S1048-9843(96)90043-0

Schein, V. E. (1973). The relationship between sex role stereotypes and requisite management characteristics. *Journal of Applied Psychology, 57*(2), 95–100. https://doi.org/10.1037/h0037128

Seegars, L., & Ramarajan, L. (2019). Blacks leading Whites. In L. M. Roberts, A. J. Mayo, & D. A. Thomas (Eds.), *Race, work, and leadership: New perspectives on the black experience*. Harvard Business Press.

Sergent, K., & Stajkovic, A. D. (2020). Women's leadership is associated with fewer deaths during the COVID-19 crisis: Quantitative and qualitative analyses of United States governors. *Journal of Applied Psychology, 105*(8), 771–783. https://doi.org/10.1037/apl0000577

Shah, A. K., & Oppenheimer, D. M. (2008). Heuristics made easy: An effort-reduction framework. *Psychological Bulletin, 134*(2), 207. https://doi.org/10.1037/0033-2909.134.2.207

Smith, J. A., & Foti, R. J. (1998). A pattern approach to the study of leader emergence. *The Leadership Quarterly, 9*(2), 147-160. https://doi.org/10.1016/S1048-9843(98)90002-9

Smith, W. J., & Joseph, S. E. (2010). Workplace challenges in corporate America: Differences in black and white. *Equality, Diversity and Inclusion: An International Journal, 29*(8), 743–765. https://doi.org/10.1108/02610151011089500

Smith, A. N., Watkins, M. B., Ladge, J. J., & Carlton, P. (2019). Making the invisible visible: Paradoxical effects on intersectional invisibility on the career experiences of executive Black women in the workplace. *Academy of Management Journal, 62*(6). https://doi.org/10.5465/amj.2017.1513

Spencer, S. J., Steele, C. M., & Quinn, D. M. (1999). Stereotype threat and women's math performance. *Journal of Experimental Social Psychology, 35*(1), 4–28. https://doi.org/10.1006/jesp.1998.1373

Staw, B. M., & Barsade, S. G. (1993). Affect and managerial performance: A test of the sadder-but-wiser vs. happier-and-smarter hypotheses. *Administrative Science Quarterly, 38*(2), 304–331. https://doi.org/10.2307/2393415

Steele, C. M., & Aronson, J. (1995). Stereotype threat and the intellectual test performance of African Americans. *Journal of Personality and Social Psychology, 69*(5), 797–811. https://doi.org/10.1037/0022-3514.69.5.797

Stewart, J. B. (2014, June). Among gay C.E.O.s, the pressure to conform. *New York Times.* https://www.nytimes.com/2014/06/28/business/john-browne-former-chief-of-bp-on-being-a-closeted-executive.html

Strachan, J. C., Poloni-Staudinger, L. M., Jenkins, S., & Ortbals, C. D. (2019). *Why don't women rule the world?* CQ Press.

Sy, T., Shore, L. M., Strauss, J., Shore, T. H., Tram, S., Whiteley, P., & Ikeda-Muromachi, K. (2010). Leadership perceptions as a function of race-occupation fit: The case of Asian Americans. *Journal of Applied Psychology, 95*(5), 902. https://doi.org/10.1037/a0019501

Tajfel, H., & Turner, J. C. (1985). The social identity theory of intergroup behavior. In S. Worchel & W. G. Austin (Eds.), *Psychology of Intergroup Relations* (pp. 7–24). Nelson-Hall.

Tharenou, P. (1999). Gender differences in advancing to the top. *International Journal of Management Reviews, 1*(2), 111–132. https://doi.org/10.1111/1468-2370.00008

Thomas, D. A. (1993). Racial dynamics in cross-race developmental relationships. *Administrative Science Quarterly, 38*(2), 169-194. https://doi.org/10.2307/2393410

Thomas, K., Robinson, A. J., Provolt, L., & Brown, B. L. (2019). When Black leaders leave. In L. M. Roberts, A. J. Mayo, & D. A. Thomas (Eds.), *Race, work, and leadership: New perspectives on the black experience.* Harvard Business Press.

Togoh, I. (2020, June). Michael Seibel becomes Reddit's first Black board member after Alexis Ohanian's resignation. *Forbes.* https://www.forbes.com/sites/isabeltogoh/2020/06/10/michael-seibel-becomes-reddits-first-black-board-member-after-alexis-ohanians-resignation/#aa27f58430a0

Travis, D. J., & Thorpe-Moscon, J. (2018). *Day-to-day experiences of emotional tax among women and men of color in the workplace.* Catalyst. https://www.catalyst.org/research/day-to-day-experiences-of-emotional-tax-among-women-and-men-of-color-in-the-workplace/

Uhlmann, E. L., & Cohen, G. L. (2005). Constructed criteria: Redefining merit to justify discrimination. *Psychological Science, 16*(6), 474–480. https://doi.org/10.1111/j.0956-7976.2005.01559.x

Underhill, C. M. (2006). The effectiveness of mentoring programs in corporate settings: A meta-analytical review of the literature. *Journal of Vocational Behavior, 68*(2), 292–307. https://doi.org/10.1016/j.jvb.2005.05.003

van Knippenberg, D., & Hogg, M. A. (2003). A social identity model of leadership effectiveness in organizations. *Research in Organizational Behavior, 25,* 243–295. https://doi.org/10.1016/S0191-3085(03)25006-1

Vial, A. C., Napier, J. L., & Brescoll, V. L. (2016). A bed of thorns: Female leaders and the self-reinforcing cycle of illegitimacy. *The Leadership Quarterly, 27*(3), 400–414. https://doi.org/10.1016/j.leaqua.2015.12.004

Vorauer, J. D., Main, K. J., & O'Connell, G. B. (1998). How do individuals expect to be viewed by members of lower status groups? Content and implications of meta-stereotypes. *Journal of Personality and Social Psychology, 75*(4), 917–937. https://doi.org/10.1037/0022-3514.75.4.917

Voyles, E., Finkelstein, L., & King, E. (2014). A tale of two theories: Stereotype threat and metastereotypes. *Industrial and Organizational Psychology*, 7(3), 419–422. https://doi.org/10.1111/iops.12171

Vroom, V. H., & Jago, A. G. (2007). The role of the situation in leadership. *American Psychologist, 62*(1), 17–24. https://doi.org/10.1037/0003-066X.62.1.17

Wemple, E. (2017, August). *Studies agree: Media gorged on Hillary Clinton email coverage.* https://www.washingtonpost.com/blogs/erik-wemple/wp/2017/08/25/studies-agree-media-gorged-on-hillary-clinton-email-coverage/

Wentling, R. M. (2004). Factors that assist and barriers that hinder the success of diversity initiatives in multinational corporations. *Human Resource Development International,* 7(2), 165–180. https://doi.org/10.1080/1367886042000243781

Wyatt, M., & Silvester, J. (2015). Reflections on the labyrinth: Investigating black and minority ethnic leaders' career experiences. *Human Relations, 68*(8), 1243–1269. https://doi.org/10.1177/0018726714550890

Yukl, G. A. (2006). *Leadership in organizations* (6th ed.). Pearson Prentice Hall.

Zhang, Z., Waldman, D. A., & Wang, Z. (2012). A multilevel investigation of leader-member exchange, informal leader emergence, and individual and team performance. *Personnel Psychology, 65*(1), 49–78. https://doi.org/10.1111/j.1744-6570.2011.01238.x

Zheng, W., Kark, R., & Meister, A. (2018, November). How women manage the gendered norms of leadership. *Harvard Business Review.* https://hbr.org/2018/11/how-women-manage-the-gendered-norms-of-leadership

Zweigenhaft, R. L., & Domhoff, G. W. (2006). *Diversity in the power elite: How it happened, why it matters.* Rowman & Littlefield.

CHAPTER 5

INCLUSIVE LEADERSHIP

The Roots of an Emerging Theory

Trevor Cox

ABSTRACT

As the workplace continues to grow more diverse, new leadership practices and theories are required. While leadership theories continue to devote attention to issues surrounding diversity, equity, and inclusion, inequities persist. Inclusive leadership is an emerging theory that addresses some of the gaps in theory and practice surrounding diversity and inclusion in organizations. Inclusive leadership as a framework addresses both the demands of such a complex workplace and puts diversity and inclusion at the center of practice. In human resources (HR), inclusive leadership fills a gap in HR practices and policies that often fail to create inclusion within the workplace. As the theory of inclusive leadership emerges, defining both leadership and inclusion is elusive. This chapter seeks to move towards a more holistic definition of inclusive leadership and explores the dynamics of inclusive leadership through leadership of the self, others, and the organization. The chapter explores inclusive leadership's roots in diversity as a positive organizational benefit and its confluence with other leadership theories such as adaptive leadership, LMX and relational leadership, and

Leadership:
Leaders, Followers, and Context, pp. 99–135

specifically authentic leadership. Finally, it proposes inclusive leadership as a root leadership construct and makes recommendations for future study.

The nature of leadership is changing in the United States. The workforce continues to grow more complex and diverse perspectives are essential to engage in the kind of innovative thinking that appreciates differences as positive resources for a more effective workforce. Yet while scholarship acknowledges this critical need for a globalized and diverse workforce as a business imperative (Geiger & Jordan, 2014), inequality in organizations and society continue to persist. Although diversity and inclusion are now getting worldwide attention, "discrimination, harassment, exclusion, and inequality in organizations persist" (Nkomo et al. 2019, p. 511). Organizational leaders see daily the misunderstandings and conflicts that are a result of the inability to value differences in others, and societal injustice and inequity remain an insidious problem (Wasserman, 2015).

While leadership is continually shifting because of these inevitable realities, still more needs to be done for organizations and societies to address ongoing exclusion and to fully benefit from the diversity present in society and the workplace. Shifts and changes in processes, boundaries, and structures require new leadership capacities that not only address the inequities so prevalent in society but reap the benefits of the growing diversity of the current workforce (Chrobot-Mason et al., 2014; Ferdman & Deane, 2014). Leaders in the current climate must develop capacities that attend to the way privilege and marginalization affect how people relate to each other, be familiar with historical and geographic patterns of discrimination, and expand their own frames of reference to include more cultural perspectives (Wasserman, 2015; Wasserman et al., 2014).

Inclusive leadership is an emerging framework that works to address some of the gaps surrounding the practice and theory of diversity and inclusion in organizations. In the last few years, there have been several leadership theories designed to meet the demands of a globalized and increasingly complex landscape (Avolio & Mhatre, 2013; Caligiuri, 2012; Heifetz & Linsky, 2002; Mendenhall et al., 2012; Worley et al., 2014), yet these theories rarely address issues of diversity, equity, and social justice (Chin, 2010). Inclusive leadership as a framework addresses both the demands of such a complex workplace and puts issues of diversity and inclusion at the center of practice.

Despite the pressing needs for leadership practice, the research on diversity, inclusion, and leadership continues to remain ambiguous and often inconsistent. As a result, organizations too often resort to the same practices that began decades ago, often resulting in making things worse rather than better (Bernstein et al., 2019). Chrobot-Mason et al. (2014) also argued that while the need for leaders to be able to work across multiple lines of difference continues to grow, many people still operate under the same stereotypes and biases which have historically torn groups apart. One underlying reason for such operation is that diversity scholarship has paid little attention to the leadership capacities needed, and leadership scholarship is underdeveloped concerning diversity.

Such a lack of clarity and ambiguous results of the presence of diversity in both research and practice creates "increasingly polarizing discourse on the relevance and impact of diversity in the workplace" (Nkomo et al., 2019, p. 499). Gotsis and Grimani (2016) argued for a solution of integrating diversity, multiple identities, and inclusion into leadership theories to optimize leadership effectiveness. As such, what is needed is a theory that moves beyond the traditional approaches to diversity and can serve to integrate the disparate research in the field (Bernstein et al., 2019; Nishii et al., 2018). Inclusive leadership not only keeps diversity at its core but provides insights into how to integrate multiple identities within a group. Further, the proposed research in this chapter integrates several streams of research.

The field of human resources (HR) also has a vested interest in the study of inclusive leadership. Jordan et al. (2019) argued that while diversity and inclusion are a continual topic of scholarship and research, there is very little work on the process of how to most benefit from diversity in organizations. As a result, HR often relies on diversity policies alone "without emphasizing the value of varying demographics, perspectives, and cultures can bring to workplace contexts" (p. 1). Further, many of these well-intended HR practices fail to actually create inclusion in organizations (Buengeler et al., 2018). What is needed is a multilevel approach to diversity that equips leaders to shape inclusive climates, strengthen social connections, build collective identification, and provide opportunities for individuals to span boundaries (Nishii et al., 2018). Nishii et al. (2018) recommend that HR practices be re-thought using targeting and recruiting efforts that would identify candidates on the ability to practice inclusive leadership. They also recommend that the ongoing training of employees should involve the skills and capacities needed for inclusive leadership and inclusive climates.

Inclusive leadership has begun to emerge as a critical theory that can integrate the necessary leadership capacities for the 21st century as well as leverage the benefits and address the issues surrounding an increasingly diverse workplace. This chapter reviews the literature on inclusive leadership in American contexts (context will be discussed in the conclusion) to determine the needed skills and capacities for inclusive leadership, examines the relationship to inclusive leadership to other leadership theories, and argues for inclusive leadership as a "root leadership construct." The chapter will conclude with recommendations for further research as the theory of inclusive leadership continues to emerge.

DEFINING INCLUSIVE LEADERSHIP

The first task of conceptualizing inclusive leadership as a unique theory is not only to define inclusive leadership but to acknowledge some of the inconsistencies in its definition as well. While inclusive leadership definitions vary, creating a more holistic definition could potentially bring several disparate streams of research together to make a more robust research and practice base; however, defining inclusive leadership is even more complicated because neither inclusion nor leadership have standardized definitions and researchers disagree about the necessity of creating formalized definitions. Much of leadership theory has pointed out the lack of a standardized definition, but as Day and Harrison (2007) asserted: "the complexity and multidimensionality of the very nature of leadership mitigate the possibility of a simple or unitary definition" (p. 360). Inclusion also lacks a clear definition (Combs et al., 2019; Shore et al., 2011), but Ferdman (2014) made a similar argument citing the complexity of the topic means there is not a pressing need for a standardized definition of inclusion. Yet Shore et al. (2011) note that the "considerable disparity" (p. 1267) about the definition hampers inclusion both theoretically and practically. As such, a thorough investigation of inclusive leadership must acknowledge the complexity and the importance of both leadership and inclusion within inclusive leadership.

Scholars have taken several approaches in the study of inclusive leadership and multiple studies have defined inclusive leadership in their own ways (see Table 5.1). Yet many of these definitions do not place diversity at the center of consideration or do not take a positive organizational perspective that sees diversity as a benefit. For example, the International Leadership Association's (ILA) 2016 conference title was *The Dynamics of Inclusive Leadership*. However, the majority of the work done during this conference did not see inclusive leadership as a primary way of leading but sought to add inclusion to whatever leadership conceptualization was presented. Such an approach is all too common. Inclusive leadership as defined here is a broader understanding which places diversity at the center, addresses barriers to inclusion, and seeks the benefits and values of diversity.

Further, a majority of the literature on inclusion and leadership is primarily pragmatic and behavioral. Other streams of research argues that inclusive leadership needs to not only concentrate on what leaders do but what they *know* and who they *are* (Booysen, 2014; Cox, 2017). The prag-

Table 5.1

Inclusive Leadership Definitions

Nembhard & Edmondson (2006)	Leader inclusiveness is words and deeds by a leader or leaders that indicate an invitation and appreciation for others' contributions" (p. 947).
Hollander (2008)	"Inclusive Leadership is a process of active followership emphasizing follower needs and expectations, with the guiding principle of 'Doing things with people, not to people,' in a two-way influence relationship" (cover).
Carmeli et al. (2010)	"Inclusive leadership refers to a specific kind of relational leadership where leaders exhibit openness, accessibility, and availability in their interactions with followers ..., inclusive leadership is at the core of relational leadership and focuses on whether followers feel that leaders are available to them, whether the leader listens, and is paying attention to follower needs" (pp. 250–251).
Booysen (2014)	"Inclusive Leadership is an ongoing cycle of learning through collaborative and respectful relational practice that enables individuals and collectives to be fully part of the whole, such that they are directed, aligned, and committed toward shared outcomes, for the common good of all, while retaining a sense of authenticity and uniqueness" (p. 306).
Wuffli (2015)	Inclusive Leadership is a dynamic and change-oriented process which enables bridge building across different sectors of society and across cultures to involve as many people and diverse situations as possible and encourages leaders to take positions related to their underlying ethics and virtues.
Wasserman (2015)	"Inclusive leadership involves particular skills and competencies for relational practice, collaboration, building inclusion for others, creating inclusive work places and work cultures, partnerships and consensus building, and true engagement of all" (p. 335).
Randel et al. (2018)	Inclusive Leadership is defined as a "set of leader behaviors that are focused on facilitating group members feeling part of the group (belongingness) and retaining their sense of individuality (uniqueness) while contributing to group processes and outcomes" (p. 191).
Ratcliff et al. (2018)	Inclusive Leadership has five dimensions: fair treatment, being open to differences, integration into the unit, leveraging unique perspectives and expertise, and developing shared understanding in communications.
Najmaei & Sadeghinejad (2019)	"Inclusive Leadership is a style of leadership which is premised on the leader's availability, acceptability and openness to all follower's contributions to the work process and to satisfy their needs for uniqueness and belongingness. Inclusive Leaders promote collaboration, coordination, and equality in all aspects to create an atmosphere where diversity is cherished and capitalized on" (p. 225).

matic approaches in the literature often cite what behavioral approaches are needed (e.g., Ferdman, 2014; Miller & Katz, 2002; Pless & Maak, 2004), but have not taken the theory further into these more holistic understandings. One of the most prominent studies (Randel et al., 2018) has attempted to create a consistent theoretical definition of inclusive leadership, but their definition is also entirely behavioral. While their definition places diversity at the core and sees it as a value, a more holistic definition is needed which takes into account the knowing, doing, and being of an individual, as well as its shared, relational capacity.

Interestingly, while there are several different approaches and understandings of inclusive leadership, these different streams rarely rely on each other. The behavioral stream has done a great deal of empirical work to show the benefits of inclusive leadership (Carmeli et al., 2010; Chen & Tang, 2018; Choi et al., 2015; Chung et al., 2020; Hirak et al., 2012; Hollander, 2008; Javed et al., 2018; Jin et al., 2017; Nembhard & Edmondson, 2006; Nishii & Mayer, 2009; Qi & Liu, 2017; Steele & Derven, 2015; Ye et al., 2019), while other streams have taken a more theoretical approach trying to develop a more robust and holistic understanding (e.g., Ferdman & Deane, 2014). Bringing these two streams together not only creates a more robust definition of inclusive leadership but can begin to show conclusive evidence of the business case for inclusive leadership.

Najmaei and Sadeghinejad (2019), in a scientometric assessment, argued tthat here are three waves of inclusive leadership research. Wave one (2009–2013) laid the foundation and introduced the term, wave two (2013–2016), tried to understand inclusion and inclusive leader behaviors, and wave three (2016–present) explicitly focused on inclusive leadership and other styles, consolidating conceptual and theoretical positioning. They argue that the concept is still in its infancy and needs a more robust theoretical construct within the leadership research to be beneficial across multiple sectors such as business, education, and health care. The current chapter is positioned in the third wave hoping to consolidate and integrate the existing literature.

Beyond the "waves" of inclusive leadership, Ratcliff et al. (2018) described three approaches to inclusive leadership in the literature. Each of the waves have common elements, but certain nuances need to be taken into account. The first approach "defines inclusive leadership as leader actions that focus on the practice of inviting and appreciating input of all members in decision-making processes" (p. 3). The role of a leader is to create safety for members to speak up and contribute to the whole. The second approach Ratcliff identified is defining inclusive leadership based on the "quality of relationships that leaders have with their followers" (p. 3). Quality relationships create more felt inclusion but can create divisions in a group based on who has the higher quality of relationship with the leader. The third approach relies on optimal distinctiveness theory where people have both the need to belong to the group and have their uniqueness honored. According to this approach, Inclusive leaders behave in such a way that followers feel that they both belong and are valued for their unique contributions.

Table 5.1 offers a list of the primary definitions of inclusive leadership currently in the literature. These definitions have either been relied on frequently in subsequent literature or are summaries of a particular approach to inclusive leadership.

Randel et al. (2018) suggested inclusive leadership should be considered its own framework distinct from other leadership theories. As mentioned several times, many leadership approaches lack an approach to diversity, and Sims (2018) argued that many traditional approaches actually perpetuate many of the problems surrounding diversity. As such, inclusive leadership is a unique approach that takes complexity and an ever-changing environment into consideration while retaining diversity as a primary value. In other words, inclusive leadership is an approach that holistically addresses twenty-first-century workplace needs and contexts. Based on the previous literature, the current chapter uses a slightly modified version of Booysen's (2014) definition as: *a style of leadership that requires an ongoing cycle of knowing, doing, and being through collaborative and respectful relational practice that enables individuals and collectives to be fully part of the whole, such that they are directed, aligned, and committed toward shared outcomes, for the common good of all, while retaining a sense of belonging and uniqueness, especially for traditionally marginalized social groups*.

This definition captures a more holistic understanding of inclusive leadership and incorporates the many aspects of the theory explored in the following.

CONCEPTUAL FOUNDATIONS AND DEFINITIONS

Diversity and Inclusion

Perhaps one of the most critical tasks of reviewing the theory of inclusive leadership is to look at its roots within the diversity and inclusion literature. The evolution of inclusive leadership comes "from a simple extension of diversity management or an approach to diversity management mainly [focused] on gender to a new leadership style imperative to success in today's world with implications for different aspects of employee's productivity and organizational performance" (Najmaei & Sadeghinejad, 2019, p. 238). Inclusive leadership can only be properly understood as a new leadership style by exploring its roots in diversity management. For the purposes of this chapter, diversity is defined as "the representation of multiple identity groups and their cultures in a particular organization or workgroup" (Ferdman, 2014, p. 3). Identity groups include (but are not limited to) culture, ethnicity, race, nationality, gender, age, ability/disability, religion, sexual orientation, personal behaviors, cognitive styles, social and cultural identity, and global dimensions within the context of a unique, complex, and whole human beings (Cox, 2017).

Since the 1960s, American organizations have been addressing the complexity of and problems surrounding diversity (Wasserman et al., 2014; Wasserman & Blake-Beard, 2010). While extraordinary strides were made during this time, the past few decades of scholarship revealed that the presence of diversity alone was not sufficient. For organizations to fully benefit from diversity in a way that works for everyone, additional conditions were required (Ferdman, 2014; Ferdman & Deane, 2014). Within the organizational literature, the two most explored conditions have been *inclusion* and *leadership*.

Inclusion first emerged "as a correlate to diversity, concerned more with ways that organizations can maximize the benefits of diversity by fostering and promoting full rights, access, and privileges of employment and advancement to all organizational members" (Combs et al., 2019, p. 279). Beginning in the 1990s and early 2000s, scholars (Cox & Blake, 1991; Ely & Thomas, 2001; Mor Barak, 2000) began to argue that diversity was not a problem to be solved, but resources from which organizations could both benefit and learn from (Ferdman, 2014). As organizations became more diverse, it became more important for diverse individuals to be able to bring their authentic selves to work (Ferdman, 2014). Scholars recognized the need for additional conditions for the presence of diversity to provide positive benefits (Ferdman, 2014) and inclusion became a vital concept to bridge the gap between representation and allowing traditionally excluded groups to bring their whole selves to work. As Randel et al. (2018) pointed out:

> In order to achieve more complete involvement of diverse individuals in the workplace and to provide the opportunity for all organizational members to reach their full potential, researchers and practitioners have increasingly looked to inclusion … as a route to accomplishing these goals. (p. 191)

Miller and Katz (2002) were some of the first to make a distinction between inclusion and diversity. Their work focuses on one primary argument: "Diversity without inclusion does not work" (p. 17). They recognized that even demographically diverse organizations "often lack the basic skills and workplace environment required to leverage that diversity" (p. 8). Without the skills for generative dialogue across difference, those who are most different from the dominant group wind up being marginalized in the organization. Too often, organizations stop at simply "leveling the playing field" by eliminating the barriers that prevent equal participation from all people. Yet a level playing field is not enough to truly benefit from diversity and can often create more divisions by trying to bring the organizations up to standards only applied to the dominant group. Inclusion means organizations "raise the playing field" where *everyone* brings "all of their talents and energies to the workplace, working together to create something greater than any individual or monocultural group could do alone" (Miller & Katz 2002, p. 15).

Roberson's (2006) study took a more empirical approach to distinguishing diversity and inclusion. She claimed inclusion is often assumed in organizations because diversity is present, but this misunderstands the nature of inclusion. Her study showed the lack of empirical support for inclusion as its own distinct concept, and that organizations have "conceptually distinct definitions of diversity and inclusion" (p. 228). Diversity was defined as the representation of people on a spectrum of differences and similarities in an organization. Inclusion, on the other hand, was defined as organizational objectives designed to leverage differences and increase the ability of all members to contribute fully and effectively.

While these two works brought the differences between diversity and inclusion to the forefront, more scholarship has been done to define inclusion fully. Ferdman (2018) described three approaches to inclusion and noted that clarifying the three brings an essential nuance to the conversation. The first approach to inclusion is "granting full and complete privileges for those deemed worthy of admission" (p. 100). In this view, people are included to the extent that they adopt the existing values and norms of the organization or group. The second view is the inclusion of everyone to the organization or group "without criteria and without processes for creating respectful and/or civil engagements across differences" (p. 100). While all perspectives are welcomed, there is no approach to bridging differences, and there is room for exclusive perspectives to crowd out others. The third approach, which Ferdman argued is the preferred view, is the

> type of inclusion that does not require conformity, but that is nonetheless characterized by strong, unifying, and egalitarian bases for ongoing engagement that allow both maintaining and assessing the meaning and limits of collective principles and values, even as these evolve and are adapted to new conditions and members. (p. 101)

Inclusion, in this view, creates engagement across differences through dynamic and proactive processes. As such, inclusion is much more of a process than at outcome (Najmaei & Sadeghinejad, 2019).

Shore et al.'s (2011) seminal review of the inclusion literature has provided perhaps the most recognized definition of inclusion: "the degree to which an employee perceives that he or she is an esteemed member of the work group through experiencing treatment that satisfies his or her needs for *belongingness* and *uniqueness*" (p. 1265, italics added). The need for belonging and uniqueness creates an interesting paradox in practice. Ferdman (2017) argued that inclusion requires embracing a paradox persective to inclusion helps create a more inclusive space. The tension of belonging and uniqueness is creating space where everyone can both belong and be the same as well as belong and be different. When a person feels they belong to the group, they are more likely to bring their full selves, while still remaining a representative of the group. In other words, "to fully belong, I need to be able to keep my separate and distinct identity; for that identity to matter and make a difference to the whole, I need to fully belong" (Ferdman, 2017, p. 14).

Inclusion, therefore, gives voice to the ways people are different by affirming the uniqueness and complexity of the individual "without losing sight of intergroup relations, intercultural dynamics, and systemic processes and structures" (Ferdman & Deane, 2014, p. xxiv) or "having to give up valuable identities or aspects of themselves" (Ferdman 2014, p. 12). Inclusion not only acknowledges and honors differences in unique, complex, and whole human beings (Ferdman, 2014) but makes space for people to bring these differences to the group to make a full contribution to the workplace or environment.

Although diversity and inclusion are distinct concepts, Ferdman (2014) encouraged not divorcing the two either, as the power of inclusion comes from its roots in diversity. Connecting the two concepts harkens back to the original goals of diversity of addressing social inequities, systemic discrimination, inequality, and "the hierarchical aspects of intergroup relations in a societal and organizational context" (p. 9). Inclusion not only expands the approach to diversity, but aids in removing some of the stigma connected with diversity and "diversity fatigue" experienced when little progress can be seen (Wasserman & Blake-Beard, 2010; Wasserman et al., 2014). Ratcliff et al. (2018) noted,

> the potential benefits of diversity can only be fully realized when members feel that they are included and their perspectives and knowledge are leveraged in the decision-making processes; thus, fostering and maintaining a climate of inclusion is integral to leverage diverse knowledge bases. (p. 1)

As Shore et al. (2018) pointed out, attention to diversity has focused on bringing underrepresented groups into the workplace, but inclusion seeks to "create equal access to decision-making, resources, and upward mobility opportunities for these individuals" (p. 2). Locating inclusion within diversity means not only appreciating and honoring people because of their difference and uniqueness but also addressing barriers within a group, organization, or society that prevents full contribution of each member, especially those of underrepresented groups (Ferdman, 2014).

Central to the current discussion, Shore et al. (2011) argued that while inclusion takes into consideration all social groups, it pays "particular attention to groups that have had fewer opportunities historically and that are stigmatized in the societies in which they live" (p. 1277). Inclusion elevates the climate where both minority and majority members feel they belong and are respected and has the potential to "create greater equality and opportunities in the workplace for diverse people by affirming the unique contribution they offer and encouraging full participation in work group activities" (p. 1281). In a more recent review, Shore et al. (2018) summarized it as follows:

> inclusion involves equal opportunity for members of socially marginalized groups to participate and contribute while concurrently providing opportunities for members of nonmarginalized groups, and to support employees in their efforts to be fully engaged at all levels of the organization and to be authentically themselves. (p. 2)

Conceptualizing inclusion as rooted in diversity and creating space for diverse individuals to contribute fully to a group requires a positive approach to diversity. In previous decades, diversity scholarship has often taken a deficit approach, which focuses on the problems associated with diversity and the lack of inclusion that happens in organizations (Shore et al., 2011). Deficit models center mostly on the problems related to diversity and how to manage them, such as eliminating bias and discrimination (Boekhorst, 2015). As a result, "workplace diversity research had generated relatively more knowledge about the experiences of exclusion than knowledge of the mechanisms, processes, or practices that foster equality and inclusion" (Nkomo et al., 2019, p. 499).

Other models claimed diversity was a hindrance to performance, and so organizations pushed for assimilation. Assimilation asks underrepresented groups to conform to the dominant culture (Williams, 2013), rather than asking what needs to be changed in the system (Ferdman, 2014). Excluded groups are often either forced or unwilling to accommodate to dominant norms for promotion. Such assimilation results in employees having to submerge important aspects of themselves, which may be stigmatized or devalued for promotion or acceptance within the organization or even accepted (Combs et al., 2019; Ferdman, 2014; Livers & Caver, 2003). Further, individuals who are forced to be "included by the group against their own will were found to be more likely to behave aggressively" (Jansen et al., 2014, p. 3).

Ferdman and Deane (2014) rooted their understanding of inclusion in positive organizational scholarship (POS) to see diversity as a benefit rather than a problem to be solved. Using a POS lens for diversity research means examining "phenomena that exemplify a just, equal, close society where difference is empowering" (Ramarajan & Thomas, 2013, p. 552). Rather than highlighting the ongoing negative processes, a positive lens looks for examples where people are being included, and negative relationships and outcomes are minimized. A positive lens appreciates and values people "*because of* and not in spite of their differences, as well as their similarities" (Ferdman, 2014, p. 5, italics in original). It is important to note here that a positive approach does not ignore the barriers to inclusion. In fact, it takes seriously knowing what obstacles are in place and seeks to identify and understand generative processes of inclusion and inclusive leadership that can help create paradigms and models for overcoming difficulties and facilitating individual and collective agency for diversity to been as a resource.

In summary, the current paradigm for inclusion roots the concept as both distinct from and related to diversity. Inclusion moves beyond representation, views diversity as a value, and creates the additional conditions necessary for diversity to provide positive benefits to the group or organization. Barriers to full contributions from diverse individuals are addressed, and diversity is leveraged in a virtuous cycle benefitting both individuals and organizations, as well as the different social identity groups the individuals in organizations represent (Ferdman & Deane, 2014; Miller & Katz, 2002).

> **Proposition 1:** Inclusive leadership will be positively related to the experience of inclusion (defined as belongingness and uniqueness), especially for diverse and historically underrepresented individuals.

Inclusion and Leadership

As important as a thorough understanding of inclusion is, such a process does not occur on its own. It requires guidance and leadership. As such, diversity scholarship and practice points to leadership as the second element necessary for diversity efforts in organizations. Leadership is "the linchpin for inclusion at other levels of the multilevel framework; it can facilitate (and perhaps even be considered a key part of) inclusion in groups, organizations and societies, as well as help translate and spread inclusion across these levels" (Ferdman, 2014, p. 17). As Randel et al. (2018) pointed out, "simply placing individuals who differ from one another in a work group or promoting diverse individuals into leadership positions does not ensure positive outcomes" (p. 11). When left unmanaged, the drive for inclusion "can also lead to status distinctions, subgrouping, outgroup discrimination ... and implicit biases against certain groups" (Buengeler et al., 2018, p. 289). Further, organizations that make intentional efforts to recruit and develop underrepresented individuals may find that inclusive policies are not enough for individuals to feel included and contribute fully to the organization. Organizations then begin to feel they have let down these individuals (Randel et al., 2018).

In order to benefit from the promise inclusion holds for organizations and groups, "such experiences are dependent in part on effective leadership" (Randel et al., 2018, p. 190). Several studies show the main difference between high performing diverse teams and low performing diverse teams is leadership (Chrobot-Mason et al., 2014; Gotsis & Grimani, 2016; Maznevski & Chui, 2012). Concentrated effort and carefully managed group processes are required to both address exclusion and leverage diversity (Gallegos, 2014; Ferdman, 2014). Leaders not only play an important role in theoretical models (Boekhorst, 2015; Nishii, 2013; Perry & Li, 2019; Shore et al., 2018) but have an essential impact on inclusion by defining inclusion in context; shaping the diversity climate at the individual, group, and organization level; and modeling inclusion (Ferdman, 2014; Perry & Li, 2019). In doing so, leaders often determine whether employees discriminate in a group and define how important group members see inclusion to their work (Perry & Li, 2019).

Individual leaders are not, however, the only ones responsible for creating inclusion in groups and organizations. Cox (2017) found that inclusive leadership is a collective responsibility rather than an approach utilized by a single person. As leadership development research begins to make the distinction between leader development (the development of capacities in an individual) and leadership development (the collective development of capacities within a group), leadership is now seen as a relational property more than an individual responsibility (Chrobot-Mason et al., 2014). An individual leader's role is to moderate the relationship between team-member resources to enhance and build leadership capacity within the team (Day & Harrison 2007). While the individual leader is not ignored, it requires a more holistic approach to understand the dynamic and multilevel process of leadership (Avolio et al., 2009). Inclusive leadership is fundamentally a team process (Morgan, 2017) where the role of inclusive leaders is to develop the capacity for inclusive leadership in themselves as well as their followers, teams, and organizations.

> **Proposition 2:** Effective, collaborative leadership is a positive antecedent to the experience of inclusion.

The need for leadership and inclusion in diverse organizations has led to the initial development of inclusive leadership theories. As mentioned in the introduction, research in leadership has developed theories to meet the demands of a globalized and increasingly complex landscape, yet none of these theories have diversity at their core. As Najmaei and Sadeghinejad (2019) noted, "Inclusive Leadership is a leadership style that promotes and capitalizes on the power of diversity ... essence, inclusive leaders maximize the gains from diversity by fostering inclusion" (p. 222).

> **Proposition 3:** Inclusive leadership moderates the relationship between organizational outcomes and the presence of diversity in an organization. When higher levels of inclusive leadership are present, diversity is more positively related to organizational outcomes.

THE DYNAMICS OF INCLUSIVE LEADERSHIP

Chrobot-Mason et al. (2014) showed that well-developed leadership studies focus on leading the self, others, and the organization. Several studies within inclusion and inclusive leadership also promote a multilevel understanding. Ferdman (2017) argued inclusion should look at

> a combination of individual behaviors and attitudes, group norms, leadership approaches, and organization policies and practices [which] enable each person to flourish and develop, providing opportunities to fully connect and engage in ways that are beneficial for both the individual and the collective. (Ferdman, 2017, pp. 4–5)

Attention should be paid to the organizational, societal, and cultural systems which influence the way identities are construed and overlap (Wasserman, 2015). Buengeler et al. (2018) argued specifically that HR practitioners consider the individual, relational, and organizational levels of inclusion to help employees feel included. In other words, leadership of the self, the group, and the organization are critical for a thorough understanding of inclusive leadership.

Leadership of the Self

Wasserman and Blake-Beard (2010) understood inclusive leadership to be a cycle involving knowing, being, and doing. *Being* refers to the relational skills and authenticity needed to translate knowledge to practice; *knowing* is the "attentive mind-set required to capture the opportunities from difference" (p. 199), and *doing* is the integration of both knowledge and practice required for inclusive leadership and navigating change. Knowing, being, and doing are all integrated and need to be continually understood in context to create a virtuous cycle of development to help leaders "expand the stewardship of their organizations" (p. 212).

Inclusive leadership is much more than a simple set of rules and behaviors, and just prescribing particular behaviors is not sufficient. While it must be "reflected in behavior rather than platitudes which celebrate diversity but don't do the hard work of inclusion" (Gallegos, 2014, p. 196), inclusive leadership is about knowing when and how to use these behavioral manifestations, rather than creating a prescriptive list. Additionally, often the actual practice of inclusive behaviors leads to other ways of knowing and being (Booysen, 2014).

Leadership of the self first requires "including oneself" (Cox, 2017; Ferdman & Roberts, 2014; Whitney et al., 2010). Including oneself starts with bringing one's whole self to work, which includes the various components, characteristics and identities which work together to make a whole self. It also means becoming aware of one's own relationship to power and privilege (Ferdman & Roberts, 2014). Those working toward helping others feel like their voices matter must first come to understand their own voice and contributions matter (Ferdman & Roberts, 2014). Leaders must consider their own ways of being in order to be more inclusive of difference (Gallegos, 2014). When leaders know, accept, and express their whole self it "creates a platform for welcoming inclusion within one's organization" (Ferdman & Roberts, 2014, p. 95).

Inclusive leadership requires ongoing self-reflection and perspective-taking (Wasserman & Blake-Beard, 2010) by both leaders and group members (Gallegos, 2014). Leadership is a complex and ongoing process of examining previously taken-for-granted ways of working and interacting and reevaluating who and what is considered normal (Ferdman, 2014). Inclusive Leaders have to be lifelong learners and consistently focus on their own development, "particularly with regard to intergroup attitudes and behavior, together with a willingness to engage in continuous learning about differences" (Wasserman et al., 2008, p. 187). As Sims (2018) argued, the more aware leaders are of the differences between themselves and others, the more they will seek to learn about others and seek out ways to empower others and mitigate conflict across differences. In other words, the more authentic one becomes and the more aware of one's own identity, the more room they will create for the authenticity of others.

Proposition 4: Self-awareness and inclusion of the self will be positively related to inclusive leadership.

The ability to attend to both the self and others is in itself a difficult task but "becomes exponentially more challenging when bridging across differences in race, gender, sexual orientation, or nationality" (Gallegos, 2014, p. 183). Inclusive leaders must attend to their own ongoing growth and learning and reflect on their ways of making meaning and relating to others (Gallegos, 2014; Wasserman, 2015). Such critical reflection keeps leaders from privileging certain perspectives and helps them continually ask the essential questions for inclusive leadership: "Whose voices or perspectives might we be missing?" or "What are the limitations to the current ways we are seeing the issue?" (Gallegos, 2014, p. 181). Inclusive leaders take a learning stance by surrendering to the fact that they often do not know everything and will make mistakes. A posture of not knowing allows one to attend to those who are different by "considering, honoring, valuing, and respecting connections, distinctions and that which one does not understand" (Wasserman, 2015, p. 342). Persons of privilege can stop and notice how they can use their position of privilege to open connections (Wasserman, 2015, p. 342). Leaders with privilege also need to be asking themselves: "To what extent can/should we rely on familiar ways of doing things (ways that may be optimal for me or us)? How much do I (and we) need to change to include you (and them)? Who decides? And what do we do considering the historical realities of such comfort?" (Ferdman, 2017, p. 23).

Leaders need to specifically focus on the role between- and within-group identities, conflict, and social and legal views of diversity all play in the enactment of inclusion (Wasserman et al., 2008). Attention must be also paid to the sociohistorical bias and marginalization of certain social identities in order to counteract the problems in their environments while respecting the unique identities of their followers (Chrobot-Mason et al., 2014). Several authors now refer to the ability to attend to social identities as diversity intelligence (Das, 2019; Sims, 2018). Leaders need to understand when and how certain identities become more salient, how the salience of those identities affects followers' responses to the leader, and be willing to "reshape and redefine the group prototype" (Chrobot-Mason et al., 2014, p. 689) of leadership. Inclusive leaders understand their expression of self affects how others express themselves and that values and judgments originate from the collective and not just the individual (Wasserman et al., 2008). They must understand how to "recognize differences between themselves and others without considering the dissimilarities as an impediment to performance" (Das, 2019, p. 16). Buengeler et al. (2018) argued that while recognizing social identity in HR policies is not enough for inclusion, it can help leaders understand how and why people may react to HR policies. Diversity intelligence can address the barriers to inclusion and enact feelings of belongingness and uniqueness by ensuring all members of the group contribute full based on their uniqueness (Das, 2019).

As leaders span the boundaries of differences, they must also attend to the various faultlines which are present as differences are encountered and have an understanding of group dynamics in order to help people embrace differences and value conflict (Wasserman et al., 2014). Inclusive leaders pay attention to "deeper emotional reactions such as fear of feeling incompetent or fear of loss of power or control" (Wasserman et al., 2008, p. 189) and guide followers through these emotions. They must be engaged in the complexity of differences while at the same time, observing the leadership process (Wasserman et al., 2014).

Attending to social identity requires an understanding of intersectionality. Facets of one's identity are not static but grow and develop to support other identities. Intersectionality explores how these multiple identities are interconnected and influenced by certain contexts to produce "unequal power distribution and structural inequities" (Wasserman et al., 2014, p. 454). Inclusive leaders understand not only that individuals have different identities but that these identities shape people's experiences in the workplace and should be seen as a benefit to the whole (Combs et al., 2019; Ferdman, 2017).

Proposition 5: Leader capacity for diversity intelligence will be positively related to inclusive leadership.

Truly inclusive leadership of the self requires a great deal of humility. Gallegos (2014) believed humility is a central tenet of inclusive leadership. Randel et al. (2016) and Cox (2017) both argued for humility as a strong indicator that a leader will engage in inclusive leadership behaviors. Humble leaders have a "high level of clarity regarding one's identity, strengths, and weaknesses" (Randel et al., 2016, p. 7). As leaders understand they are not the center of the universe, their self-focus decreases, and empathy and appreciation for others increase. Specifically for inclusive leadership, "Humble leaders will not be threatened by members' differences, or strengths and abilities that may be different from their own, and will therefore be likely to observe ways to integrate member uniqueness into the group" (p. 8). Cox (2017) further argues that humility is an important reminder that inclusive leadership is more than a set of behaviors, especially since it often requires sacrifice and difficulty.

Proposition 6: Humility will be positively related to inclusive leadership.

Leadership of Others

The leadership of others in inclusive leadership requires understanding how to create inclusive environments (Chrobot-Mason et al., 2014; Gotsis & Grimani, 2016). Climate "refers to employees' shared perceptions of the formal and informal organizational policies, practices, and procedures with respect to a strategic focus of interest" (Nishii & Rich, 2014, p. 331). For the purposes of this section, the "strategic focus of interest" is inclusion. An inclusive climate occurs when people are treated fairly, valued for who they are, and included in decision making (Nishii, 2013). The environment must be inclusive of people of all backgrounds, not only those in positions of power. However, a single-minded concentration on improving the status of underrepresented groups often has the "unintended effect of exacerbating negative stereotypes and perceived intergroup competition" (p. 1755). Nishi (2013) further suggests a more relational approach for inclusive climates.

Nishii and Rich (2014) established three elements of a relational, inclusive climate. First, there must be perceived equal status. Second, individuals have to know each other in personal ways that establish cross-cutting ties across identities and reduce stereotyping. Creating equal status in these relationships requires mutual adaptations for both dominant and nondominant groups while still retaining cultural identities. Finally, groups must work together across boundaries to solve problems with participative and inclusive decision making.

Inclusive leaders strive to create such a climate where full participation is encouraged, different groups have equal access to power and decision making, and safe space is provided for authentic dialogue to occur. Leaders both model and encourage the appreciation of the perspectives of others and willingness to see other's views as valid and important (Chrobot-Mason et al., 2014). Leaders pay attention to the varying manifestations of diversity in their teams, shine light on them, show how they are valuable, and "provide the support and resources for the team to engage in deeper dialogue and constructive conflict in service of establishing a cohesive environment where all can being their best ideas to the table" (Gallegos, 2014, p. 190).

Several studies have looked at the necessary elements inclusive leaders must take to create inclusive climates. Randel et al. (2018) offered five leadership behaviors for facilitating inclusion at the group level. Facilitating belongingness requires: "1) supporting group members, 2) ensuring that justice and equity are part of each member's experience, and 3) providing opportunities for shared decision making on relevant issues" (p. 4). Shared decision making often requires leader to share power and broaden consultation on decision making and how work is conducted, which creates a sense of psychological ownership and interdependence within the group. Facilitating uniqueness requires "1) encouraging diverse contributions to the work group and 2) helping group members fully offer their unique talents and perspectives to enhance the work of the group" (p. 4).

Facilitating uniqueness is also closely related to authenticity. The literature continually points to authenticity as a core element of inclusive leadership (Gallegos, 2014; Wasserman & Blake-Beard 2010). Inclusive leaders create a context where everyone is fully engaged in collaborative pursuits, yet do not have to compromise or hide parts of their true selves (Gallegos, 2014). Authenticity requires building relationships that foster new ways of relating, sense-making, learning, engagement, and creativity (Gallegos, 2014). Again, this is a difficult process, especially when dealing with difference and diversity. Inclusive leaders have to overcome many layers of distrust by investing the time and energy required for people to work together in unfamiliar circumstances. Diverse, authentic relationships are neither easy nor comfortable because they challenge our taken for granted assumptions and familiarity and force us to seek out others who are radically different (Gallegos, 2014).

Ferdman's (2017) paradox of safety and comfort helps explain the tension of diverse relationships. Inclusion increases individual and collective comfort, while at the same time forcing individuals and the collective to leave their comfort zones. Managing this paradox requires balancing comfort and discomfort, along with the need for safety and the ability to take risks. Leaders must understand safety always has limits, and creating space for differences requires some discomfort. Feeling too safe loses people's attention and can perpetuate inequity while feeling too uncomfortable can make it difficult to perform. Ferdman articulated:

> I am included to the extent I can move beyond my comfort zone and engage in challenging situations that test my biases and open my mind, so that I can fully belong, safely participate, and thoroughly engage across differences. Moreover, for me to be included, I must accept others for who they are, even if that might cause me discomfort and require me to adapt. (p. 23)

Inclusion requires *mutual adaptation* where people are willing to engage in ongoing dialogue and learning, and see that those whom they do not understand are essential to individual and collective growth (Ferdman, 2017). Cox (2017) terms the process of mutual adaptation as co-authenticity. Co-authenticity extends the idea of being oneself fully, yet also creating room for others to be fully themselves as well. Much like Ferdman above, Cox (2017) argued that co-authenticity requires "brave space" (Arao & Clemens, 2013) where dominant identities do not define safety, and there is room for the discomfort and challenge.

Co-authenticity means being aware of the impact of one's authenticity while also being willing to adapt to the other authentic selves, without losing valuable parts of oneself. It is not losing a sense of one's own identities, but adapting for the sake of another (Ferdman, 2017; Nishii & Rich, 2014). Each person must make space within themselves for the other. Much like a dance, each person retains their own unique self while incorporating some of others' selves into their selves. Rather than a focus on what is of value for each individual, authenticity focuses on what is of value for the collective, and together the collective forges understandings of equity, fairness, justice, belongingness, and inclusion. Creating shared meaning across difference requires the "capacity to stay engaged at a meta-level to the multiple ways in which people interpret a situation or relationship" (Wasserman et al., 2008, p. 184). Inclusive leaders see themselves as responsible for their relationships, and shift their focus from the self to others.

> **Proposition 7:** Co-authenticity (the ability to be authentic and adapt to the authenticity of others) is positively related to inclusive leadership.

As co-authenticity happens, leaders need to able to slow down, define how differences will be engaged, and pay attention to "the container" where inclusive leadership is taking place (Cox, 2017; Wasserman, 2015). Managing the container means creating the rules of engagement and describe the boundaries for inclusive behavior. Yet at the same time, leaders must be willing to adapt those boundaries to make sure they still work for the actual people present in the group (Ferdman, 2017; Gallegos, 2014). As Ferdman (2018) put it, this means no one fully owns the boundaries, and once these boundaries are marked, they need to be reexamined based on the continual changes in the people and the organization. Both Buengeler et al. (2018) in the human resource management literature and Cox (2017) in the leadership development literature argue that the best way to adaptively approach boundaries is co-constructing the environment. Co-construction not only empowers those in the group but mitigates the problem of ownership of boundaries and ensures the space works for those present.

An adaptive approach for diversity embraces another of Ferdman's (2017) inclusion paradoxes: boundaries and norms. Inclusion requires stable and well-defined boundaries and norms, which are also open and shifting. As mentioned previously, true inclusion does not mean "everything goes ... [but] constitutes a particular way of being and working together—with and across differences" (Ferdman, 2018, p. 100). Inclusion means being able to invite people into a well-defined system (Ferdman, 2017) that is "precise in clarifying both the meaning and limits of inclusion (Ferdman, 2018, p. 100). Rules and boundaries are necessary, but rules and boundaries are no longer clear and predictable (Gallegos, 2014). Boundaries have the potential to produce automatic ways of interaction that prevent people from seeing the value of people who are different (Wasserman & Blake-Beard, 2010).

Cox (2017) argued that dialogue across differences is critical for the group level of inclusive leadership. Dialogue creates authenticity and inclusion but requires well-defined containers (Ferdman, 2017; Isaacs, 1999). The work of the leader for such containers is creating ground rules, modeling vulnerability, engaging social identity, bringing in multiple perspectives, sharing power, navigating conflict, and asking which voices are missing (Cox, 2017). Dezenberg (2017) further argued that inclusive climates required: interacting collaboratively, communicating, empowering stakeholders, painting the picture, individualizing, inclusive thinking and action, facilitating positive interventions, thinking broadly, and involving people.

Proposition 8: Leader capacity to create a dialogic, inclusive climate will be positively related to inclusive leadership.

Leadership of the Organization

Leading the organization involves the strategy, structure, rules, and procedures of an organization (Chrobot-Mason et al., 2014). Cox (2017) argued that the organizational level needs the mission, vision, and policies of the organization to be aligned with the practice of inclusive leadership. Policies need to have accountability and address barriers and inequities. Organizations need to create space for authenticity where diversity is seen as a strength for the organization, create diverse pipelines to provide supports for marginalized individuals to have access to resources and conditions for success, readily available institutional training, and developmental relationships in order to infuse inclusive leadership into day-to-day operations.

Offerman and Basford (2014) suggest six best practices at the organizational level to create an inclusive culture through organizational commitments. First, organizations should develop a pipeline of diverse, high-quality talent. Specifically, they propose that this requires retention efforts for members of underrepresented groups. Second, organizations should not only confront explicit acts of discrimination but have policies for confronting microinequities and microaggressions as well. Third, organizations should treat diversity as a valued asset to business performance. Fourth, there should be accountability embedded into the organization for diversity and inclusion. Fifth, training organizational members for inclusion is critical. Sixth, formal training is insufficient on its own, there needs to be peer-to-peer, or we might say relational, influence in everyday work situations.

Another important theme for the organizational level of inclusive leadership is being able to lead change (Booysen, 2014; Morgan, 2017). Assumptions, values, and beliefs must be assessed throughout the structure, culture, systems, strategies, and practice of the organization. Organizations need to be able to reflect on their existing culture in order to gain the full value of diversity. Only when organizations engage in the difficult conversations of what barriers might be in place will inclusion occur throughout the organization (Gallegos, 2014). As mentioned earlier, even in already inclusive organizations, norms and boundaries must again take an adaptive approach where boundaries are constantly reevaluated, thus leaders will continually need the capacity for change. Training intervention is not enough; there must be a structural transformation that changes the way people engage one another within the organization (Wasserman et al., 2008).

In keeping with the importance of creating inclusive climates, two of the only empirical studies on the practice of inclusive leadership suggest change occurs from the group level outward. Dezenberg (2017) argued that creating positive climates cause the positive cluster to spread throughout the organization. Similarly, Cox (2017) argued that the main work and the development of inclusive leadership is done on the group level by creating space for dialogue across difference. Just as leadership is the "linchpin" for inclusion, inclusion on the group level is the linchpin for inclusive leadership. As followers become more co-authentic and become more aware of their taken-for-granted ways of relating, thinking, and acting, Inclusive leadership is developed within the individual and the group, thus creating a positive spiral within the environment or organization. Further, experiencing inclusion creates the desire to be more inclusive, and can lead to the further practice of inclusive leadership (Cox, 2017).

Other studies support the conclusion that change occurs on the group level (Chung et al., 2020; Perry & Li, 2019), but further research asserts that bottom-up approaches also require top-down support (Combs et al., 2019; Das, 2019; Nkomo et al., 2019). Bernstein et al. (2019) argued that continual generative interactions across differences, along with strong organizational support, creates organizational inclusion and equity. Specifically, for human resource management, Buengeler et al. (2018) argued that HR leaders need to work dialogically with employees to discover contextual best practices for diversity.

Proposition 9: Leader capacity to lead dialogic change will be positively related to inclusive leadership.

Alongside change, inclusive leaders must be able to deal with conflict and resistance. Since meaning is socially constructed within the workgroup and workgroup climate is learned through social interactions, workgroup members tend to rely on leaders to make sense of interactions and behaviors in the workplace. As such, one of the primary functions of inclusive leaders us to help shape employee perceptions construct shared meaning (Boekhorst, 2015). Using a positive framework, Wasserman et al. (2008) saw leaders' primary role as "dancing with resistance." Leaders must not only challenge existing norms, but provide a metanarrative for the organization where diversity is valued, boundaries are provided, modeled, and continuously questioned to make sure they work for all involved. A metanarrative of inclusion allows leaders to reframe conflicts for the advantage of the group or organization and helps coordinate shared meaning. Dancing with resistance requires the ability to "boundary span" and understand the faultlines across multiple lines of difference. When leaders broaden their perspectives and practice collaboration, difference can be embraced and conflicts valued (Wasserman et al., 2014). Chrobot-Mason et al. (2014) also pointed out the need for reflection and learning once the conflict is resolved.

Proposition 10: Leader capacity for dealing with conflict and resistance will be positively related to inclusive leadership.

CONFLUENCE WITH OTHER LEADERSHIP THEORIES

Inclusive leadership builds on and expands several leadership theories. As has been mentioned several times, many of the current leadership theories stop short of seeing diversity as a critical part of leadership. In order to build the case for inclusive leadership as an emerging and root theory, it is important to look at how it both transcends and includes other leadership theories.

Adaptive Leadership

Adaptive leadership is a framework of leadership that helps mobilize people "to tackle tough challenges and thrive" (Heifetz et al., 2009, p. 14). This framework is especially crucial in the competitive, complex, and continually changing environments where there are no simple solutions or prescriptive ways of leading. Particularly important for Adaptive leadership is Heifetz and Laurie's (2001) distinction between technical and adaptive solutions. Prescriptive responses are considered technical solutions that provide simplistic answers in order to restore order and maintain organizational norms. Adaptive solutions challenge norms and look for innovative solutions. Rather than leaders being the people with "all the answers," Adaptive leadership helps people ask the right questions and adapt to their situations. Adaptive leaders need the ability to move back and forth from seeing the larger picture "on the balcony" to the day-to-day operations "on the dance floor" (Chrobot-Mason et al., 2014; Heifetz & Laurie, 2001).

A diverse workforce adds further layers of ambiguity, uncertainty, and complexity that must be taken into account for inclusive leadership. There are no blanket rules for inclusion (Wasserman et al., 2008), and diversity requires leaders to manage the complex relational dynamics of diverse groups and stakeholders (Wasserman & Blake-Beard, 2010). Adaptive solutions often require leaders to make judgment calls in the moment, and the "identities, culture, experiences, and stories that emerge in such moments are complex, multifaceted, and fluid" (Wasserman & Blake-Beard 2010, p. 200). Many leaders try to respond to diversity with technical solutions rather than adaptive (Gallegos, 2014; Wasserman & Blake-Beard, 2010). Leaders often make the mistake of thinking more information will solve any problems encountered along with inclusion, or that creating simplistic rules to guide behavior and training managers to act accordingly is enough to create inclusion. Yet these technical fixes often come across as lacking authenticity and create more distance between groups.

Inclusive leadership as a theory builds on the unique relationship between adaptive leadership and diversity and inclusion. The presence of diversity creates unique challenges that require an adaptive approach and the ability to include diverse perspectives and people requires leaders to continually adapt their boundaries, norms, and the containers where leadership takes place.

LMX and Relational Leadership

Relational leadership has emerged over the last decade as a way of thinking about leadership as a "more dynamic socially-constructed system of interdependent relations in which shared leadership and organizational change can occur" (Offerman, 2012, p. 362; Uhl-Bien, 2006). Relational leadership developed as an extension to leader-member exchange (LMX) theory. LMX theory was initially conceived of as "effective leadership processes [that] occur when leaders and followers are able to develop mature leadership relationships (partnerships) and thus gain access to the many benefits these relationships bring" (Graen & Uhl-Bien, 1995, p. 225). The higher quality the relationship is between the leader and follower, the more significant impact on leader and follower outcomes (Avolio et al., 2009). Initial versions of inclusive leadership were based on LMX theory citing that by establishing high-quality relationships, leaders can promote equality, inclusion, and power-sharing to improve relationship exchanges (Hollander, 2008; Nishii & Mayer, 2009). Nishii and Mayer (2009) even go as far as to say that "high-quality exchanges with leaders [is] one form of inclusion, since those individuals in high-quality LMX relationships are more likely to experience ... inclusion" (p. 1416). Much of the "second wave" of inclusive leadership relied heavily on LMX theory.

Relational leadership developed through critiques of LMX theory for not considering social contexts by focusing more on the interdependent nature of relationships within an organization rather than the simplistic look at the leader-follower dyad (Avolio et al., 2009). Relational leadership is a way of being and relating with others which considers the context and emerges from relational dialogue with others (Cunliffe & Eriksen, 2011). It is a "way of being-in-the-world that embraces an intersubjective and relationally-responsive way of thinking and acting" (p. 1445), which cannot be formalized into policies or job descriptions. It is both a way of theorizing leadership and a way of practicing it in which draws upon the relational resources in a given setting.

Relational leadership takes responsibility for drawing out differences in dialogue and then "being both *responsive* to differences and *responsible* for acting on them. This sense of responsibility—*to be responsive, responsible and accountable to others in our everyday interactions with them*—contrasts to individualized heroic models of leadership" (Cunliffe & Eriksen, 2011, p. 1439, italics in original). Creating spaces for moments of dialogue that surface and address differences and being responsible to those differences creates a way forward for the group or organization.

Chrobot-Mason et al. (2014) believed relational-based leadership is one of the primary drivers for leading across differences in diverse groups. Booysen (2014) and Carmeli et al. (2010) also saw inclusive leadership as primarily a relational leadership approach. Developing a relational view of leadership moves beyond just the behavioral adjustments of cultural competence, to paying attention to how meaning is coordinated for others in relationship.

Several studies argue that inclusive leadership is both practiced and developed at the relational level. Cox (2017) argued that inclusive leadership is developed through "relational disorienting dilemmas" where individuals encounter those who are different and allow them to challenge their assumptions. Bernstein et al. (2019) argued that in order to facilitate inclusion, leaders must create contextually relevant practices for positive relationships and engage in overcoming the barriers to those relationships. Combs et al. (2019) also argued that in studying the failure of diversity and inclusion efforts in organizations, relationships played an instrumental role "in fostering work cultures where marginalized groups can flourish, and diversity and inclusion programs find meaning and purpose...environments that promote and provide avenues for the development of positive and meaningful relationships between individual and employee groups are desperately needed" (pp. 283–284). Dezenberg (2017) further connects relational leadership with adaptive leadership arguing that inclusive leadership has a critically human thrust that takes into consideration an "evolving context" and the need for continual change and adaptation.

Inclusive leadership, as a theory, extends the relational leadership literature in several ways. First, while relational leadership is helpful for drawing out difference and taking context into consideration, Cunliffe and Erikson (2011) note it does not yet address issues of power or identity the way inclusive leadership does. By keeping diversity at the center, inclusive leadership must deal with the identities of people in the environment, which also means attention to power dynamics and addresses barriers to inclusion.

Authentic Leadership

Drawing on George's (2004) original theory, Luthans and Avolio (2003) define authentic leadership as "a process that draws from both positive psychological capacities and a highly developed organizational context, which results in both greater self-awareness and self-regulated positive behaviors on the part of leaders and associates, fostering positive self-development" (p. 243). Although seemingly focused on the self, authentic leadership assumes knowing, accepting and remaining true to one's self results in more genuine social transactions (Avolio & Mhatre, 2013). It is a multilevel construct which includes "the leader, follower, and context very specifically in the way it was conceptualized and measured" (Avolio et al., 2009, p. 424).

Currently, many leadership scholars argue for Authentic Leadership to be seen as a "root construct" which means it "represents the base of good leadership regardless of form" (Avolio et al., 2009, p. 424) and is "capable of grounding other leadership frameworks" (Avolio & Mhatre, 2013, p. 775). The grounding of leadership theory is especially important as research now points away from a one-size-fits-all theory of leadership. Scholars believe what is needed is a root construct that can span across different leadership theories and provide particular ways of knowing, doing, and being for leaders in the current workforce. As such, theorists argue the four root constructs of authentic leadership (self-awareness, unbiased processing, relational authenticity, and authentic behavior) should be built into every leadership development intervention program, regardless of the focus (Avolio & Mhatre, 2013).

Authentic leadership also comes out of POS, as it builds on the strengths and identity of a leader rather than correcting what is wrong with the leader (Avolio et al., 2009). As such, authentic leadership has several areas of congruence with inclusive leadership such as a multilevel approach, positive relationships, and of course: authenticity. However, notably absent from the authentic leadership literature are issues surrounding diversity and inclusion (Berkovich, 2014). While some see inclusive leadership as a subset of authentic leadership (Boekhorst, 2015; Cottrill et al., 2014), authenticity does not guarantee diversity is represented and ignores important considerations for diversity and inclusion.

In summary, inclusive leadership extends the literature on adaptive, relational, and authentic leadership. While inclusive leadership requires all three kinds of leadership, it centralizes issues related to diversity and ensures diverse individuals have both a presence and a voice in the environment. As such, the metaphor of "the table" is helpful for a better understanding of the role of diversity, inclusion, and leadership in defining inclusive leadership. Diversity efforts tend to be concerned with *who* is at the table, but these efforts often stop short of being concerned with *what happens* at the table. Leadership theories such as adaptive, relational, and authentic leadership, care deeply about what happens at the table but are often unconcerned with who is present at the table. inclusive leadership as a theory connects the concern for who is at the table and what happens when they are there, ensuring both representation of diversity and the ability for all individuals to contribute fully. The ability of inclusive leadership to advance these theories leads then to the proposition of inclusive leadership as a root construct.

INCLUSIVE LEADERSHIP AS A ROOT CONSTRUCT

The current chapter has described inclusive leadership as a dynamic process with important theoretical roots. Based on the theoretical influences of a more holistic definition, inclusive leadership is ideally poised to be considered a *root construct* for leadership.In keeping with Avolio and Gardner's (2005) proposal for a root construct, this chapter will close by addressing Hunt's (2006) six points of defining leadership: purpose, definitions, historical roots and context, dynamic and processual approach, and the level of analysis.

Purpose

The primary purpose of proposing inclusive leadership as an emerging theory is its importance in practice. The introduction to this chapter highlighted that while diversity, inclusion, and leadership have been studied for decades, inequities still exist. The current chapter argues that one primary reason for these inequities is that diversity has not been central to leadership theory. The diversity and leadership literature propose more intertwining of leadership theory with scholarship on diversity and inclusion (Chrobot-Mason et al., 2016), but such intertwining has been limited. Sims (2018) argued that many have connected transformational leadership and LMX theory because they promote inclusive behaviors but much like authentic leadership, diversity is still not at the center. Others (Chin & Trimble, 2014; Sims, 2018) also argued that these leadership styles might be able to promote diversity but "are rife with value judgments and are based on narrow non-inclusive demographics" (Sims, 2018, p. 317). Boekhorst (2015) tried to incorporate diversity and inclusion into authentic leadership by making inclusion the primary value for authentic leadership, but inclusion is still not the primary goal of leadership. Gotsis and Grimani (2016) argued that inclusiveness is a critical element in authentic, ethical, servant, and spiritual leadership and showed how the relational aspects of transformational and LMX leadership are beneficial to diversity outcomes.

Inclusive leadership is thus positioned as a new form of leadership that places inclusion at the center in ways other theories do not. Randel et al. (2018) proposed that "inclusive leadership enables the effective functioning of diverse work groups in ways that are not sufficiently addressed by other forms of leadership" (p. 191), and Najmaei and Sadeghinejad (2019) suggested that inclusive leadership should be considered a "new kind of leadership which differs from traditional styles and helps overcome the barriers other styles struggle with" (p. 229).

Definitions

The current study proposed a definition which has a more holistic understanding of inclusive leadership that moves beyond a behavioral approach and centralizes diversity and the work of addressing the challenges that keep diverse individuals and organizations from thriving. This definition also incorporates the importance of an adaptive, relational, and authentic approach to leadership, and extends these to doing the work of creating equitable environments for everyone.

The root constructs of authentic leadership center around the importance of authenticity within leadership. Authenticity still plays a crucial role in leadership, but inclusive leadership extends the idea of authenticity to that of "co-authenticity" for the sake of others. Even Berkovich's (2014) critiques of developing critically aware authentic leadership are answered through the dialogic development of inclusive leadership (Cox, 2017).

With this in mind, inclusive leadership has the potential to become a more effective root construct because it addresses not only the problems of inequity but values and leverages diversity for the sake of the whole. Further, while "authenticity" can be subverted for the sake of personal gain, inclusive leadership at its core is for the sake of others where justice and equity are defined and worked out in relationship.

Historical Roots and Context

The current study extends several bodies of work. First, it extends the research on Authentic Leadership in its quest to find a root construct. Avolio and Gardner (2005) argue that if authentic leadership became a root construct, it would enrich the study of other kinds of leadership. The same would be true of inclusive leadership, but inclusive leadership adds the important dimension of diversity within the study. As the field of leadership continues to grow, there continues to be a call to examine leadership in light of diversity (Chrobot-Mason et al., 2014), yet there has been no consistent way of doing so. inclusive leadership takes into consideration both the presence and participation of diversity, ensuring a more holistic look at diversity within leadership.

This chapter also extends the inclusive leadership literature. The various waves and practices of inclusive leadership can make inclusive leadership illusive, and often this results in inclusive leadership having very little meaning at all. Just as inclusion is in need of common understandings, the current study combines the different streams of inclusive leadership into one definition to create more common ground for future study. This approach is thus inclusive of each stream of inclusive leadership in order to find shared ground and a way forward.

Relational Aspects and Dynamic and Processual Approach

Avolio and Gardner (2005) further argue that authentic leadership should be considered a root construct because of its relational focus on leadership and dynamic processes. As has been shown, inclusive leadership is relational at its core, and several authors argue that it can only be developed relationally (Booysen, 2014; Cox, 2017). Further, the relational approach to inclusive leadership is one that goes beyond the leader-follower dyad and considers the interconnectedness of people in organizations and society, making it a much more dynamic theory. Avolio and Gardner (2005) themselves argue that part of the challenge of authenticity is the dynamics of the organizational and societal context that impede the ability of traditionally underrepresented groups to achieve authenticity. inclusive leadership directly addresses these barriers and creates space for co-authenticity.

Level of Analysis

Several studies have shown the importance of inclusive leadership being a multilevel construct (Buengeler et al., 2018; Cox, 2017; Ferdman, 2014; Wasserman, 2015). Leadership of the self (individual), others (dyads, groups), and the organizations have been explored throughout this work. Further research should continue to understand how inclusive leadership is developed and practiced on each level.

FURTHER RESEARCH (AND LIMITATIONS)

As mentioned in the introduction, one main issue surrounding the scope and focus of the current chapter should be mentioned. Throughout the chapter, the primary literature has been focused on an American context. The lack of a more global context is one distinct limitation within all of the literature on inclusive leadership, although it is improving. While Randel et al. (2016) found only 17 quantitative studies outside of the U.S., the current author has found 7 more since the time of that publishing (Adams et al., 2019; Brewis, 2019; Chen & Tang, 2018; Javed et al., 2018; Qi & Liu, 2017; Ye et al., 2018, 2019). Boitano et al. (2017) have also attempted an edited work to bring a "global perspective that transcends cultures, disciplines, nations states, and other artificial boundaries" (p. xiii). Further, almost all of the non-U.S. studies take a behavioral approach where diversity is not necessarily the center. While the current model attempts to take context and culture into consideration, it is possible inclusive leadership could look different in other cultures. As an example, Prime and Salib, (2014) define inclusion as the perception of both uniqueness and belongingness. Yet research in India revealed that uniqueness and belongingness were not separate concepts as they were in other countries. Different cultures affect both what is meant by inclusion and how inclusion should be practiced. Historical marginalization and inequity are also different in various countries, so some of the issues surrounding equity could affect the practice of inclusive leadership. However, if the current streams of literature could continue to be in conversation, rich insights into a more global understanding of inclusive leadership could be discovered.

Exploration of the propositions would create a more cohesive theory. Not only would future research validate the propositions, but that validation would also continue to bring a more cohesive approach to inclusive leadership as a whole. With this in mind, more work should be done to bridge the various streams of inclusive leadership. Current empirical studies that take the more behavioral approach could begin to think about expanding their definitions and scales. The more holistic theoretical models currently lack empirical evidence. Najmaei and Sadeghinejad's (2019) literature review notes that more work within inclusive leadership is called for in how it relates to psychological safety, creativity, learning from failures, strategic decision making, employee turnover, and voice-related work issues and concerns. These areas reflect the need for continuing to understand the impact of inclusive leadership. Much of the current literature either concentrates on this impact or is trying to define and understand inclusive leadership simply. Cox (2017) recommends there be more research on how inclusive leadership is developed on the individual, group, and organization level. As the propositions made in this chapter are verified, these dynamics then become the very things needed to develop in individuals and organizations.

CONCLUSION

As organizations continue to grow more diverse and globalized, inclusive leadership becomes a critically important way of practicing leadership. As Najmaei and Sadeghinejad (2019) articulated: "As the breadth and depth of diversity in our societies continues to rise, so does the importance and value of Inclusive Leadership" (p. 222). inclusive leadership offers an opportunity for leaders to begin to leverage the diversity present in their environments.

Yet beyond the theory and research, inclusive leadership must address the very real harm, injustice, inequity, and violence that exist in our world. Taking a positive approach to something as difficult as inclusive leadership can feel idealistic in a broken and fractured world where differences threaten to divide human beings and the world every day. While the workplace continues to grow more diverse and globalized, inequity and discrimination persist, and the result of exclusion fills news headlines daily. Inclusive leadership taking a positive stance envisions a future where inclusion is at the heart of leadership practice and inequity and injustice are addressed and eliminated for the benefit of all.

REFERENCES

Adams, B. G., Meyers, M. C., & Sekaja, L. (2019). Positive leadership: Relationships with employee inclusion, discrimination, and well-being. *Applied Psychology, 69*(4). https://doi.org/10.1111/apps.12230

Arao, B., & Clemens, K. (2013). From safe spaces to brave spaces: A new way to dialogue around diversity and social justice. In L. M. Landreman (Ed.), *The art of effective facilitation: reflections from social justice educators* (pp. 135–150). Stylus.

Avolio, B. J., & Gardner, W. L. (2005). Authentic leadership development: Getting to the root of positive forms of leadership. *The Leadership Quarterly, 16*(3), 315–338.

Avolio, B. J., & Mhatre, K. H. (2013). Advances in theory and research on authentic leadership. In K. S. Cameron & Spreitzer (Eds.), *The Oxford handbook of positive organizational scholarship* (reprint ed, pp. 773–783). Oxford University Press.

Avolio, B. J., Walumbwa, F. O., & Weber, T. J. (2009). Leadership: Current theories, research, and future directions. *Annual Review of Psychology, 60*, 421–449. https://doi.org/10.1146/annurev.psych.60.110707.163621

Berkovich, I. (2014). Between person and person: Dialogical pedagogy in authentic leadership development. *Academy of Management Learning & Education, 13*(2), 245–264.

Bernstein, R. S., Bulger, M., Salipante, P., & Weisinger, J. Y. (2019). From diversity to inclusion to equity: A theory of generative interactions. *Journal of Business Ethics*. https://doi.org/10.1007/s10551-019-04180-1

Boekhorst, J. A. (2015). The role of authentic leadership in fostering workplace inclusion: A social information processing perspective. *Human Resource Management, 54*(2), 241– 264. https://doi.org/10.1002/hrm.21669

Boitano, A., Dutra, R. L., & Schockman, H. E. (Eds.). (2017). *Breaking the zero-sum game: Transforming societies through inclusive leadership*. Emerald.

Booysen, L. (2014). The development of inclusive leadership: Practice and processes. In B. M. Ferdman & B. R. Deane (Eds.), *Diversity at work: The practice of inclusion* (1st ed., pp. 296–329). Jossey-Bass.

Brewis, D. N. (2019). Duality and fallibility in practices of the self: The 'inclusive subject' in diversity training. *Organization Studies, 40*(1), 93–114. https://doi.org/10.1177/0170840618765554

Buengeler, C., Leroy, H., & De Stobbeleir, K. (2018). How leaders shape the impact of HR's diversity practices on employee inclusion. *Human Resource Management Review, 28*(3), 289–303. https://doi.org/10.1016/j.hrmr.2018.02.005

Caligiuri, P. (2012). *Cultural agility: Building a pipeline of successful global professionals*. Jossey-Bass.

Carmeli, A., Reiter-Palmon, R., & Ziv, E. (2010). Inclusive leadership and employee involvement in creative tasks in the workplace: The mediating role of psychological safety. *Creativity Research Journal, 22*(3), 250–260. https://doi.org/10.1080/10400419.2010.504654

Chen, C., & Tang, N. (2018). Does perceived inclusion matter in the workplace? *Journal of Managerial Psychology, 33*(1), 43–57. https://doi.org/10.1108/JMP-02-2017-0078

Chin, D. J. L., & Trimble, J. E. (2014). *Diversity and leadership* (1st ed.). SAGE.

Chin, J. L. (2010). Introduction to the special issue on diversity and leadership. *American Psychologist, 65*(3), 150–156. https://doi.apa.org/doiLanding?doi=10.1037%2Fa0018716

Choi, S. B., Tran, T. B. H., & Park, B. I. (2015). Inclusive leadership and work engagement: Mediating roles of affective organizational commitment and creativity. *Social Behavior and Personality: An International Journal, 43*(6), 931–943. https://doi.org/10.2224/sbp.2015.43.6.931

Chrobot-Mason, D., Gerbasi, A., & Cullen-Lester, K. L. (2016). Predicting leadership relationships: The importance of collective identity. *The Leadership Quarterly, 27*(2), 298–311. https://doi.org/10.1016/j.leaqua.2016.02.003

Chrobot-Mason, D., Ruderman, M. N., & Nishii, L. H. (2014). leadership in a diverse workplace. In D. Day (Ed.), *The oxford handbook of leadership and organizations* (1st ed, pp. 683–708). Oxford University Press.

Chung, B. G., Ehrhart, K. H., Shore, L. M., Randel, A. E., Dean, M. A., & Kedharnath, U. (2020). Work group inclusion: Test of a scale and model. *Group & Organization Management, 45*(1), 75–102. https://doi.org/10.1177/1059601119839858

Combs, G. M., Milosevic, I., & Bilimoria, D. (2019). Introduction to the special topic forum: Critical discourse: Envisioning the place and future of diversity and inclusion in organizations. *Journal of Leadership & Organizational Studies, 26*(3), 277–286. https://doi.org/10.1177/1548051819857739

Cottrill, K., Lopez, P. D., & Hoffman, C. C. (2014). How authentic leadership and inclusion benefit organizations. *Equality, Diversity & Inclusion, 33*(3), 275–292. http://dx.doi.org/10.1108/EDI-05-2012-0041

Cox, T. H., Jr., & Blake, S. (1991). Managing cultural diversity: Implications for organizational competitiveness. *Executive (19389779), 5*(3), 45–56.

Cox, T. (2017). *Learning from and for "the other": The development of inclusive leadership capacity by faculty members*. [Doctoral dissertation, Trinity International University]. ProQuest Dissertation Publishing.

Cunliffe, A. L., & Eriksen, M. (2011). Relational leadership. *Human Relations, 64*(11), 1425– 1449. https://doi.org/10.1177%2F0018726711418388

Das, A. (2019). Diversity intelligence for inclusive leadership: A conceptual framework. *Global Journal of Management and Business Research, 19*(9), 7. https://journalofbusiness.org/index.php/GJMBR/article/view/2832

Day, D. V., & Harrison, M. M. (2007). A multilevel, identity-based approach to leadership development. *Human Resource Management Review, 17*(4), 360–373. https://doi.org/10.1016/j.hrmr.2007.08.007

Dezenberg, M. E. (2017). *Inclusive leadership's evolving context: organizational climate and culture connect* [Doctoral dissertation, Antioch University]. ProQuest Dissertations Publishing.

Ely, R. J., & Thomas, D. A. (2001). Cultural diversity at work: The effects of diversity perspectives on work group processes and outcomes. *Administrative Science Quarterly, 46*(2), 229–273. https://doi.org/10.2307/2667087

Ferdman, B. M. (2014). The practice of inclusion in diverse organizations: Toward a systemic and inclusive framework. In B. M. Ferdman & B. R. Deane (Eds.), *Diversity at work: The practice of inclusion* (1st ed., pp. 3–54). Jossey-Bass.

Ferdman, B. M. (2017). Paradoxes of inclusion: Understanding and managing the tensions of diversity and multiculturalism. *The Journal of Applied Behavioral Science, 53*(2), 235– 263. https://doi.org/10.1177/0021886317702608

Ferdman, B. M. (2018). In Trump's shadow: Questioning and testing the boundaries of inclusion. *Equality, Diversity and Inclusion: An International Journal, 37*(1), 96–107. https://doi.org/10.1108/EDI-09-2017-0177

Ferdman, B. M., & Deane, B. R. (Eds.). (2014). *Diversity at work: The practice of inclusion* (1st ed). Jossey-Bass.

Ferdman, B. M., & Roberts, L. M. (2014). Creating inclusion for oneself: Knowing, accepting, and expressing one's whole self at work. In B. M. Ferdman & B. R. Deane (Eds.), *Diversity at work: The practice of inclusion* (1st ed., pp. 3–54). Jossey-Bass.

Gallegos, P. V. (2014). The work of inclusive leadership: Fostering authentic relationships, modeling courage and humility. In B. M. Ferdman & B. R. Deane (Eds.), *Diversity at work: The practice of inclusion* (1st ed., pp. 177–202). Jossey-Bass.

Geiger, K. A., & Jordan, C. (2014). The role of societal privilege in the definitions and practices of inclusion. *Equality, Diversity & Inclusion, 33*(3), 261–274. https://doi.org/10.1108/edi-12-2013-0115

George, B. (2004). *Authentic leadership: Rediscovering the secrets to creating lasting value* (1st ed.). Jossey-Bass.

Gotsis, G., & Grimani, K. (2016). Diversity as an aspect of effective leadership: Integrating and moving forward. *Leadership & Organization Development Journal, 37*(2), 241–264. https://doi.org/10.1108/lodj-06-2014-0107

Graen, G. B., & Uhl-Bien, M. (1995). Relationship-based approach to leadership: Development of leader-member exchange (LMX) theory of leadership over 25 years: Applying a multi- level multi-domain perspective. *The Leadership Quarterly, 6*(2), 219–247. https://doi.org/10.1016/1048-9843(95)90036-5

Heifetz, R. A., & Laurie, D. L. (2001). The work of leadership. *Harvard Business Review, 79*(11), 131–141.

Heifetz, R. A., & Linsky, M. (2002). *Leadership on the line: Staying alive through the dangers of leading* (1st ed). Harvard Business Review Press.

Heifetz, R. A., Linsky, M., & Grashow, A. (2009). *The practice of adaptive leadership: Tools and tactics for changing your organization and the world* (1 ed.). Harvard Business Press.

Hirak, R., Peng, A. C., Carmeli, A., & Schaubroeck, J. M. (2012). Linking leader inclusiveness to work unit performance: The importance of psychological safety and learning from failures. *The Leadership Quarterly, 23*(1), 107–117. https://doi.org/10.1016/j.leaqua.2011.11.009

Hollander, E. (2008). *Inclusive leadership: The essential leader-follower relationship* (Applied Psychology Series). Routledge.

Hunt, J. G. (2004). What is leadership? In J. Antonakis, T. Cianciolo, & R. J. Sternberg (Eds.), *The nature of leadership* (pp. 19–47). SAGE

Isaacs, W. (1999). *Dialogue: The art of thinking together* (1 ed.). Crown Business.

Jansen, W. S., Otten, S., Zee, K. I., & Jans, L. (2014). Inclusion: Conceptualization and measurement. *European Journal of Social Psychology, 44*(4), 370–385. https://doi.org/10.1002/ejsp.2011

Javed, B., Khan, A. K., & Quratulain, S. (2018). Inclusive leadership and innovative work behavior: Examination of LMX perspective in small capitalized textile firms. *The Journal of Psychology, 152*(8), 594–612. https://doi.org/10.1080/00223980.2018.1489767

Jin, M., Lee, J., & Lee, M. (2017). Does leadership matter in diversity management? Assessing the relative impact of diversity policy and inclusive leadership in the public sector. *Leadership & Organization Development Journal, 38*(2), 303–319. https://doi.org/10.1108/LODJ-07-2015-0151

Jordan, S. L., Ferris, G. R., & Lamont, B. T. (2019). A framework for understanding the effects of past experiences on justice expectations and perceptions of human resource inclusion practices. *Human Resource Management Review, 29*(3), 386–399. https://doi.org/10.1016/j.hrmr.2018.07.003

Livers, A. B., & Caver, K. A. (2003). Leader development across race. In C. D. McCauley & E. Van Velsor (Eds.), *The Center for Creative Leadership handbook of leadership development* (2nd ed.). Jossey-Bass.

Luthans, F., & Avolio, B. J. (2003). Authentic leadership development. In J. E. Dutton, R. E. Quinn, & K. S. Cameron (Eds.), *Positive organizational scholarship: Foundations of a new discipline* (1st ed., pp. 241–258). Berrett-Koehler.

Maznevski, M. L., & Chui, C. (2012). Leading global teams. In M. E. Mendenhall, J. S. Osland, A. Bird, G. R. Oddou, M. L. Maznevski, M. J. Stevens, & G. K. Stahl (Eds.), *Global leadership 2e: Research, practice, and development* (2nd ed., pp. Loc 3062–3506). Routledge.

Mendenhall, M. E., Osland, J. S., Bird, A., Oddou, G. R., Maznevski, M. L., Stevens, M. J., & Stahl, G. K. (2012). *Global leadership 2e: Research, practice, and development* (2nd ed). Routledge.

Miller, F. A., & Katz, J. H. (2002). *The inclusion breakthrough* (1st ed.). Berrett-Koehler.

Mor Barak, M. E. (2000). The inclusive workplace: An ecosystems approach to diversity management. *Social Work, 45*(4), 339–353. https://doi.org/10.1093/sw/45.4.339

Morgan, E. (2017). Breaking the zero-sum game: Transforming societies through inclusive leadership. In A. Boitano, R. L. Dutra, & H. E. Schockman (Eds.), *Breaking the zero- sum game: Transforming societies through inclusive leadership* (pp. 5–27). Emerald.

Najmaei, A., & Sadeghinejad, Z. (2019). Inclusive leadership: A scientometric assessment of an emerging field. In A. Georgiadou, M. A. Gonzalez-Perez, & M. R. Olivas-Lujan (Eds.), *Diversity within diversity management: Types of diversity in organizations* (Vol. 22, pp. 221–245). Emerald.

Nembhard, I. M., & Edmondson, A. C. (2006). Making it safe: The effects of leader inclusiveness and professional status on psychological safety and improvement efforts in health care teams. *Journal of Organizational Behavior, 27*(7), 941–966. http://doi.wiley.com/10.1002/job.413

Nishii, L. H. (2013). The benefits of climate for inclusion for gender-diverse groups. *Academy of Management Journal, 56*(6), 1754–1774. https://doi.org/10.5465/amj.2009.0823

Nishii, L. H., Khattab, J., Shemla, M., & Paluch, R. M. (2018). A multi-level process model for understanding diversity practice effectiveness. *Academy of Management Annals, 12*(1), 37–82. https://doi.org/10.5465/annals.2016.0044

Nishii, L. H., & Mayer, D. M. (2009). Do inclusive leaders help to reduce turnover in diverse groups? The moderating role of leader-member exchange in the diversity to turnover relationship. *Journal of Applied Psychology, 94*(6), 1412–1426. https://doi.org/10.1037/a0017190

Nishii, L. H., & Rich, R. E. (2014). Creating inclusive climates in diverse organizations. In B. M. Ferdman & B. R. Deane (Eds.), *Diversity at work: The practice of inclusion* (1st ed., pp. 330–363). Jossey-Bass.

Nkomo, S. M., Bell, M. P., Roberts, L. M., Joshi, A., & Thatcher, S. M. B. (2019). Diversity at a critical juncture: New theories for a complex phenomenon. *Academy of Management Review*, *44*(3), 498–517. https://doi.org/10.5465/amr.2019.0103

Offerman, L. R. (2012). Relational leadership: Creating effective leadership with diverse staff. In M. Uhl-Bien & S. M. Ospina (Eds.), *Advancing relational leadership research: A dialogue among perspectives* (pp. 361–380). Information Age Publishing.

Offerman, L. R., & Basford, T. E. (2014). Inclusive human resource management: Best practices and the changing role of human resources. In B. M. Ferdman & B. R. Deane (Eds.), *Diversity at work: The practice of inclusion* (1st ed., pp. 229–259). Jossey-Bass.

Perry, E. L., & Li, A. (2019). Diversity climate in organizations. In E. L. Perry & A. Li, *Oxford research encyclopedia of business and management*. Oxford University Press. https://doi.org/10.1093/acrefore/9780190224851.013.45

Pless, N. M., & Maak, T. (2004). Building an inclusive diversity culture: Principles, processes and practice. *Journal of Business Ethics*, *54*(2), 129–147. https://doi.org/10.1007/s10551-004-9465-8

Prime, J., & Salib, E. R. (2014). *Inclusive leadership: The view from six countries* (Research Study No. D127). Catalyst Research Center. http://www.catalyst.org/knowledge/inclusive-leadership-view-six-countries

Qi, L., & Liu, B. (2017). Effects of inclusive leadership on employee voice behavior and team performance: The mediating role of caring ethical climate. *Frontiers in Communication*, *2*. https://doi.org/10.3389/fcomm.2017.00008

Ramarajan, L., & Thomas, D. (2013). A positive approach to diversity in organizations. In K. S. Cameron & Spreitzer (Eds.), *The Oxford handbook of positive organizational scholarship* (reprint ed., pp. 552–565). Oxford University Press.

Randel, A. E., Dean, M. A., Ehrhart, K. H., Chung, B., & Shore, L. (2016). Leader inclusiveness, psychological diversity climate, and helping behaviors. *Journal of Managerial Psychology*, *31*(1), 216–234. https://doi.org/10.1108/jmp-04-2013-0123

Randel, A. E., Galvin, B. M., Shore, L. M., Ehrhart, K. H., Chung, B. G., Dean, M. A., & Kedharnath, U. (2018). Inclusive leadership: Realizing positive outcomes through belongingness and being valued for uniqueness. *Human Resource Management Review*, *28*(2), 190–203. https://doi.org/10.1016/j.hrmr.2017.07.002

Ratcliff, N. J., Key-Roberts, M., Simmons, M. J., & Jimenez-Rodriguez, M. (2018). Inclusive leadership survey item development. *United States Army Research Institute for the Behavioral and Social Sciences*, 26.

Roberson, Q. M. (2006). Disentangling the meanings of diversity and inclusion in organizations. *Group & Organization Management*, *31*(2), 212–236. https://doi.org/10.1177/1059601104273064

Shore, L. M., Randel, A. E., Chung, B. G., Dean, M. A., Holcombe Ehrhart, K., & Singh, G. (2011). Inclusion and diversity in work groups: A review and model for future research. *Journal of Management, 37*(4), 1262–1289. https://doi.org/10.1177/0149206310385943

Shore, L. M., Cleveland, J. N., & Sanchez, D. (2018). Inclusive workplaces: A review and model. *Human Resource Management Review, 28*(2), 176–189. https://doi.org/10.1016/j.hrmr.2017.07.003

Sims, C. M. (2018). The diversity intelligent servant leader: Developing leaders to meet the needs of a diverse workforce. *Advances in Developing Human Resources, 20*(3), 313– 330. https://doi.org/10.1177/1523422318778009

Steele, R., & Derven, M. (2015). Diversity & inclusion and innovation: A virtuous cycle. *Industrial and Commercial Training, 47*(1), 1–7. https://doi.org/10.1108/ICT-09-2014- 0063

Uhl-Bien, M. (2006). Relational leadership theory: Exploring the social processes of leadership and organizing. *The Leadership Quarterly, 17*(6), 654–676. https://doi.org/10.1016/j.leaqua.2006.10.007

Wasserman, I. C. (2015). Dialogic OD, diversity, and inclusion: Aligning mindsets, values, and practices. In D. A. Noumair & A. B. (Rami) Shani (Eds.), *Research in organizational change and development* (Vol. 24, pp. 329–356). Emerald.

Wasserman, I. C., & Blake-Beard, S. (2010). Leading inclusively: Mind-sets, skills and actions for a diverse, complex world. In K. Bunker, D. T. Hall, & K. E. Kram (Eds.), *Extraordinary leadership: Addressing the gaps in senior executive development* (1st ed., pp. 197–212). Jossey-Bass.

Wasserman, I. C., Gallegos, P., & Taylor, E. (2014). Diversity and inclusion in organizational practice. In B. B. Jones & M. Brazzel (Eds.), *The NTL handbook of organization development and change* (pp. 445–465). Wiley.

Wasserman, I. C., Gallegos, P. V., & Ferdman, B. M. (2008). Dancing with resistance: Leadership challenges in fostering a culture of inclusion. In K. M. Thomas (Ed.), *Diversity resistance in organizations.* (2008-06292-007; pp. 175–200). Taylor & Francis Group/Lawrence Erlbaum Associates.

Whitney, D., Trosten-Bloom, A., & Rader, K. (2010). *Appreciative leadership: Focus on what works to drive winning performance and build a thriving organization* (1st ed.). McGraw-Hill Education.

Williams, D. A. (2013). *Strategic diversity leadership: Activating change and transformation in higher education.* Stylus.

Worley, C. G., Williams, T., & Lawler, E. E., III. (2014). *The agility factor: Building adaptable organizations for superior performance* (Kindle ed.). Jossey-Bass.

Wuffli, P. A. (2015). *Inclusive leadership: A framework for the global era* (1st ed.). Springer.

Ye, Q., Wang, D., & Guo, W. (2019). Inclusive leadership and team innovation: The role of team voice and performance pressure. *European Management Journal, 37*(4), 468–480. https://doi.org/10.1016/j.emj.2019.01.006

Ye, Q., Wang, D., & Li, X. (2018). Inclusive leadership and employees' learning from errors: A moderated mediation model. *Australian Journal of Management, 44*(3), 20. https://doi.org/10.1177/0312896218805796

CHAPTER 6

KNOWING ME, KNOWING YOU

Immigrant Ethnic Identity and Leader-Member Relationships

Monica M. Sharif and Terri A. Scandura

ABSTRACT

Many countries around the world have experienced an influx of talented immigrants that are joining the workforce and, therefore, important to today's economy. Leadership scholars have investigated the importance of leader-member dyads for several years. However, research has largely omitted the consideration of immigrant diversity with regard to leader-member relationships. These individuals come from unique cultural backgrounds and have unique ethnic identities. We propose that immigrant ethnic identity influences the formation of dyadic relationships with host-country natives. Additionally, immigrant ethnic identity interacts with several variables that affect leader-member exchange (LMX). We introduce a model of the ethnic identity-LMX relationship. Two moderators are proposed: surface-level diversity, and cultural intelligence. The aim of this theory is to discuss the implications of immigrant-host-country native leader-member relationships

Leadership:
Leaders, Followers, and Context, pp. 137–156

in the organizational context. Additionally, we introduce the importance of the examination of immigrant ethnic identity for leadership theory. This theory provides the basis for many directions for future research.

> The immigrant world has always been a difficult one, torn between old loyalties and new realities.
>
> —Portes and Rumbaut, 2006, p. 120

Richard Florida (2004) wrote

> of critical importance to American success in this last century has been a tremendous influx of talented immigrants … [and] today's global economy centers on competition for people rather than for goods or services.… We no longer think of immigration as a gatekeeping function but as a talent attraction function necessary for economic growth. (p. 2)

There has been a huge growth in the number of international migrants worldwide—a jump from 173 million in 2000 to 258 million in 2017 (United Nations International Migration Report, 2017). The largest number of immigrants chose the U.S. as their new home, followed by Saudia Arabia, Germany, Russia, and the United Kingdom. Immigrants also represent a huge percentage of the growth in the labor force. For example in the U.S. between 2000 and 2010, immigrants represented 47% of the growth (Organization for Economic Co-operation and Development [OECD], 2012a, 2012b). A similar pattern exists in several countries around the world. Thus, immigration is both common and important to today's global economy. Yet, research and the study of domestic cultural differences in the context of organizations, especially with regard to leader-member relations, has not kept pace with these trends.

A recent article highlighted the importance of research on marginalized groups that have been overlooked in all of the top industrial-organizational psychology journals (Ruggs et al., 2013). In a response to this article, Binggeli, Dietz, and Krings (2013) emphasized that immigrants are "a forgotten minority" and despite calls for research on the topic for over 30 years (Bell et al., 2010; Dietz, 2010; Hirschman, 1982; Pettigrew, 1998), the Ruggs et al. (2013) review did not identify even one article in these journals that addressed the discrimination of immigrants. Due to the growing size of the immigrant population, competition for immigrant employees in areas such as information technology and engineering, income disparities, and the increasing number of employee discrimination claims, Binggeli et al. (2013) emphasized the importance of research on the topic of immigration in the organizational context. Immigrants have unique ethnic identities (Phinney, 1990; Schwartz et al., 2007) and these identities affect their performance and behaviors in the workplace (Schwartz et al., 2010). According to social identity theory, individuals identify with groups in order to simultaneously fulfill the need to be unique and the need to belong (Brewer, 1991; Roccas & Brewer, 2002). They differentiate their in-group and out-group in order to decrease uncertainty and increase self-esteem (Tajfel & Turner, 1986). Ethnic identity is defined as "a sense of self as a group member that develops over time through an active process of investigation, learning and commitment" (Phinney & Ong, 2007, p. 279) and "includes a sense of attachment or belonging ... the development concept of an achieved identity ... and involvement in ethnic practices" (Phinney & Ong, 2007, p. 275). Therefore, ethnic identity captures a huge part of one's sense of being. It is distinct from personality and self-identity (Ryder et al., 2000) yet dictates a significant amount of individuals' daily behaviors, perceptions, and interpretations (D'Andrade, 1984).

The way in which individuals identify with culture should play a role in their interaction with their leaders and their subsequent relationship quality (leader-member exchange, LMX). The specific experiences that immigrants accumulate in the process of moving to a new country has an important impact on the way in which they develop their new identities. This is unique from the experiences of ethnic minorities living in the host country. Employing a social identity perspective, this chapter examines the ways in which immigrant ethnic identity influences the formation of dyadic relationships within the organization. Specifically, we propose that immigrant ethnic identity influences leader member relationship quality in the organization. We develop rationale for the importance of the examination of LMX in immigrant-host-country native leader-member dyads. We first review the importance of studying LMX in relation to immigrants. We then detail our definition of immigration and review the ethnic identity framework set forth by Fitzsimmons (2013). Next, the importance of the interaction between LMX and ethnic identity is highlighted, and we present a model of LMX in immigrant-host-country native leader-member dyads. Last, we propose cultural intelligence as a moderator of the ethnic identity—LMX relationship. In this chapter, we further the discussion on immigration in the organizational context.

THEORY AND PROPOSITIONS

Immigration is prevalent in North America and is continually increasing world-wide (OECD, 2012a). Individuals are not only working in globally distributed teams that include individuals from diverse cultures (Gajendran & Joshi, 2012; Earley & Mosakowski, 2004; Mohammed & Angell, 2004) and/or having expatriate experiences (Feldman & Thomas, 1992; Mendenhall & Oddou, 1985), most individuals have worked one-on-one, within their own office, with an immigrant who possesses a unique ethnic identity.

The Oxford dictionary defines an immigrant as "a person who comes to live permanently in a foreign country." Immigrants have unique motivations and reasons for immigration and come from different backgrounds. They face discrimination in many forms based on skin color, country of origin, education level and cultural values among others (Stone et al., 2020). This in turn affects their job expectancies, job ratings and employment decisions.

Research on LMX has identified the importance of high-quality leader-member relationships for most organizational outcome variables including performance, organizational citizenship behavior (OCBs) and turnover (Gerstner & Day, 1997; Sin et al., 2009). Scandura and Lankau (1996) developed a theoretical framework identifying the importance of considering diversity in LMX relationships and outlined the impact that diversity may have on the different role development stages of role taking, role making and role routinization (Graen & Scandura, 1987). This research laid the foundation for future research on diversity in LMX relationships. Research has also shown that culture influences the role taking process in several ways including on work-related scripts, role conceptions, role behavior and its consequences (Stone-Romero et al., 2003). However, further research is needed to examine what influences immigrants relationships with their leaders.

Immigrants behavior in the organization will differ depending on many factors. One primary factor is ethnic identity. In a recent theoretical piece, Fitzsimmons (2013) discussed the increasing number of immigrants in the workplace and emphasized the contribution of these individuals to their organizations via personal, social, and task outcomes. The author introduced a four-category typology of ethnic identity (*prioritizing*, *aggregating*, *compartmentalizing*, and *hybridizing*) that we will employ in this chapter. Our research will focus on the importance of subordinate immigrant status in the evaluation of leader-member relationships. We propose that immigrant ethnic identity will influence the dyadic relationship. Although immigrants may have cultural similarities with host-country ethnic minorities such as collective values (Stone et al., 2015), the process of immigration itself provides them with a different acculturation process. Additionally, different than expatriates who move to a country on a short-term basis (and have the intention to eventually return home), many immigrants possess (whether it is voluntary or forced) a long-term commitment to a new life in an unfamiliar country (Portes & Rumbaut, 2006) and therefore, ethnic identities. This research will present a theoretical model addressing the influence of immigrant ethnic identity on LMX.

The theoretical argument that we present in the following sections has one boundary condition. For the purposes of this chapter, the immigrant is the follower. Given differences in the power and status of leaders and subordinates, we chose to focus on the cases in which the immigrants are the subordinates. However, we recognize that the processes we discuss may be relevant to immigrant supervisors as well, and this is an area for future theory and research. We begin our discussion with a definition of immigrants and then describe our relational ethnic identity framework.

ETHNIC IDENTITY INTEGRATION

Based on social identity theory, Fitzsimmons (2013) developed a four-category typology of cultural identity that incorporates *identity integration* and *identity plurality*. Identity integration spans from separated to integrated and identity plurality spans from single to multiple highly accessible identities. In the first category, *prioritizing* (single accessible identity), immigrant individuals choose a primary identity after hierarchically organizing their cultural identities. These individuals have a simplified identity structure, and their everyday interactions and interpretations are made primarily with one cultural identity with traces of their other cultures. For the purposes of this chapter, we will focus on prioritizing individuals who have chosen their heritage culture (value and traditions of ancestors) identity as primary.

In the second category, *aggregating* (multiple accessible identities), individuals give importance to three or more cultural identities. Fitzsimmons (2013) described this category as merged (Roccas & Brewer, 2002), marginal and fused (Phinney & Devich-Navarro, 1997), integrated (Pratt & Foreman, 2000) and cosmopolitan (Hannerz, 1990). Therefore, aggregating individuals have less differentiation between in-groups and out-groups because their "in-group" spans across many individuals.

In the third category, *compartmentalizing* (separated identity integration), individuals consider their identities to be separate and contingent on the context. They identify with one culture or another. Fitzsimmons (2013) described this to be similar to alternating (Phinney & Devich-Navarro, 1997) and compartmentalized (Pratt & Foreman, 2000; Roccas & Brewer, 2002). Lastly, in the fourth category, *hybridizing* (integrated identity integration), individuals see their identities as integrated. Therefore, they identify with the intersection of cultures.

The leadership literature has just begun to address the role of differing ethnic identities in the workplace. Our purpose is to extend this line of inquiry and to highlight the importance of immigrant ethnic identity with respect to LMX. The immigrant experience is unique and worthy of discussion. It is important to note that we are assuming that ethnic identity will regularly affect individuals' perceptions and behaviors in the organization. As shown in cross-cultural research (Tsui et al., 2007), individuals' unique backgrounds and motivations influence leadership and dyadic relationships in the organization. Therefore, we suggest that immigrants' ethnic identities also influence LMX. We first review the literature on LMX and then discuss ethnic identity.

LMX

Sparrowe and Liden (1997) described LMX as an active role making process where leaders and followers make offers and provide stimulus to move the relationship away from being contractually defined. Accordingly, high quality relationships develop over time if offers are accepted, and the responses are well received by the leader. In cases where offers are not made and/or not accepted by a dyad member, the relationship does not have the opportunity to develop. When both members of the relationship make a conscious effort to improve and maintain the relationship, the highest levels of LMX are achieved. Therefore, high LMX requires *both* parties to accept increased social exchange (Maslyn & Uhl-Bien, 2001; Uhl-Bien & Maslyn, 2003). Beneficial outcomes are less likely to occur when both parties view the relationship in a contractual fashion (Graen & Uhl-Bien, 1995). However, in the opposite case where both view the relationship in balanced, mutual, favorable and social exchange terms, there are beneficial outcomes (Sparrowe & Liden, 1997).

Several studies examined the influence of cultural differences in LMX (Dulebohn et al., 2011; Rockstuhl et al., 2012). For example, Zhang et al. (2012) indicated that supervisor-subordinate relationships in China, different from the United States, mainly involve "non-work exchange" in which the exchanged benefits are social and material in nature. Therefore, leader-member interaction usually flourishes as a result of social interactions such as after-hour visits to the home (Chen & Tjosvold, 2006; Law et al., 2000). Cultural differences in expectations and behaviors may significantly affect the development of positive relationships between immigrant followers and their leaders. However, we propose that this will depend on his/her ethnic identity (whether it is prioritizing, aggregating, compartmentalizing, or hybridizing). We suggest that immigrants' ethnic identity will influence role expectations in leader-member relationships and also the quality of the relationship. The next section will elaborate the importance of ethnic identity and LMX.

LMX AND RELATIONAL ETHNIC IDENTITY

Research has shown that culture determines how managers assess their employees (DeVoe & Iyengar, 2004; Martinko & Douglas, 1999; Snape et al., 1998). For example, individuals from Western cultures concentrate on dispositional causes for behavior whereas individuals from East Asian cultures largely consider situational information and are inclined to make situational attributions (Choi et al., 1999; Lee et al., 1996; Morris & Peng, 1994). Mok et al. (2010) found managers from American versus East Asian cultures to be less sensitive to employees' circumstances in performance evaluations. The extent to which individuals identify with their heritage culture should, therefore play a role in LMX.

We propose that ethnic identity will significantly influence relationship quality, one's evaluation of relationships and, therefore, LMX. This is due to relationship favorability. Some relationships are easier than others to develop than others (Uhl-Bien, 2003). Particularly some relationships develop with ease due to similarities within the relationship such as value congruence. When differences occur within the relationship such as demographic dissimilarity, value incongruence, or difference in experience, such relationships are more difficult to develop. The higher the relationship favorability (ease of relationship development), the higher likelihood of high-quality relationship development (Uhl-Bien, 2003).

Different types of ethnic identity will have different relationships with LMX. Specifically, followers who hold a prioritizing (heritage cultural dominant) identity may have a difficult time establishing high LMX with a host-country native dyadic partner. This would be the case for a German female subordinate with a prioritizing identity who is working with a U.S. native male manager. Differences in ethnic identity could lead to different perceptions and evaluation of the leader-member relationship. Although this individual immigrated to the United States, she has no (or little) interest in adopting American cultural values and may therefore have difficulty working with an American dyadic partner. This will largely be due to differing perceptions and behaviors, which ultimately influence LMX. Therefore,

> **Proposition 1a.** Prioritizing (heritage culture dominant) immigrant ethnic identity is negatively related to LMX.

Followers with aggregating identities experience less differentiation between in-groups and out-groups because they prioritize several identities (Park & Rothbart, 1982). Because of their tendency to give worth to multiple identities, immigrants with aggregating identities strongly identify with the host country culture, just as they do with their other identities.

In a work relationship with a host-country native manager, the follower will be able to understand and effectively communicate in accounting for cultural leniencies and preferences. This is because of aggregating individuals' ability to integrate both cultures successfully in their everyday lives (LaFromboise et al., 1993; Phinney & Devich-Navarro, 1997). Therefore,

> **Proposition 1b.** Aggregating immigrant ethnic identity is positively related to LMX.

Individuals with compartmentalizing identities are very aware of differences in their cultural identities and experience internal conflict (Phinney & Devich-Navarro, 1997). In certain situations, these individuals experience a type of cultural clash (tension) in which they behaviorally or affectively react against cultural expectations (Chavez, 1994; Durczak, 1997; O'Hearn, 1998; Roth, 1969). Compartmentalized individuals have a highly valenced perception of social cues (Phinney & Devich-Navarro, 1997; Vivero & Jenkins, 1999) and tend to recall these cultural cues (Benet-Martinez et al., 2002). If an individual continually displays culturally oppositional behaviors the dyadic partner will misconstrue the action and/or misattribute the behavior as some type of counterproductive behavior or inability. Compartmentalized individuals will purposely seek differences with their host-country native counterpart and acknowledge themselves as different when rating relationship quality. This is because they see their cultural identities as separate and incompatible and therefore put forth an increased amount of cognitive effort in handling situational cultural cues (Benet-Martinez et al., 2002). Therefore,

> **Proposition 1c.** Compartmentalizing immigrant ethnic identity is negatively related to LMX.

Followers with hybridizing identities feel that their identities are integrated and identify with the intersection of the cultures (Fitzsimmons, 2013). Therefore, when considering leader-member relationships, we propose that hybridizing followers will have high LMX. Followers in this category engage in frame switching behavior and respond to situationally relevant cues (Cheng et al., 2006; Cheng et al., 2008). A dyadic partner that continually displays culturally congruent behavior will have the basis to develop a high-quality leader member relationship and have a dyadic partner who feels similarly. For example, a hybridizing Turkish-German female who is working with a German host-country native manager will continually display a German ethnic identity in the work relationship. Therefore,

Proposition 1d. Hybridizing immigrant ethnic identity is positively related to LMX.

In the next section, we introduce cultural intelligence as a moderator of the ethnic identity-LMX relationship. Figure 6.1 presents the model for this chapter.

CULTURAL INTELLIGENCE

Cultural intelligence may influence LMX in culturally diverse dyads. Cultural intelligence is defined as "an individual's capability to function and manage effectively in culturally diverse settings" (Ang et al., 2007, p. 336) and " 'an outsider['s] seemingly natural ability to interpret someone's unfamiliar and ambiguous gestures the way that person's compatriots would' " (Earley & Mosakowski, 2004, p. 139). Cultural intelligence specifically applies to situations involving race, ethnicity, and nationality. In dyadic relationships with individuals from unique cultures, it is important to consider the extent to which the partners have the intelligence to appropriately handle interactions with individuals of diverse cultures. Culturally intelligent immigrants may have the ability to effectively work with dyadic partners from different nationalities despite apparent cultural differences. Additionally, culturally intelligent native individuals working with immigrants may manage cultural differences and prevent these differences from severely hurting leader-member relations. Research has indicated that cultural intelligence is significant beyond other individual differences. For example, studies of cultural intelligence have shown its empirical distinctiveness from and relationship with the Big Five personality traits (Ang et al., 2006).

Figure 6.1

Moderation Model of Immigrant Ethnic Identity and LMX

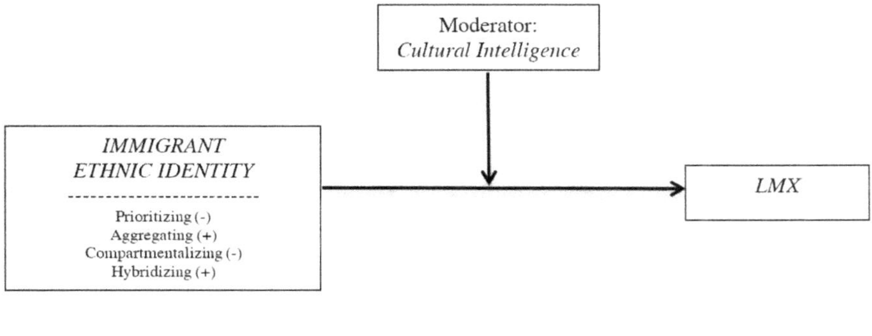

Earley and Ang (2003) suggested that cultural intelligence is composed of four dimensions: metacognitive, cognitive, motivational, and behavioral. The metacognitive dimension refers to the comprehension and command of individual thought processes to obtain and interpret cultural knowledge (Flavell, 1979). Metacognitive capabilities include planning, monitoring, and amending mental models of cultural norms for countries or groups of people (Ang et al., 2007). Therefore, individuals who have high metacognitive capabilities are mindful of others' cultural preferences both before and during interactions. In addition, they adjust their cultural assumptions during and after interactions (Brislin et al., 2006; Triandis, 2006). The cognitive dimension of cultural intelligence refers to attained norms, practices, and conventions in other cultures by means of education and personal experience (Ang et al., 2007). Individuals high on the cognitive dimension have knowledge of economic, legal, and social systems of a variety of cultures and subcultures (Triandis, 1994). Additionally, they have an understanding of the frameworks for basic cultural values (e.g., Hofstede, 2001). These individuals are able to comprehend similarities and differences across cultures (Brislin et al., 2006). The motivational component of cultural intelligence refers to the ability to direct attention and energy towards understanding and behaving properly in culturally different situations (Ang et al., 2007). These individuals tend to have an intrinsic interest in learning about cross-cultural interactions (Deci & Ryan, 1985). Additionally, they have confidence in their ability to handle cross-cultural interactions (Bandura, 2002). The behavioral dimension of cultural intelligence demonstrates individuals' ability to display proper verbal and nonverbal actions in cross-cultural situations (Ang et al., 2007). These individuals tend to display the culturally appropriate words, tones, gestures, and facial expressions in applicable situations. After conducting three studies in two national contexts, Ang et al. (2007) found that metacognitive and cognitive cultural intelligence predicted cultural judgment and decision making. Additionally, they found motivational and behavioral cognitive intelligence to predict cultural adaptation. Also, metacognitive and behavioral cultural intelligence predicted task performance.

Dyadic members who have a high degree of cultural intelligence are able to manage cultural differences even from the beginning of the relationship. Culturally intelligent individuals are more understanding and willing to work with culturally diverse partners. Therefore, misperceptions and misunderstandings will be limited.

We propose that when both the host-country leader and immigrant follower have high cultural intelligence, the positive relationship between LMX and ethnic identity will increase. Regardless of the type of ethnic identity, prioritizing, aggregating, compartmentalizing, or hybridizing, LMX will be higher for those dyads with culturally intelligent members.

This is because cultural intelligence allows dyadic partners to effectively interpret cultural differences. Culturally intelligent individuals are able to understand different social cues and efficiently work with individuals from different cultures. This helps create relationship favorability.

> **Proposition 2.** When the immigrant follower has high cultural intelligence and the host-country native manager has high cultural intelligence, ethnic identity (prioritizing, aggregating, compartmentalizing, hybridizing) will be positively related to high LMX.

DISCUSSION

Leader-member relationships composed of immigrants and host-country natives deserve additional attention in the leadership literature. The theory introduced in this chapter provides a new lens for examining LMX via immigrant ethnic identity. We articulated the theoretical linkages between ethnic identity (prioritizing, aggregating, compartmentalizing, and hybridizing) and LMX. Additionally, we proposed that cultural intelligence will influence the LMX quality of immigrant-host-country native dyads.

The development of this theory provides the foundation for future research examining immigrant managers and employees' LMX. There is an emphasis on the relative adaptability and strength of immigrant individuals who have aggregating or hybridizing identities versus those that have prioritizing or compartmentalizing identities. Depending on the existing situational context, managers adjust the ways in which they evaluate their employees (Jawahar, 2005). When evaluating LMX, both subordinates and managers will rely on their ethnic identity and the current context to arrive at their judgment of relationship quality. For example, hybridizing employees effectively switch between cultural cues and settings when evaluating their subordinates (Mok & Morris, 2010). In addition to the evaluation process, hybridizing individuals provide the means for high quality diverse relationships because of their ability to detect and respond to cultural cues on a day-to-day basis. Compartmentalizing individuals, on the other hand, are generally counterproductive in leader-member relationships because of their constant display of contrasting cultural cues.

The extent to which there is a climate of diversity in an organization is important for the moderating effects of cultural intelligence. Being in an organization that is tolerant and supportive of diversity is very different than being in one that is discriminatory. For example, being the only culturally diverse dyad in a workgroup of multiple homogenous dyads may have different dynamics than being one of several culturally diverse dyads. When an organization does not implement fair employee policies and/

or encourage integration of underrepresented employees (McKay et al., 2009), employees from minority groups may feel marginalized, excluded or discriminated against (Blank & Slip, 1994; Goldman et al., 2006). Diversity climates are important because they enhance creativity, cooperation and problem solving among other things (Cox, 1994; Cox & Blake, 1991; Gilbert & Ivancevich, 2000; Robinson & Dechant, 1997).

Additionally, surface level diversity in another factor to consider. Surface level diversity refers to apparent differences in biological characteristics that are seen in physical features including age, sex, and race/ethnicity (Harrison et al., 1998). Research has shown that rater-ratee ethnic similarity was related to higher performance ratings (Kraiger & Ford, 1985). On the other hand, a meta-analytic study only found small and inconsistent effects (Pulakos et al., 1989). Tsui and O'Reilly (1989) found that racial dyadic differences were marginally related to leaders' liking of subordinates and were not related to leaders' ratings of members' effectiveness. With regards to immigrants, this could be represented in such things as accent, clothing (i.e., scarf, turban), skin color, ethnic features and/or any outward and apparent physical indicator of a difference in nationality.

Seng et al. (2016) examined surface level diversity (race) and found differences in cross-race and minority dyads versus dyads where both members were part of the racial majority with regard to the relationship attributes of professional respect, affect, loyalty and contribution. Additionally, research has shown that a high degree of similarity is related to high quality LMX, just as low similarity is related to low quality LMX (Green et al., 1996; Liden et al., 1993). Therefore, when considering our model, immigrant surface level diversity may also affect the host-country native manager's impression in a dyadic relationship. Due to racism, discrimination or stereotyping, surface-level diversity will play a significant moderating role in the relationship between immigrant ethnic identity and LMX. Future research should explore the importance of diversity climate and surface-level diversity considering employee ethnic identity and LMX.

Additionally, studying LMX differentiation within a workgroup that has immigrants is a direction for future research. For example, it would be important to study situations in which there is only one immigrant follower and the rest of the employees in the organization are from the host-country, including the leader. Overall, future theory should develop upon the application of our model in differing diversity climates.

The LMX literature is also in need of a deeper study of indicators of LMX. This chapter added to this discussion by incorporating the topic of immigrant ethnic identity. Beyond research on expatriates and research on international collaboration, there is a need for the study of immigrants' ethnic identities on organizational outcomes. Interpersonal relationships (relationships between coworkers, team members, manager-employee relationships) in the organization are affected by the ethnic identity of employees. Further research should apply the study of immigrants and ethnic identity to other domains of organizational behavior such as teams and networks.

Research is needed to expand the theory that was introduced in this chapter and to address other means of discrimination with regards to immigration in the workplace. Tsui et al. (2007) conducted a review of cross-national, cross-cultural research in organizational behavior. However, surprisingly, the authors disregarded articles with cross-cultural domestic relationships specifically stating that "cross-cultural studies in cross-national contexts are more complex than domestic cross-cultural studies" (p. 427) and "we define cross-national, cross-cultural organizational behavior as the study of individual behavior and team processes in which national cultural characteristics play a major role as independent or moderating variables" (p. 428). After identifying the importance of immigrants (especially with regards to ethnic identity) in this chapter, these comments are especially perplexing. When considering differences in ethnic identity, domestic cross-cultural interactions may in fact involve the same (if not more) complexity than cross-cultural interactions across countries. National culture plays a strong role in immigrants' identity (Schwartz et al., 2006) and our theory delineated the importance of examining immigration in the workplace.

Future theory and research with a specific focus on supervisor immigrants is also needed. Considering their positions of power and authority, immigrant leaders' ethnic identity might affect LMX in different ways, especially considering the cultural moderators. For example, immigrant supervisors might be less sensitive to diversity climate because they feel as though they are large contributors to the climate.

CONCLUSION

Immigrants are increasingly present in organizations around the U.S. and the world. Leadership scholars and organizations need to dedicate significant research to studying immigrants in the work environment. In this chapter, we explained the relationship between ethnic identity and LMX considering surface-level diversity and cultural intelligence as moderating variables. Specifically, we developed theory for the influence of immigrant ethnic identity on leader member relationship quality in the organization. Our hope is that future research will build upon our conceptualization and investigate the importance of immigrant ethnic identity in leader-member relationships.

REFERENCES

Ang, S., Van Dyne, L., & Koh, C. (2006). Personality correlates of the four-factor model of cultural intelligence. *Group & Organization Management, 31*(1), 100–123. https://doi.org/10.1177/1059601105275267

Ang, S., Van Dyne, L., Koh, C., Ng, K. Y., Templer, K. J., Tay, C., & Chandrasekar, N. A. (2007). Cultural intelligence: Its measurement and effects on cultural judgment and decision making, cultural adaptation and task performance. *Management and Organization Review, 3*(3), 335–371. https://doi.org/10.1111/j.1740-8784.2007.00082.x

Bandura, A. (2002). Social cognitive theory in cultural context. *Applied Psychology, 51*(2), 269–290. https://doi.org/10.1111/1464-0597.00092

Bell, M. P., Kwesiga, E. N., & Berry, D. P. (2010). Immigrants: The new. *Journal of Managerial Psychology, 25*(2), 177–188. https://doi.org/10.1108/02683941011019375

Benet-Martínez, V., Leu, J., Lee, F., & Morris, M. W. (2002). Negotiating biculturalism: Cultural frame switching in biculturals with oppositional versus compatible cultural identities. *Journal of Cross-cultural Psychology, 33*(5), 492–516. https://doi.org/10.1177/0022022102033005005

Binggeli, S., Dietz, J., & Krings, F. (2013). Immigrants: A forgotten minority. *Industrial and Organizational Psychology, 6*(1), 107–113. https://doi.org/10.1111/iops.12019

Blank, R., & Slipp, S. (1994). *Voices of diversity*. AMACOM.

Brewer, M. B. (1991). The social self: On being the same and different at the same time. *Personality and Social Psychology Bulletin, 17*(5), 475–482. https://doi.org/10.1177/0146167291175001

Brislin, R., Worthley, R., & Macnab, B. (2006). Cultural intelligence: Understanding behaviors that serve people's goals. *Group & Organization Management, 31*(1), 40–55. https://doi.org/10.1177/1059601105275262

Chavez, D. (1994). *Face of an angel*. Farrar, Straus, and Giroux.

Chen, Y. F., & Tjosvold, D. (2006). Participative leadership by American and Chinese managers in China: The role of relationships. *Journal of Management Studies, 43*(8), 1727–1752. https://doi.org/10.1111/j.1467-6486.2006.00657.x

Cheng, C. Y., Lee, F., & Benet-Martínez, V. (2006). Assimilation and contrast effects in cultural frame switching: Bicultural identity integration and valence of cultural cues. *Journal of Cross-Cultural Psychology, 37*(6), 742–760. https://doi.org/10.1177/0022022106292081

Cheng, C. Y., Sanders, M., Sanchez-Burks, J., Molina, K., Lee, F., Darling, E., & Zhao, Y. (2008). Reaping the rewards of diversity: The role of identity integration. *Social and Personality Psychology Compass, 2*(3), 1182–1198. https://doi.org/10.1111/j.1751-9004.2008.00103.x

Choi, I., Nisbett, R. E., & Norenzayan, A. (1999). Causal attribution across cultures: Variation and universality. *Psychological Bulletin, 125*(1), 47. https://doi.org/10.1037/0033-2909.125.1.47

Cox, T. H. (1994). *Cultural diversity in organizations: Theory, research and practice*. Berrett-Koehler.

Cox, T. H., & Blake, S. (1991). Managing cultural diversity: Implications for organizational competitiveness. *Academy of Management Perspectives, 5*(3), 45–56. https://doi.org/10.5465/ame.1991.4274465

D'Andrade, R. G. (1984). Cultural meaning systems. In R. A. Shweder & R. A. LeVine (Eds.), *Cultural theory: Essays on mind, self, and emotion* (pp. 88-119). Cambridge University Press.

Deci, E. L., & Ryan R. M. (1985). *Intrinsic motivation and self-determination in human behavior.* Plenum.

DeVoe, S. E., & Iyengar, S. S. (2004). Managers' theories of subordinates: A cross-cultural examination of manager perceptions of motivation and appraisal of performance. *Organizational Behavior and Human Decision Processes, 93*(1), 47–61. https://doi.org/10.1016/j.obhdp.2003.09.001

Dietz, J. (2010). Introduction to the special issue on employment discrimination against immigrants. *Journal of Managerial Psychology, 25*(2), 104–112. https://doi.org/10.1108/02683941011019320

Dulebohn, J. H., Bommer, W. H., Liden, R. C., Brouer, R. L., & Ferris, G. R. (2012). A meta-analysis of antecedents and consequences of leader-member exchange: Integrating the past with an eye toward the future. *Journal of Management, 38*(6), 1715–1759. https://doi.org/10.1177/0149206311415280

Durczak, J. (1997). *Selves between cultures: Contemporary American bicultural autobiography*. International Scholars Publications.

Earley, P. C., & Ang, S. (2003). *Cultural intelligence: Individual interactions across cultures*. Stanford University Press.

Earley, P. C., & Mosakowski, E. (2004). Cultural intelligence. *Harvard Business Review, 82*(10), 139–146.

Feldman, D. C., & Thomas, D. C. (1992). Career management issues facing expatriates. *Journal of International Business Studies, 23*(2), 271–293. https://doi.org/10.1057/palgrave.jibs.8490268

Fitzsimmons, S. R. (2013). Multicultural employees: A framework for understanding how they contribute to organizations. *Academy of Management Review, 38*(4), 525–549. https://doi.org/10.5465/amr.2011.0234

Flavell, J. H. (1979). Metacognition and cognitive monitoring: A new area of cognitive–developmental inquiry. *American Psychologist, 34*(10), 906–911. https://doi.org/10.1037/0003-066x.34.10.906

Florida, R. (2004). America's looming creativity crisis. *Harvard Business Review, 82*(10), 122–136.

Gajendran, R. S., & Joshi, A. (2012). Innovation in globally distributed teams: The role of LMX, communication frequency, and member influence on team decisions. *Journal of Applied Psychology, 97*(6), 1252–1261. https://doi.org/10.1037/a0028958

Gerstner, C. R., & Day, D. V. (1997). Meta-Analytic review of leader–member exchange theory: Correlates and construct issues. *Journal of Applied Psychology, 82*(6), 827–844. https://doi.org/10.1037/0021-9010.82.6.827

Gilbert, J. A., & Ivancevich, J. M. (2000). Valuing diversity: A tale of two organizations. *Academy of Management Perspectives, 14*(1), 93–105. https://doi.org/10.5465/ame.2000.2909842

Goldman, B. M., Gutek, B. A., Stein, J. H., & Lewis, K. (2006). Employment discrimination in organizations: Antecedents and consequences. *Journal of Management, 32*(6), 786–830. https://doi.org/10.1177/0149206306293544

Graen, G. B., & Scandura, T. A. (1987). Toward a psychology of dyadic organizing. *Research in Organizational Behavior, 9*, 175–208.

Graen, G. B., & Uhl-Bien, M. (1995). Relationship-based approach to leadership: Development of leader-member exchange (LMX) theory of leadership over 25 years: Applying a multi-level multi-domain perspective. *The Leadership Quarterly, 6*, 219–247. https://doi.org/10.1016/1048-9843(95)90036-5

Green, S. G., Anderson, S. E., & Shivers, S. L. (1996). Demographic and organizational influences on leader–member exchange and related work attitudes. *Organizational Behavior and Human Decision Processes, 66*(2), 203–214. Doi:10.1006/obhd.1996.0049

Hannerz, U. (1990). Cosmopolitans and locals in world culture. In M Featherstone (Ed.) *Global culture: Nationalism, globalism and modernity*. SAGE.

Harrison, D. A., Price, K. H., & Bell, M. P. (1998). Beyond relational demography: Time and the effects of surface-and deep-level diversity on work group cohesion. *Academy of Management Journal, 41*(1), 96–107. https://doi.org/10.2307/256901

Hirschman, C. (1982). Immigrants and minorities: Old questions for new directions in research. *International Migration Review, 16*(2), 474–490. https://doi.org/10.1177/019791838201600209

Hofstede, G. (2001) *Culture's consequences: Comparing values, behaviors, institutions, and organizations across nations*. SAGE.

Jawahar, I. M. (2005). Do raters consider the influence of situational factors on observed performance when evaluating performance? Evidence from three experiments. *Group & Organization Management, 30*(1), 6–41. https://doi.org/10.1177/1059601104267664

Kraiger, K., & Ford, J. K. (1985). A meta-analysis of ratee race effects in performance ratings. *Journal of Applied Psychology, 70*(1), 56–65. https://doi.org/10.1037/0021-9010.70.1.56

LaFromboise, T., Coleman, H. L., & Gerton, J. (1993). Psychological impact of biculturalism: Evidence and theory. *Psychological Bulletin, 114*(3), 395–412. https://doi.org/10.1037/0033-2909.114.3.395

Law, K. S., Wong, C. S., Wang, D., & Wang, L. (2000). Effect of supervisor-subordinate guanxi on supervisory decisions in China: An empirical investigation. *International Journal of Human Resource Management, 11*(4), 751–765. https://doi.org/10.1080/09585190050075105

Lee, F., Hallahan, M., & Herzog, T. (1996). Explaining real-life events: How culture and domain shape attributions. *Personality and Social Psychology Bulletin, 22*(7), 732–741. https://doi.org/10.1177/0146167296227007

Liden, R. C., Wayne, S. J., & Stilwell, D. (1993). A longitudinal study on the early development of leader-member exchanges. *Journal of Applied Psychology, 78*(4), 662–674. https://doi.org/10.1037/0021-9010.78.4.662

Martinko, M.J.& Douglas, S.C. (1999). Culture and expatriate failure: An attributional explication. *International Journal of Organizational Analysis, 7*, 265–293. https://doi.org/10.1108/eb028903

Maslyn, J. M., & Uhl-Bien, M. (2001). Leader-member exchange and its dimensions: Effects of self-effort and other's effort on relationship quality. *Journal of Applied Psychology, 86*, 697–708. https://doi.org/10.1037/0021-9010.86.4.697

McKay, P. F., Avery, D. R., & Morris, M. A. (2009). A tale of two climates: Diversity climate from subordinates' and managers' perspectives and their role in store unit sales performance. *Personnel Psychology, 62*, 767–791. https://doi.org/10.1111/j.1744-6570.2009.01157.x

Mendenhall, M., & Oddou, G. (1985). The dimensions of expatriate acculturation: A review. *Academy of Management Review, 10*(1), 39–47. https://doi.org/10.5465/amr.1985.4277340

Mohammed, S., & Angell, L. C. (2004). Surface- and deep-level diversity in workgroups: Examining the moderating effects of team orientation and team process on relationship conflict. *Journal of Organizational Behavior, 25*(8), 1015–1039. https://doi.org/10.1002/job.293

Mok, A., Cheng, C. Y., & Morris, M. W. (2010). Matching versus mismatching cultural norms in performance appraisal: Effects of the cultural setting and bicultural identity integration. *International Journal of Cross Cultural Management, 10*(1), 17–35. https://doi.org/10.1177/1470595809359584

Mok, A., & Morris, M. W. (2010). Asian-Americans' creative styles in Asian and American situations: Assimilative and contrastive responses as a function of bicultural identity integration. *Management and Organization Review, 6*(3), 371–390. https://doi.org/10.1111/j.1740-8784.2010.00190.x

Morris, M. W., & Peng, K. (1994). Culture and cause: American and Chinese attributions of social and physical events. *Journal of Personality and Social Psychology, 67*, 949–971. https://doi.org/10.1037/0022-3514.67.6.949

OECD. (2012a). *International migration outlook 2012*. OECD Publishing. http://dx.doi.org/10.1787/migr_outlook-2012-en

OECD. (2012b). *Key statistics on migration in OECD countries*. http://www.oecd.org/document/4/0,3746,en_2649_37415_48326878_1_1_1_37415,00.html

O'Hearn, C. C. (1998). *Half and half: Writers on growing up biracial and bicultural*. Pantheon.

Park, B., & Rothbart, M. (1982). Perception of out-group homogeneity and levels of social categorization: Memory for the subordinate attributes of in-group and out-group members. *Journal of Personality and Social Psychology, 42*, 1051–1068. https://doi.org/10.1037/0022-3514.42.6.1051

Pettigrew, T. F. (1998). Reactions toward the new minorities of Western Europe. *Annual Review of Sociology, 24*, 77–103. https://doi.org/10.1146/annurev.soc.24.1.77

Phinney, J. S. (1990). Ethnic identity in adolescents and adults: Review of research *Psychological Bulletin, 108*(3), 499–514. https://doi.org/10.1037/0033-2909.108.3.499

Phinney, J., & Devich-Navarro, M. (1997). Variations in bicultural identification among African American and Mexican American adolescents. *Journal of Research on Adolescence, 7*, 3–32. https://doi.org/10.1207/s15327795jra0701_2

Phinney, J., & Ong, A. D. (2007). Conceptualization and measurement of ethnic identity: Current status and future directions. *Journal of Counseling Psychology, 54*(3), 271–281. https://doi.org/10.1037/0022-0167.54.3.271

Portes, A., & Rumbaut, R.G. (2006). *Immigrant America: A portrait*. University of California Press.

Pratt, M. G., & Foreman, P. O. (2000). Classifying managerial responses to multiple organizational identities. *Academy of Management Review, 25*, 18–42. https://doi.org/10.5465/amr.2000.2791601

Pulakos, E. D., Oppler, S. H., White, L. A., & Borman, W. C. (1989). Examination of race and sex effects on performance ratings. *Journal of Applied Psychology, 74*, 770–780. https://doi.org/10.1037/0021-9010.74.5.770

Robinson, G., & Dechant, K. (1997). Building a business case for diversity. *Academy of Management Executive, 11*, 21–31. https://doi.org/10.5465/ame.1997.9709231661

Roccas, S., & Brewer, M.B. (2002). Social identity complexity. *Personality and Social Psychology Review, 6*, 88–106. https://doi.org/10.1207/s15327957pspr0602_01

Rockstuhl, T., Dulebohn, J. H., Ang, S., & Shore, L. M. (2012). Leader-member exchange (LMX) and culture: A meta-analysis of correlates of LMX across 23 countries. *Journal of Applied Psychology, 97*, 1097–1130. https://doi.org/10.1037/a0029978

Roth, P. (1969). *Portnoy's complaint*. Random House.

Ruggs, E. N., Law, C., Cox, C. B., Roehling, M. V., Wiener, R. L., Hebl, M. L., & Barron, L. (2013). Gone fishing: I-O psychologists' missed opportunities to understand marginalized employees experiences with discrimination. *Industrial and Organizational Psychology, 6*(1), 39–60. https://doi.org/10.1111/iops.12007

Ryder, A. G., Alden, L. E., & Paulhus, D. L. (2000). Is acculturation unidimensional or bidimensional? A head-to-head comparison in the prediction of personality, self-identity, and adjustment. *Journal of Personality and Social Psychology, 79*(1), 49–65. https://doi.org/10.1037/0022-3514.79.1.49

Scandura, T. A., & Lankau, M. J. (1996). Developing diverse leaders: A leader-member exchange approach. *The Leadership Quarterly, 7*(2), 243–263. https://doi.org/10.1016/s1048-9843(96)90043-0

Schwartz, S. J., Pantin, H., Prado, S., Sullivan, G., & Szapocznik, J. (2006). Nativity and years in receiving culture as markers of acculturation in ethnic enclaves. *Journal of Cross-Cultural Psychology, 37*(3), 345–353. https://doi.org/10.1177/0022022106286928

Schwartz, S. J., Unger, J. B., Zamboanga, B. L., & Szapocznik, J. (2010). Rethinking the concept of acculturation. *American Psychologist, 65*(4), 237–251. https://doi.org/10.1037/a0019330

Schwartz, S. J., Zamboanga, B. L., Rodriguez, L., & Wang, S. C. (2007). The structure of cultural identity in an ethnically diverse sample of emerging adults. *Basic and Applied Social Psychology, 29*(2), 159–173. https://doi.org/10.1080/01973530701332229

Seng, B. R., Cogliser, C. C., Randolph, A. F., Scandura, T. A., Miller, C. D., & Smith-Genthos, R. (2016). Diversity in leadership relationships: Race in leader-member exchanges. *Leadership & Organization Development Journal, 37*(6), 750–773. https://doi.org/10.1108/lodj-10-2014-0201

Sin, H. P., Nahrgang, J. D., & Morgeson, F. P. (2009). Understanding why they don't see eye to eye: An examination of leader-member exchange (LMX) agreement. *Journal of Applied Psychology, 94*, 1048–1057. https://doi.org/10.1037/a0014827

Snape, E., Thompson, S., Yan, F. K. C., & Redman, T. (1998). Performance appraisal and culture: Practice and attitudes in Hong Kong and Great Britain. *International Journal of Human Resource Management, 9*, 841–861. https://doi.org/10.1080/095851998340838

Sparrowe, R. T., & Liden, R. C. (1997). Process and structure in leader-member exchange. *Academy of Management Review, 22*(2), 522–552. https://doi.org/10.5465/amr.1997.9707154068

Stone, D. L., Harrison, T. L., Canedo, J., Lukaszewski, K. M., & Suazo, M. (2015). The difference between HIspanic-American and Anglo-American small business owners' values, beliefs and use of financial planning. *Southern Management Association Conference Proceedings*, St. Petersburg, FL.

Stone, D. L., Lukaszewski, K. M., Krueger, D. C., & Canedo, J. C. (2020). A model of factors thought to influence unfair discrimination against immigrants in organizations. In D. L. Stone, J. H. Dulebohn, & K. M. Lukaszewski (Eds.), *Diversity and inclusion in organizations* (pp. 331–360). Information Age Publishing.

Stone-Romero, E. F., Stone, D. L., & Salas, E. (2003). The influence of culture on role conceptions and role behavior in organisations. *Applied Psychology, 52*(3), 328–362. https://doi.org/10.1111/1464-0597.00139

Tajfel, H., & Turner, J. (1986). The social identity theory of intergroup behavior. In S. Worchel & W. Austin (Eds.), *Psychology of intergroup relations* (pp. 7–24). Nelson-Hall.

Triandis, H. C. (1994). *Culture and social behavior.* McGraw-Hill.

Triandis, H. C. (2006). Cultural intelligence in organizations. *Group & Organization Management, 31*, 20–26. https://doi.org/10.1177/1059601105275253

Tsui, A. S., Nifadkar, S. S., & Ou, A. Y. (2007). Cross-national, cross-cultural organizational behavior research: Advances, gaps, and recommendations. *Journal of Management, 33*(3), 426–478. https://doi.org/10.1177/0149206307300818

Tsui, A. S.. & O'Reilly, C. A. (1989). Beyond simple demographic effects: The importance of relational demography in superior-subordinate dyads. *Academy of Management Journal 32*, 402–423. https://doi.org/10.2307/256368

Uhl-Bien, M. (2003). Relationship development as a key ingredient for leadership development. In S. E. Murphy & R. E. Riggio (Eds.), *The future of leadership development*, (pp. 129–147). Lawrence Erlbaum Associates.

Uhl-Bien, M., & Maslyn, J. M. (2003). Reciprocity in manager-subordinate relationships: Components, configurations, and outcomes. *Journal of Management, 29*, 511–532. https://doi.org/10.1016/s0149-2063_03_00023-0

United Nations International Migration Report. (2018). *International Migration Report 2017–Highlights*. United Nations.

Vivero, V. N., & Jenkins, S. R. (1999). Existential hazards of the multicultural individual: Defining and understanding "cultural homelessness." *Cultural Diversity and Ethnic Minority Psychology, 5*, 6–26. https://doi.org/10.1037/1099-9809.5.1.6

Zhang, X., Fu, P., Xi, Y., Li, L., Xu, L., Cao, C., Li, G., Ma, L., & Ge, J. (2012). Understanding indigenous leadership research: Explication and Chinese examples. *The Leadership Quarterly, 23*, 1063–1079. https://doi.org/10.1016/j.leaqua.2012.10.009

CHAPTER 7

USING LMX-ALLIANCE TO ENHANCE FOLLOWER AND TEAM PERFORMANCE

George Graen, Julio C. Canedo, Andrew F. Johnson, and Miriam Grace

ABSTRACT

Leader-member exchange (LMX) theory is a well-established lens through which to understand the relation between leaders and followers in organizations. For decades, research has shown LMX to be consistently related with important job-related outcomes. While remaining true to the dyadic relationship underpinning LMX, this chapter extends the theory to consider multiple levels of analysis. Using the LMX framework, we identify two types of leader-follower relationships at different organizational levels and consider alliances and relations in each of them. Further, we introduce and develop the concept of LMX-alliance (LMX-A) and provide a process to use it to improve the relationship between leader and follower and enhance follower and team performance. The chapter concludes with implications for theory, research, and practice.

Leadership:
Leaders, Followers, and Context, pp. 157–180

Leader-member exchange (LMX) theory is a well-established lens through which to better understand the relation between leaders and followers within organizations. Over time, this theory has expanded our understanding of this dyadic relationship. Importantly, the theory has consistently shown that organizational outcomes can be traced to these relationships. Thus, the theory has significant implications for organizational performance in practical settings.

As LMX theory continues to evolve, there remain important questions to be considered, theoretical developments to contemplate, and continued application of concepts in organizational settings to ensure viability for researchers and practitioners alike. This chapter aims to further LMX theory in each of these areas. First, in the next section we briefly review the existing literature on LMX. In the subsequent section we provide theory for a new development to extend LMX into the team environment by introducing the LMX-alliance model (LMX-A). We illustrate this important theoretical extension and describe a process for improving the relation between leader and follower and, as a consequence, the performance of the latter. The following section discusses implications for theory, research, and practice. Finally, the last section highlights the main ideas discussed in the chapter.

LITERATURE REVIEW

For decades, researchers have endeavored to better understand the relation between leaders and followers. The numerous outcomes tied to this relation have made this pursuit particularly important as human capital is increasingly central to building organizational value. This is true for industries such as high-tech, but also more broadly, as the economy shifts towards services and knowledge creating activities. LMX focuses on leader-member relations, its antecedents, and outcomes.

Organizations stand to benefit greatly from good relations between leaders and followers (members). Good leader-member relations between supervisors and subordinates increase subordinates' job satisfaction, organizational commitment, organizational citizenship behaviors, affective commitment, innovation, distributive justice, and job performance, and decrease turnover and absenteeism (Chaudhry et al., 2020; Dulebohn et al., 2012; Gerstner & Day, 1997; Gottfredson & Aguinis, 2017; Henderson et al., 2009; Martin et al., 2016; Nandedkar & Brown, 2018).

To better understand how to achieve these positive outcomes (or reduce negative consequences), scholarship has transformed to gain knowledge on the relationships among employees. Leadership research and practice relative to leader style and the enhancement of follower performance has moved away from consideration, initiation of structure, and contingent rewards (Piccolo et al., 2012; Podsakoff et al., 2006). Conversely, LMX theory, has gained support thanks to meta-analyses and comprehensive literature reviews (e.g., DeRue et al., 2011; Dulebohn et al., 2012; Gottfredson & Aguinis, 2017; Henderson et al., 2009; Judge et al., 2004; Martin et al., 2016). Further, longitudinal studies conducted as natural experiments for over 20 years, in organizational settings, showed that performance and speed-of-promotion were predicted by a measure of LMX (Graen et al., 2006; Wakabayashi & Graen, 1984).

In addition, leaders' behaviors have proven to be functional in improving teams' learning, performance, effectiveness, and productivity (Burke et al., 2006). In agreement with these findings, we present a proposal to enhance followers' performance through LMX and leaders' behaviors.

THEORETICAL DEVELOPMENT

The LMX-A model is based on the idea that the capacity to lead teams can be developed and provide resources that help teams thrive (Day et al., 2004). In Figure 7.1, we depict our proposal of the LMX-A system of alliances necessary for optimal team and individual performance. The model shows both position and influence power relationships operating effectively within their respective spheres.

Using this model, we extend our understanding of LMX through inclusion of teams and the coordinator/leader of leaders, thus providing for an additional level of analysis and extending beyond dyadic-based studies. As shown in Figure 7.1, the multilevel model includes two types of relations (alliances) that we consider relevant for performance: (1) relations among individuals and their supervisors (individual-leader, individual-coordinator, and leader-coordinator) and (2) relations among teams and their supervisors (team of individuals-leader and team of leaders-coordinator). These alliances should be analyzed to better understand followers' motivation to achieve quality work.

The relation among individuals (Type 1 in our model) has been traditionally studied in the leadership literature. Some of the major findings in this type of leadership were discussed in the previous section and are presented throughout the chapter. It is the typical supervisor-subordinate (leader-member) relationship. In addition, research on the antecedents and consequences of teamwork in organizations has also a long history in academic research (see, for example, Breuer et al., 2016; De Jong et al., 2016; Hackman & Morris, 1975; Morrissette & Kisamore, 2020). We believe that the relation among teams and their supervisors (Type 2 in our model) is in need of more exploration to gain understanding of the

Figure 7.1

LMX-A Model: Alliances to Improve Individual and Team Performance

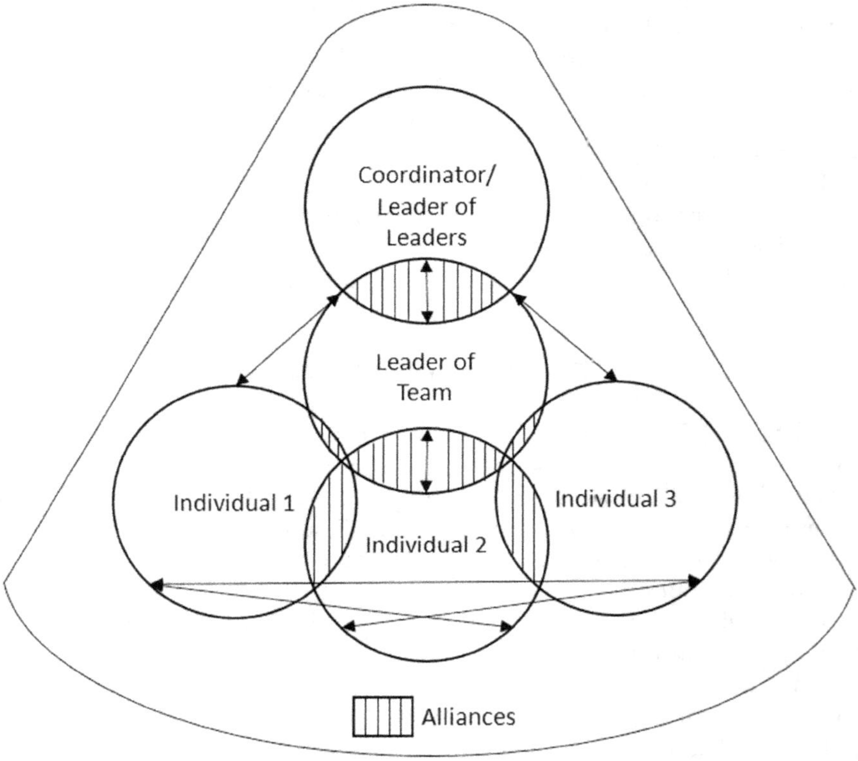

relation between teamwork and performance and other desired outcomes. For example, teamwork has shown to have stronger relations to attitudinal outcomes compared to performance outcomes (Richter et al., 2011). In addition, shared leadership in teams has proven strongly related to attitudinal outcomes, behavioral processes, and emergent team states but not to team performance (Wang et al., 2014). We believe that the incorporation of LMX theory to the relation between teams and their supervisors will help to improve teams' performance and other desired outcomes. Although our model considers the two types of relations (individuals to supervisors and teams to supervisors), we will focus on the latter, given that the former have been largely studied.

In our model, a leader is responsible for the processes and outcomes of a team of individuals. He or she and other leaders report to a coordinator, who is responsible for multiple interdependent teams and typically works with human resource managers to administer the various functions of the employment process. These functions include talent acquisition, appraisal, evaluation, succession planning, and career management. In addition, this level of management uses formal power to achieve team assignments and informal influence through the leader of each of the teams. Our model also suggests other types of relations as possible in a work environment. For example, we acknowledge that, at the individual-supervisor level, interaction among individuals and coordinators is feasible. At the team-supervisor level, the relation between teams of individuals and coordinators is also possible. Despite the type of relation, we believe that LMX-A can help to improve team outcomes. Next, we will elaborate on this idea.

Assumptions Underlying LMX-A

A psychological alliance at work is a relation between two individuals who are engaged with each other in the search for mutual benefit with no explicit declaration of this intention. People construct psychological alliances when working on the same mutually rewarding and interdependent enterprise. They develop a shared understanding with their team members of actions, behaviors, and context. Alliance constructions are dynamic and serve as guides to both instrumental and emotional decisions. In the team context, these constructions are useful in identifying each other's strengths, weaknesses, opportunities, and threats relevant to decision making related to the objectives of the enterprise. It should be noted that this reality emerges when their psychological alliances are successful. In addition to understanding the growth of agreement on the utility of promises, the instrumentality model is helpful in this endeavor (Graen, 1969; Vroom & Deci, 1970).

Measuring enterprise performance at the team-level is a function of the utility of performance to the team members at their individual levels of performance and that of others who are also contributing to the enterprise with their respective talents and interrelationships. The quality of relationships and reliability of the performance-reward system are mediating conditions. This model of team performance is useful in descriptions from offer to performance, mediated by the LMX-A perceptions (Canedo et al., 2018).

Psychological alliance is an important construct to be used in the next generation of organizational arrangements, which focus on emerging teamwork arrangements (e.g., subcontractor services, workplace variety, flexibility of different functions, and new technology creations) (Grace & Graen, 2014). The interpersonal exchange model was useful for dyadic (leader and follower) bartering, but for team-level and organization-level interactions, we recommend the LMX-A model (Graen et al., 2018). The alliance model of team performance focuses on the team as composed mainly of team leadership functions, psychological alliances between leader and members, and utility of outcomes offered compared to the current situation. This model can be tested using available data on both team-level and organization-level results of team (and follower) performance (Gottfredson & Aguinis, 2017). The model requires that several of the team's inputs and processes be available to best predict follower team performance and other outcomes. LMX-A serves as a behavioral model for peer-to-peer alliances that knit a team together and strengthen the weave for overall team performance improvement.

The LMX-A leadership model is a relational model focused on the developmental system of relations between the team leader and each team member in terms of actions, behaviors, contexts, time, and the processes from antecedents to consequences (Graen, 1976; Graen & Cashman, 1975). Relational leadership models are based on the discovery that followers develop differing qualities of relationship with their leaders, and this changes the understanding of how managers structure their team for the best overall follower performance. Previous accepted theory was that leaders should treat all of their unit members the same and that followers would react the same (Riggio & Ono, 2013). The paradigm shift that relational theory highlighted drove researchers to study each relationship in a team by placing a value on individual level data. This approach contrasts with others that aggregate or average data at the team-level (Stogdill, 1950).

LMX-A as a utility for building positive interpersonal relationships represents, arguably, one of the most important factors in organized human behavior (Uhl-Bien, 2006). Humans are social beings who must rely on their caretakers during their early years and on their tribal community throughout their entire lives. They are loved, socialized, educated, cared for, and motivated by the quality of their interpersonal relationships. For example, in the workplace, those who make their relationships useful to their team, and especially their leader, advance more quickly in their careers (Graen et al., 2006). By making their teams more effective and engaging, team members are recognized as being more valuable to their organizations and are awarded higher positions as a result (Yukl, 2012).

Ehrhardt and Ragins (2019) studied the utility of social relations of employees in the workplace. Their findings suggest that the overall quality of interpersonal attraction was associated with engagement, satisfaction, and retention. The study focused on different levels of relational identification among immediate leaders and workers in general. The authors further considered the quality of the relation between the leader and the follower. A quality relationship is one where leader and follower have a good relationship with high levels of engagement. Results recognized that the LMX-A quality accounted for up to 61% of the total variance in relational identification, suggesting that the overwhelming influence on overall engagement in work was due to the quality of LMX (Ehrhardt & Ragins, 2019).

At the team level, research has found that mean LMX has a positive relation with team potency (the shared belief of team members that they can be effective) and a negative relation with team conflict (Boies & Howell, 2006). In addition, leadership differentiation (differences in the relations among leaders and members) moderated these relations (Boies & Howell, 2006). Differences in LMX quality have also been found related to reputation, labor costs, turnover, influence, career success, commitment, and satisfaction (Henderson et al., 2009). Finally, a meta-analysis found that LMX is positively related to task performance and citizenship performance, and negatively related to counterproductive performance (Martin et al., 2016). In this same study, authors found that trust, motivation, empowerment, and job satisfaction mediated the relation between LMX and task and citizenship performance. These results suggest that alliances with immediate leaders may be among the most significant social influencers in the organization.

Individual Follower Performance

In the context of the instrumentality model (Graen, 1969; Vroom, 1964), LMX-A leadership theory suggests that the decision-making process of followers is related to enhancement offers. The model describes the decision-making process as multidimensional, dynamic, cognitive, emotional, and relational. It assumes that people are different in their preferences for outcomes, evaluate the utility of an outcome package, and decide on the outcome offered as compared to a current situation. Specifically, the utility of an offered outcome is a function of the sum of valences (value given to outcomes), times their instrumentalities (contingencies), times the expectation that the action will lead to achieving the outcome. It should be noted that the utility of an entirely new situation is the worth to the person, at that time, and in that context, which may change given reliable new information. When the utility of an offer is greater than that of the current situation by an attractive amount, the person is likely to perform the action. For example, when the outcome is money, the utility of a fixed sum may differ among team members. These individual differences allow offers to be tailored to each person for maximum effect. One size does not fit all.

The implications of individual decision making for follower performance are a function of perceived utility of leader intervention. The most important concern is its impact on the development of alliances. When a leader is perceived to be producing low expectations of achieving attractive utilities, the difficulties in developing the quality of alliances are magnified. For example, when the leader is seen as a person who routinely does not keep promises or defines follower performance arbitrarily and in self-serving ways, followers will see the assignment as an attempted trap. In addition, when the leader does not ask about follower plans for their careers, he/she is understood to be uninterested in the follower as a unique person. Other factors, based on personal perceptions, such as unconscious bias, abuse, prejudice, and unfairness may play a huge role in the process of the follower's belief in a promised reward system. Yet another set of variable concerns is the leader's know-how, including experience with the system. In sum, a leader's perceived LMX-A factors affect perceptions of the upper limits of reward attractiveness and overall expectancy of receiving the promised package and thus, ultimately, reduces the quality of the outcomes.

LMX-A Training Model

A limitation with the LMX framework is that it does not include specific leader and follower training models to promote high quality relations (Gerstner & Day, 1997; Jawahar et al., 2019), although some evidence suggests leaders can develop LMX qualities (Kangas, 2013). The search for a "teachable" method of instructing supervisors how to intervene with each of their followers to enhance overall performance and engagement has a long and uneven history (Day & Antonakis, 2012). For example, the scientific management framework was found useful for routine and repetitive machine-like work (Taylor, 1911). Recently, the "just-in-time" model was found useful for quality-first manufacturing (Liker & Hoseus, 2008). More recently, a new approach may be found to be useful for the new generation of knowledge workers operating within innovative teams (Doyle, 2015). Given this background, we describe and cite the evidence for our proposed relational model of LMX-A, which suggests that the intentional enhancement of teamwork alliances among leaders and followers will improve follower performance and engagement. Our propositions are based on a comprehensive review of literature (Graen & Canedo, 2017) that strongly points to the necessary mediation model (LMX-A) as a precondition for individual performance enhancement and leaders expected positive outcomes. Research by scientists (e.g., Campbell, 2012; Erdogan & Bauer, 2014; Wang et al., 2005) and practitioners (e.g., Rozovsky, 2015) supports this proposal.

Figure 7.2 provides a model for enhancing the relationship between leaders and followers. This model identifies leader and follower behaviors that can be used to improve dyadic and team alliances and enhance follower performance. The model suggests that a leadership relationship aimed at helping followers succeed should start with leaders and followers establishing common ground by sharing inputs (e.g., agendas, goals, tasks, activities, rewards) and achieving a shared understanding of the purpose of the work. Later, both parties should work to identify mutually authentic, safe, and know-how (ASK) characteristics to support the process. Finally, because of this process, followers should deliver performance (e.g., behaviors, results, and effectiveness) in agreement with expectations. In addition, the model postulates that the process of offering help to coworkers has a strong influence on team members' expectation of achieving contingent rewards (Graen et al., 2018).

During the inputs stage, leaders set the agenda by explaining structure, giving consideration, discussing career transformation, and promising contingent rewards (Gottfredson & Aguinis, 2017; Graen et al., 1982). We call the inputs in this model ENHANCE (E) factors because they help to increase the quality of the relation between leader and follower. These input factors drive and energize identified need-fulfilling outcomes and increase the chances of followers to perform at desired levels. The process has been found to be best described as a leader-follower alliance encompassing mutually agreeable strategy, goals, expectations, activities, and tasks.

Figure 7.2

Process for Improving LMX-A to Enhance Followers' Performance

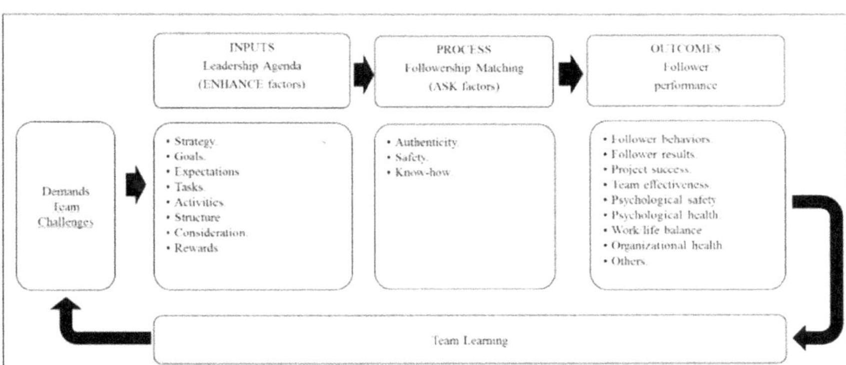

Note 1. All variables at project team level (see Gottfredson & Aguinis, 2017).
Note 2. Figure 7.2 was adapted from Graen, Canedo, and Grace (2018).

The second stage of the model (process) instructs a leader in the proper exchange of information. The phase should consider what individuals seek to accomplish given their professional work situation and aspects that may be improved to increase engagement. Leaders need to understand what their followers desire. In order to get to this level of human interaction, leaders need to establish a team culture that is Authentic, Safe, and that demonstrates Know-how about the work to be done. We call these the ASK (A) factors. We propose that these factors are the three key behavioral factors that determine the quality of the work relationship. Authenticity is the belief by both that the other will keep promises and give trustworthy feedback. Safety is a necessary condition, present when leaders and followers develop a trust relationship and feel free to express themselves. Finally, know-how provides the knowledge, skills, and abilities (competencies) leaders and followers need to perform the work and deliver the expected outcomes (behaviors and results) (Graen et al., 2019).

ASK factors will mediate both performance and effectiveness at the individual and team levels (Graen et al., 2019; Rozovsky, 2015). This suggests that the driver of follower performance happens at the human-to-human interface, influenced by the ASK and ENHANCE (A+E) factors. These factors aim to instruct leader-follower innovators who possess shared goals and agendas to perform successfully as a team (Vroom, 1964; Vroom & Jago, 1988). The A+E factors are used to establish dyadic mutually agreed upon perceptions of inputs, process, and desired outputs. Once this goal is accomplished, the resulting alliances mediate the relationships between a leader's agenda for project success and follower performance. When the necessary conditions are met, the instrumental process of developing a shared perception of success criteria is mediated by the team strength of commitment to alliances.

During the process, leaders and followers learn to work in creating an authentic safe environment and recognize each other's knowledge and potential contribution. The follower outcomes include improved performance and engagement in a number of factors as shown in Figure 7.2. Overall, the driver is the behavior of the leader towards team members. The most effective leaders are those who correctly identify and support what followers want in terms of desired outcomes. Next, we present a leader and follower protocol (collection of ideas) that has been suggested by gains in empirical follower performance and engagement (Graen, 1989):

1. Find a design that fits the specific team of actors, behaviors, and context that you are dealing with.
2. Train participants on the available agenda, assets, and a creative flexible design.

3. Instruct the team on competence networks relevant to the team's agenda.
4. Grant latitude to team members that allows them to take proper actions alone, when necessary, and when that action supports positive outcomes.
5. Give top priority to developing communication quality by clarifying each received message in terms of both denotation and connotation.
6. Reorganize team structure, as appropriate, given the changing nature of the mission.
7. Reward followers fairly.
8. Develop competence networks with coordinators, leaders, and professionals both inside and outside.
9. Keep an open door, walk around, over-communication policy in place, with both inside and outside people, by inviting and participating in an ongoing and informal communication model that stimulates and welcomes new ideas.
10. Keep track of team members and support their career aspirations.
11. Maintain honest communication with all people and promote them as soon as possible.
12. Honor the promises made.
13. Keep formal performance management honest by giving frequent performance feedback.
14. Encourage followers and leaders to become helpful to each other.
15. Celebrate participant and team successes.
16. Enjoy and reward small individual successes.
17. Maintain a climate where mistakes or failures are seen as learning opportunities.

Improving LMX-A scores by one standard deviation (.85) and employing initiating structures wanted by individual followers is projected to improve objective performance at the organization level (Gottfredson & Aguinis, 2017). This suggests a need to train leaders in a different set of interpersonal skills. When potential organizational gains become noticeable by C-suite members, change in training design should follow to capitalize on that performance growth (Graen et al., 2019). We suggest a training program to fill this need, focused on why, what, when, where, and how to enhance professional growth. Similar protocols proved successful by college graduates as they worked their careers toward the top of their organization over twenty years (Graen et al., 2006). Thus, we have evidence indicating that practicing these principles will lead to more successful careers in management.

We believe that our model is plausible and future research is needed to elaborate its fundamental usefulness. For instance, longitudinal field studies and natural experiments similar to those conducted by Graen and colleagues (2006), Graen, Hui, and Taylor (2006), and Graen and colleagues (1982) are necessary. This will help to determine how training and practice in the A+E factors improve worker relationships in all organizational directions and their impact on overall team performance and other desired outcomes.

We also believe that another advantage of our proposal is that it describes specific behaviors that can be used to yield positive results in organizational settings (e.g., leaders and followers use authentic and benevolent communications in interactions, seek agreement and feel safe when discussing work-related processes). Before implementing this idea, we caution that a detailed and tailored research design be conducted considering the specific organizational context (people, processes, structures). Implementations should consider, at least, the following recommendations:

1. Flexible teams of professionals are better performers in today's more complex and creative assignments than command-and-control supervision of assignments.
2. A team is a social organizational mechanism designated to achieve the best team design for successful outcomes.
3. Competence networks across teams are formed informally according to unwritten rules and make a difference for leaders, followers, teams, and organizations.
4. Equitable payoffs should be offered and granted based on unique knowledge, flexibility, and advancement. One size does not fit all.
5. A manager/team leader formally appointed to a team is expected to create and maintain a unit that employs all of its assets in the most productive design.
6. The team leader is expected to supply, support, and guide teams in the most productive manner, according to ongoing dynamic strategic objectives.
7. A leader is an asset who plans the agenda, organizes, and directs available assets into the most effective team structure, given the constraints on people, support, and circumstance.
8. The tools of the leader should provide adequate latitude in managing resources and leading the team as unique people with individual differences in genetic endowment, past history, and current circumstance.
9. Growth-driven participants in a team are encouraged to help create and maintain a unit that employs all of its assets in the most productive design.

10. Each follower expected performance is best described by the instrumentality-expectancy theory with mediation by the ASK model.
11. Followers develop different levels of ASK factors because of leaders treating each of them as holding a unique strategic alliance.

Action Team Alliance

Organizations need new designs for teams of knowledge professionals, who develop innovative products and services (Canedo et al., 2017). To be most productive, these teams must have a high level of psychological safety (Rozovsky, 2015) and their leaders need to be aware of team dynamics in each stage of the team development processes (Webber & Webber, 2015). The new model pretends to create and maintain safe conditions in employing all participants as a team, and is based on developing alliances within a team of knowledge professionals who are proficient in using technology and are trained in team functioning (Graen et al., 2019). The process of administering alliances might be demanding and challenging. To alleviate it, leaders should focus on (a) cultivating relationships with subordinates, (b) creating and using objective metrics, (c) embracing differences, (d) enabling collaborative behavior, and (e) managing internal stakeholders (Hughes & Weiss, 2007).

In organizational practice, corporate alliances continue to increase, yet their success rates are less than 40%, mainly due to focusing more on business plans than on designing systems for people to work together (Hughes & Weiss, 2007). We believe that ideas consistent with LMX-A can improve success in these endeavors. For example, using team-level compensation, team members and leaders are paid at their job level and rewarded additionally by the value of their innovative work. This way, individuals are fairly compensated in their individual jobs and according to their contributions in a successful team-project. This assumes players are paid fairly for their individual and mission-related work. The apparent problem with alliances between organizations may be that those negotiating the alliance are not the same people who will implement it and, thus, potential disagreements in the administration process are overlooked. With team-level alliances, those who find agreement initially are likely to be those who will implement. In addition, the quality of the interpersonal relationship seems to make a sizable difference in the quality of leader-follower alliances.

Instrumentality Theory in Relation to the LMX-A Model

We believe every prospective follower should be asked about their preferred hierarchy of outcomes in terms of utility. The underlying hierarchy of needs may be clarified by showing an honest interest (authenticity) in the person as a team member and continually asking what they hope to achieve through participation in the team process. As relevant questions are asked and discussed, the three ASK characteristics of the interacting pair become clearer. During this getting-to-know-each-other period, both test each other informally and the results become obvious when tasks are assigned and accepted. Our proposal of LMX-A model assumes that the perceived utility of an offer is mediated by a composite of the three ASK dimensions of the alliance. This way, all three dimensions are required to establish full mediation. For example, although mutual trust is helpful, authenticity, safety, and know-how are more comprehensive and reliable as predictors of positive outcomes. Mutual trust will be unlikely when the leader is seen as false, dangerous, or incompetent.

An earlier version of the LMX-A model was originally described by what was then identified as a new theoretical construct labeled "role-making process" (Graen, 1976). This construct contrasted with the Katz and Kahn (1966) role-taking theory. The difference is that role taking is the process of "role acceptance" and role making is the process of "role working outs" during team construction and process. Before the introduction of the idea of role making (Graen, 1976), scholarship focused on average leadership style. Subsequently, the focus turned to each "role making" agreement in the unit (Riggio & Ono, 2013). Accordingly, the assumption developed was that if leaders treat each follower the same, they would act predictably. Underlying this was the idea that to reward the more productive was unfair and all needed to be rewarded the same. This role-making alternate hypothesis was that followers should be graded on a curve and be given A, B, C, D, and F contingent rewards to be fair and equitable (Graen & Uhl-Bien, 1995). Since the introduction of the idea of role making, leadership theories moved toward collecting individual-level data and unit-level analyses (Graen & Canedo, 2017). This meant the focus shifted to the dyadic-level, initially, followed by the unit and organizational-levels of analysis.

Current ASK Measure

Table 7.1 shows an instrument to measure the ASK factors. It can be used with supervisors, subordinates, and peers. Use of this measure in previous research (e.g., Graen & Schiemann, 2013) showed that the Max IIF scale revealed the most information is delivered by "confidence in ideas" and "help with job problems," followed by "respect my capabilities" and "trust that I would carry out my work load", and less by "excellent working relationship" and "satisfaction with work." Agreement between leader and member (and among members) reached 68% with higher percentages in higher scores (Graen & Schiemann, 2013). This measure can be used to investigate the mediation of influence attempts by peers and subordinates.

Measuring ASK factors is relevant because the interpersonal relationship between a member and his/her leader mediates the relation between inputs (ENHANCE factors in our model) and follower performance and other desired outcomes (Gottfredson & Aguinis, 2017). Once ASK factors are measured for each relationship, team leaders can start working on molding the culture of their teams (design of work and motivation of members). If needed, leaders can be trained to understand how they can give followers the opportunities to help beyond doing their formal jobs (Graen et al., 2019). By doing so, leaders will help to improve overall team

Table 7.1

The ASK Measure

Six item (short form)	CITC	M	SD	Max IIF
My (colleague, supervisor, or subordinate) is satisfied with my work.	0.84	3.52	1.12	2.92
My (colleague, supervisor, subordinate) would help me with my job problem.	0.90	3.61	1.16	8.06
My (colleague, supervisor, subordinate) has confidence in my ideas.	0.89	3.59	1.09	8.44
My (colleague, supervisor, subordinate) has trust that I would carry my workload	0.88	3.64	1.12	5.38
My (colleague, supervisor, subordinate) has respect for my capabilities.	0.89	3.65	1.09	5.44
I have an excellent working relationship with my (colleague, supervisor, and subordinate).	0.85	3.59	1.08	3.55

Notes: CITC – corrected item total correlation, Max IIF – maximum value of information; n = 486; results of modified parallel analysis = unidimensional scale; internal consistency of responses = α = 0.95; slight negative skewness = do not interpret both mean and variance of LMX-SLX (results will be uninterruptable for variance); this skewness produces spuriously high correlations between LMX mean and variance within groups, and correlations of LMX variance within groups as a predictor are spurious; linear agreement correlation between supervisor and subordinate reports on same scales was 0.68 (p < 0.001) indicating good agreement across the range; agreement between peers also correlated 0.68 (p < 0.001); moreover, agreement for high LMX dyad is significantly better; LMX differentiation as measured by LMX variance within groups is an artifact of this skewness; finally, permission is granted by Dr. Graen for all professional use of this 360°, LMX team measure (a summary of findings is expected in return).

Note. Table 7.1 was copied from Graen and Schiemann (2013).

performance thanks to taking advantage of each member's unique competencies and drive.

LMX-A Dynamics

How does the LMX-A process develop in project teams? This was investigated over three different sets of actors, behaviors, and contexts (Graen et al., 2006). Findings showed that the process begins to predict performance when the team puts the project ahead of personal goals. In the experiment, teams of engineers worked on solving industrial problems for paying users with a six-month deadline for completion. Too late, engineers realized that when the first problem-solving part of the process was completed, they would not have enough time to complete their project reports unless they agreed to work faster and longer than planned. This heavier workload was accepted in the strong, but not in the weak, LMX-A teams. Teams validated a high relationship between LMX-A and team product. In fact, in all three experiments, the proportion of high LMX-A members with acceptably high scores was related to product usefulness.

The dynamics of constructing an authentic, safe, and knowledgeable identity of each other that permits a leader and a follower to believe in and experience an enhanced alliance is facilitated by progressively testing each other and the relationship. These dynamics of asking for help and receiving feedback concerning helpfulness, authenticity, safety, and know-how, based partly on continuous performance feedback, is desirable. These human dynamics enable two people to develop an alliance of helpfulness and fairness that is seen as more attractive than the employment contract alliance. Additionally, team members who identify themselves as learning professionals, learn by doing more advanced tasks, and allow themselves to be vulnerable through demonstration of ASK behaviors to become increasingly more valuable to their organizations. This social learning process is as old as modern humans and natural as collaboration in an interdependent problem-solving task that requires new learning to be successful. Learning by helping each other is facilitated by asking. Leveraging the LMX-A model, thus, is a demonstration of mature social skills that enhances the overall performance of the team.

ASK Training Field Experiments

Graen et al. (1982) carried out two field experiments designed to test the effort of ASK leader training on follower performance by computer workers. The experiments involved 106 employees of a large public service organization in the U.S. Midwest. The training consisted of four once-a-week sessions. Two randomly assigned conditions were contrasted as (1) an ASK course and (2) a transformational leadership course. In each session, leaders were asked for their main supervision challenges and how they dealt with them. Next, instructions were provided and leaders practiced the assigned protocols on each other. Follower performance was measured once a week by accessing the computer records of each operator. After six months, the trends showed a 16% gain in follower performance with no loss of quality for ASK-trained unit leaders compared to those trained in a transformational protocol. Finally, a measure of "career aspiration" was found to mediate follower performance producing a 50% gain from before to after ASK training of unit supervisors. This was taken to mean that the overall gain in performance was attributable to those high-growth workers who accepted the ASK alliance offered—those with strong developmental goals. This study was repeated later and found the same results (Graen et al., 1986). In sum, these experiments supported and replicated the superior effect of training of leaders on the gain in follower performance using the ASK protocol, compared to the transformative method. Next we will discuss the implications of this proposal has for theory, research, and practice.

IMPLICATIONS

Implications for Theory

The LMX-A model theory predicts that improved team performance can result from team leaders creating unique reciprocal alliances with each team member that include agreement to abide by the principles of their agreement, reinforced through habits of frequent feedback. The alliance encourages team members to model the behavior in peer-to-peer alliances that strengthen team interrelationships and reinforce positive expectations for team outcomes.

Several characteristics are required for an acceptable alliance-driven team. For example, leaders and team members must learn from each other what they hope to achieve in their jobs and careers, search for ways to realize them, find out what they seek as team contributors, and act as interested investors in an ongoing team enterprise.

The most useful scientific findings related to individuals in team performance contexts have come from the dyad-level. We first examined the case of the average style of leaders (Stogdill, 1950), later the team-level, combined with the dyadic-level (Graen, 1976; Graen et al., 2019). The dyadic leadership data were collected at the sender and receiver levels. Both follower and leader in formal interdependent assignments were asked about each of their personal drivers regarding short- and long-term development. Both parties would first ASK and then, after decision making, offer tailored contingent enhancements of their alliance. The idea was to infuse their human investments in a longer-term commitment. The strength of the dyadic alliances predicts the overall success of the team. This is taken to mean that the outcomes of the process are promised by the leader, contingent on the success of the alliance overall and the follower's evaluation of the results (e.g., fairness to followers, personnel, organization, and community) (Hughes & Weiss, 2007). Thus, research revealed the entire process from design of team structure to the development of relevant results at the individual and dyadic levels. This model has remained consistent across many different scenarios, actors, behaviors, and contexts.

Implications for Research

Long-term research is needed on the efficacy of the A+E factors. For example, how does an alliance-driven team player manage to signal to the leader that he/she is prepared to help manage the team enterprises, or how does she/he signal teammates that she wants to help them contribute to the success of the assignment? We have seen that early promotions characterize those engaging in the alliance process, but more research is required that spans experiences from the first day of employment to the achievement of management- or leader-level scenarios. We also call for research that helps develop the A+E factors in field experiments, where the values of the new generation are essential contextual elements. Learned respect for a diversity of perspectives, especially listening for the voices of Gen X and Gen Y, is an essential element of educational processes and encouraged behaviors patterns.

In addition, we need process research on the dyadic level of measurement. Research has shown that the two-person reciprocal alliance drives positive performance outcomes. Each member of the dyad influences the outcomes through their individual behavior, which, in turn, encourages the team as a whole. This type of aggregation of alliance quality needs to be weighted by each follower as contributors to team-level success, which means the employment of a contributor matrix averaging team-level alliances as measures of the quality of team-level processes. Finally, we need to remember that LMX differentiation is a consequence, not a driver, of the A+E factors. The variation within teams is a function of intentionally including consideration of individual differences in ability and motivation to tailor work design of the team. LMX differentiation should not be considered when designing teams using the A+E factors. LMX is an output, not an input.

Organizations benefit from using the best processes available. Accordingly, many organizations are open to examination of the A+E factors and structure over time. Organizations engaging in this type of research may benefit from adhering to certain strategies in their approach. First, begin on a small scale, contrasting teams that are involved initially in the process to similar teams not yet involved. Use instrumentality thinking to encourage participation (see Vroom, 1964). Second, negotiate an alliance with those in charge. Executive and MBA programs may be instrumental in carrying out this step. Third, plan the investigation to capture the before, during, and after processes using both qualitative and quantitative descriptors of relevant events using trained observers. Fourth, analyze the processes as soon as data are collected and employ early findings to add new measures. It is important to give workers the rationale for the study before collecting the data and ask each participant for their consent to be a part of the study. Employ proper analytic procedures and report the results and implications. Statistical results should fit together and reflect qualitative findings. Align your research protocols with the A+E factors; for example, provide feedback regularly and listen to the voices of younger and more junior employees.

Implications for Practice

The digital revolution is changing the relation of employment from a location of role taking to an activity of role-making. The role-taking approach defined the job as a set of rules and processes with command-and-control behaviors of management that treated workers as fixed machine-like elements. Employees signed agreements to follow rules and procedures as defined by supervisors. Rigid scenarios of actors, behaviors, and context were enforced by threat of termination at the pleasure of the organizational agent. This model worked well for static, simple, and repetitive work tasks overseen by more knowledgeable supervisors. As the machine model was transformed into the knowledge-worker model, where decisions are made at the point of work, the need emerged for greater flexibility in the design of work enterprises. The search for innovative digital applications for all aspects of life called for the use of the latest technology by teams of experts who are all leaders in their own rights, but who need to collaborate with other experts to address the complex solution spaces that challenge today's technology-driven enterprises.

One model of project attachment is relying on imagination to create the concept of a program of useful applications and finding the needed talent to contribute as additional investors in a work alliance. Project leaders would be trained in the new design of project management using an LMX-A training model, which blends well with work design methods, such as design thinking processes (Brown, 2008), to fully enable knowledge worker contexts.

DISCUSSION

Teams are social constructions designed to perform a common enterprise of interdependent work with two or more people, often with one providing direction. An important characteristic with the team environment is the exchange of influence information and behavior. The input-process-output model described in this chapter advances our understanding of this dynamic process. Underlying this model is the instrumentality algorithm, which outlines the personal driver system.

LMX continues to provide a valuable means for studying relationships within an organization. Just as organizations and relationships have changed over time, the theory continues to evolve to provide for the most current abilities and tools to understand dyadic interactions. Based on research, we introduced a comprehensive, effective, supervisory, and team interrelationship formation process to enhance individual and team performance in a team-based environment. We have detailed a rational, practical, and integrative model of leadership. In addition, we identified the instrumentality theory as a contingency model. Finally, we argue that the LMX-A model and the A+ E factors are based on solid evidence and, accordingly, will serve as the foundation of future talent management systems. In turn, these systems will lead us to employ leader-member exchange alliances that will encourage team members to engage in productivity enhancing behaviors. This must entail mutually energizing alliances directed at team effectiveness with authentic, safe, and knowledgeable colleagues. Through these processes, advances in LMX theory will provide additional value to organizations and the people within.

REFERENCES

Boies, K., & Howell, J. M. (2006). Leader-member exchange in teams: An examination of the interaction between relationship differentiation and mean LMX in explaining team-level outcomes. *The Leadership Quarterly, 17*, 246–257. https://doi.org/10.1016/j.leaqua.2006.02.004.

Breuer, C., Huffmeier, J., & Hertel, G. (2016). Does trust matter more in virtual teams? A meta-analysis of trust and team effectiveness considering virtuality and documentation as moderators. *Journal of Applied Psychology, 8*, 1151–1177. https://doi.org/10.1037/apl0000113.

Brown, T. (2008, June). Design thinking. *Harvard Business Review,* 1–10.

Burke, C. S., Stagl, K. C., Klein. C., Goodwin, G. F., Salas, E., & Halpin, S. M. (2006). What type of leadership behaviors are functional in teams? A meta-analysis. *The Leadership Quarterly, 17,* 288–307. https://doi.org/10.1016/j.leaqua.2006.02.007

Campbell, J. (2012). Leadership, the old, the new, and the timeless: A commentary. *The Oxford Handbook of Leadership,* https://doi.org/10.1093/oxfordhb/9780195398793.013.0024.

Canedo, J. C., Graen, G., & Grace, M. (2018). Let's make performance management work for new hires: They are the future. *Organizational Dynamics, 47,* 229–233. https://doi.org/10.1016/j.orgdyn.2017.11.003.

Canedo, J. C., Graen, G., Grace, M., & Johnson, R. D. (2017). Navigating the new workplace: Technology, millennials, and accelerating HR innovation. *Transactions in Human-Computer Interaction, 9,* 243–260. https://aisel.aisnet.org/thci/vol9/iss3/4.

Chaudhry, A., Vidyarthi, P. R., Liden. R. C., & Wayne, S. J. (2020). Two to tango? Implications of alignment and misalignment in leader and follower perceptions of LMX. *Journal of Business and Psychology.* https://doi.org/10.1007/s10869-020-09690-8.

Day, D. V., & Antonakis, J. (2012). Leadership: Past, present, and future. In J. Antonakis & D. V. Day (Eds.), *The nature of leadership* (pp. 3–25). SAGE.

Day, D. V., Gronn, P., & Salas, E. (2004). Leadership capacity in teams. *The Leadership Quarterly, 15,* 857–880. https://doi.org/10.1016/j.leaqua.2004.09.001

De Jong, B. A., Gillespie, N., & Dirks, K. T. (2016). Trust and team performance: A meta-analysis of main effects, moderators, and covariates. *Journal of Applied Psychology, 8,* 1134–1150. https://doi.org/10.1037/apl0000110

DeRue, D. S., Nahrgang, J. D., Wellman, N., & Humphrey, S. E. (2011). Trait and behavioral theories of leadership: An integration and meta-analytic test of their relative validity. *Personnel Psychology, 64,* 7–52. https://doi.org/10.1111/j.1744-6570.2010.01201.x

Doyle, M. (2015). Deloitte survey: Global organizations face looming crisis in engagement and retention of employees. *CSRWire.* Retrieved March 4, 2015, from http://www.csrwire.com/press_releases/37737-Deloitte-Survey-Global-Organizations-Face-Looming-Crisis-in-Engagement-and-Retention-of-Employees

Dulebohn, J. H., Bommer, W. H., Liden. R. C., Brouer, R. L., & Ferris, G. R. (2012). A meta-analysis of antecedents and consequences of leader-member exchange integrating the past with an eye toward the future. *Journal of Management, 38,* 1715–1759. https://doi.org/10.1177/0149206311415280.

Ehrhardt, K., & Ragins, B. R. (2019). Relational attachment at work: A complimentary fit perspective on the role of relationships in organizational life. *Academy of Management Journal, 62,* 248–282. https://doi.org/10.5465/amj.2016.0245

Erdogan, B., & Bauer, T. N. (2014). Leader-member exchange (LMX) theory: The relational approach to leadership. In D. V. Day (Ed.), *The Oxford handbook of leadership and organizations* (pp. 407–433). University Press.

Gerstner, C. R., & Day, D. V. (1997). Meta-analytic review of leader-member exchange theory: Correlates and construct issues. *Journal of Applied Psychology, 82,* 827–844.

Gottfredson, R. K., & Aguinis, H. (2017). Leadership behaviors and follower performance: Deductive and inductive examination of theoretical rationales and underlying mechanisms. *Journal of Organizational Behavior, 38*, 558–591. https://doi.org/10.1002/job.2152

Grace, M., & Graen, G. B. (2014). *Millennial spring: Designing the future of organizations*. Vol. IX. LMX Leadership: The Series. Information Age.

Graen, G. (1969). Instrumentality theory of work motivation: Some experimental results and suggested modifications. *Journal of Applied Psychology, 53,* 1–25. https://doi.org/10.1037/h0027100

Graen, G. B. (1976). Role-making processes within complex organizations. In M. D. Dunnette (Ed.), *Handbook of industrial and organizational psychology* (pp. 1202–1245). Rand McNally.

Graen, G. B. (1989). *Unwritten rules for your career: The 15 secrets for fast-track success*. John Wiley & Sons.

Graen, G. B., & Canedo, J. C. (2017). Charismatic and innovative team leadership by and for millennials. *Oxford University Press.* https://doi.org/10.1093/OBO/9780199846740-0127

Graen, G., Canedo, J. C., & Grace, M. (2018, September 20). Adapting LMX theory to forthcoming changes: Two different frameworks. *Industrial and Organizational Psychology: Perspectives on Science and Practice, 11,* 531–535. https://doi.org/10.1017/iop.2018.107

Graen, G., Canedo, J. C., & Grace, M. (2019). Team coaching can enhance psychological safety and drive organizational effectiveness. *Organizational Dynamics*. https://doi.org/10.1016/j.orgdyn.2019.01.003

Graen, G., & Cashman, J. (1975). A role-making model of leadership in formal organizations: A development approach. In J. G. Hunt & L. L. Larson (Eds.), *Leadership Frontiers* (pp. 143–165). Kent State University Press.

Graen, G., Dharwadkar, R., Grewal, R., & Wakabayashi, M. (2006). Japanese career programs: An empirical examination. *Journal of International Business Studies, 37,* 148–161.

Graen, G. B., Hui, C., & Taylor, E. A. (2006). Experience-based learning about LMX leadership and fairness in project teams: A Dyadic directional approach. *Academy of Management Learning and Education, 5,* 448–460. https://doi.org/10.5465/amle.2006.23473205

Graen, G. B., Novak, M., A., & Sommerkamp, P. (1982). The effects of leader-member exchange and job design on productivity and satisfaction: Testing a dual attachment model. *Organizational Behavior and Human Performance, 30,* 109–131. https://doi.org/10.1016/0030-5073(82)90236-7

Graen, G. B., Scandura, T. A., & Graen, M. R. (1986). A field experimental test of the moderating effects of growth need strength on productivity. *Journal of Applied Psychology, 71,* 484–491. https://doi.org/10.1037/0021-9010.71.3.484

Graen, G. B., & Schiemann, W. A. (2013). Leadership-motivated excellence theory: An extension of LMX. *Journal of Managerial Psychology, 28,* 452–469. https://doi.org/10.1108/JMP-11-2012-0351

Graen, G. B., & Uhl-Bien, M. (1995). Relationship-based approach to leadership: Development of leader-member exchange (LMX) theory of leadership over

25 years: Applying a multi-level multi-domain perspective. *The Leadership Quarterly, 6,* 219–247. https://doi.org/10.1016/1048-9843(95)90036-5

Hackman, J. R., & Morris, C. G. (1975). Group tasks, group interaction process, and group performance effectiveness: A review and proposed integration. *Advances in Experimental Social Psychology, 8,* 45–99. https://doi.org/10.1016/S0065-2601(08)60248-8

Henderson, D. J., Liden, R. C., Glibkowksi, B. C., & Chaudhry, A. (2009). LMX differentiation: A multilevel review and examination of its antecedents and outcomes. *The Leadership Quarterly, 20,* 517–534. https://doi.org/10.1016/j.leaqua.2009.04.003

Hughes, J., & Weiss, J. (2007). Simple rules for making alliances work. *Harvard Business Review, 85*(11), 122–126.

Jawahar, I. M., Stone, T. H., & Kluemper, D. (2019). When and why leaders trust followers: LMX as a mediator and empowerment as a moderator of the trustworthiness-trust relationship. *Career Development International, 24,* 702–716. https://doi.org/10.1108/CDI-03-2019-0078

Judge, T. A., Piccolo, R. F., & Ilies, R. (2004). The forgotten ones? The validity of consideration and initiating structure in leadership research. *Journal of Applied Psychology, 89,* 36–51. https://doi.org/10.1037/0021-9010.89.1.36

Kangas, H. M. (2013). The development of the LMX relationships after a newly appointed leader enters an organization. *Human Resource Development International, 16,* 575–589. https://doi.org/10.1080/13678868.2013.825438

Katz, D., & Kahn, R. L. (1966). *The social psychology of organizations.* Wiley.

Liker, J. K., & Hoseus, M. (2008). *Toyota culture: The heart and soul of the Toyota Way.* McGraw-Hill.

Martin, R., Guillaume, Y., Thomas, G., Lee, A., & Editropaki, O. (2016). Leader-member exchange (LMX) and performance: A meta-analytic review. *Personnel Psychology, 69,* 67–121. https://doi.org/10.1111/peps.12100

Morrissette, A. M., & Kisamore, J. L. (2020). Trust and performance in business teams: A meta-analysis. *Performance Management: An International Journal, 26,* 287–300. https://doi.org/10.1108/TPM-02-2020-0012

Nandedkar, A., & Brown, R. S. (2018). Transformational leadership and positive work outcomes: A framework exploring the role of LMX and distributive justice. *International Journal of Organizational Theory & Behavior, 21,* 315–327. https://doi.org/10.1108/IJOTB-09-2018-0105

Piccolo, R. F., Bono, J. E., Heinitz, K., Rowold, J., Duehr, E., & Judge, T. A. (2012). The relative impact of complementary leader behaviors: Which matter most? *The Leadership Quarterly, 23,* 567–581. https://doi.org/10.1016/j.leaqua.2011.12.008

Podsakoff, P. M., Bommer, W. H., Podsakoff, N. P., & MacKenzie, S. B. (2006) Relationships between leader reward and punishment behavior and subordinate attitudes, perceptions, and behaviors: A meta-analytic review of existing and new research. *Organizational Behavior and Human Decision Processes, 99,* 113–142. https://doi.org/10.1016/j.obhdp.2005.09.002

Richter, A. W., Dawson, J. F., & West, M. A. (2011). The effectiveness of teams in organizations: a meta-analysis. *International Journal of Human Resource Management, 22,* 2749–2769. https://doi.org/10.1080/09585192.2011.573971

Riggio, R. E., & Ono, M. (2013). Leadership. In *Oxford bibliographies in management.* Oxford: University Press. https://www.oxfordbibliographies.com/view/document/obo-9780199828340/obo-9780199828340-0130.xml

Rozovsky, J. (2015, November 17). *The five keys to a successful Google team.* https://rework.withgoogle.com/blog/five-keys-to-a-successful-google-team/

Stogdill, R. M. (1950). Leadership, membership and organization. *Psychological Bulletin, 47,* 1–14. https://doi.org/10.1037/h0053857

Taylor, F. W. (1911). *The principles of scientific management.* Harper & Brothers.

Uhl-Bien, M. (2006). Relational leadership theory: Exploring the social processes of leadership and organizing. *The Leadership Quarterly, 17,* 654–676. https://doi.org/10.1007/978-90-481-9014-0_7

Vroom, V. H. (1964). *Work and motivation.* Wiley.

Vroom, V. H., & Deci, E. L. (1970). *Management and motivation.* Penguin.

Vroom, V. H., & Jago, A. G. (1988). *The new leadership. Managing participation in organizations.* Prentice-Hall.

Wakabayashi, M., & Graen, G. B. (1984). The Japanese career progress study: A 7-year follow-up. *Journal of Applied Psychology, 69,* 603–614. https://doi.org/10.1037/0021-9010.69.4.603

Wang, H., Law, K. S., Hackett, R. D., Wang, D., & Chen, Z. X. (2005). Leader-member exchange as a mediator of the relationship between transformational leadership and followers' performance and organizational citizenship behavior. *Academy of Management Journal, 48,* 420–432. https://doi.org/10.5465/amj.2005.17407908

Wang, D., Waldman, D. A., & Zhang, Z. (2014). A meta-analysis of shared leadership and team effectiveness. *Journal of Applied Psychology, 2,* 181–198. https://doi.org/10.1037/a0034531

Webber, S. S., & Webber, D. S. (2015). Launching and leading intense teams. *Business Horizons, 58,* 449–457. https://doi.org/10.1016/j.bushor.2015.03.009

Yukl, G. (2012). Effective leadership behavior: What we know and what questions need more attention. *Academy of Management Perspectives, 26,* 66–85. https://doi.org/10.5465/amp.2012.0088

CHAPTER 8

BARRIERS TO AUTHENTIC LEADER-FOLLOWER RELATIONSHIPS

Implications for Human Resource Management

William L. Gardner, Daniel P. Gullifor, James D. Carlson, Claudia C. Cogliser, and Margaret L. Williams

ABSTRACT

Over the past 15 years, scholarly and practitioner interest in the construct of authentic leadership has rapidly expanded. At the same time, one of the implicit assumptions underlying authentic leadership theory—that it is possible to achieve authenticity and authentic leadership across spatial, cultural, and temporal contexts—has not been fully appreciated or challenged. For theory to advance, the boundary conditions of that theory must be identified to understand the parameters within which the theory does, and does not, apply, along with other contextual moderators that may impact the extent to which leaders and their followers are able to establish authentic relationships.

Leadership:
Leaders, Followers, and Context, pp. 181–218

In this chapter we adopt Johns's (2006) perspective on organizational context to consider elements of the omnibus (temporal, physical, and cultural boundaries) and discrete (follower competence, perceived social distance, frequency of leader-follower interaction, virtuality, and "Dark Triad" personalities) context that serve as potential barriers to the formation of authentic leader-follower relationships. To do so we draw on the leader-member exchange (LMX) and leader and follower identity theories to consider the implications of these barriers for leaders and followers who strive to be authentic at work. We also consider the implications of these barriers to authentic leadership and followership for human resource management (HRM) within organizations. Finally, we identify potential directions for future research to ascertain the effects of these and other barriers to the development of authentic leader-follower relationships.

Leaders who strive to stay true to their core values and beliefs and remain truthful, transparent, and developmental in their dealings with others are said to be engaging in authentic leadership (Avolio & Gardner, 2005). Over the last decade, authentic leadership has received extensive theoretical and empirical interest (Banks et al., 2016; Gardner et al., 2011; Lemoine et al., 2019), resulting in considerable support for positive relationships with a host of favorable work outcomes, including leader and follower well-being (Rahimnia & Sharifirad, 2015; Weiss & Cropanzano, 1996; Mona Weiss et al., 2018; Matthias Weiss et al., 2018), employee job satisfaction (Azanza et al., 2013; Leroy et al., 2015), organizational commitment (Guerrero et al., 2015), organizational citizenship behaviors (Mehmood et al., 2016; Pastor Álvarez et al., 2019), work engagement (Wei et al., 2018), work role performance (Leroy et al., 2015), team performance (Lyubovnikova et al., 2017), and firm level performance (Clapp-Smith et al., 2009). These relationships with critical workplace outcomes have stimulated an expansion and integration of authentic leadership research into scholarship in human resource management (HRM; Gill et al., 2018; Karam et al., 2017).

The surge of interest in authentic leadership has created much excitement for further theory development and testing (Avolio & Walumbwa, 2014; Banks et al., 2016; Lemoine et al., 2019). While this fervor constitutes a positive development for the field, the continued advancement of authentic leadership research requires greater exposure of underlying assumptions and boundary conditions (Bacharach, 1989; Van de Ven, 2007). One of these underlying assumptions is that the development of authentic leadership and its characteristic authentic relationships generalize across settings. This assumption that authentic leadership is achievable, regardless of context, is both unsubstantiated, and questionable, as barriers to authentic relationships may not only exist, but persist at varying levels (Alvesson & Einola, 2019; Gardner & Cogliser, 2018; Yagil & Medler-Liraz, 2013).

The organizational context presents potential barriers to the development of authentic relationships at what Johns (2006, p. 391) described as the omnibus (i.e., "the context broadly considered") and the discrete (i.e., "the particular contextual variables or levers that shape behavior or attitudes") levels. Omnibus level barriers might include misalignment between national cultures, economic conditions, or temporal restrictions, whereas the barriers at the discrete level might include temporary affective displays (e.g., emotional labor; Gardner et al., 2009) or more permanent hindrances such as stable personality traits (e.g., narcissism, Machiavellianism, psychopathy; O'Boyle et al., 2012). Despite preliminary empirical support for the predictions of authentic leadership theory (Banks et al., 2016; Gardner et al., 2011), there is a dearth of literature that examines the potential barriers to authentic leadership and authentic relationship development. This gap will not only expose authentic leadership theory to criticism (Alvesson & Einola, 2019; Iszatt-White & Kempster, 2018; Sidani & Rowe, 2018), but it is also likely to hinder its further development (Bacharach, 1989; Van de Ven, 2007).

The purpose of this chapter is twofold. First, we make explicit the implicit assumption that authentic leadership and authentic relationships are achievable in any setting. Second, we question the soundness of this assumption by proposing several boundary conditions that are likely to serve as barriers to authentic leadership development. To do so, we consider the following question: *Under what circumstances will individuals be unwilling or unable to develop authentic leader-follower relationships?* To provide a conceptual answer to this question, we first present a model of how authentic leader-follower relationships are formed, followed by a discussion of the contextual factors that may serve to erect barriers to such relationships. Throughout this discussion, we consider the implications of these barriers for HRM practices to make the significance of the boundary conditions and discrete contextual moderators of authentic leadership more concrete. We proceed to develop and present theoretical propositions to explicate the relationships between the proposed barriers and authentic leader-follower relationship development. It should be noted this chapter's aim is not to provide an exhaustive examination of contextual moderators, but to instead highlight the potential obstacles to authentic leader-follower relationship development and their HRM implications. It is our intention to lay the groundwork for future empirical testing of contextual moderators and further development of the authentic leadership theory.

AUTHENTIC LEADER-FOLLOWER RELATIONSHIP VERIFICATION

Defined as "a pattern of leader behavior that draws upon and promotes both positive psychological capacities and a positive ethical climate, to foster greater self-awareness, an internalized moral perspective, balanced processing of information, and relational transparency on the part of leaders working with followers, fostering positive self-development" (Walumbwa et al., 2008, p. 94), authentic leadership is characterized by its four core dimensions of self-awareness, internalized moral perspective, balanced processing of information, and relational transparency (Gardner et al., 2005; Walumbwa et al., 2008). To be true to oneself, one must first know oneself. Thus, self-awareness provides a foundation upon which authentic leadership can be built. Possessing an internalized moral perspective involves remaining true to one's internal standards by resisting temptation and pressure to compromise one's values and convictions. Balanced processing of information is the ability and practice of accepting both positive and negative forms of information, in a nondefensive manner, and incorporating that information into the decision-making process. Relational transparency involves being open and forthcoming in conveying information about the self and associated entities to close others. While no one is completely authentic or inauthentic across all situations (Erickson, 1994), the extent to which a leader possesses and exhibits varying degrees of these components determines the degree to which he or she achieves authenticity.

To adequately discuss and identify barriers to authentic leadership, we must first consider the process whereby authentic leader-follower relationships develop over time. To do so, we discuss one major theoretical perspective on authentic leadership (Avolio & Gardner, 2005; Gardner et al., 2011; Karam et al., 2017) and its evolution to gain insight into the current status of the field and the need to clarify boundary conditions. As is the case for other theories of leadership (Gardner & Avolio, 1998; Graen & Uhl-Bien, 1995), authentic leadership focuses on the relationship between leaders and followers. Kernis and Goldman (2006, p. 300) characterize this relational orientation as, "valuing and striving for openness, sincerity, and truthfulness in one's close relationships," thus serving as the basis for the relational transparency component of authentic leadership. Relational transparency emphasizes the presentation of a true, authentic self, as compared with a fake or distorted self, to others (Gardner et al., 2005; Walumbwa et al., 2008). Despite this relational focus, the role that the follower plays in authentic leader-follower relationship development has only recently been empirically explored (Leroy et al., 2015). Leroy and colleagues (2015) demonstrate that the interplay between authentic leadership and authentic followers serves to promote follower need satisfaction and performance. Further, the development of psychological attachment styles over time is proposed to have differential outcomes on the formation of authentic leadership and relationships (Hinojosa et al., 2014).

One literature stream that informs the developmental process whereby leader-follower relationships form derives from leader-member exchange (LMX) theory (Dulebohn et al., 2012; Graen & Scandura, 1987; Graen & Uhl-Bien, 1995). LMX theory posits that leaders form unique, differential relationships with each of their followers such that the quality of these relationships varies, with higher-quality relationships being characterized by higher levels of affect, loyalty, contribution, and professional respect (Liden & Maslyn, 1998). Extensive research focused on LMX (Gerstner & Day, 1997; Graen & Uhl-Bien, 1995; Ilies et al., 2005) has generated both empirical support and enhanced confidence in our understanding of LMX's relationship with critical workplace outcomes (e.g., job performance, satisfaction, organizational citizenship behaviors, etc.), as well as greater conceptual clarity regarding the relationship development process.

According to Graen and Scandura (1987) and Graen and Uhl-Bien (1995), the quality of the LMX relationship is developed through a three-stage dyadic process that includes role-taking ("stranger" phase; Graen & Uhl-Bien, 1995), role-making ("acquaintance" phase; Graen & Uhl-Bien, 1995), and role-routinization ("mature partnership" phase; Graen & Uhl-Bien, 1995). Prior to the commencement of the first stage of role-taking, both parties (i.e., a leader and a member) must opt into the process, bringing with them their own histories, personalities, and current circumstances. Additionally, this process would take place in an environment that would be "laden with the trappings of the formal structural arrangements, part organization history, and current circumstances" (Graen & Scandura, 1987, p. 179) with strangers occupying independent organizational roles (Graen & Uhl-Bien, 1995). Once both parties embark on the relationship development process, the role-taking, -making, and -routinization process commences.

In the role-taking or acquaintance phase, individuals attempt to discover the abilities and motivations of the other party. This typically includes the iterative process of the leader initiating the interaction by offering various tasks and assignments to probe the member's strengths and weaknesses with an offer of increased social exchanges. Next, the member reacts by behaving in some manner relevant to the assigned task or assignment and the leader evaluates this behavior, either explicitly or implicitly, to determine whether the member should be considered for the in-group (i.e., those with high-quality exchange relationships) or the out-group (i.e., those with low-quality exchange relationships). In the second phase of role-making, the leader and member begin to establish mutual expectations for their dyadic relationship based on the undertaking and completion of tasks. As the leader and member continue to engage in unstructured tasks, their dyadic interdependencies are identified, and patterns of beneficial behaviors and exchanges emerge beyond just the contractual level. In the final role-routinization or mature partnership phase, the previously established expectations regarding the beneficial exchange of resources becomes increasingly predictable and highly developed because of the longer time frame of reciprocity with both behavioral and emotional support. By adhering to the negotiated roles and expectations, both parties are better able to leverage a well-defined and high-quality LMX relationship. Graen and Scandura (1987) note this process typically proceeds sequentially; failure in any phase (e.g., poor performance) may result in the return to the previous phase.

Overall, this role-based model of LMX development suggests that LMX relationships will vary and yet likely develop quickly, then stabilize (Dienesch & Liden, 1986; Graen & Scandura, 1987), with the quality of the relationship typically increasing over time (Liden et al., 1993; Nahrgang et al., 2009; Nahrgang & Seo, 2016). Liden and colleagues (1993) found that perceptions of LMX quality two weeks into the process were predictive of LMX quality at six weeks, and LMX quality at six weeks was predictive of LMX quality at six months. Similarly, Bauer and Green (1996) found that the quality of the relationship at two months was a strong predictor of the relationship quality at six months. Indeed, the quality of the LMX relationship most commonly develops in a positive manner over time before stabilizing.

This LMX relationship development process informs the authentic leader-follower relationship development process in two fundamental ways. The first involves the leader's and follower's decisions to opt into the relationship development process, bringing with them their self-views, personalities, and history. Just as both parties must opt into the role-based LMX relationship development process, leaders and followers who strive for authenticity must embrace situations that are likely to foster more authentic leader-follower relationships. Heightened levels of self-awareness among more authentic leaders (Gardner et al., 2005), allow them to exert greater self-control by pursuing situations that are conducive to conduct that is aligned with core values. Such choices promote feelings of authenticity by the leader, while simultaneously enacting the positive behavior modeling (Gardner et al., 2005; Ilies et al., 2005) that is critical to the development of authentic leader-follower relationships.

The second connection arises from the iterative nature of the interactions between the leader and follower and how they support enhanced clarity in the subsequent relationship. Just as the expectations and role requirements that define the LMX relationship require probing, so too do open and transparent communications that reflect each party's true, inner selves. Through the leader's consistent communication and enactment of her or his values, the follower is likely to perceive greater coherence between who the leader claims to be and how she or he behaves. Common results of this process of positive behavioral modeling include the follower reinforcing the leader's self-views and granting her or him an identity as an authentic leader, while simultaneously inferring permission to claim an identity as an authentic follower. Gardner and colleagues (2005, p. 348) underscore the importance of this process by stating that it is "through their interactions the authentic leader and follower both come to know who they are, and how each impacts the other." Indeed, it is through these transparent, iterative interactions that an "authentic relationship" is formed (p. 348).

The iterative interactions that characterize the development of leader-follower relationships are impacted by the individual attributes and personal identities of leaders and followers. In addition to the individual identities of each party, it has been suggested that the *interpersonal* identity, formed jointly over time, is equally important (DeRue & Ashford, 2010). This perspective posits that leader and follower identities are claimed and granted through repeated interactions. According to this perspective, a social actor initially exhibits a behavior that represents a claim to a leader identity. If this claim is accepted, the target of this claim grants a leader identity to the actor. Moreover, the target may in turn exhibit a behavior that represents a claim to a follower identity. If this claim is accepted, the leader grants the desired follower identity. As this process iterates over time, and these identities are continually claimed and granted, the leader and follower internalize these identities and cement their relationship.

DeRue and Ashford's (2010) model provides insight into the interpersonal processes that are operative in forming authentic leader-follower relationships. While authentic leadership theory suggests that authentic interactions will promote awareness and clarity regarding leader and follower identities, the critical elements of "openness, transparency, loyalty, and trust" (Gardner et al., 2005) embodied in authentic leader-follower relationships reveal inherent limits to their formation. For example, although other leaders selectively disclose, and may at times misrepresent, personal information in claiming a leader identity, leaders who strive for authenticity, provide an open, honest, and balanced self-appraisal in conveying their identities. Thus, whereas a commitment to authenticity constrains the identities that leaders and followers can claim, the absence of such a commitment expands the identity claims that are possible, but at the price of an authentic leader-follower relationship. As such, potential inter- and intrapersonal barriers become evident since the formation of authentic leader-follower relationships requires both the ability and willingness to achieve authenticity on the part of both parties.

As the process of leader and follower identity claiming and granting unfolds, each party attempts to ascertain the extent to which the other party actually possesses the claimed identity. We refer to this process as *verification*. We posit that this relational "authenticating" process of verification grows out of individual self-verification (Swann, 1983). Self-verification assumes that "stable self-views provide people with a crucial source of coherence and continuity," which is useful as individuals engage in social interaction processes to define their identity (Swann & Buhrmester, 2012, p. 407). Some self-verification is undertaken to create self-confirmatory scenarios as individuals prefer interaction partners that confirm their own self-views (Swann & Buhrmester, 2012). However, individuals' self-views may not be accurate, and hence they may not be fully aware of who they are and how they appear to others.

Although verification does not require that all self-views are confirmed to be accurate, self-awareness will heighten the probability that they will be. Persons who claim a leader identity tend to select self-verifying situations to confirm that identity. So, leaders who possess a high degree of self-awareness, as authentic leaders do, will select self-verifying situations and interaction partners that reinforce a relatively accurate self-view. As leaders exhibit the components of authentic leadership (self-awareness, internalized moral code, balanced processing, and relational transparency), the interaction partner develops a perception of coherence between who the leader is and the behaviors exhibited. If the leader exhibits these behaviors and followers detect consistency between these actions and the individual, over time followers are more likely to grant the leader an "authentic" identity. We suggest this continuance of claiming and granting of behaviors that contribute to the identification of the leader as "authentic" is the point where authentic leadership is enacted.

Because it is our intention to examine authentic leader-follower relationships, not just authentic relationships in general, we refer to authentic leadership and authentic followership as arising when the leader-follower relationship has been constructed, and also verified. Figure 8.1 depicts this model of the process whereby authentic leader-follower relationships are developed and verified. As Figure 8.1 reflects, this model integrates the authentic leadership (Gardner et al., 2005), LMX (Graen & Scandura, 1987; Graen & Uhl-Bien, 1995), and identity (DeRue & Ashford, 2010) perspectives on the formation of leader-follower relationships described above. During the role-taking/stranger stage of the LMX process, based on an open and honest self-appraisal, the leader and follower claim and grant their respective identities. However, because the parties are not well acquainted, these identities are only tentatively granted and based primarily on faith that the other party is being genuine. As the relationship matures and the leader and follower move into the role-making/acquaintance phase, both the leader and the follower are in a position to verify their own identity and confirm that the identity claimed by the other party is authentic. Finally, in the role-routinization/maturity phase of LMX development, assuming both the leader and the follower have been authentic in their interactions, an authentic relationship between the parties is solidified. While Figure 8.1 does not reflect the various contextual influences discussed below, the development of authentic leader-follower relationships does require a context that allows for the identification of leader and follower, as well as the verification of authenticity. It is our intention to explicate various contexts that potentially enact barriers to authenticity with a focus on the implications for HRM practices. However, we first discuss the role of boundary conditions and the contextual framework employed to facilitate this theoretical refinement.

BOUNDARY CONDITIONS, AND CONTEXTUAL MODERATORS

Calls for the examination of boundary conditions and context are common in the field of management (Liden & Antonakis, 2009; Walter et al., 2012; Yammarino & Dubinsky, 1994). To facilitate our discussion of potential boundary conditions, we draw from Bacharach's (1989) influential discussion of theory building. Bacharach defines theory as "a statement of relations among concepts within a set of boundary assumptions and constraints" (p. 496). These boundary conditions "set the limitations in applying the theory" (p. 498) and failure to specify a theory's boundaries may result in its overapplication and overstated explanatory power. A theory's boundaries are based on the theorist's assumptions regarding values, time, and space. Assumptions regarding values influence the types of research questions that are selected, examined, and interpreted. Unfortunately, theorists rarely state their value assumptions, and this leads to unresolved debates due to the implicit nature of this type of boundary. Boundary conditions regarding time restrict generalizability based on the assumption that certain phenomena occur in a specific time period. Assumptions based on time are often made more explicit than those of values. An example of a time-based boundary might include theory that is based on a period of time in which a production economy is dominant that would not generalize to an era characterized by a knowledge-based economy. The final assumption that creates theoretical boundaries, and often overlaps with time-based assumptions, pertains to spatial boundaries. Spatial boundaries restrict the application of theory to a specific unit of analysis, such as specific types of organizations. Like time-based assumptions, spatial assumptions are often made more explicit than those based on values. An example of how the boundaries between time and space can overlap is provided by the COVID-19 pandemic. Because it is restricted to a particular time period and its effects are uniquely manifest within particu-

Figure 8.1

Model of the Authentic Leader-Follower Relationships Verification Process

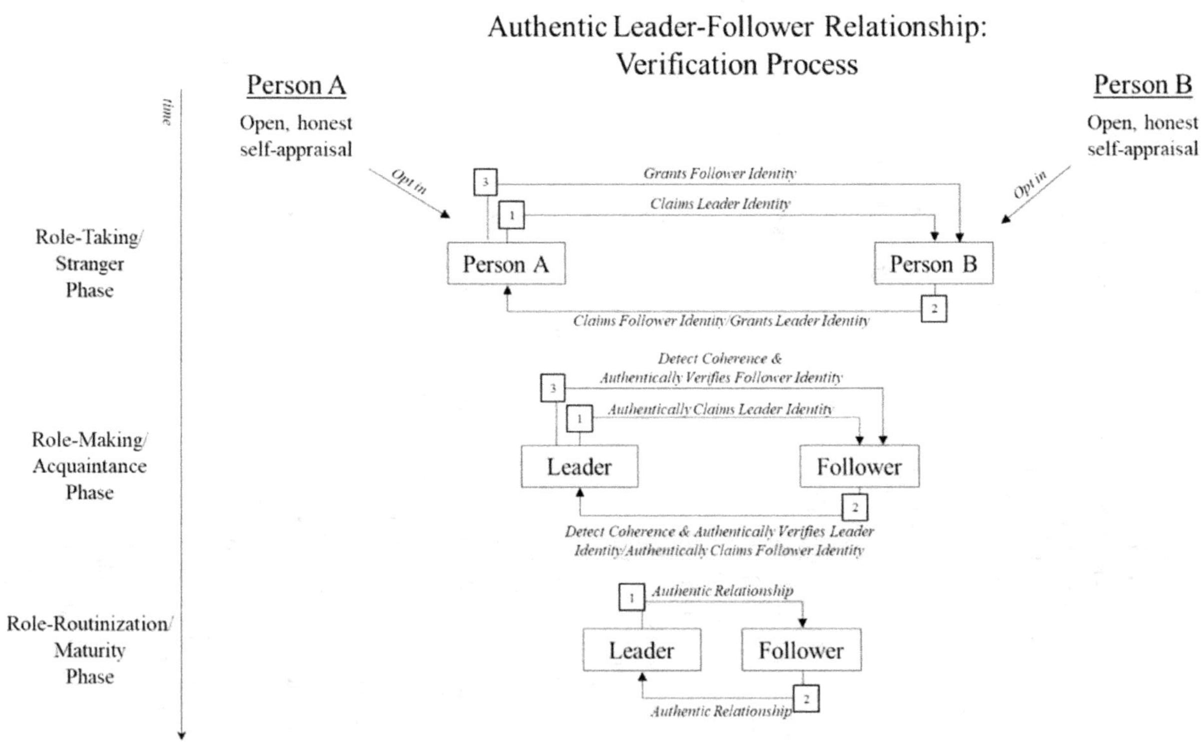

lar organizations to alter how they function, the pandemic can be viewed as creating new boundaries regarding time and space.

As noted above, temporal and spatial based assumptions are made explicit more often than value-based assumptions. However, it is not uncommon for theorists to fail to make any of these types of assumptions explicit. Bacharach (1989) notes that the under-articulation of theoretical assumptions can lead to dire consequences, such as the application and testing of a theory in settings or contexts that are not consistent with the original theory. This, in turn, could result in misinterpretations of results and a field attempting to build upon a foundation that is no longer theoretically or empirically sound. There is also potential for stagnation of a field based on misapplication of the theory; the theory may be overgeneralized, resulting in a subsequent decrease in rigor in the peer-review and critical thought process. Thus, making explicit the assumptions and boundaries of a theory and its application is imperative to the continued development of the associated field of study.

It is important to note that we do not believe the authentic leadership literature necessarily suffers from any of these adverse outcomes. Nor do we believe the field is traveling a path that is strewn with trivial findings destined for scientific gridlock. We do, however, observe that sound science demands that authentic leadership researchers make the assumptions and boundaries of the theory explicit to remove potential obstacles to the development and maturation of the authentic leadership literature.

CONTEXTUAL BARRIERS TO AUTHENTIC LEADERSHIP

We now identify and discuss potential barriers to authentic leadership and an associated set of propositions. Each barrier identified is posited to have an impact on authentic leadership and the development of authentic leader-follower relationships. We anticipate that these barriers will not only have the potential to impact the development of authentic leadership, but also its relationships with HRM practices (e.g., recruitment, selection, evaluation, socialization, training, and development; Karam et al., 2017) and the positive outcomes that have been linked to authentic leadership (e.g., job satisfaction, organizational commitment and organizational citizenship behaviors, work role performance, and firm level performance; Banks et al., 2016; Gardner et al., 2011; Karam et al., 2017). To facilitate the discussion of contextual moderators, we draw upon Gary Johns's (2006, 2017, 2018) framework of contextual factors that influence organizational behavior. As noted in our introduction, Johns identified two distinct levels of context. The *omnibus* context refers to the broadly considered context that comprises many features and particulars (e.g., who, where, when, and why). The *discrete* context refers to the particular, more specific variables that shape behavior or attitudes (e.g., task characteristics, social environment, and physical environment). According to Johns (2006), "discrete context can be viewed as nested within omnibus context such that the effects of omnibus context are mediated by discrete contextual variables or their interactions, thus reflecting Rousseau and Fried's (2001) configurational portrayal of context" (p. 391).

To further explicate the differences between the omnibus and discrete context, as well as the role of boundary conditions, we depict their influence on a focal set of relationships in Figure 8.2. As Figure 8.2 indicates, the boundaries (e.g., assumptions about time, space, and values) designate the conditions under which the relationships posited by the theory are applicable. Within these boundaries, the omnibus and discrete context serve to influence the focal relationships. Note that these boundaries may at times be "fuzzy," as depicted in Figure 8.2. That is, although theoretical boundaries may at times be absolute (in or out; land versus sea), in other cases they may be gradual (land/marsh land/sea; plains/foothills/mountains). As an example of a "fuzzy" temporal boundary, consider the temporal progression of the COVID-19 pandemic. Rather than being a definitive pre- versus post-pandemic boundary, it is more accurate to recognize pre-, during, and post-pandemic stages.

The omnibus context is especially relevant when identifying the boundaries of a theory. For instance, in answer to the "Who?" question in describing the omnibus context, Johns (2006) asserts that there may be some occupations for which a theory applies, and others where it does not. Hence, occupation would serve as a boundary for the theory. With respect to the "Where?" question, Johns suggests that there may be some cultures, industries, or geographic regions within which a theory is more or less applicable. Regarding the "When?" question, he suggests that there may be temporal boundaries (e.g., pre-, during, and post-pandemic) that reflect underlying assumptions about when the posited relationships are present. Finally, Johns asserts that *why* a research question is being investigated (e.g., the rationale for the research) reflects underlying assumptions that may impact how the findings are interpreted.

Note that, consistent with Johns (2006) assertion that the discrete context is nested within the omnibus context, Figure 8.2 depicts the omnibus context as influencing the discrete context. Additionally, the figure indicates that the omnibus context (e.g., the occupation, time period, etc.) may also serve as a direct moderator of the focal set of relationships. Finally, consistent with the preceding discussion of the discrete context, the figure indicates elements of the proximal context that impact the nature of the relationships between the independent, mediating, and dependent variables. Elements of the discrete context identified by Johns (2006) include the task (e.g.,

Figure 8.2

Omnibus Contextual Boundaries and Discrete Contextual Moderators

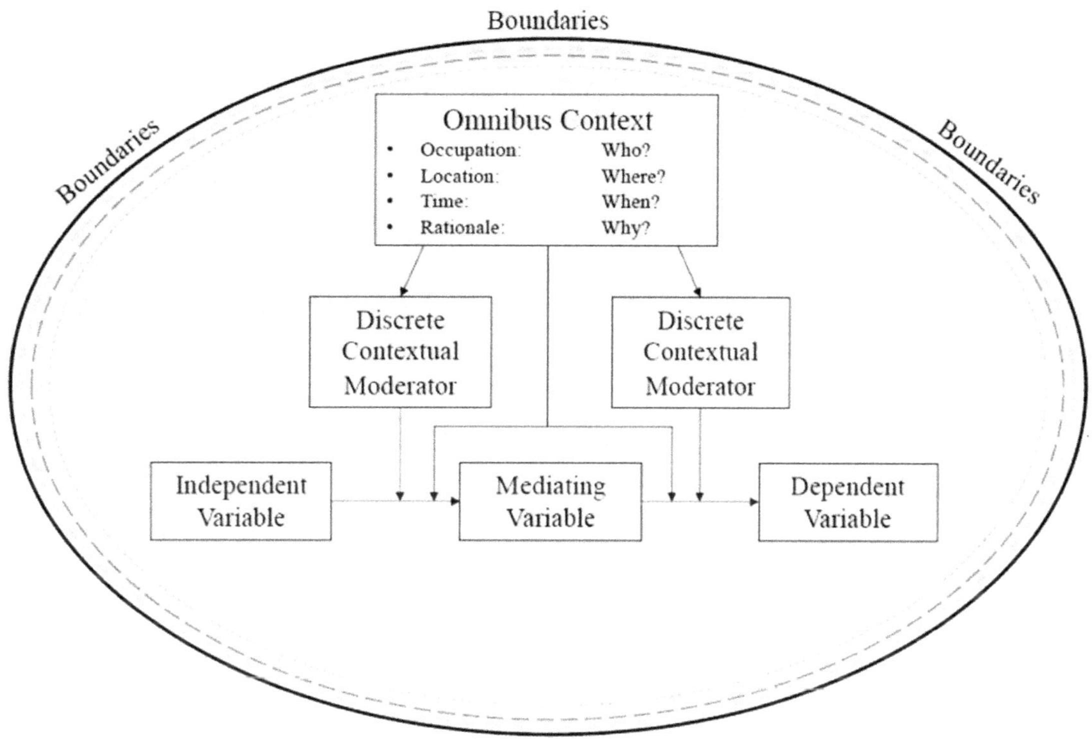

autonomy, uncertainty, accountability, resources), social (e.g., social density, social structure, social influence), and physical (e.g., temperature, light, built environment, décor). In the sections below, we consider how elements of the omnibus and discrete context may emerge as barriers to the formation and continuation of authentic leader-follower relationships.

Omnibus Context

With regard to the omnibus context, we suggest that the boundary conditions of time, physical distance, and cultural friction will have an impact on authentic leadership and the ability to develop authentic leader-follower relationships.

Temporal Boundaries: Insufficient Time

Time is an important contextual variable because it "affects the web of social and economic relationships that surrounds any aspect of organizational behavior" (Johns, 2006, p. 392). Time has implications for authentic leadership as it is required for authentic leader-member relationships to emerge. In particular, as suggested by Figure 8.1, time requirements and constraints have implications for the proposed model of verification of authentic leader and follower identities and the development of authentic leader-follower relationships.

With regard to the development of authentic leader-follower identities and relationships, we assert that the process of verification relies on the knowledge gained over time about the coherence and consistency of the interaction partner's identity. The verification process requires time for a sufficient number of iterative personal interactions between a leader and follower to unfold for attributions to be made. Consider, for example, the popular HRM practice of formalized mentorship programs that pair proteges with assigned mentors (Allen et al., 2004). Though it has long been established that mentoring is related to enhanced work effectiveness (Kram, 1985; Scandura & Williams, 2000), the importance of authenticity to effective mentoring has only recently been made explicit. According to Fries-Britt and Snider (2015, p. 9), "[m]entoring relationships that seek authenticity will strengthen and not diminish over time." As such, temporal restrictions (i.e., inadequate time) that prevent the compilation of enough interactions to develop a sense of coherence and consistency will undermine the utility of mentoring programs in building authentic leader-follower relationships.

As the model depicted in Figure 8.1 indicates, both the process of claiming and granting identities, as well as the verification process, require repeated interactions. For instance, in the role-taking phase of the LMX relationship development process, both parties engage in simple transactional exchanges that primarily serve as a means of discovering the other party's strengths and weaknesses. Though this is a critical phase of relationship development, it is essentially a process of discovery to establish the most basic tenets of the working relationship that are based primarily on economic transactions and hierarchical role-defined behaviors. It is only through repeated interactions and advancement of both the role-making and routinization phases where the relationship extends beyond economic transactions and becomes more personal and revelatory of one's true, inner selves. So, even in situations that may otherwise be conducive to the development of authentic leader-follower relationships (e.g., mentoring assignments), insufficient time for the requisite number of repeated interactions will prevent the formation of an authentic leader-follower relationship. Note that this is an example of a "fuzzy boundary" in that the amount of time that is sufficient for authentic leader-follower relationships to form is not absolute; however, as the amount of available interaction time declines to approach zero, there will clearly be a point where the leader-follower relationship crosses the temporal boundaries of the omnibus context such that the underlying assumptions of authentic leadership theory regarding the formation of authentic relationships no longer apply. Accordingly, we advance:

> **Proposition 1.** The shorter the duration of the leader-follower relationship, the less likely authentic leader-follower relationships will form.

Physical Distance

Physical distance is the first of three, distinctly different forms of distance that we propose as boundaries to authentic leadership. Antonakis and Atwater (2002, p. 684) define physical distance as "how far or how close followers are located from their leader." This is identified as an omnibus contextual boundary because it helps to address the question of *where*, which is an important part of the story a theory should tell (Johns, 2006; Shepherd & Sutcliffe, 2015) and certainly constitutes a spatial boundary (Bacharach, 1989). We assert that a discussion of physical distance has important implications for the proposed model of the verification of authentic leadership and the formation of authentic leader-follower relationships.

To develop authentic leader-follower relationships, the process of claiming and granting leader and follower identities, and verification beyond these claims, requires repeated interactions. As previously noted, authentic relationships generally require more time to develop than the claiming and granting of more general leader-follower identities. If followers are physically located at a distance from their leaders, there is a reduction in exposure of the parties to one another. For instance, in response to the COVID-19 pandemic, many organizations have enacted "work from home" policies whereby employees are not required to physically come to the workplace (Kramer & Kramer, 2020). While flexible job design programs have had so much success that companies are considering permanently implementing work from home options (Brownlee, 2020), they are likely to diminish the types of interaction necessary to establish authentic leader-follower relationships—whether of high LMX or not. Indeed, it may be difficult to not only grant authenticity, but also for leaders and followers to make such claims in the first place. Even in situations that are otherwise conducive to the development of authentic relationships, if the physical distance is great enough, it will become impossible to form the desired authentic relationship. This requires an intentional focus on the onboarding of remote workers, including taking steps to "jumpstart" the leader-follower relationship, to counteract the isolation associated with the physical distancing inherent in remote work (Maurer, 2020).

Notice that our focus here is on the initial formation of the leader-follower relationship; once an authentic relationship has formed, it may be more resistant to the physical distance imposed by environmental challenges such as the COVID-19 pandemic. Thus, we suggest:

> **Proposition 2:** The greater the physical distance between a leader and follower, the more likely too few interactions have transpired to form an authentic relationship.

Cultural Friction

Authentic leadership is considered to be a "root" construct underlying many different positive forms of leadership (Avolio & Gardner, 2005). This characterization as a root construct implies authentic leadership possesses extensive generalizability, such that its application is not limited to a small number of cultures. In fact, extensive research has been completed using samples from around the world, including Australia, Belgium, Brazil, Kenya, China, Germany, Greece, Pakistan, Portugal, the United Kingdom and the United States, to provide evidence for the validity of the authentic leader construct and its most commonly used measure, the Authentic Leadership Questionnaire (Gill & Caza, 2018; Leroy et al., 2015; Leroy et al., 2012; Lyubovnikova et al., 2017; Mehmood et al., 2016; Peus et al., 2012; Rego et al., 2015; Rego et al., 2013; Walumbwa et al., 2008). Additionally, self-concordance, a construct that is fundamental to the notion of authenticity, has been found to be important to well-being in numerous cultures (Sheldon et al., 2004). Despite these preliminary findings, it has been suggested that the manifestation of authenticity, and authentic leadership in particular, may be influenced by national culture, as different cultures contain different display rules that mandate emotional labor in certain situations (Gardner et al., 2009). Thus, consideration of the "who?" component of the omnibus context suggests that cultural differences may serve as a barrier to the realization of authentic leader-follower relationships.

Cultural friction (Shenkar, 2012; Shenkar et al., 2008) is a metaphor based on an encounter of cultural systems that are not in harmonious agreement. This metaphor is receiving increased attention given the globalization of business and extensive interaction of cultures (Chen et al., 2010). In Johns's (2006,) discussion of context, he states that "being an individualist in an individualistic culture might engender different attitudes and behavior than being an individualist in a collectivist culture" (p. 388). Research has shown that Eastern cultures (e.g., China, Japan, Korea, India) are more collectivistic than Western cultures (e.g., United States, Canada, United Kingdom) (Barkema et al., 2015). Additionally, Eastern cultures have different communication styles, attitudes towards the treatment of out-group members, and views on the distance reflected in vertical relationships than do Western cultures (Barkema et al., 2015). These contextual differences, which are broad compared to more specific forms of subcultures, are important to authentic leadership research because culture helps define the self (Erickson, 1994; Mead, 1934).

One particular situation where the importance of cultural awareness and alignment can be clearly seen is the HRM practice of making expatriate leadership assignments. Typically, expatriates who occupy administrative roles are provided with an opportunity to claim a particular identity, such as those associated with leadership and authenticity. However, if such claims are not recognized by the recipient, or worse, the behavior whereby the claim is made is inconsistent with cultural norms, they will not be granted and the identity the expatriate seeks will be denied. An example of this would be an American expatriate in China who strives to lead in a way that is congruent with his/her conception of leadership within an individualistic culture. While this may be successful in a Western country, such as the United States, it will likely not achieve the desired results in China, which embraces Eastern cultural values. Indeed, in China's highly collectivistic culture, the word "self" has a negative connotation that does not exist in individualistic cultures (House et al., 2004). Clearly, exhibiting such ethnocentric and culturally insensitive behavior on the part of the expatriate would make it more difficult to form authentic leader-follower relationships. Ethnocentrism is not limited to multinational firms, however, and we acknowledge that despite calls for greater efforts in diversity, equity, and inclusion efforts in organizations (Rabl et al., 2020), cultural friction remains.

Thus, we expect that in situations characterized by high cultural friction, leader claiming behavior is less likely to be recognized and subsequently granted, halting the process required to claim, grant, and verify identities and develop authentic leader-follower relationships.

> **Proposition 3:** The higher the level of cultural friction between two interaction partners, the less likely leader identity claims will be recognized and granted, and authentic leader-follower relationships will ensue.

Discrete Context

Within the discrete context, we suggest that follower competence, perceived social distance, perceived frequency of leader-follower interaction, virtuality, narcissistic interaction partners, Machiavellian personalities, and psychopathic personalities will serve to impede the development of authentic leader-follower relationships.

Follower Competence

As noted previously, leaders form differential quality relationships with each of their followers, with some relationships being higher-quality and some being lower-quality. The extent to which these relationships differ is referred to as LMX differentiation (Henderson et al., 2009). Even when they are willing to invest in the development of high-quality exchange relationships, leaders may lack the resources (e.g., time, opportunities, funding) to reciprocate and develop multiple social exchanges. As such, leaders are required to make decisions regarding the social exchanges and relationships for which they reciprocate and invest resources. One criterion that leaders consider when making this decision is the follower's capacity to contribute (i.e., competence).

Consistent with Liden and Maslyn's (1998) multidimensional conceptualization of LMX, contribution (i.e., the level of work-related activity each party puts forth) is a critical component of the LMX relationship. One of the most influential predictors of a higher-quality LMX relationship is the follower's competence and ability to perform the job. Indeed, multiple studies have provided support for the strong, positive relationship between follower ability (Day & Crain, 1992; Dockery & Steiner, 1990) and performance. There is also meta-analytic support for a moderately strong, positive relationship between follower competence and LMX quality (Dulebohn et al., 2012; Nahrgang et al., 2009). This evidence underscores the importance of follower's competence and the leader's continued investment in the LMX relationship. It should be noted that follower's competence is not the only predictor of relationship quality, nor do leaders cast aside followers with limited competence. Rather, when resources are limited, leaders may be more likely to invest themselves and their resources in the individuals and relationships that are most likely to yield greater returns. Yu et al. (2018) refer to this approach as the equity perspective of LMX differentiation in workgroups.

Similar to the importance of follower competence in establishing higher-quality LMX relationships, we suggest follower's competence influences the establishment of more authentic leader-follower relationships. While authentic interactions between leaders and moderately competent individuals occur, the continued investment in followers who are the more capable performers fosters more personal disclosure and hence an increased likelihood that leaders will reveal their true inner selves. As such, when followers possess a greater capacity for performance, a more authentic leader-follower relationship is more likely to form. Conversely, low levels of follower ability may serve to block the formation of authentic relationships with the leader. Here, it is important to reiterate that ample evidence from the LMX literature confirms that open and high trust relationships are more likely to emerge when the follower's competence is high (see the meta-analysis by Dulebohn et al., 2012). Accordingly, we advance:

> **Proposition 4:** As the level of follower competence increases, the likelihood of an authentic leader-follower relationship forming rises; low levels of follower competence may serve as a barrier to the formation of an authentic relationship with the leader.

Perceived Social Distance

The second form of distance, as outlined by Antonakis and Atwater (2002), is that of perceived social distance which was originally described by Park (1924, p. 339) as the degree of "understanding and intimacy which characterize personal and social relations." There have since been many refinements to the definition of this construct. Here, we adopt Antonakis and Atwater's (2002, p. 682) definition of social distance in the leadership domain as "the perceived differences in status, rank, authority, social standing, and power, which affect the degree of intimacy and social contact that develop between followers." Note that although Johns (2006) identifies location as an element of the omnibus context, we consider perceived social distance to be part of the discrete context because it reflects the interaction partners' perceptions of social distance, rather than the physical location per se.

Bogardus (1927) was the first scholar to apply the idea of social distance to the leadership domain. He speculated that social distance developed as a result of a follower's recognition of the leader's outstanding achievements. He also notes that if leadership is solely propped up based on excessive recognition and prestige, it may be knocked down by a reduction in this social distance. Indeed, as social distance is reduced, the leader, and all of his/her strengths and weaknesses, become more visible. In contrast to Bogardus's (1927) account of the vulnerability of the leader-follower relationship as it relates to reductions in social distance, Yagil (1998) views such reductions as being beneficial because they grant the leader an opportunity to communicate with followers in an individualized manner. Such customized communication affords the leader an opportunity to tailor the content and delivery of information to meet the needs of an individual, as opposed to attempting to meet the many, often conflicting, needs of the collective group. Additionally, Yagil (1998), in accordance with Aronson et al. (1966), argued that a reduction in social distance may make the leader appear vulnerable, human, and fallible. This humanization, she argues, provides support for the identification process.

We argue that a decrease in social distance demystifies leadership and provides followers with a more realistic, and humanistic understanding of the leader. As discussed previously, more as opposed to less authentic leaders are more likely to select into self-verifying situations that reinforce accurate self-views. A reduction in social distance may provide followers a clearer understanding of these self-views. Additionally, as argued by Yagil (1998), the vulnerability of the leader will aid the claiming and granting process whereby leader-follower identities, as well as authentic identities, are established. In terms of discrete contextual moderators, this discussion suggests that increases in social distance between the leader and follower will have the opposite effect; that is, they will serve to impede the process of forming authentic leader-follower relationships. Accordingly, we advance the following:

> **Proposition 5:** As the perceived social distance increases, the leader's self-views, even when accurate, become less visible, thereby impeding the process where claims of authenticity are made and granted, and hence the development of authentic leader-follower relationships.

Perceived Frequency of Leader-Follower Interaction

The final form of distance, as presented by Antonakis and Atwater (2002, p. 686), involves "the perceived degree to which leaders interact with their followers." While this definition does not reflect the traditional conception of "distance," it is distinctly different from the previously discussed forms of distance. Moreover, it is necessary to understand how psychologically close or distant a leader may be from followers. This necessity becomes apparent when considering that a leader who is physically located in close proximity to followers, but does not frequently interact with them, is not close with them. Conversely, a leader who is physically distant, but interacts frequently with followers, is thus, relatively close to them. Here again, we consider perceived frequency of leader-follower interaction to be an element of the discrete context, rather than the omnibus context, because it is based on perceptions of distance and interaction frequency rather than the actual physical location of the interaction partners.

Frequency of interaction could be influenced by any number of factors. A common explanation for decreased interaction is group size, such that the larger the group, the greater the number of relationships a leader must manage. Yu and colleagues (2018) found that larger groups and the resulting demands on the leader's time and energy enhanced the negative influence of LMX differentiation on group harmony and solidarity. Ashford and Cummings (1985) note that increases in leader-follower interactions could be a result of role ambiguity or inexperienced employees. This demonstrates the impact that followers could have on the frequency of interactions with leaders. However, Antonakis and Atwater (2002) proposed that leaders who possess a high achievement orientation may be susceptible to not only high frequency of contact with followers, but also an increased susceptibility to micromanagement. Moreover, a recent study by Weiss and colleagues (2018) revealed that authentic leadership was related to decreased mental depletion for leaders and that the strength of this relationship increased with more frequent interactions with followers. These findings suggest that both the leader and the follower may serve as a source of not only verification, but also the personal resources necessary to achieve enhanced authenticity. These examples illustrate the roles that both the leader and the follower play in determining the frequency of interaction and suggest that leadership development programs provide clear recommendations related to frequency of interactions between new leaders and followers.

As noted previously, the development of an authentic relationship requires not only time, but repeated interactions. It is through these iterative interactions that leaders and followers come to grant and claim identities, and authentic leader-follower relationships develop. Relationships characterized by infrequent interactions make it less likely that a leader will be verified as authentic. Accordingly, we advance:

> **Proposition 6:** As the frequency of leader-follower interactions declines, it becomes more difficult to form authentic leader-follower relationship decreases.

Virtuality

To date, the extent to which leaders and followers are able to achieve authentic relationships within virtual environments has not been investigated. However, given the rise in virtual work necessitated by the COVID-19 pandemic (Rego et al., 2015; Rego et al., 2013), the potential effects of virtuality on authentic leadership and followership merit examination. The extant literature suggests that virtuality may indeed serve as a barrier to authenticity, as members of virtual teams repeatedly express frustration that their unique contributions are too often ignored or not integrated into team decision making (Gilson et al., 2015; Martins et al., 2004). A recent study by Maynard et al. (2019) of 63 global virtual supply chain teams provides preliminary insight into the extent to which virtuality may serve as a discrete contextual barrier to authentic relationships. This study examined the moderating effects of team virtuality on the relationships between personal and professional familiarity among team members, information elaboration, and both manager-rated team effectiveness and team leader-rated viability. The results revealed that professional familiarity among team members was positively associated with team information elaboration, which in turn was positively related to both team effectiveness and viability. In contrast, personal familiarity was unrelated to information elaboration, perhaps because it is just as likely to lead to process losses due to informal socializing as it is gains. When team virtuality is taken into account, however, these relationships change. Specifically, increasing team virtuality appears to enhance the influence of personal familiarity on information elaboration, thereby reducing the relationship between professional familiarity and information elaboration. The authors speculate that the challenges in virtual settings may constrain the benefits of professional familiarity as team members become increasingly reliant on technology for information exchange. In contrast, in low virtuality contexts, personal familiarity appears to pull members off task, whereas in high virtuality contexts, personal knowledge of other members enhances communication and promotes process gains. One implication for the formation of authentic leader-follower relationships within virtual settings is that such settings may dampen the otherwise positive effects of professional familiarity on information exchange and thereby create fewer opportunities for authentic interactions. In contrast, personal familiarity among leaders and followers may offset virtual barriers to communication and thereby allow more authentic relationships to form.

These findings suggest the importance of developing and emphasizing virtual team-building skills among remote workers. In addition to building these skills, it is also critical for leaders to recognize that time devoted to teambuilding is not "lost" but will pay-off in terms of stronger leader-follower relationships and associated benefits.

> **Proposition 7a:** The relationship between professional familiarity and authentic leader-follower relationships is mediated by information elaboration and moderated by virtuality such that a lack professional familiarity inhibits information elaboration, which in turn discourages the formation of authentic relationships, in high versus low virtual contexts.

> **Proposition 7b:** The relationship between personal familiarity and authentic leader-follower relationships is mediated by information elaboration and moderated by virtuality such that a lack of personal familiarity inhibits greater information elaboration, which in turn discourages the formation of authentic relationships, in low versus high virtual contexts.

Interaction Partners With "Dark Triad" Personalities

Of the offensive but non-pathological personalities, three that are known as the "dark triad" have gained the most attention in the literature: narcissism, Machiavellianism, and psychopathy (Paulhus & Williams, 2002). Each of these personality types involve, to varying degrees, "a socially malevolent character with behavior tendencies towards self-promotion, emotional coldness, duplicity, and aggressiveness" (Paulhus & Williams, 2002, p. 557). O'Boyle and colleagues (2012) meta-analyzed these dark personalities and found that all were positively related to counterproductive work behavior, and most were related to diminished job performance. Though this study identified conditions where dark personalities may be advantageous to organizations, the authors compared the recruitment and selection of individuals with these dark personalities to welcoming likeable serial killers into the organization or recommending smoking as a weight loss strategy, where the costs would clearly outweigh the potential benefits. While each of these personality types share similar characteristics and conceptual overlap, each is considered to be its own distinct construct, as has been repeatedly shown in the literature (O'Boyle et al., 2012). Despite these distinctions, we anticipate that each will have a similar effect on authentic leader-follower relationships, so we combine them in the following propositions.

Judge et al. (2006, p. 762) reference the APA's *Diagnostic and Statistical Manual of Mental Disorders* (IV) in describing narcissists as individuals who are "preoccupied with fantasies of unlimited success, believe they are special and unique, require excessive admiration, have a sense of entitlement, are interpersonally exploitative, lack empathy, and are arrogant and haughty." Research on leaders who possess narcissistic personalities indicates that they are more likely to engage in abusive leadership (Tepper, 2007; Tepper, 2016; Tepper et al., 2017). Although some research suggests that there are positive aspects of narcissism that may enhance leadership effectiveness, provided the leader can suppress more negative aspects of this trait (Paunonen et al., 2006), "even at their best, narcissistic leaders are bound to leave damaged … relationships in their wake" (Rosenthal & Pittinsky, 2006, p. 619).

Most of the attention devoted to narcissism within the leadership literature focuses on the influence of this trait on leader behavior, and the influence of narcissism as a trait of the leader and/or follower on leader-follower relationships has received less attention. Because narcissists are interpersonally exploitative, they form relationships to take advantage of others and use them for achieving the unlimited success they believe they deserve. So, although narcissists may be able to successfully form relationships in the short-term, the quality of these relationships tends to erode over time (Campbell et al., 2002).

While narcissists face major challenges within interpersonal relationships, particularly long-term relationships, perhaps the intrapersonal relationship with the self is most challenging. This is because they have a difficult time reconciling the differences between their inflated and idealized self-views and their actual selves (Rosenthal & Pittinsky, 2006). Such distorted self-views reflect a lack of self-awareness and balanced processing, which are core components of authentic leadership (Gardner & Cogliser, 2018). Together, their warped sense of reality and inaccurate self-views thwart the development of authentic relationships.

Machiavellianism is widely considered to be an especially manipulative personality trait; it reflects a social strategy where the actor treats others entirely as a means to an end. Similar to narcissism, the study of Machiavellianism within the leadership literature has focused primarily on the leader (Den Hartog & Belschak, 2012; Furnham et al., 2013), and the role Machiavellianism plays within the leader-follower relationship has received less attention. Machiavellianism has been associated with a desire to excel at the expense of others (Stewart & Stewart, 2006) and it is negatively related to agreeableness (Paulhus & Williams, 2002). These findings suggest that Machiavellian individuals simply seek to use individuals to achieve their desired goals and that Machiavellian personalities will impede the development of authentic relationships. Due to the manipulative tendencies associated with this trait, we propose that the relational transparency component of authentic leadership will be neglected because being open and forthcoming with information provides others with material that could potentially be used for personal gain at the leader's expense. This lack of openness will, in turn, provide few opportunities for the verification of authentic leader and follower identities.

The final dark triad personality trait that may impede the development of authentic leader-follower relationships is psychopathy, which is characterized by low empathy and high levels of anxiety (Paulhus & Williams, 2002). The relevant literature for our interests here pertains to non-clinical (as opposed to clinically diagnosed), and emergent, psychopathy. While psychopathy theory is at an early stage of development, there are already important implications of this trait for leader-follower relationships. Empirical research has demonstrated that psychopathy is associated with a hostile and dominant interpersonal style (Blackburn, 1998). This dominant interpersonal style, coupled with a lack of empathy, reflects a very individualistic perspective that is not conducive to forming and sustaining relationships.

These findings suggest that psychopathy on the part of leaders and/or followers will inhibit the development of authentic relationships. Given the lack of empathy, we posit that the persons who possess this trait will be unable to engage in balanced processing due to an inability to take multiple perspectives into account when making decisions. Moreover, when highly biased information processing is paired with the dominant interpersonal style that characterizes psychopathy, we anticipate the granting and claiming process of verification that is required for the formation of authentic leader-follower relationships will be impaired. Thus, we advance:

> **Proposition 8a:** Narcissistic, Machiavellian, and psychopathic interaction partners are less likely to engage in verification or grant authentic leader and/or follower identities to others.

> **Proposition 8b:** Narcissistic, Machiavellian, and psychopathic interaction partners are less likely to be granted authentic leader and/or follower identities by others because they are: a) less likely to be perceived as authentic, and b) less likely to seek authentic leader and follower identities.

DISCUSSION AND FUTURE RESEARCH

Reviews of the authentic leadership literature suggest that to advance the field and sustain the interest of researchers and practitioners, theoretical refinements and more rigorous empirical research are needed (Banks et al., 2016; Gardner et al., 2011; Lemoine et al., 2019); thus, further explication of the contextual moderators of the theory is required. While this chapter constitutes a step in that direction, it is important to recognize other efforts in this regard. Hinojosa and colleagues (2014), for example, examined boundary conditions at the individual level as suggested by various attachment styles, as well as at the organizational level in the form of organizational culture. Gardner and colleagues (2009) likewise incorporated several contextual elements in their examination of authentic leadership and emotional labor. More recently, Sendjaya et al. (2016) examined the role of Machiavellianism as a barrier to the development of leader morality. While results of this study are consistent with our propositions regarding Machiavellianism, further research is needed to flesh out the impact of this and the other traits that make up the dark triad on authentic leadership.

It is our intention to build upon and expand these initial considerations of contextual barriers to further advance authentic leadership theory. By making the boundary conditions for the theory more explicit, we seek to replace the implicit assumption that authentic leadership is achievable in any context, with greater recognition of the limits of this form of leadership. Ignoring these limits and perpetuating this unrealistic assumption could retard the development of authentic leadership theory (Alvesson & Einola, 2019). Making the boundary conditions and discrete contextual moderators known may help scholars avoid potential impediments to the theory's maturation.

To this point, the processes whereby authentic leader-follower relationships develop has not been fully explicated. Drawing upon DeRue and Ashford's (2010) model of claiming and granting behaviors that produce leader and follower identities, as well as Graen and Scandura's (1987) model of the stages of LMX development, we have attempted to further clarify these relational processes by identifying potential obstacles to the development of authentic leader-follower relationships and also noting implications for HRM practices. Nevertheless, this is a preliminary effort and hence more work in this direction is needed, as several questions about such processes remain unanswered. For example, as is the case for DeRue and Ashford's (2010) and Graen and Scandura's (1987) models, our model is dyadic in nature. Is an expanded model of claiming and granting behaviors for leader and follower identities and/or LMX development that reflects interactions among multiple parties (e.g., groups) needed for more complex work settings? If so, how would this process unfold in comparison to the dyadic process we described? Is the leader verified in the same way and over the same timeline as in a dyadic relationship? And how does this process change when developing an authentic leader-follower relationship and not just a leader-follower relationship? Given the number of unanswered questions, it is clear that future refinements and extensions of the proposed model are necessary.

Future research on authentic relationships should continue to focus on both the roles of the leader and follower (Hernandez et al., 2011). Throughout much of our discussion, an implicit assumption is made that the leader makes an initial claim to a leader identity that is then granted by the follower. Further examination of the initial steps in this process, as well as the process whereby leaders grant follower identities, is required. Additionally, how are follower behaviors selected to claim certain identities within the authentic relationship? For example, Carsten et al. (2010) found that the identities of followers and their behaviors are socially constructed and depend heavily on contextual factors. Similar insights into the processes whereby authentic followership (Avolio & Reichard, 2008; Gardner et al., 2005; Karam et al., 2017; Leroy et al., 2015) develops is merited.

Though we make progress in this chapter, continued integration and empirical investigation of the intersection of authentic leadership and HRM is warranted. Karam and colleagues (2017) made conceptual progress in their integration of authentic leadership and high-performance HR practices as a means to explain work engagement. In a recent study, Luu (2020) provided empirical evidence of a positive relationship between authentic leadership and job crafting; that relationship was moderated by HR system flexibility such that it was more positive when HR flexibility was low versus high. Luu (2020) suggested that lower levels of HR system flexibility meant that followers were more reliant on their leaders for resources. Moreover, because more authentic leaders served as better sources for resource support, they elicited greater motivation to engage in job crafting behaviors to maximize performance. Although these findings provide preliminary evidence that HR practices have important implications for authentic leadership, further empirical research is needed. Also, as the workplace becomes increasingly relational and knowledge-based (Grant & Parker, 2009), combined with the effects of digital technology growth in the workplace quite broadly (Cortellazzo et al., 2019) and the very specific COVID-19 pandemic-related shifts to work arrangements (Spurk & Straub, 2020), accumulating evidence of effective HR practices and authentic leadership is critical to effective workplace functioning.

Other potential barriers to authenticity related to the diversity of interaction partners also merit attention. For instance, the types of friction we describe as arising from cultural differences might emerge from other types of demographic differences as well. Indeed, given that people prefer interaction partners that confirm their own self-views (e. g., Pelled & Xin, 2000) it seems likely that similarity across dimensions such as gender, race, ethnicity, and gender identity, might enhance authentic relationships, whereas differences in these attributes might create a boundary condition for the formation of authentic relationships. Research on diversity in the workplace suggests that group members who are demographically different will have lower relationship quality because of in-group favoritism and a dislike for those who are different (DiTomaso et al., 2007; Luksyte & Avery, 2015; et al., 2002). A relational approach which guides practitioners into taking into account biases that emerge from demographic similarities and differences is warranted (Tsui et al., 1995; Tsui & O'Reilly, 1989).

Likewise, a focus on representation of one's individual ethnicity within the organization, especially for those whose demographic group faces under-representation, is called for (King et al., 2017). Because the dominant culture in the U.S. workplace has developed to support the behavior and preferences of White men (Kimmel, 2013), women and minoritized workers may find it difficult to be or may choose not to be "authentic" at work (especially in terms of relational transparency) when interacting with persons from the majority group (Storberg-Walker & Gardiner, 2017). The behavior of "code-switching" (McCluney et al., 2019) in which one alters one's appearance, style of speech, expressions, and/or behavior in ways that optimize the comfort levels of others is one example. It is not known if these pressures limit the formation of authentic leader-follower relationships.

Further consideration of research findings from the diversity, equity, and inclusion literature might also be taken into account in terms of gender and racial stereotypes. A contextual moderator might exist such that pressure to conform to the stereotype of the "ideal leader" and pressure to not conform to the gender and racial stereotypes of one's group (i.e., stereotype threat; Spencer et al., 2016) would impact a leader's ability and motivation to engage in relational transparency. These pressures would be stronger the more "under-represented" an individual is within the organization (Ely, 1995). Such considerations are illustrative of the kinds of factors that future researchers could explore in an effort to better explicate contextual influences on authentic leader-follower relationships.

The field of HRM is uniquely positioned to generate these kinds of insights, as evidenced by multiple conceptual examinations of the intersection of authentic leadership and HRM. According to Boekhorst (2015), as the organization's workforce continues to become increasingly diverse, the need to foster a climate of inclusivity is paramount and one of the most effective ways to do this is for authentic leadership (i.e., characterized by relational transparency), organizational reward systems (i.e., those which promote knowledge sharing), and workforce composition (i.e., degree of cultural homogeneity) to work in concert with another to reinforce the practice of workplace inclusion. Further supporting the complementary role of authentic leadership and HRM is the work of Gill and colleague's (2018). These authors suggest that managers who display authentic leadership behaviors can strengthen HR systems by promoting greater authenticity, consistency, and legitimacy of HRM practices. Continued research regarding specific HR practices and their interaction with authentic leadership is necessary for the advancement of both theory and practice.

CONCLUSION

Well-developed theories make it a point to make their assumptions explicit (Bacharach, 1989). By providing some preliminary articulation of the boundary conditions and contextual moderators of authentic leadership, we believe research in this area can avoid the traps of over-application, less rigorous peer review processes, and other missteps that impair the maturation of theory. We hope future researchers will build upon the initial work presented here to systematically advance authentic leadership theory and promote rigorous empirical investigations. Doing so would constitute a significant step toward realizing the considerable promise of authentic leadership theory.

REFERENCES

Allen, T. D., Eby, L. T., Poteet, M. L., Lentz, E., & Lima, L. (2004). Career benefits associated with mentoring for proteges: A meta-analysis. *Journal of Applied Psychology, 89*, 127–136. https://doi.org/10.1037/0021-9010.89.1.127

Alvesson, M., & Einola, K. (2019). Warning for excessive positivity: Authentic leadership and other traps in leadership studies. *The Leadership Quarterly, 30*, 383–395. https://doi.org/10.1016/j.leaqua.2019.04.001

Antonakis, J., & Atwater, L. (2002). Leader distance: A review and a proposed theory. *The Leadership Quarterly, 13*, 673–704. https://doi.org/10.1016/S1048-9843(02)00155-8

Aronson, E., Willerman, B., & Floyd, J. (1966). The effect of a pratfall on increasing interpersonal attractiveness. *Psychonomic Science, 4*, 227–228. https://doi.org/10.3758/BF03342263

Ashford, S. J., & Cummings, L. L. (1985). Proactive feedback seeking: The instrumental use of the information environment. *Journal of Occupational Psychology, 58*, 67–79. https://doi.org/10.1111/j.2044-8325.1985.tb00181.x

Avolio, B. J., & Gardner, W. L. (2005). Authentic leadership development: Getting to the root of positive forms of leadership. *The Leadership Quarterly, 16*, 315–338. https://doi.org/10.1016/j.leaqua.2005.03.001

Avolio, B. J., & Reichard, R. J. (2008). The rise of authentic followership. In R. E. Riggio, I. Chaleff, & J. Lipman-Blumen (Eds.), *The art of followership: How great followers create great leaders and organizations.* (pp. 325–337). Jossey-Bass.

Avolio, B. J., & Walumbwa, F. O. (2014). Authentic leadership theory, research, and practice: Steps taken and steps that remain. In D. Day (Ed.), *The Oxford handbook of leadership and organizations* (pp. 331–356). Oxford University Press. https://doi.org/10.1093/oxfordhb/9780199755615.001.0001

Azanza, G., Moriano, J. A., & Molero, F. (2013). Authentic leadership and organizational culture as drivers of employees' job satisfaction. *Journal of Work and Organizational Psychology, 29*, 45–50. https://doi.org/10.5093/tr2013a7

Bacharach, S. B. (1989). Organizational theories: Some criteria for evaluation. *Academy of Management Review, 14*, 496–515. https://doi.org/10.5465/AMR.1989.4308374

Banks, G. C., McCauley, K. D., Gardner, W. L., & Guler, C. E. (2016). A meta-analytic review of authentic and transformational leadership: A test for redundancy. *The Leadership Quarterly, 27*, 634–652. https://doi.org/10.1016/j.leaqua.2016.02.006

Barkema, H. G., Chen, X.-P., George, G., Luo, Y., & Tsui, A. S. (2015). West meets East: New concepts and theories. *Academy of Management Journal, 58*, 460–479. https://doi.org/10.5465/amj.2015.4021

Bauer, T. N., & Green, S. G. (1996). Development of leader–member exchange: A longitudinal test. *Academy of Management Journal, 39*, 1538–1567. https://doi.org/10.2307/257068

Blackburn, R. (1998). Psychopathy and personality disorder: Implications of interpersonal theory. In D. J. Cooke, A. E. Forth, & R. D. Hare (Eds.), *Psychopathy: Theory, research, and implications for society* (pp. 269–301). Kluwer. https://doi.org/10.1007/978-94-011-3965-6_13

Boekhorst, J. A. (2015). The role of authentic leadership in fostering workplace inclusion: A social information processing perspective. *Human Resource Management, 54*, 241–264. https://doi.org/10.1002/hrm.21669

Bogardus, E. S. (1927). Leadership and social distance. *Sociology and Social Research, 12*, 173–178.

Brownlee, D. (2020). Twitter, Square announce work from home forever option: What are the risks? *Forbes*. Retrieved May 18, 2020, from https://www.forbes.com/sites/danabrownlee/2020/05/18/twitter-square-announce-work-from-home-forever-optionwhat-are-the-risks/#6170660e2565

Campbell, W. K., Foster, C. A., & Finkel, E. J. (2002). Does self-love lead to love for others? A story of narcissistic game playing. *Journal of Personality and Social Psychology, 83*, 340–354. https://doi.org/10.1037/0022-3514.83.2.340

Carsten, M. K., Uhl-Bien, M., West, B. J., Patera, J. L., & McGregor, R. (2010). Exploring social constructions of followership: A qualitative study. *The Leadership Quarterly, 21*, 543–562. https://doi.org/10.1016/j.leaqua.2010.03.015

Chen, G., Kirkman, B. L., Kim, K., Farh, C. I. C., & Tangirala, S. (2010). When does cross-cultural motivation enhance expatriate effectiveness? A multilevel investigation of the moderating roles of subsidiary support and cultural distance. *Academy of Management Journal, 53*, 1110–1130. https://doi.org/10.5465/AMJ.2010.54533217

Clapp-Smith, R., Vogelgesang, G. R., & Avey, J. B. (2009). Authentic leadership and positive psychological capital: The mediating role of trust at the group level of analysis. *Journal of Leadership & Organizational Studies, 15*, 227–240. https://doi.org/10.1177/1548051808326596

Cortellazzo, L., Bruni, E., & Zampieri, R. (2019). The role of leadership in a digitalized world: A review. *Frontiers in Psychology, 10*, 1938. https://doi.org/10.3389/fpsyg.2019.01938

Day, D. V., & Crain, E. C. (1992). The role of affect and ability in initial exchange perceptions. *Group and Organization Management, 17*, 380–397. https://doi.org/10.1177/1059601192174005

Den Hartog, D. N., & Belschak, F. D. (2012). Work engagement and Machiavellianism in the ethical leadership process. *Journal of Business Ethics, 107*, 35–47. https://doi.org/10.1007/s10551-012-1296-4

DeRue, D. S., & Ashford, S. J. (2010). Who will lead and who will follow? A social process of leadership identity construction in organizations. *The Academy of Management Review, 35*, 627–647. https://doi.org/10.5465/amr.35.4.zok627

Dienesch, R. M., & Liden, R. C. (1986). Leader-member exchange model of leadership: A critique and further development. *Academy of Management Review, 11*, 618–634. https://doi.org/10.5465/AMR.1986.4306242

DiTomaso, N., Post, C., & Parks-Yancy, R. (2007). Workforce diversity and inequality: Power, status, and numbers. *Annual Review of Sociology, 33*, 473–501. https://doi.org/10.1146/annurev.soc.33.040406.131805

Dockery, T. M., & Steiner, D. D. (1990). The role of the initial interaction in leader-member exchange. *Group & Organization Studies, 15*, 395–413. https://doi.org/10.1177/105960119001500405

Dulebohn, J. H., Bommer, W. H., Liden, R. C., Brouer, R. L., & Ferris, G. R. (2012). A meta-analysis of antecedents and consequences of leader-member exchange. *Journal of Management, 38*, 1715–1759. https://doi.org/10.1177/0149206311415280

Ely, R. J. (1995). The power of demography: Women's social construction of gender identity at work. *Academy of Management Journal, 38*, 589–634. https://doi.org/10.2307/256740

Erickson, R. J. (1994). Our society, our selves: Becoming authentic in an inauthentic world. *Advanced Development Journal, 6*, 27–39.

Fries-Britt, S., & Snider, J. (2015). Mentoring outside the line: The importance of authenticity, transparency, and vulnerability in effective mentoring relationships. *New Directions for Higher Education, 171*, 3–11. https://doi.org/10.1002/he.20137

Furnham, A., Richards, S. C., & Paulhus, D. L. (2013). The dark triad of personality: A 10 year review. *Social and Personality Psychology Compass, 7*, 199–216. https://doi.org/10.1111/spc3.12018

Gardner, W. L., & Avolio, B. J. (1998). The charismatic relationship: A dramaturgical perspective. *Academy of Management Review, 23*, 32–58. https://doi.org/10.5465/AMR.1998.192958

Gardner, W. L., Avolio, B. J., Luthans, F., May, D. R., & Walumbwa, F. (2005). "Can you see the real me?" A self-based model of authentic leader and follower development [Article]. *The Leadership Quarterly, 16*, 343–372. https://doi.org/10.1016/j.leaqua.2005.03.003

Gardner, W. L., & Cogliser, C. C. (2018). "Walking the talk" alone: Leading and following authentically in an inauthentic world. *The Journal of Character & Leadership Development, 5*, 45–56. https://jcli.scholasticahq.com/article/5031-walking-the-talk-alone-leading-and-following-authentically-in-an-inauthentic-world

Gardner, W. L., Cogliser, C. C., Davis, K. M., & Dickens, M. P. (2011). Authentic leadership: A review of the literature and research agenda. *The Leadership Quarterly, 22*, 1120–1145. https://doi.org/10.1016/j.leaqua.2011.09.007

Gardner, W. L., Fischer, D., & Hunt, J. G. (2009). Emotional labor and leadership: A threat to authenticity? *The Leadership Quarterly, 20*, 466–482. https://doi.org/10.1016/j.leaqua.2009.03.011

Gerstner, C. R., & Day, D. V. (1997). A meta-analytic review of leader-member exchange theory. *Journal of Applied Psychology, 82*, 827–844. https://doi.org/10.1037/0021-9010.82.6.827

Gill, C., & Caza, A. (2018). An investigation of authentic leadership's individual and group influences on follower responses. *Journal of Management, 44*, 530–544. https://doi.org/10.1177/0149206314566461

Gill, C., Gardner, W., Claeys, J., & Vangronsvelt, K. (2018). Using theory on authentic leadership to build a strong human resource management system. *Human Resource Management Review, 28*, 304–318. https://doi.org/10.1016/j.hrmr.2018.02.006

Gilson, L. L., Maynard, M. T., Young, N. C. J., Vartianen, M., & Hakonen, M. (2015). Virtual teams research: 10 years, 10 themes, and 10 opportunities. *Journal of Management, 41*, 1313–1337. https://doi.org/10.1177/0149206314559946

Graen, G. B., & Scandura, T. A. (1987). Toward a psychology of dyadic organizing. *Research in Organizational Behavior, 9*, 175–208. http://terriscandura.com/redesign/wp-content/uploads/2017/08/Toward-a-Psychology-of-Dyadic-Organizing-Graen-Scandura87.pdf

Graen, G. B., & Uhl-Bien, M. (1995). Relationship-based approach to leadership: Development of leader-member exchange (LMX) theory of leadership over 25 years: Applying a multi-level multi-domain perspective. *The Leadership Quarterly, 6*, 219–247. https://doi.org/10.1016/1048-9843(95)90036-5

Grant, A. M., & Parker, S. K. (2009). Redesigning work design theories: The rise of relational and proactive perspectives. *The Academy of Management Annals, 3*, 317–375. https://doi.org/10.1080/19416520903047327

Guerrero, S., Lapalme, M.-È., & Séguin, M. (2015). Board chair authentic leadership and nonexecutives' motivation and commitment. *Journal of Leadership & Organizational Studies, 22*, 88–101. https://doi.org/10.1177/1548051814531825

Henderson, D. J., Liden, R. C., Glibkowski, B. C., & Chaudhry, A. (2009). LMX differentiation: A multilevel review and examination of its antecedents and outcomes. *The Leadership Quarterly, 20*, 517–534. https://doi.org/10.1016/j.leaqua.2009.04.003

Hernandez, M., Eberly, M. B., Avolio, B. J., & Johnson, M. D. (2011). The loci and mechanisms of leadership: Exploring a more comprehensive view of leadership theory. *The Leadership Quarterly, 22*, 1165–1185. https://doi.org/10.1016/j.leaqua.2011.09.009

Hinojosa, A. S., Davis McCauley, K., Randolph-Seng, B., & Gardner, W. L. (2014). Leader and follower attachment styles: Implications for authentic leader–follower relationships. *The Leadership Quarterly, 25*, 595–610. https://doi.org/10.1016/j.leaqua.2013.12.002

House, R. J., Hanges, P. J., Javidan, M., Dorfman, P. W., & Gupta, V. (2004). *Culture, leadership, and organizations. The GLOBE Study of 62 Societies*. SAGE.

Ilies, R., Morgeson, F. P., & Nahrgang, J. D. (2005). Authentic leadership and eudaemonic well-being: Understanding leader-follower outcomes. *The Leadership Quarterly, 16*, 373–394. https://doi.org/10.1016/j.leaqua.2005.03.002

Iszatt-White, M., & Kempster, S. (2018). Authentic leadership: Getting back to the roots of the 'root construct'? *International Journal of Management Reviews, 21*, 356–369. https://doi.org/10.1111.ijmr.12193

Johns, G. (2006). The essential impact of context on organizational behavior. *Academy of Management Review, 31*, 386–408. https://doi.org/10.5465/AMR.2006.20208687

Johns, G. (2017). Reflections on the 2016 decade award: Incorporating context in organizational research. *The Academy of Management Review, 42*, 577–595. https://doi.org/10.5465/amr.2017.0044

Johns, G. (2018). Advances in the treatment of context in organizational research. *Annual Review of Organizational Psychology and Organizational Behavior*, 21–46. https://doi.org/10.1146/annurev-orgpsych-032117-104406

Judge, T. A., LePine, J. A., & Rich, B. L. (2006). Loving yourself abundantly: Relationship of the narcissistic personality to self- and other perceptions of workplace deviance, leadership, and task and contextual performance. *Journal of Applied Psychology, 91*, 762–776. https://doi.org/10.1037/0021-9010.91.4.762

Karam, E. P., Gardner, W. L., Gullifor, D. P., Tribble, L. L., & Li, M. (2017). Authentic Leadership and High-Performance Human Resource Practices: Implications for Work Engagement. In *Research in Personnel and Human Resources Management* (pp. 103–153). https://doi.org/10.1108/s0742-730120170000035004

Kernis, M. H., & Goldman, B. M. (2006). A multicomponent conceptualization of authenticity: Theory and research. In M. P. Zanna (Ed.), *Advances in experimental social psychology* (Vol. 38, pp. 283–357). Academic Press. https://doi.org/10.1016/S0065-2601(06)38006-9

Kimmel, M. S. (2013). *Angry white men: American masculinity at the end of an era*. Nation Books.

King, E., Dawson, J., Jensen, J., & Jones, K. (2017). A socioecological approach to relational demography: How relative representation and respectful coworkers affect job attitudes. *Journal of Business and Psychology, 32*, 1–19. https://doi.org/10.1007/s10869-016-9439-8

Kram, K. E. (1985). Improving the mentoring process. *Training and Development Journal, 39*, 40, 42–43.

Kramer, A., & Kramer, K. Z. (2020). The potential impact of the Covid-19 pandemic on occupational status, work from home, and occupational mobility. *Journal of Vocational Behavior, 119*, 103442. https://doi.org/10.1016/j.jvb.2020.103442

Lemoine, G. J., Hartnell, C. A., & Leroy, H. (2019). Taking stock of moral approaches to leadership: An integrative review of ethical, authentic, and servant leadership. *Academy of Management Annals, 13*, 148–187. https://doi.org/10.5465/annals.2016.0121

Leroy, H., Anseel, F., Gardner, W. L., & Sels, L. (2015). Authentic leadership, authentic followership, basic need satisfaction, and work role performance: A cross-level study. *Journal of Management, 41*, 1677–1697. https://doi.org/10.1177/0149206312457822

Leroy, H., Palanski, M. E., & Simons, T. (2012). Authentic leadership and behavioral integrity as drivers of follower commitment and performance. *Journal of Business Ethics, 107*, 255–264. https://doi.org/10.1007/s10551-011-1036-1

Liden, R. C., & Antonakis, J. (2009). Considering context in psychological leadership research. *Human Relations, 62*, 1587–1605. https://doi.org/10.1177/0018726709346374

Liden, R. C., & Maslyn, J. M. (1998). Multidimensionality of leader-member exchange: An empirical assessment through scale development. *Journal of Management, 24*, 43–72. https://doi.org/10.1016/S0149-2063(99)80053-1

Liden, R. C., Wayne, S. J., & Stilwell, D. (1993). A longitudinal study of the early development of leader-member exchanges. *Journal of Applied Psychology, 78*, 662–674. https://doi.org/10.1037/0021-9010.78.4.662

Luksyte, A., & Avery, D. R. (2015). Exploring burnout and work-family facilitation as factors influencing why and when relational demography diminishes employee citizenship. *Journal of Occupational and Organizational Psychology, 88*, 750–772. https://doi.org/10.1111/joop.12096

Luu, T. T. (2020). Linking authentic leadership to salespeople's service performance: The roles of job crafting and human resource flexibility. *Industrial Marketing Management, 84*, 89–104. https://doi.org/10.1016/j.indmarman.2019.06.002

Lyubovnikova, J., Legood, A., Turner, N., & Mamakouka, A. (2017). How authentic leadership influences team performance: The mediating role of team reflexivity. *Journal of Business Ethics, 141*, 59–70. https://doi.org/10.1007/s10551-015-2692-3

Martins, L. L., Gilson, L. L., & Maynard, M. T. (2004). Virtual teams: What do we know and where do we go from here? *Journal of Management, 30*, 805–835. https://doi.org/10.1016/j.jm.2004.05.002

Maurer, R. (2020). Virtual onboarding of remote workers more important than ever: The power of connection during this time cannot be overstated. Retrieved September 15, 2020, from https://www.shrm.org/resourcesandtools/hr-topics/talent-acquisition/pages/virtual-onboarding-remote-workers.aspx

Maynard, M. T., Mathieu, J., Gilson, L. L., Sanchez, D. R., & Dean, M. A. (2019). Do I really know you and does it matter? Unpacking the relationship between familiarity and information elaboration in global virtual teams. *Group & Organization Management, 44*, 3–37. https://doi.org/10.1177/1059601118785842

McCluney, C. L., Robotham, K., Lee, S., Smith, R., & Durkee, M. (2019). The costs of code-switching. *Harvard Business Review*. https://hbr.org/2019/11/the-costs-of-codeswitching

Mead, G. H. (1934). *Mind, self, and society from the standpoint of a social behaviorist*. University of Chicago Press.

Mehmood, Q., Hamstra, M. R. W., Nawab, S., & Vriend, T. (2016). Authentic leadership and followers' in-role and extra-role performance: The mediating role of followers' learning goal orientation. *Journal of Occupational and Organizational Psychology, 89*, 877–883. https://doi.org/10.1111/joop.12153

Nahrgang, J. D., Morgeson, F. P., & Ilies, R. (2009). The development of leader-member exchanges: Exploring how personality and performance influence leader and member relationships over time. *Organizational Behavior and Human Decision Processes, 108*, 256–266. https://doi.org/10.1016/j.obhdp.2008.09.002

Nahrgang, J. D., & Seo, J. J. (2016). How and why high leader-member exchange (LMX) relationships develop: Examining the antecedents of LMX. In T. N. Bauer & B. Erdogan (Eds.), *The Oxford handbook of leader-member exchange* (pp. 87–117). Oxford University Press.

O'Boyle, E. H., Jr., Forsyth, D. R., Banks, G. C., & McDaniel, M. A. (2012). A meta-analysis of the Dark Triad and work behavior: A social exchange perspective. *Journal of Applied Psychology, 97*, 557–579. https://doi.org/10.1037/a002567910.1037/a0025679.supp

Park, R. E. (1924). The concept of social distance as applied to the study of racial attitudes and racial relations. *Journal of Applied Sociology, 8*, 339–344.

Pastor Álvarez, A., Molero Alonso, F., Bardera Mora, M. d. P., & Moriano León, J. A. (2019). Authentic leadership and its relationships with work engagement and organizational citizenship behaviors in military units: The role of identification as a mediating variable. *Military Psychology, 31*, 412–424. https://doi.org/10.1080/08995605.2019.1646078

Paulhus, D., L., & Williams, K. M. (2002). The dark triad of personality: Narcissism, Machiavellianism, and psychopathy. *Journal of Research in Personality, 36*, 556–563. https://doi.org/10.1016/S0092-6566(02)00505-6

Paunonen, S. V., Lönnqvist, J.-E., Verkasalo, M., Leikas, S., & Nissinen, V. (2006, 10//). Narcissism and emergent leadership in military cadets. *The Leadership Quarterly, 17*, 475–486. https://doi.org/10.1016/j.leaqua.2006.06.003

Pelled, L. H., & Xin, K. R. (2000). Relational demography and relationship quality in two cultures. *Organization Studies, 21*, 1077–1094. https://doi.org/10.1177/0170840600216003

Peus, C., Wesche, J., Streicher, B., Braun, S., & Frey, D. (2012, 05/15/). Authentic leadership: An empirical test of its antecedents, consequences, and mediating mechanisms. *Journal of Business Ethics, 107*, 331–348. https://doi.org/10.1007/s10551-011-1042-3

Rabl, T., del Carmen Triana, M., Byun, S.-Y., & Bosch, L. (2020). Diversity management efforts as an ethical responsibility: How employees' perceptions of an organization integration and learning approach to diversity affect employee behavior. *Journal of Business Ethics, 161*, 531–550. https://doi.org/10.1007/s10551-018-3849-7

Rahimnia, F., & Sharifirad, M. S. (2015). Authentic leadership and employee well-being: The mediating role of attachment insecurity. *Journal of Business Ethics, 132*, 363–377. https://doi.org/10.1007/s10551-014-2318-1

Rego, A., Reis Júnior, D., & Pina e Cunha, M. (2015). Authentic leaders promoting store performance: The mediating roles of virtuousness and potency. *Journal of Business Ethics, 128*, 617–634. https://doi.org/10.1007/s10551-014-2125-8

Rego, A., Vitória, A., Magalhães, A., Ribeiro, N., & e Cunha, M. P. (2013). Are authentic leaders associated with more virtuous, committed and potent teams? *The Leadership Quarterly, 24*, 61–79. https://doi.org/10.1016/j.leaqua.2012.08.002

Rosenthal, S. A., & Pittinsky, T. L. (2006). Narcissistic leadership. *The Leadership Quarterly, 17*, 617–633. https://doi.org/10.1016/j.leaqua.2006.10.005

Rousseau, D. M., & Fried, Y. (2001). Location, location, location: Contextualizing organizational research. *Journal of Organizational Behavior, 22*, 1–13. https://doi.org/10.1002/job.78

Scandura, T. A., & Williams, E. A. (2000). Research methodology in management: Current practices, trends, and implications for future research. *Academy of Management Journal, 43*, 1248–1264. https://doi.org/10.5465/1556348

Sendjaya, S., Pekerti, A., Härtel, C., Hirst, G., & Butarbutar, I. (2016). Are authentic leaders always moral? The role of Machiavellianism in the relationship between authentic leadership and morality. *Journal of Business Ethics, 133*, 125–139. https://doi.org/10.1007/s10551-014-2351-0

Sheldon, K. M., Elliot, A. J., Ryan, R. M., Chirkov, V., Kim, Y., Wu, C., Demir, M., & Sun, Z. (2004). Self-concordance and subjective well-being in four cultures. *Journal of Cross-Cultural Psychology, 35*, 209–233. https://doi.org/10.1177/0022022103262245

Shenkar, O. (2012). Cultural distance revisited: Towards a more rigorous conceptualization and measurement of cultural differences. *Journal of International Business Studies, 43*, 1–11. https://doi.org/10.1057/jibs.2011.40

Shenkar, O., Luo, Y., & Yeheskel, O. (2008). From "distance" to "friction": Substituting metaphors and redirecting intercultural research. *Academy of Management Review, 33*, 905–923. https://doi.org/10.5465/AMR.2008.34421999

Shepherd, D. A., & Sutcliffe, K. M. (2015). The use of anthropomorphizing as a tool for generating organizational theories. *The Academy of Management Annals, 9*, 97–142. https://doi.org/10.5465/19416520.2015.1011510

Sidani, Y. M., & Rowe, W. G. (2018). A reconceptualization of authentic leadership: Leader legitimation via follower-centered assessment of the moral dimension. *The Leadership Quarterly, 29*, 623–636. https://doi.org/10.1016/j.leaqua.2018.04.005

Spencer, S. J., Logel, C., & Davies, P. G. (2016, 2016/01/04). Stereotype Threat. *Annual Review of Psychology, 67*(1), 415–437. https://doi.org/10.1146/annurev-psych-073115-103235

Spurk, D., & Straub, C. (2020). Flexible employment relationships and careers in times of the COVID-19 pandemic. *Journal of Vocational Behavior, 119*. https://doi.org/10.1016/j.jvb.2020.103435

Stewart, A. E., & Stewart, E. A. (2006, Fal 2006). The preference to excel and its relationship to selected personality variables. *The Journal of Individual Psychology, 62*, 270–284. https://doi.org/10.1037/t06561-000

Storberg-Walker, J., & Gardiner, R. A. (2017). Authentic leadership in HRD - Identity matters! Critical explorations on leading authentically. *Advances in Developing Human Resources, 19*, 350-361. https://doi.org/10.1177/1523422317728731

Swann, W. B., Jr. (1983). Self-verification: Bringing social reality into harmony with the self. In J. R. Suls & A. G. Greenwald (Eds.), *Psychological perspectives on the self* (Vol. 2, pp. 33–66). Erlbaum.

Swann, W. B., Jr., & Buhrmester, M. D. (2012). Self-verification: The search for coherence. In M. R. Leary & J. P. Tangney (Eds.), *Handbook of self and identity* (2nd ed., pp. 405–424). The Guilford Press.

Tepper, B. J. (2007). Abusive supervision in work organizations: Review, synthesis, and research agenda. *Journal of Management, 33*, 261–289. https://doi.org/10.1177/0149206307300812

Tepper, B. J. (2016). Abusive supervision in work organizations: Review, synthesis, and research agenda. *Journal of Management, 33*, 261–289. https://doi.org/10.1177/0149206307300812

Tepper, B. J., Simon, L., & Park, H. M. (2017). Abusive supervision. *Annual Review of Organizational Psychology and Organizational Behavior, 4*, 123–152. https://doi.org/10.1146/annurev-orgpsych-041015-062539

Tsui, A. S., Ashford, S. J., St. Clair, L., & Xin, K. R. (1995). Dealing with discrepant expectations: Response strategies and managerial effectiveness. *Academy of Management Journal, 38*, 1515–1543. https://doi.org/10.2307/256842

Tsui, A. S., & O'Reilly, C. A., III. (1989). Beyond simple demographic effects: The importance of relational demography in superior-subordinate dyads. *Academy of Management Journal, 32*, 402–423. https://doi.org/10.2307/256368

Van de Ven, A. H. (2007). *Engaged scholarship: A guide for organizational and social research*. Oxford University Press.

Walter, F., Cole, M. S., der Vegt, G. S. v., Rubin, R. S., & Bommer, W. H. (2012, 2012/10/01/). Emotion recognition and emergent leadership: Unraveling mediating mechanisms and boundary conditions. *The Leadership Quarterly, 23*, 977–991. https://doi.org/https://doi.org/10.1016/j.leaqua.2012.06.007

Walumbwa, F. O., Avolio, B. J., Gardner, W. L., Wernsing, T. S., & Peterson, S. J. (2008). Authentic leadership: Development and validation of a theory-based measure. *Journal of Management, 34*, 89–126. https://doi.org/10.1177/0149206307308913

Wei, F., Li, Y., Zhang, Y., & Liu, S. (2018). The interactive effect of authentic leadership and leader competency on followers' job performance: The mediating role of work engagement. *Journal of Business Ethics, 153*, 763–773. https://doi.org/10.1007/s10551-016-3379-0

Weiss, H. M., & Cropanzano, R. (1996). *Affective events theory: A theoretical discussion of the structure, causes and consequences of affective experiences at work* (Vol. 18). JAI Press. https://doi.org/10.1016/j.leaqua.2017.09.002

Weiss, M., Kolbe, M., Grote, G., Spahn, D. R., & Grande, B. (2018, June 1). We can do it! Inclusive leader language promotes voice behavior in multi-professional teams. *The Leadership Quarterly, 29*, 389–402. https://doi.org/https://doi.org/10.1016/j.leaqua.2017.09.002

Weiss, M., Razinskas, S., Backmann, J., & Hoegl, M. (2018). Authentic leadership and leaders' mental well-being: An experience sampling study. *The Leadership Quarterly, 29*, 309–321. https://doi.org/10.1016/j.leaqua.2017.05.007

Yagil, D. (1998). Charismatic leadership and organizational hierarchy: Attribution of charisma to close and distant leaders. *The Leadership Quarterly, 9*, 161–176. https://doi.org/10.1016/S1048-9843(98)90003-0

Yagil, D., & Medler-Liraz, H. (2013). Moments of truth: Examining transient authenticity and identity in service encounters. *Academy of Management Journal, 56*, 473–497. https://doi.org/10.5465/amj.2011.0252

Yammarino, F. J., & Dubinsky, A. J. (1994). Transformational leadership theory: Using levels of analysis to determine boundary conditions. *Personnel Psychology, 47*, 787–811. https://doi.org/10.1111/j.1744-6570.1994.tb01576.x

Yu, A., Matta, F. K., & Cornfield, B. (2018). Is leader-member exchange differentiation beneficial or detrimental for group effectiveness? A meta-analytic investigation and theoretical integration. *Academy of Management Journal, 61*, 1158–1188. https://doi.org/10.5465/amj.2016.1212

CHAPTER 9

ENOUGH ALREADY!

The Role of Authentic Leadership in Improving the Management of Workplace Harassment in Organizations

James M. Schmidtke and Fred O. Walumbwa

ABSTRACT

Harassment continues to be a significant problem in organizations. Research on harassment in organizations—whether directed toward legally protected groups or more general workplace harassment, suggests that leadership plays a key role in the management and reduction of such behaviors. However, there are no theoretical frameworks for understanding how leadership affects the management and prevalence of harassment in organizations. In this paper, we develop a theoretical framework of the relation between authentic leadership and the policies and practices designed to manage workplace harassment. We review the relevant leadership research to develop this model that incorporates both theories and dimensions of authentic leadership as well as behaviors that are aimed at reducing the frequency of harassment in the workplace.

Leadership:
Leaders, Followers, and Context, pp. 219–254

It has been 30 years since Anita Hill brought the issue of sexual harassment, and general workplace harassment, to the public consciousness and stimulated the discussion of work environments and employee treatment. It has also generated a plethora of research designed to examine issues related to this phenomena. Unfortunately, there has been minimal progress in eliminating such behavior in the workplace (Quick & McFadyen, 2017; Robotham & Cortina, 2019). In 1992, 10,532 complaints were made to the Equal Employment Opportunities Commission (EEOC) regarding harassment based upon sex; in 2019 there were 12,739 complaints (EE0C, 2019a, 2019b). Similarly, harassment complaints based upon race were 5,783 in 1997 and 8682 in 2019 (EEOC, 2019c). While the relative percent of cases per workforce has decreased, the absolute number of cases remains high suggesting that organizations still have much work to do to eradicate harassment. This may be particularly concerning considering that the majority of targets do not make formal complaints (Bergman et al., 2002). Further, Robotham and Cortina (2019) suggest that while policies and practices designed to deter harassment are commonplace, they are not achieving their goals.

Harassment, broadly defined as negative interpersonal interactions that create an intimidating or hostile work environment, which can lead to adverse job conditions or outcomes (Bowling & Beehr, 2006; Rospenda & Richman, 2004), has received significant research attention in the past two decades including multiple meta-analyses and reviews, examining the antecedents and consequences of harassment (Bowling & Beehr, 2006; Dhanani & LaPalme, 2019; Fitzgerald & Cortina, 2018; McCord et al., 2018; Neall & Tuckey, 2014). This research has focused mainly on one of two forms of harassment: one that is geared toward legally protected groups (e.g., sexual or racial harassment) and the second often termed "workplace harassment," which specifically excludes behaviors that are directed toward legally protected groups. Further, research in this area tends to focus on a specific type of harassment (e.g., sexual harassment, racial harassment) rather than harassment in the aggregate. One reason for this focused research is that it reflects the way federal and state agencies track harassment claims and it makes obtaining certain types of data easier. A second reason is that these categories reflect salient dimensions of targets' identities and is often a feature on which harassers focus.

It is important to recognize that workplace harassment is both a legal construct and a social/psychological phenomenon. According to the U.S. EEOC, harassment is defined as unwelcomed conduct directed toward members of a protected class ("Harassment," n.d.). However, many states expand the federal standard to include general behavior that threatens, intimidates, or puts a person's safety at risk regardless of membership in particular social categories (Gilani et al., 2014). In state laws, these behaviors are referred to as either workplace harassment or bullying. As a social/psychological experience, harassment can be defined as unwanted behavior at work that targets see as either offensive or threatening, and damage their well-being and interfere with the ability to perform their job (Fitzgerald et al., 1997). This definition focuses on individuals' reactions to harassment situations. These two standpoints are often conflated. Leaders may believe that creating policies that shield organizations against legal liability will eliminate workplace harassment. Similarly, individuals may label every negative interpersonal interaction as harassment.

LEADERSHIP GOALS

One reason this distinction between the two constructs is important is that it suggests three leadership goals for managing harassment (see Figure 9.1). First, they must reduce the prevalence of harassment to protect their members from harm and promote a climate of inclusivity and respect. Workplace harassment negatively affects both individuals and the organizations for which they work. Individuals who are harassed often experience negative health consequences such as anxiety, depression, and stress (Bowling & Beehr, 2006; Matthiesen & Einarsen, 2004; Raver & Nishii, 2010), which can lead to burnout and withdrawal. Ultimately, these individual consequences can lead to low productivity and organizational commitment (Bowling & Beehr, 2006) as well as absenteeism and turnover (Merkin & Shah, 2014; Nielsen & Einarsen, 2012). In addition, organizations with toxic environments may have more difficulty recruiting new employees. Consequently, leaders need to take actions that minimize the occurrence of incidents of workplace harassment.

Second, leaders must help increase understanding and sensitivity to the issues surrounding workplace harassment. This helps employees identify and address situations that might be perceived as harassment. It also helps potential targets of harassment differentiate between behaviors that are legitimately harassing and those that are simply negative, awkward, or uncomfortable. This is not to suggest that targets, who are experiencing harassment, should not seek support. However, individuals who file claims without merit as a result of negative interpersonal interactions create other potential problems. They burden the reporting system slowing down the investigations of valid harassment incidents. In addition, they may undermine the legitimacy of other targets' genuine claims and affect the others' willingness to take those claims seriously. Finally, they can damage the reputation of the accused individuals particularly when such accusations are unfounded.

Figure 9.1

Proposed Framework for the Relation Between Authentic Leadership and the Management of Workplace Harassment

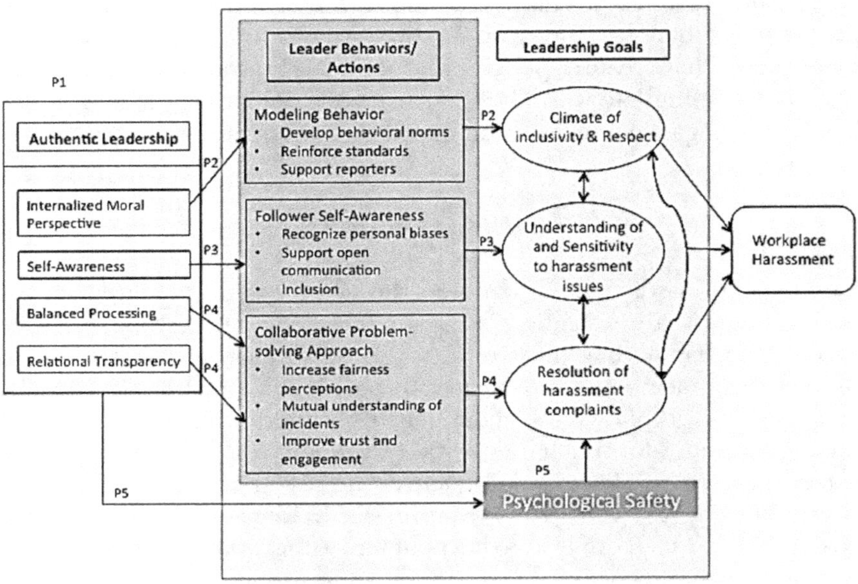

Finally, leaders must protect the organization from legal liability through the successful resolution of harassment complaints. Although most instances of workplace harassment may not result in legal claims, cases that end up in court can be expensive. In 2019, the EEOC received approximately 72,675 complaints involving harassment and discrimination (EEOC, 2019d). Of the claims that were successful, employers paid $347 million to plaintiffs (EEOC, 2019d). It should be noted that these are only federal claims; they do not include state lawsuits or cases settled out of court. Most claims are made at the state level since filing federal claims is more expensive. Further, these amounts do not include legal fees. Thus, organization leaders must consider the potential legal costs in managing situations involving workplace harassment.

The current chapter focuses on the social/psychological definition of sexual harassment for two reasons. First, policies and practices aimed at protecting organizations against legal liability often do not address the fundamental causes of harassment. A common approach to managing workplace harassment is zero tolerance policies (Borgwald & Theixos, 2013; Stockdale et al., 2004). The specific content of these policies varies but the essential component is that any validated claim or harassment will result in the perpetrators' termination. Legal experts found that these policies do shield organizations from legal liability, but they do little to reduce harassment or address the underlying issues (Firestone & Harris, 2003; Stockdale et al., 2004). Second, legally defined harassment is a subset of socially/psychologically defined harassment; any organizational practice that effectively resolves harassment claims or reduces their occurrence should be consistent with legal requirements for protecting organizations. Since this definition of harassment relies on targets' perceptions, it may lead to complaints that do not violate company policy. It might include comments or behaviors that individuals find offensive or irritating that do not constitute workplace harassment or warrant disciplinary action. As suggested earlier, managers still need to process these complaints and resolve them.

PREVIOUS RESEARCH ON WORKPLACE HARASSMENT

Research on harassment in organizations suggests that contextual factors such as the climate and leadership are associated with the prevalence of such behavior in organizations (Hart et al., 2018; Porter et al., 2018). For example, Fitzgerald et al. (1999) found organizational tolerance for sexual harassment was positively related to reported prevalence of harassment. Individuals reported experiencing sexual harassment in organizations that were perceived to be more tolerant. Further, meta-analyses revealed a positive relation between workplace aggression (including harassment) and poor leadership (e.g., Hershcovis et al., 2007).

Given that leadership is associated with the incidents of aggressive and antisocial behaviors such as harassment, it is likely that leaders' actions play a key role in the reduction of such behaviors (Hart et al., 2018). For example, some literature on leadership and aggression suggests that leaders help reduce negative behaviors by modeling appropriate behaviors (Brown et al., 2005). However, modeling appropriate behavior is only one aspect of managing harassment. Leaders must not only model appropriate behavior, they must also respond to incidents of harassment. Leaders' responses to incidents of harassment might influence organizational members' interpretation of events, what they learn from the event, and how they behave in the future (Hart et al., 2018). If leaders do not adequately address harassment incidents, organizational members may perceive organizational initiatives (e.g., discipline, training, etc.) as inauthentic and an attempt to avoid liability.

Further, specific leadership behaviors might deter future incidents of workplace harassment. Unfortunately, there are few theoretical frameworks for understanding leadership's influence on workplace harassment and few empirical studies examining the relation between leaders' behaviors and the prevalence of harassment. Porter et al. (2018) examined the relation between leader-member exchange and workplace bullying. Higher quality relationships between leaders and followers were associated with fewer incidents of workplace bullying. Perry et al. (2020) proposed a model of the relation between inclusive leadership and sexual harassment. They theorized that inclusive leadership behaviors would lead to higher feelings of inclusion and lower levels of sexual harassment. Two limitations of these papers are that they focus on specific forms of harassment and focus on only one of the leadership goals for harassment. We believe that a more comprehensive model of the relation between leadership and workplace harassment makes a stronger contribution to both the leadership and workplace harassment literatures. For example, although researchers have highlighted the importance of leadership in deterring or eliminating workplace harassment (Hart et al., 2018; Hershcovis et al., 2007; Perry et al., 2020; Porter et al., 2018), to date, relatively few studies have examined how specific leadership behaviors deter or eliminate workplace harassment. Given the costs, prevalence, and negative consequences associated with workplace harassment (Bowling & Beehr, 2006; Dhanani & LaPalme, 2019; Fitzgerald & Cortina, 2018; McCord et al., 2018; Quick & McFadyen, 2017), organizational leaders desperately require a comprehensive framework that they can use as a guide to reduce workplace harassment. From a theoretical perspective, such a comprehensive model will advance the literature by highlighting links between specific leader actions and goals related to workplace harassment.

Accordingly, we propose and develop a theoretical framework of the relationship between leadership and harassment highlighting potential mediators of these relationships. Specifically, our model links the components of authentic leadership to specific managerial behaviors and actions that can help individuals to better understand harassment and effectively resolve complaints as well as foster more inclusive and respectful environments (see Figure 9.1). As the model shows, the components of authentic leadership specify particular leader behaviors and actions that are related to the three leadership goals previously identified. Achieving these goals will lead to organizations that have fewer incidents of workplace harassment.

Before discussing the specifics of the model, we note that our model encompasses both forms of harassment: those that are directed toward legally protected groups and more general workplace harassment. More specifically, and for the purposes of this chapter, we conceptualize workplace harassment as verbal or physical behavior that is perceived negatively by the target and leads to emotional, psychological, or work-related harm. Important in this conceptualization is that the determination is based upon targets' perceptions and not harassers' intentions. The degree of harm may range from feeling offended to the target experiencing mental or physical health related problems. This definition includes behaviors focused on the target's membership in a particular social category as well as general negative interpersonal behaviors. Further, our definition specifically excludes egregious harassment incidents (e.g., threats of violence) that would be considered criminal as well as other explicit criminal behaviors such as assault or rape. We exclude criminal behavior, as these would likely be initially referred to law enforcement for investigation before determining if organizational leaders would need to become involved.

THE ROLE OF AUTHENTIC LEADERSHIP

There is extensive literature examining theories of leadership as well as their influence on important organizational outcomes, such as performance, attitudes, organizational citizenship behaviors and organizational culture (e.g., Avolio et al., 2004; Avolio et al., 2009; Hoch et al., 2018; Lemoine et al., 2019; Zhang et al., 2019). Research has also examined the effects of leadership on broader issues such as organizational decline, crisis, and several counterproductive and antisocial behaviors (e.g., Mackey et al., 2017; Ng & Feldman, 2015; O'Reilly & Banki, 2016; Tepper et al., 2017; Zhang et al., 2019).

Authentic leadership, ethical leadership and servant leadership behaviors all underscore the importance of ethical behavior (Hoch et al., 2018). Consequently, we would expect that these theories would be most relevant for managing workplace harassment. The focus of each of these forms of leadership is slightly different. Ethical leadership focuses on the character and behavior of the leader as a role model for followers (Brown et al., 2005) while servant leadership focuses on followers and their developmental needs (Stone et al., 2004). Authentic leadership considers the character and behavior of leaders and the needs of the organization and followers (Avolio et al., 2004). Further, authentic leadership is considered the foundation for positive leadership theories such as ethical and servant leadership (Avolio & Gardner, 2005). Consequently, we utilize an authentic leadership lens as it is the most likely to provide a more systematic integrative framework that explains how specific leadership behaviors can help leaders accomplish the three goals for managing workplace harassment. Authentic leadership refers to

> a pattern of leader behavior that draws upon and promotes both positive psychological capacities and a positive ethical climate, to foster greater self-awareness, an internalized moral perspective, balanced processing of

> information, and relational transparency on the part of leaders working with followers, fostering positive self-development. (Walumbwa et al., 2008, p. 94)

Further, authentic leaders have been described as architects of real change (Misati & Walumbwa, 2018) and advocates of others' well-being and act in line with others' needs and interests (Braun et al., 2018). Therefore, we believe that this leadership perspective has the potential to deter harassment in organizations. While the term "change agent" is often associated with transformational leadership, authentic leaders are theorized to be self-aware, transparent, to act in line with their core beliefs, and to not succumb to pressure to act otherwise. These qualities distinguish authentic leadership from transformational leadership. For instance, whereas transformational leaders focus on leading followers to a higher purpose through the use of an inspiring vision and challenging goals (Burns, 1978), authentic leaders focus on leading followers to achieve higher levels of authenticity by leading with purpose, values, and integrity (Avolio et al., 2004; Gardner et al., 2005).

In addition, authentic leaders suspend judgment and keep their options open as they solicit, carefully listen to, and genuinely consider alternative points of view. Theoretically, they are not afraid to take action on what they believe is right (Avolio et al., 2004; Gardner et al., 2005). In other words, authentic leaders know and act upon their true values and beliefs and help others do the same. They solicit group members' participation in decision making and facilitate active interactions among group members (Avolio et al., 2004; Avolio & Walumbwa, 2014). Such leaders are legitimate and trustworthy role models who set the stage for the cultivation of followers' positive attitudes and behaviors through their positive role modeling (Gardner et al., 2005; Luthans & Avolio, 2003). Authentic leadership encompasses leaders' integrity—that is, the alignment of leaders' espoused values, principles, and conduct with those that they enact—which influences greater self-awareness, an internalized moral perspective, balanced processing of information, and relational transparency (Walumbwa et al., 2008). When followers perceive that leaders embody integrity through their words and actions, they are more likely to adopt strategies and behaviors modeled by leaders (Bandura, 1977, 1986). As such, authentic leadership is a valuable leadership lens to examine the relation between leadership and harassment in organizations. There is some research evidence suggesting that this specific leadership behavior may play a key role in reducing antisocial behaviors such as harassment (e.g., Laschinger & Read, 2016; Warszewska-Makuch et al., 2015).

AUTHENTIC LEADERSHIP COMPONENTS

Authentic leadership is conceptualized to have four components including an internalized moral perspective, self-awareness, balanced processing, and relational transparency (Walumbwa et al., 2008). An *internalized moral perspective* refers to leaders being guided by their internal morals and standards, as opposed to being pressured into decisions by others (Gardner et al., 2005). Authentic leaders are more apt to resist social pressures and act in accord with their internal values and beliefs (Avolio & Walumbwa, 2014). Accordingly, employees are expected to identify more with leaders when they witness them engaging in consistent, values-based behaviors (Gardner et al., 2005; Ilies et al., 2005). The second dimension of authentic leadership, *self-awareness* involves leaders understanding their own strengths and weaknesses, their motivations, beliefs, and feelings, and knowing how their actions affect those around them. Leaders with high self-awareness are able to draw upon this accurate self-knowledge (Campbell et al., 1996) while knowing how others are likely to perceive their actions. Gardner et al. (2005) theorized that authenticity requires leaders to possess a solid base of emotional, moral, and cognitive development. The third dimension, *balanced processing*, refers to the ability to objectively analyze information from many sources before making a decision. Authentic leaders are willing to seek out information from others that challenge their positions because they are not manipulative or defensive. Employees are more likely to take ownership of ideas and their work because of their solicited voice in the decisions that affect them (Wagner et al., 2003). Finally, the fourth dimension, *relational transparency*, refers to leaders openly sharing their true feelings and thoughts. Transparency in thoughts and information sharing encourages openness by others and leads to more trusting relationships (Gardner et al., 2005). Transparency and openness also helps to reduce hidden agendas between people and builds more effective relationships (Dirks & Ferrin, 2002). As shown in Figure 9.1, these components form the foundation of our model.

AUTHENTIC LEADERSHIP AND CHALLENGES OF WORKPLACE HARASSMENT

A growing number of empirical studies have reported that authentic leadership is related to a variety of follower attitudes and behaviors at different levels of analysis (see Banks et al., 2016; Hoch et al., 2018; Lemoine et al., 2019, for both qualitative and quantitative reviews). Avolio and colleagues (e.g., Avolio et al., 2004; Gardner et al., 2005) suggested that social learning theory (Bandura, 1977, 1986) provides one of the main theoretical explanations for the influence of authentic leadership on followers. Specifically, Gardner et al. (2005) noted that authentic leaders model "positive values, psychological states, behaviors, and self-development" (p. 358). Followers observe leaders engaging in transparent decision-making, showing self-awareness, and displaying integrity and commitment to deep-seated values. These engender trust in the leader and allow the leader to be seen as credible, prestigious, and trustworthy—thereby gaining followers' attention and motivation to learn from them (Bandura, 1977, 1986). Authentic leaders are in a prime position for followers to emulate their motivations, goals, values, emotions, and behaviors, and influence followers' positive behaviors (Avolio & Walumbwa, 2014). Empirical studies support the theoretical argument that through authentic leaders' positive modeling, followers are more likely to reach several outcomes, including performing organizational citizenship behaviors, being more satisfied and committed to the organization, demonstrating team and supervisor helping behaviors, being more creative and performing productively (Braun & Peus, 2018; Hirst et al., 2016; Leroy et al., 2013; Ribeiro et al., 2020).

Lack of Clearly Defined Standards of Conduct

One of the reasons why workplace harassment is often ignored or mismanaged is that individuals lack understanding of the social dynamics that might lead one to perceive a behavior as harassing. Currently, there are no studies that have examined harassers' actual intent; it is inferred based upon contextual factors. Thus, it may be possible that harassers are unaware that their behavior is offensive or of the negative effects it has on targets. Many workplace policies fail to recognize the indeterminate and perceptual nature of harassment. The social/psychological definition suggests that harassment does not consist of objective standards but rather target perceptions. The *same* behavior (e.g., jokes or lewd comments) may be harassing in some situations (when it is unwelcomed) but not in others. Individual factors often affect whether a particular situation is considered harassment. For example, research has indicated that gender and status often affect individuals' perceptions of sexual harassment (see Rotundo et al., 2001 for a meta-analysis). Women and individuals with low organizational status are more likely than men and high-status individuals to perceive social sexual situations as harassment. This difference is greater for less severe forms of harassment (e.g., sexual comments, jokes, etc.). This is particularly important considering that surveys (e.g., Morral et al., 2018) indicate that the most common types of harassing behaviors experienced are verbal while the least common types experienced are physical.

In some cases, certain categories of behavior may always be unambiguously unacceptable, such as lewd language or gestures. The determination of suitability for other types of behavior will be completely dependent on the context and specific individuals involved. Take for example humor a normal part of many social interactions. Humor can play an important role in the workplace: it can used to communicate; it can help build social relationships and group cohesiveness; and it can also relieve stress and improve creativity (Romero & Cruthirds, 2006). In some cases, jokes can be interpreted as bullying or harassing when they are targeted at either particular social groups or some individual flaw or weakness (Hodson et al., 2010). Whether humor is harassment or not, will be dependent, in large part, on the perspective of the individuals present in the situation and the context. Consequently, in some cases, harassers and bystanders in the work environment have no idea that they have offended the target or how.

Problems of Traditional Policies and Procedures

Traditional policies and practices created to manage workplace harassment (i.e., prevent, report, discipline, etc.) are designed to deter harassment and shield the employer from legal liability. This approach often creates divisions between targets and alleged harassers and fails to promote a deeper understanding or sensitivity of the issues. Several researchers (Bies & Tyler, 1993; Sitkin & Bies, 1994; Sitkin & Roth, 1993) suggest that legalistic remedies are limited in their ability to promote harmony. These efforts fail to change organizational culture because they do not help individuals learn why particular behaviors are problematic nor do they address the broader workplace environment. Policies and procedures in and of themselves do not create organizational climates. Rather, it is the interaction of behaviors, policies and organizational values and culture. Organizational leaders play a critical role in this interaction. As mentioned earlier, much of the workplace harassment discusses the importance of organizational leadership in addressing the issue (Bowling & Beehr, 2006; Hershcovis et al., 2007; Neall & Tuckey, 2014; Zhang & Bednall, 2016). However, the literature does little to specify how leaders can affect the climate or the mechanisms through which this occurs.

Through social learning, authentic leaders may help individuals gain a better appreciation of different perspectives and perceptions of others' behavior as well as their own. Consequently, individuals might develop a more thorough understanding of the factors that affect perceptions of harassment. This improved understanding can guide individuals' behavior and thus, lower the incidence of workplace harassment. Further, this broader understanding may help shape the climate of the organization.

Thus, as leaders increase the degree to which they enact the components of authentic leadership, their organizations are likely to see a decrease in the frequency of workplace harassment.

> **Proposition 1:** There will be a negative relationship between the enacted components of authentic leadership and the frequency of workplace harassment incidents.

Leadership Behaviors/Actions

Modeling Behavior

An authentic leader's moral perspective can diminish workplace harassment by modeling positive appropriate behavior (Avolio et al., 2004; Gardner et al., 2005; Walumbwa et al., 2008). Organizational members look to leaders as indicators of norms for appropriate conduct. Their status in the organization makes their actions visible and salient such that even individuals who do not directly observe their behavior often learn about what leaders have done through coworkers' descriptions. As suggested earlier by social learning theory (Bandura, 1977, 1986), organizational members pay attention to the actions of leaders and model their own behavior after them. Research has demonstrated that leadership can influence both counterproductive behaviors (Detert et al., 2007; Erkutlu & Chafra, 2013; Ng & Feldman, 2015) and prosocial behaviors in organizations (Hannah et al., 2011; Ng & Feldman, 2015; Valsania et al., 2012). Valsania et al. (2012) found a significant correlation between moral perspective and organizational citizenship behaviors. Further, women experience less harassment in the military when leaders demonstrated respectful behavior (Buchanan et al., 2014).

Develop Behavioral Norms

In addition to modeling, authentic leaders can help to establish norms for acceptable and unacceptable behavior. Although this may appear to be straightforward, establishing norms for harassment may be challenging because of the indeterminate nature of certain forms of harassment. As mentioned earlier, jokes might be considered harassment under certain conditions. In this case, establishing norms for appropriate humor will require leaders to display or discuss the nuance in certain situations. Further, authentic leaders may also need to model emotional intelligence, that is, the ability to monitor the social environment and receive feedback regarding the appropriateness of behavior (Goleman, 1995; Mayer et al., 2016). A meta-analysis by Miao et al. (2018) showed a strong correlation between authentic leadership and emotional intelligence. Accordingly, authentic leaders may encourage emotional intelligence in their followers which will, in turn, help them monitor social cues as they determine the boundaries of appropriate behavior in their interpersonal interactions.

Reinforce Standards

In addition to setting norms for behavior, authentic leaders, can use their internalized moral perspective by encouraging others to resist social pressures to engage in questionable behaviors. The majority of workplace harassment behaviors occur among peers in organizations (Caskey, 2001; Fevre et al., 2012). Harassers often use the power provided to them legitimated by either workplace or societal norms (Cortina & Magley, 2009; Lee & Brotheridge, 2011;). In such cases, the harassment is being used to reinforce the existing power structure (either formal or informal) in the organization (Jenkins, 2011; Wilson & Thompson, 2001). Harassers may encourage others to participate in behavior that helps to reinforce the status quo at the expense of less powerful organizational members.

This is particularly important as organizations become increasingly diverse. Gotsis and Grimani (2016) argued that authentic leaders can promote an environment of equity and fairness among diverse group members, especially those that are particularly vulnerable. In such situations, existing norms for behavior may reflect opinions, values, and belief systems of the pre-existing majority. New entrants with differing views may, at a minimum, feel excluded, and in the extreme may find behavior norms associated with the existing culture to be intolerant and harassing. In such cases, older organizational members may be pressured to maintain the status quo regardless of the consideration for new members. Authentic leaders can help to break these old standards and foster new ones that are inclusive of new, diverse organizational members.

Support Reporters

Finally, authentic leaders can support those individuals who report workplace harassment. These individuals often face isolation and informal social retaliation for reporting harassers. Research has demonstrated that authentic leadership can mitigate the negative effects of workplace harassment by providing social support (Rossiter & Sochos, 2018; Warszewska-Makuch et al., 2015). Further, authentic leaders can encourage individuals to be proactive in ways that improve the climate with respect to workplace harassment. Walumbwa and Schaubroeck (2009) found that ethical leadership had a positive effect on voice behavior. By providing social and emotional support to individuals who report harassment, authentic leaders send the message that this behavior is valued. This may encourage others to come forward. Through these multiple mechanisms a leader's moral perspective can help foster an improved workplace climate that promotes civility and reduces workplace harassment.

> **Proposition 2:** Leaders internalized moral perspective will be positively related to their modeling appropriate behavior. This will, in turn, lead to organizational climates that are inclusive and respectful.

Follower Self-Awareness

We now turn next to the role authentic leaders can play to improve organizational members' understanding and sensitivity toward workplace harassment.

Problems Defining Harassment

As stated earlier, workplace harassment is in the eye of the beholder. An important factor for organizations that are trying to manage workplace harassment need to consider is that targets and harassers are likely to have different definitions and perceptions of workplace harassment. Most policies designed to address harassment rarely offer targets and harassers an opportunity to discuss the situation in a controlled environment. Doing so might allow them to come to a common understanding, or at a minimum, reveal the other party's point of view. In reality, most processes for resolving harassment complaints involve a manager or human resource professional discussing the situation with the target and alleged harasser separately focusing on their understanding and perspective of the situation without regard to the other party's viewpoint. This understanding is critical. Harassers who do not understand the problems associated with their behavior are likely to repeat it and possibly engage in similar behaviors with other targets. Further, they may encourage others to participate in similar behavior. When harassers do not understand targets' perceptions, it may be easier to attribute complaints to targets' oversensitivity or dispositional qualities, rather than their own behavior. Self-serving attribution biases (see Snyder et al., 1976) would suggest that harassers are likely to attribute the causes of harassment complaints (negative outcome) to external forces (e.g., the target is oversensitive) rather than internal forces (e.g., I behaved badly). Thus, they may be less willing to accept responsibility for their behaviors.

Recognizing Personal Biases

Conversely, it may be possible for targets to define any ambiguous interpersonal interactions as an offense and an instance of workplace harassment. This is critical since both legal and social/psychological definitions place the determination of whether the behavior is indeed harassment as a judgment made by the target. However, both definitions also recognize that some type of reasonable person standard must be applied to assess the veracity of the claim of harassment. That is, would a reasonable person in the same situation find the particular behavior to be harassment. In addition, targets may make internal attributions for harassers' behaviors (Parzefall & Salin, 2010; Wilkerson & Meyer, 2019). That is, targets may believe that the harasser possesses a character or personality flaw that motivates them to engage in such behavior with the intent to harm (Parzefall & Salin, 2010). Consequently, targets may believe that the harasser is incapable of understanding the significance of their behavior and altering it. In this case, the goal of leaders may be to get targets to realize that in some cases the harasser did not understand the offensive nature of their behavior or that the harm was unintended. Further, leaders may try to get targets to see that harassers may be able to learn, alter their behavior and improve their interpersonal sensitivity.

Self-awareness is the leaders ability to be aware of their strengths, weaknesses, emotions and personality. Embedded in this idea of self-awareness is the concept of an individual's identity (Avolio & Gardner, 2005; Gardner et al., 2005). Self-categorization theory (Tajfel & Turner, 1984; Turner, 1982) posits that individuals have both a personal and social identity. Personal identity encompasses the individual characteristics the make them unique (e.g., intelligence, personality) while social identities are the individuals memberships in social groups or categories that help to define the self (e.g., female, father). Authentic leaders have a strong sense of what makes them unique and their membership in social categories (Gardner et al., 2005). This self-awareness allows leaders to recognize their personal biases that might affect their interpretation of and reactions to a situation (Harvey et al., 2006; Mazutis & Slawinski, 2008). Consequently, authentic leaders will possess the sensitivity to understand how others in the workplace might interpret their words and actions and modulate their behavior in ways that foster inclusion and positive social relationships. Authentic leaders, in turn, may help their followers develop self-awareness such that they may be able to understand how their identity influences their perceptions. Further, increasing follower self-awareness might help individuals understand potentially harassing behaviors from multiple viewpoints. Yammarino et al. (2008) suggested that authentic leaders can help individuals develop social judgment skills that allow them to evaluate how others might react to a situation. Further, they can help shape shared perceptions of what is respectful and civil treatment within the workplace (Dickson et al., 2001). Ultimately, "authentic leadership can make a fundamental difference in organizations by helping people find meaning and connection at work through greater self-awareness" (Avolio & Gardner, 2005, p. 331).

Supportive Open Communication

There is emerging literature demonstrating that authentic leadership can positively influence collective interests, inclusion, and positive attitudes toward diversity (Boekhorst, 2015; van Loon & van Dijk, 2015). Authentic leadership can help promote understanding by eliciting different viewpoints from followers (Walumbwa et al., 2008) and fostering an open, authentic dialog that specifically includes those who are vulnerable or marginalized in the organization (Hu et al., 2018; Nembhard & Edmondson, 2006). Puente et al. (2007) found that leader self-awareness lead individuals to engage in open and honest communication in the aftermath of a "triggering" event. Mazutis and Slawinski (2008) suggested that this open dialog supports the effective exchange of ideas, especially in the case of discussing difficult issues. Further, these conversations can lead to organizational learning and long-term change. This is particularly important for managing workplace harassment, as it is a sensitive complex issue and engaging in conversations to promote understanding may lead individuals to feel vulnerable.

Inclusion

Authentic leadership can foster feelings of inclusion among organizational members. In their model of inclusive workplaces, Shore et al. (2018) specifically linked the authenticity of leadership to the practices and processes that foster inclusion. They identified six themes that would create inclusive organizations: psychological safety, involvement in the workgroup, feeling respected and valued, influence on decision-making, authenticity and recognizing, honoring, and advancing diversity. Further, they suggested that leadership is critical to promoting these themes. As authentic leaders take actions that promote these themes, the inclusiveness of the organization increases. In their model, leaders establish standards for suitable behavior and model inclusive behavior. Although they do not specifically identify authentic leadership, they suggested that the leaders' values and transparency are critical to fostering inclusion. Empirical research has found positive correlations between authentic leadership and inclusion (Boekhorst, 2015; Cottrill et al., 2014). Inclusion is an important component in fostering a meaningful understanding of and sensitivity to workplace harassment. It increases the likelihood that all members, even those with perspectives that differ from the organizational norms or majority opinion, will be more comfortable expressing those viewpoints. If participation in dialog regarding workplace harassment issues and perspectives is limited, the recognition of these matters will also be constrained.

> **Proposition 3:** Leader self-awareness will be positively associated with follower self-awareness. Increased follower self-awareness will be associated with an improved understanding and greater sensitivity to harassment issues.

In conjunction with modeling appropriate behavior, authentic leaders who have followers develop an understanding of and sensitivity to potentially harassing behaviors will not only change the climate but will also reduce the incidents of workplace harassment. When incidents of workplace harassment do occur, authentic leadership principles can be infused into the resolution process to ensure voice and fair treatment of all parties and reinforcing the climate of respect and civility. We turn next to a discussion of resolution of harassment complaints.

Collaborative Problem-Solving Approach to Resolving Complaints

One more direct way authentic leaders can help better manage workplace harassment is to refocus the process for how complaints are resolved. When an employee makes a complaint of workplace harassment (either formally or informally), three determinations must be made: (1) what specifically occurred during the situation; (2) does the behavior constitute a violation of the company's workplace harassment policy; and (3) for substantiated complaints, what action should the organization take with respect to the harasser (Arnow-Richman, 2019).

Problems With Traditional Policies

Research has demonstrated that individuals do not report harassment (McDonald et al., 2011). For example, McDonald et al. found that less than

17% of individuals who experienced sexual harassment either reported or made a formal complaint. One of the reasons why the traditional approaches do little to change behavior or promote a respectful climate is that it forces the harasser and target into an adversarial process (Fitzgerald, 1993); both parties are trying to prove that their version and understanding of the situation is correct. Targets try to prove that harassers engaged in inappropriate behaviors while harassers try to suggest that targets misunderstood the harassers' behaviors or are hyperbolizing situations. Under this approach, targets usually in a lower position of power may fear that they will not be believed or will experience re-victimization (Fitzgerald, 1993). This antagonistic model may lead others in the workplace to choose sides supporting either the target or the harasser (Hughes, 1998). Fitzgerald (1993) suggested this antagonistic process is one of the reasons targets do not choose formal complaint mechanisms.

A second reason why targets do not file formal complaints is that they often fear retaliation. Cortina and Magley (2009) provided support that this fear may be warranted. Although they found that targets who reported were not likely to experience work-related retaliation (e.g., change in assignments, poor performance ratings, etc.), they did experience social retaliation (e.g., ostracism, name-calling, etc.) from other organizational members. This was particularly true when the harasser was a powerful individual in the organization.

A third reason targets do not report harassment is that they perceive a loss of control over the outcomes of the complaint resolution process. Once targets file formal complaints, organizations assume control and dictate both process and outcomes (Marshall, 2005). Researchers (e.g., Marshall, 2005; Rowe, 1996) suggest that most procedural systems set up to receive harassment complaints are not target friendly and, in fact, discourage targets from reporting because of the lack of power or control they perceive in the process. Lind and Tyler (1988) suggested that individuals perceive procedures as fairer when they have a voice in the process. Further, Shestowsky (2004) found that individuals preferred dispute resolution processes that were facilitative (e.g., mediation) over those that were evaluative (e.g., arbitration). One particular area that targets of harassment are concerned with is the formal complaint outcomes. One reason targets cite for not reporting is that they do not want to cause trouble for the harasser (Gadlin, 1991; Gutek, 1985). Policies that limit target control are less likely to lead to successful complaint resolution because they may not be utilized.

Finally, traditional procedures tend to ignore the interpersonal dynamics of a situation, specifically, the relationship between the harasser and target. Research has indicated that one of the negative consequences associated with harassment is the harm caused to the interpersonal and working relationships among coworkers (Gutek, 1985; Loy & Stewart, 1984).

For example, many women indicate that they do not use formal mechanisms to report sexual harassment because they do not want to disrupt working relationships (Gadlin, 1991; Gruber & Smith, 1995; Gutek, 1985). Therefore, practices that focus on stopping the behavior to the exclusion of the interpersonal dynamics are not likely to result in successful resolution of harassment complaints in a manner that repairs the parties' working relationship.

In addition to targets' unwillingness to engage in the formal complaint process, accused harassers may also be apprehensive in engaging in the process. In the era of the "me too" movement, legal experts suggest that low status alleged harassers may be at risk for becoming a scapegoat for organizations' needs to appear responsive to complaints regardless of the severity behavior or the situational context in which it occurred (Arnow-Richman, 2019). In such cases, alleged harassers may try to deny the situation occurred or mislead others about the details of the situation in an attempt to protect themselves from punishment or dismissal.

In cases of harassment, involved parties often have differing accounts as to what specific actions occurred, what each party's intentions were and how the situation should be interpreted and managed (Catley et al., 2017; Mikula & Wenzel, 2000). Alleged harassers tend to view their behavior as acceptable and a result of external circumstances while targets tend to view the behavior as more serious and attribute more blame to harassers' dispositions (Mikula & Wenzel, 2000). To resolve these incidents, managers must gather information from the target, alleged harasser, and any witnesses that exist. Once information is gathered managers must assess and interpret it in order to make their own determinations as to what occurred. When targets and alleged harassers are not willing to engage in the process, these tasks become difficult. Further, complainants in dispute often are unwilling to accept judgments of the situation that conflict with their viewpoints (Catley at al., 2017); this may also discourage them from participating.

Fostering a Collaboration Problem Solving Approach

A second way authentic leaders may help to improve the process is by understanding the desired outcomes of the target and harasser. In cases where a complaint is deemed a policy violation, some type of action needs to be taken. In traditional approaches, harassers often receive some type of punishment for their behavior (Arnow-Richman, 2019; Becton et al., 2017). However, this is often not the resolution targets seek (Gadlin, 1991). Targets often want validation of their perceptions of offensiveness of the behavior (Lewis, 2006; Lutgen-Sandvik, 2008) and a sincere apology (Okimoto & Wenzel, 2014). Put to the point, many targets of harassment simply want the behavior to stop and repair the relationship (Gadlin, 1991). Shifting the goals of the process to reconciliation may increase the use of the complaint procedure and produce more positive outcomes for the affected parties and the organization as a whole.

Increasing Perceptions of Fairness

Research suggests that having an effective complaint process is a critical component of any organization's harassment policy (Butler & Schmidtke, 2010; Compton, 2007; Peirce et al., 1997; Zugelder et al., 2006). Peirce et al. (1997) found that the effectiveness of the complaint process affected individuals' willingness to report. Accordingly, organizations need to improve perceptions of the complaint process to increase individuals' willingness to use them and engage in the process. This is why the issues of due process and fair treatment are critical. Due process is the ability of individuals to participate in a formal process that is free from arbitrary or unreasonable treatment. Fair treatment in the process suggests that individuals are treated equally and with respect. The limited research on managerial effectiveness during the complaint resolution process (Catley et al., 2017; Harrington et al., 2015) suggests that impartiality and trust are critical. This is consistent with the theories of procedural justice (Thibaut & Walker, 1975) and interactional justice (Bies & Moag, 1986). When procedures are fair, individuals are more accepting of undesirable outcomes (Lind & Tyler, 1988). Interpersonal treatment during processes also affects individuals' perceptions of the fairness of outcomes (Bies & Moag, 1986). One of the ways organizations might encourage participation in some type of incident resolution process is to ensure that both parties have a voice and are treated respectfully.

Balanced processing can help to improve complaint procedures by shifting the goals of the process. Rather than simply adjudicating complaints, the process could be used more developmentally to help both alleged harassers and targets to understand the dynamics of workplace harassment and each other's perspectives. A more developmental approach may promote more individuals to utilize the process. Fotohabadi and Kelly (2018) found that authentic leadership was correlated with more a collaborative conflict resolution style, which requires a high degree of engagement and cooperation (Thomas & Kilmann, 1978). In addition, several studies have found a positive correlation between authentic leadership and perceptions of procedural justice (Hsiung, 2012; Kampa et al., 2017; Kiersch & Byrne 2015). Thus, authentic leaders may help to create a complaint resolution process that engages both targets and alleged harassers in a way that increases voice and perceptions of fairness. Consequently, authentic leaders may be able to shift the complaint resolution process to a more problem-solving approach that is less judgmental and adversarial than traditional approaches. All parties are allowed a voice in the process and consequently, may perceive this process as fairer even when the outcome is not favorable to them.

Promoting a Mutual Understanding of Incidents

One of the aspirations of authentic leaders is to balance the perspectives, needs and goals of various organizational participants (Avolio & Gardner, 2005). To accomplish this, they engage in behaviors that promote balanced processing and relational transparency. Balanced processing involves taking multiple perspectives into account before assessing the situation. Relational transparency involves leaders displaying openness and trust in relationships, encouraging followers to do the same. These two principals will work in tandem in the process of resolving complaints; leaders can encourage the target, the alleged harasser, and any bystanders to reflect and discuss the situation in an open and honest matter, without inserting their own views or judgments in the process. Hinojosa et al. (2014) proposed that authenticity helps to create secure attachments between leaders and followers. This attachment style facilitates the sharing of information in ways that promote more accurate recollections that are consistent with one's actual experience (Gentzler & Kerns, 2006). Further, it also helps promote healthy processing of negative emotions (Shaver et al., 2009), which are typically present in workplace harassment situations. Consequently, balanced processing may facilitate engagement of the affected parties in the resolution of a complaint in a manner that limits the biased recollection of events and limits the adversarial nature of more traditional processes. This, in turn, allows for more honest and accurate information to be shared during the complaint resolution process, which should lead to better judgments and higher perceptions of fairness.

In addition, this balanced processing may help facilitate parties to share their interpretation and perspective of the situation in a nonjudgmental, nonconfrontational manner. Edmondson (2003, 2004) found that leaders who engage in open and honest communication and demonstrate their own vulnerability diminish defensiveness. When leaders model the desired approach in this manner, it encourages followers to share accurate and relevant information about their concerns (Edmondson, 2003, 2004; Meyer et al., 2017). Further, authentic leaders who are willing to discuss the effect of their social identities and biases on their judgments may foster followers' awareness of their preconceived notions in social judgments. In the resolution of harassment complaints, this may help all parties identify their assumptions and biases in the interpretations of the situation. This can foster discussion of the situation that promotes a respectful dialog and does not belittle the targets' reactions or disparage harassers' character. It also may allow targets and alleged harassers to understand each other's perspective on the situation. Of course, this does not necessitate that the parties agree on the interpretation of the incident(s), but it allows for a shared understanding of both viewpoints. From a social learning perspective, this shared understanding may lead to outcomes favorable to all parties such as validation, respect, apology, and relationship restoration as they are able to learn appropriate behaviors by mimicking their authentic leader. It also may help harassers develop empathy so they not only understand the consequences of their behavior in this particular situation, but they also are able to generalize this understanding to other circumstances.

Improve Trust and Engagement

In addition to the indirect role relational transparency may play in fostering balanced processing through facilitating honest and open communication during the complaint resolution process, it can also directly help to facilitate trust and engagement in the process as well as increase perceptions of fairness. Research has demonstrated a significant correlation between authentic leadership and trust and employee engagement (Datta, 2015; Gatling et al., 2017; Hassan & Ahmed, 2011; Vogelgesang et al., 2013; Wang & Hsieh, 2013). Relational transparency appears to be particularly important in developing these reactions (Gatling et al., 2017; Vogelgesang et al., 2013). Recall that two reasons individuals do not report incidents of harassment is that they perceive a loss of control in the process and fear potential retaliation (Cortina & Magley, 2009; Marshall, 2005; Rowe, 1996). Trust in the leader and the process may assuage these concerns and increase the willingness of individuals to report harassment. Transparency also leads to engagement (Vogelgesang et al., 2013). Consequently, it may foster individuals' active participation in the resolution process, which is a critical element of a collaborative conflict resolution style (Thomas & Kilmann, 1978).

> **Proposition 4:** Leaders who facilitate the sharing or multiple perspectives in a more open and honest manner are likely to facilitate a more collaborative problem-solving approach. As the complaint process shifts from adversarial to collaborative, the process will be perceived as fairer, will promote understanding and foster trust and engagement. These will ultimately lead to more successful resolution of harassment complaints.

In addition to these explicit effects of balanced processing and relational transparency on the complaint resolution process, authentic leadership may also help facilitate the process through increased psychological safety (Hsiung, 2012; Liu et al., 2015; Walumbwa & Schaubroeck, 2009), positive affect (Zhou et al., 2014). Psychological safety (Kahn, 1990) is the willingness of individuals to express themselves without fear, shame or punishment. As psychologically safety increases, individuals will be more willing to be engaged and share information (Frazier et al., 2017). The effect of psychological safety is particularly important as it has a demonstrated effect of voice behavior and whistleblowing (Hsiung, 2012; Liu et al., 2015; Walumbwa & Schaubroeck, 2009). This is particularly important in the complaint resolution process. For example, because of the interpersonal nature of harassment, individuals may feel particularly vulnerable, and consequently, may be hesitant to be honest and open in their communication. Increased psychological safety may mitigate this.

> **Proposition 5:** Leaders who facilitate sharing or multiple perspectives more openly and honestly are likely are likely to foster feelings of increased psychological safety in the complaint resolution process which will increase the likelihood of successful complaint resolutions.

Taken together, this research suggests that authentic leadership may help to promote more effective workplace harassment resolution procedures. Such a process not only ends the behavior, but also fosters cooperation between the parties and facilitates open, honest dialog through balanced processing of multiple perspectives and relational transparency. This, in turn, leads to three positive outcomes. First, it gives both parties voice in the process and more control over the outcomes, which enhances perceptions of fairness. This may increase targets' motivation to report workplace harassment and harassers' willingness to engage in the process. Second, this process fosters a mutual understanding of the incident. While parties may still not agree on the interpretation of the incident, they may understand why the behavior was problematic. This might help parties generalize why certain behaviors might be perceived as harassment, preventing future incidents from occurring. Finally, it can help improve trust and engagement creating a more positive, cooperative process rather than the traditional adversarial approach, which propagates defensiveness and the potential for retaliation. It should be noted that there are certainly limitations to this approach. Obviously, these practices might not be appropriate in cases involving egregious, malicious harassment or violence. However, these types of cases are typically rare (Neall & Tuckey, 2014).

DISCUSSION

In the current chapter, we explore the relation between authentic leadership and the management of workplace harassment. While we have attempted to link the specific components of authentic leadership with specific leadership behaviors/actions and goals related to harassment management, there is likely to be overlap between the elements and their effects. For example, leaders' internalized moral perspectives will not only affect the way they model behavior to establish norms that create a positive climate, but this perspective will also likely have an effect on the manner in which they resolve harassment complaints. We propose the specific relations because they allow for better specification of the connection between authentic leadership, leaders' behaviors, and actions (i.e., modeling behavior, improving follower awareness, and collaborative problem solving) and the management workplace harassment.

Authentic leadership, specifically, the internalized moral perspective component will direct leaders to model appropriate behavior. This will, in turn, help create a climate of inclusivity and respect by setting behavioral norms, reinforcing standards for behavior, and supporting reporters. While the existing authentic leadership and workplace harassment literatures have not examined this specific connection. As highlighted above, followers are likely to emulate authentic leaders' prosocial and organizational citizenship behaviors. We expect that followers will also engage in more respectful and inclusive behaviors with respect to workplace harassment when leaders' actions set the tone. This should lead to lower levels of harassment. Buchanan et al. (2014) found that women experienced less sexual harassment when leaders demonstrated respectful behavior. Future research needs to examine this relationship with the broader concept of workplace harassment.

Authentic leaders' self-awareness will help and encourage followers to become more self-aware and consequently, identify their personal biases, engage in more open communication, and increase the inclusion of all organizational members. This follower self-awareness will help them to understand how their potentially harassing behaviors might be perceived by someone else and thus, will be more sensitive to the issues involving workplace harassment. This understanding and sensitivity should help to reduce the levels of sexual harassment. While research has demonstrated a relationship between authentic leadership and inclusion (Cottrill et al., 2014), there is no research that has examined how authentic leadership, or its components might affect followers understanding of and sensitivity to workplace harassment issues. Further, there is no research that has examined the link between leaders' and followers' self-awareness. Future research is needed to explore these relationships. Self-awareness is a critical piece in reducing workplace harassment. Individuals who have an awareness of the effects their behavior has on others are less likely to engage in activities that others might find objectionable.

Finally, authentic leaders might play a critical role in resolving harassment complaints. Balanced processing and relational transparency might help create and facilitate a resolution process that is more collaborative than adversarial. A less antagonistic process might facilitate increase perceptions of fairness, promote learning, and improve trust between the parties involved. Given there is limited research demonstrating a relation between authentic leadership and a collaborative conflict resolution style (Fotohabadi & Kelly, 2018), more work is needed in this area. Further, future research should also examine the relationship between authentic leadership and satisfaction with complaint resolution outcomes. A complaint resolution processes that facilitates positive outcomes increases the likelihood that individuals will utilize and engage in the process.

In addition to these specific mechanisms, we also recognize the link between authentic leadership and psychological safety. While this factor affects a multitude of issues such as creativity, performance and work-related attitudes they also are important considerations for the management of workplace harassment. This will influence the effectiveness of the specific mechanisms used to achieve the goals of the harassment reduction programs and procedures. For example, having meaningful discussions that help organizational members understand the dynamics underlying workplace harassment require that individuals feel safe in expressing their opinions. Thus, we included them in the model even though they may not have a direct effect on the reduction of workplace harassment.

In our framework, we identify three important leadership goals for organizations' management of workplace harassment: facilitating an inclusive and respectful climate, promoting understanding, and sensitivity to harassment issues and effectively resolving harassment complaints. While these are distinct components of a harassment reduction program, they are interrelated and mutually reinforcing. For example, encouraging understanding and sensitivity of workplace harassment is likely to have an effect on the climate of the organization. Resolving complaints of harassment in a positive developmental manner is likely to promote sensitivity and understanding for involved parties, which are likely to spread to other organizational members. Further, the specific mechanisms that are identified to achieve these goals are also likely to affect each other as well. For example, follower awareness of personal biases is likely to influence the collaborative approach to resolving complaints. Individuals who have a better understanding of the underlying issues may have an easier time understanding the perspective of the other party during a complaint resolution.

CONCLUSION

While much of the harassment literature identifies organizational leadership as a key factor in helping to reduce its prevalence, researchers have failed to identify the specific mechanisms for accomplishing this goal. Consequently, there is a paucity of empirical research that examines the mechanisms leaders utilize to reduce harassment in their organization beyond generalized perceptions. For example, Buchanan et al. (2014, p. 695) asked targets whether, "leadership makes an honest and reasonable effort to stop sexual harassment." While this research is important in understanding targets perceptions of the leadership, it does not identify the specific actions leaders can take to influence these perceptions or reduce harassment.

In conclusion, the purpose of this chapter is to close this gap in the literature by providing a framework for understanding the relations among the components of authentic leadership and the specific actions that leaders can take to manage workplace harassment. In doing so, we hope to provide guidance to managers who are actively trying to reduce workplace harassment and create a respectful, inclusive climate. We also offer this framework for researchers who are examining the role of leadership in ending workplace harassment. We believe that examining the specific elements of authentic leadership and their influence on leaders' actions and behaviors for managing workplace is a fruitful area for future research.

REFERENCES

Arnow-Richman, R. S. (2019). Harassers' rights and employer best practices: The quest for a calibrated approach in the era of MeToo. *University of San Francisco Law Review*; *U Denver Legal Studies Research Paper No. 19–08*. Retrieved from https://ssrn.com/abstract=3416760

Avolio, B. J., Gardner, W. L., Walumbwa, F. O., Luthans, F., & May, D. R. (2004). Unlocking the mask: A look at the process by which authentic leaders impact follower attitudes and behaviors. *The Leadership Quarterly*, *15*(6), 801–823. https://doi.org/10.1016/j.leaqua.2004.09.003

Avolio, B. J., & Gardner, W. L. (2005). Authentic leadership development: Getting to the root of positive forms of leadership. *The Leadership Quarterly*, *16*(3), 315–338. https://doi.org/10.1016/j.leaqua.2005.03.001

Avolio, B. J., & Walumbwa, F. O. (2014). Authentic leadership theory, research and practice: Steps taken and steps that remain. In D. V. Day (Ed.), *The Oxford handbook of leadership and organizations* (pp. 332–357). Oxford University Press. https://doi.org/10.1093/oxfordhb/9780199755615.013.017

Avolio, B. J., Walumbwa, F. O., & Weber, T. J. (2009). Leadership: Current theories, research, and future directions. *Annual Review of Psychology, 60*, 421–449. https://doi.org/10.1146/annurev.psych.60.110707.163621

Bandura, A. (1977). Self-efficacy: toward a unifying theory of behavioral change. *Psychological Review, 84*(2), 191–215. https://doi.org/10.1037/0033-295x.84.2.191

Bandura, A. (1986). *Social foundations of thought and action*. Prentice Hall.

Banks, G. C., McCauley, K. D., Gardner, W. L., & Guler, C. E. (2016). A meta-analytic review of authentic and transformational leadership: A test for redundancy. *The Leadership Quarterly, 27*(4), 634–652. https://doi.org/10.1016/j.leaqua.2016.02.006

Becton, J. B., Gilstrap, J. B., & Forsyth, M. (2017). Preventing and correcting workplace harassment: Guidelines for employers. *Business Horizons, 60*(1), 101–111. https://doi.org/10.1016/j.bushor.2016.09.005

Bergman, M. E., Langhout, R. D., Palmieri, P. A., Cortina, L. M., & Fitzgerald, L. F. (2002). The (un) reasonableness of reporting: Antecedents and consequences of reporting sexual harassment. *Journal of Applied Psychology, 87*(2), 230–242. https://doi.org/10.1037/0021-9010.87.2.230

Bies, R. J., & Moag, J. S. (1986). Interactional communication criteria of fairness. *Research in Organizational Behavior, 9*, 289–319.

Bies, R. J., & Tyler, T. R. (1993). The "litigation mentality" in organizations: A test of alternative psychological explanations. *Organization Science, 4*(3), 352–366. https://doi.org/10.1287/orsc.4.3.352

Boekhorst, J. A. (2015). The role of authentic leadership in fostering workplace inclusion: A social information processing perspective. *Human Resource Management, 54*(2), 241–264. https://doi.org/10.1002/hrm.21669

Borgwald, K., & Theixos, H. (2013). Bullying the bully: Why zero-tolerance policies get a failing grade. *Social Influence, 8*(2-3), 149–160. https://doi.org/10.1080/15534510.2012.724030

Bowling, N. A., & Beehr, T. A. (2006). Workplace harassment from the victim's perspective: a theoretical model and meta-analysis. *Journal of Applied Psychology, 91*(5), 998–1012. https://doi.org/10.1037/0021-9010.91.5.998

Braun, S., & Peus, C. (2018). Crossover of work–life balance perceptions: Does authentic leadership matter? *Journal of Business Ethics, 149*(4), 875–893. https://doi.org/10.1007/s10551-016-3078-x

Braun, S., Peus, C., & Frey, D. (2018). Connectionism in action: Exploring the links between leader prototypes, leader gender, and perceptions of authentic leadership. *Organizational Behavior and Human Decision Processes, 149*, 129–144. https://doi.org/10.1016/j.obhdp.2018.10.003

Brown, M. E., Treviño, L. K., & Harrison, D. A. (2005). Ethical leadership: A social learning perspective for construct development and testing. *Organizational Behavior and Human Decision Processes, 97*(2), 117–134. https://doi.org/10.1016/j.obhdp.2005.03.002

Buchanan, N. T., Settles, I. H., Hall, A. T., & O'Connor, R. C. (2014). A review of organizational strategies for reducing sexual harassment: Insights from the US military. *Journal of Social Issues, 70*(4), 687–702. https://doi.org/10.1111/josi.12086

Burns, J. M. (1978). *Leadership*. Harper & Row.

Butler, J. S., & Schmidtke, J. M. (2010). Theoretical traditions and the modeling of sexual harassment within organizations: The military as data. *Armed Forces & Society*, *36*(2), 193–222. https://doi.org/10.1177/0095327x09344062

Campbell, J. D., Trapnell, P. D., Heine, S. J., Katz, I. M., Lavallee, L. F., & Lehman, D. R. (1996). Self-concept clarity: Measurement, personality correlates, and cultural boundaries. *Journal of Personality and Social Psychology*, *70*(1), 141–156. https://doi.org/10.1037/0022-3514.70.1.141

Caskey, C. R. (2001). Workplace violence. *Clinical Laboratory Science*, *14*(2), 95–100.

Catley, B., Blackwood, K., Forsyth, D., Tappin, D., & Bentley, T. (2017). Workplace bullying complaints: Lessons for "good HR practice." *Personnel Review*, *46*(1), 100–114. https://doi.org/10.1108/pr-04-2015-0107

Compton, N. (2007). How workplace managers can protect against hostile environment claims from their female and male employees: A legal review of decisional law. *Journal of Diversity Management (JDM)*, *2*(1), 41–48. https://doi.org/10.19030/jdm.v2i1.5005

Cortina, L. M., & Magley, V. J. (2009). Patterns and profiles of response to incivility in the workplace. *Journal of Occupational Health Psychology*, *14*(3), 272–288. https://doi.org/10.1037/a0014934

Cottrill, K., Denise Lopez, P., & C. Hoffman, C. (2014). How authentic leadership and inclusion benefit organizations. *Equality, Diversity and Inclusion: An International Journal*, *33*(3), 275–292. https://doi.org/10.1108/edi-05-2012-0041

Datta, B. (2015). Assessing the effectiveness of authentic leadership. *International Journal of Leadership Studies*, *9*(1), 19–32. http://citeseerx.ist.psu.edu/viewdoc/download?doi=10.1.1.675.4155&rep=rep1&type=pdf#page=27

Detert, J. R., Treviño, L. K., Burris, E. R., & Andiappan, M. (2007). Managerial modes of influence and counterproductivity in organizations: A longitudinal business-unit-level investigation. *Journal of Applied Psychology*, *92*(4), 993–1005. https://doi.org/10.1037/0021-9010.93.2.328

Dhanani, L. Y., & LaPalme, M. L. (2019). It's not personal: A review and theoretical integration of research on vicarious workplace mistreatment. *Journal of Management*, *45*(6), 2322–2351. https://doi.org/10.1177/0149206318816162

Dickson, M. W., Smith, D. B., Grojean, M. W., & Ehrhart, M. (2001). An organizational climate regarding ethics: The outcome of leader values and the practices that reflect them. *The Leadership Quarterly*, *12*(2), 197–217. https://doi.org/10.1016/s1048-9843(01)00069-8

Dirks, K. T., & Ferrin, D. L. (2002). Trust in leadership: Meta-analytic findings and implications for research and practice. *Journal of Applied Psychology*, *87*(4), 611–628. https://doi.org/10.1037/0021-9010.87.4.611

Edmondson, A. C. (2003). Speaking up in the operating room: How team leaders promote learning in interdisciplinary action teams. *Journal of Management Studies*, *40*(6), 1419–1452. https://doi.org/10.1111/1467-6486.00386

Edmondson, A. C. (2004). Learning from mistakes is easier said than done: Group and organizational influences on the detection and correction of human error. *The Journal of Applied Behavioral Science*, *40*(1), 66–90. https://doi.org/10.1177/0021886304263849

Equal Employment Opportunities Commission. (2019a). *Sexual harassment charges EEOC & FEPAs Combined: FY 1992–FY 1996*. https://www. https://www.eeoc.gov/statistics/sexual-harassment-chargeseeoc-fepas-combined-fy-1992-fy-1996_

Equal Employment Opportunities Commission. (2019b). *Charges alleging sex-based harassment (Charges filed with EEOC) FY 2010–FY 2019*. https://www.eeoc.gov/statistics/charges-alleging-sex-based-harassment-charges-filed-eeoc-fy-2010-fy-2019

Equal Employment Opportunities Commission. (2019c). *Charges alleging race and harassment (Charges filed with EEOC) FY 2010–FY 2019*. https://www.eeoc.gov/statistics/charges-alleging-race-and-harassment-charges-filed-eeoc-fy-1997-fy-2019

Equal Employment Opportunities Commission. (2019d). *Charges alleging race and harassment (charges filed with EEOC) FY 1997–FY 2019*. https://www.eeoc.gov/statistics/all-statutes-charges-filed-eeoc-fy-1997-fy-2019

Erkutlu, H., & Chafra, J. (2013). Effects of trust and psychological contract violation on authentic leadership and organizational deviance. *Management Research Review*, *36*(9), 828–848. https://doi.org/10.1108/mrr-06-2012-0136

Fevre, R., Lewis, D., Robinson, A., & Jones, T. (2012). Insight into ill-treatment in the workplace: Patters, causes and solutions. *Contemporary Readings in Law & Social Justice*, *4*(2), 245–277. http://tinyurl.com/socsi-insight

Firestone, J. M., & Harris, R. J. (2003). Perceptions of effectiveness of responses to sexual harassment in the US military, 1988 and 1995. *Gender, Work & Organization*, *10*(1), 42–64. https://doi.org/10.1111/1468-0432.00003

Fitzgerald, L. F. (1993). Sexual harassment: Violence against women in the workplace. *American Psychologist*, *48*(10), 1070–1076. https://doi.org/10.1037/0003-066x.48.10.1070

Fitzgerald, L. F., & Cortina, L. M. (2018). Sexual harassment in work organizations: A view from the 21st century. In C. B Travis, J. W. White, A. Rutherford, W. S. Williams, S. L. Cook, & K. F. Wyche (Eds.), *APA handbook of the psychology of women: Perspectives on women's private and public lives* (pp. 215–234). American Psychological Association. https://doi.org/10.1037/0000060-012

Fitzgerald, L. F., Magley, V. J., Drasgow, F., & Waldo, C. R. (1999). Measuring sexual harassment in the military: the sexual experiences questionnaire (SEQ—DoD). *Military Psychology*, *11*(3), 243–263. https://doi.org/10.1207/s15327876mp1103_3

Fitzgerald, L. F., Swan, S., & Magley, V. J. (1997). But was it really sexual harassment?: Legal, behavioral, and psychological definitions of the workplace victimization of women. In W. O'Donohue (Ed.), *Sexual harassment: Theory, research, and treatment* (pp. 5–28). Allyn & Bacon.

Fotohabadi, M., & Kelly, L. (2018). Making conflict work: Authentic leadership and reactive and reflective management styles. *Journal of General Management*, *43*(2), 70–78. https://doi.org/10.1177/0306307017737363

Frazier, M. L., Fainshmidt, S., Klinger, R. L., Pezeshkan, A., & Vracheva, V. (2017). Psychological safety: A meta-analytic review and extension. *Personnel Psychology*, *70*(1), 113–165. https://doi.org/10.1111/peps.12183

Gadlin, H. (1991). Careful maneuvers: Mediating sexual harassment. *Negotiation Journal*, *7*, 139--153. https://doi.org/10.1111/j.1571-9979.1991.tb00610.x

Gardner, W. L., Avolio, B. J., Luthans, F., May, D. R., & Walumbwa, F. (2005). "Can you see the real me?" A self-based model of authentic leader and follower development. *The Leadership Quarterly*, *16*(3), 343–372. https://doi.org/10.1016/j.leaqua.2005.03.003

Gatling, A., Shum, C., Book, L., & Bai, B. (2017). The influence of hospitality leaders' relational transparency on followers' trust and deviance behaviors: Mediating role of behavioral integrity. *International Journal of Hospitality Management*, *62*, 11–20. https://doi.org/10.1016/j.ijhm.2016.11.010

Gentzler, A., & Kerns, K. (2006). Adult attachment and memory of emotional reactions to negative and positive events. *Cognition & Emotion*, *20*(1), 20–42. https://doi.org/10.1080/02699930500200407

Gilani, S. R. S., Cavico, F. J., & Mujtaba, B. G. (2014). Harassment at the workplace: A practical review of the laws in the United Kingdom and the United States of America. *Public Organization Review*, *14*(1), 1–18. https://doi.org/10.1007/s11115-012-0202-y

Goleman, D. (1995). *Emotional intelligence*. Bantam.

Gotsis, G., & Grimani, K. (2016). Diversity as an aspect of effective leadership: Integrating and moving forward. *Leadership & Organization Development Journal*, *37*(2), 241–264. https://doi.org/10.1108/lodj-06-2014-0107

Gruber, J. E., & Smith, M. D. (1995). Women's responses to sexual harassment: A multivariate analysis. *Basic and Applied Social Psychology*, *17*(4), 543–562. https://doi.org/10.1207/s15324834basp1704_7

Gutek, B. A. (1985). *Sex and the workplace*. Jossey-Bass.

Hannah, S. T., Avolio, B. J., & Walumbwa, F. O. (2011). Relationships between authentic leadership, moral courage, and ethical and pro-social behaviors. *Business Ethics Quarterly*, *21*(4), 555–578. https://doi.org/10.5840/beq20112143

Harassment. (n.d.). U.S. Equal Employment Opportunity Commission. Retrieved from *https://www.eeoc.gov/laws/types/harassment.cfm*

Harrington, S., Warren, S., & Rayner, C. (2015). Human resource management practitioners' responses to workplace bullying: cycles of symbolic violence. *Organization*, *22*(3), 368–389. https://doi.org/10.1177/1350508413516175

Hart, C. G., Crossley, A. D., & Correll, S. J. (2018). Leader messaging and attitudes toward sexual violence. *Socius: Sociological Research for a Dynamic World*, *4*, 1–11. https://doi.org/10.1177/2378023118808617

Harvey, P., Martinko, M. J., & Gardner, W. L. (2006). Promoting authentic behavior in organizations: An attributional perspective. *Journal of Leadership & Organizational Studies*, *12*(3), 1–11. https://doi.org/10.1177/107179190601200301

Hassan, A., & Ahmed, F. (2011). Authentic leadership, trust and work engagement. *International Journal of Human and Social Sciences*, *6*(3), 164–170. https://www.researchgate.net/profile/Forbis_Ahamed/publication/300040844_Authentic_Leadership_Trust_And_Employees'_Work_Engagement/links/5addbb504585l5c60f5f6f68/Authentic-Leadership-Trust-And-Employees-Work-Engagement.pdf

Hershcovis, M. S., Turner, N., Barling, J., Arnold, K. A., Dupré, K. E., Inness, M., LeBlanc, M. M., & Sivanathan, N. (2007). Predicting workplace aggression: A meta-analysis. *Journal of Applied Psychology*, *92*(1), 228–238. https://doi.org/10.1037/0021-9010.92.1.228

Hinojosa, A. S., McCauley, K. D., Randolph-Seng, B., & Gardner, W. L. (2014). Leader and follower attachment styles: Implications for authentic leader–follower relationships. *The Leadership Quarterly*, *25*(3), 595–610. https://doi.org/10.1016/j.leaqua.2013.12.002

Hirst, G., Walumbwa, F., Aryee, S., ButarButar, I., & Chen, C. J. H. (2016). A multilevel investigation of authentic leadership as an antecedent to helping behavior. *Journal of Business Ethics*, *139*(3), 485–499. https://doi.org/10.1007/s10551-015-2580-x

Hoch, J. E., Bommer, W. H., Dulebohn, J. H., & Wu, D. (2018). Do ethical, authentic, and servant leadership explain variance above and beyond transformational leadership? A meta-analysis. *Journal of Management*, *44*(2), 501–529. https://doi.org/10.1177/0149206316665461

Hodson, G., Rush, J., & MacInnis, C. C. (2010). A joke is just a joke (except when it isn't): Cavalier humor beliefs facilitate the expression of group dominance motives. *Journal of Personality and Social Psychology*, *99*(4), 660–682. https://doi.org/10.1037/a0019627

Hsiung, H. H. (2012). Authentic leadership and employee voice behavior: A multi-level psychological process. *Journal of Business Ethics*, *107*(3), 349–361.https://doi.org/10.1007/s10551-011-1043-2

Hu, Y., Wu, X., Zong, Z., Xiao, Y., Maguire, P., Qu, F., Wei, J., & Wang, D. (2018). Authentic leadership and proactive behavior: The role of psychological capital and compassion at work. *Frontiers in Psychology*, *9*, 1–12. https://doi.org/10.3389/fpsyg.2018.02470

Hughes, P. (1998). Workplace speech and conduct policies: Reconsidering the legal model. *Canadian Bar Review*, *77*, 105–125. https://cbr.cba.org/index.php/cbr/article/download/3751/3744

Ilies, R., Morgeson, F. P., & Nahrgang, J. D. (2005). Authentic leadership and eudaemonic well-being: Understanding leader–follower outcomes. *The Leadership Quarterly*, *16*(3), 373–394. https://doi.org/10.1016/j.leaqua.2005.03.002

Jenkins, M. (2011). Practice note: Is mediation suitable for complaints of workplace bullying?. *Conflict Resolution Quarterly*, *29*(1), 25–38. https://doi.org/10.1002/crq.21035

Kahn, W. A. (1990). Psychological conditions of personal engagement and disengagement at work. *Academy of Management Journal*, *33*(4), 692–724. https://doi.org/10.5465/256287

Kampa, J., Rigotti, T., & Otto, K. (2017). Mechanisms linking authentic leadership to emotional exhaustion: The role of procedural justice and emotional demands in a moderated mediation approach. *Industrial health*, *55*(2), 95–107. https://doi.org/10.2486/indhealth.2016-0046

Kiersch, C. E., & Byrne, Z. S. (2015). Is being authentic being fair? Multilevel examination of authentic leadership, justice, and employee outcomes. *Journal of Leadership & Organizational Studies*, *22*(3), 292–303. https://doi.org/10.1177/1548051815570035

Laschinger, H. K. S., & Read, E. A. (2016). The effect of authentic leadership, person-job fit, and civility norms on new graduate nurses' experiences of coworker incivility and burnout. *JONA: The Journal of Nursing Administration*, *46*(11), 574–580. https://doi.org/10.1097/nna.0000000000000407

Lee, R. T., & Brotheridge, C. M. (2011). Sex and position status differences in workplace aggression. *Journal of Managerial Psychology, 26*(5), 403–418. https://doi.org/10.1108/02683941111139010

Lemoine, G. J., Hartnell, C. A., & Leroy, H. (2019). Taking stock of moral approaches to leadership: An integrative review of ethical, authentic, and servant leadership. *Academy of Management Annals, 13*(1), 148–187. https://doi: 10.1097/NNA.0000000000000407

Leroy, H., Anseel, F., Dimitrova, N. G., & Sels, L. (2013). Mindfulness, authentic functioning, and work engagement: A growth modeling approach. *Journal of Vocational Behavior, 82*(3), 238–247. https://doi.org/10.1016/j.jvb.2013.01.012

Lewis, D. (2006). The contents of whistleblowing/confidential reporting procedures in the UK: Some lessons from empirical research. *Employee Relations, 28*(1), 76–86. https://doi.org/10.1108/01425450610633073

Lind, E. A., & Tyler, T. R. (1988). *The social psychology of procedural justice.* Plenum Press. https://doi.org/10.1007/978-1-4899-2115-4

Liu, S. M., Liao, J. Q., & Wei, H. (2015). Authentic leadership and whistleblowing: Mediating roles of psychological safety and personal identification. *Journal of Business Ethics, 131*(1), 107–119. https://doi.org/10.1007/s10551-014-2271-z

Loy, P., & Stewart, L. (1984). The extent and effects of the sexual harassment of working women. *Sociological Focus, 17*, 31–43. https://doi.org/10.1080/00380237.1984.10570460

Lutgen-Sandvik, P. (2008). Intensive remedial identity work: Responses to workplace bullying trauma and stigmatization. *Organization, 15*(1), 97–119. https://doi.org/10.1177/1350508407084487

Luthans, F., & Avolio, B. J. (2003). Authentic leadership: A positive developmental approach. In K. S. Cameron, J. E. Dutton & R. E. Quinn (Eds.), *Positive organizational scholarship* (pp. 241–261). Barrett-Koehler.

Mackey, J. D., Frieder, R. E., Brees, J. R., & Martinko, M. J. (2017). Abusive supervision: A meta-analysis and empirical review. *Journal of Management, 43*(6), 1940–1965. https://doi.org/10.1177/0149206315573997

Marshall, A. M. (2005). Idle rights: Employees' rights consciousness and the construction of sexual harassment policies. *Law & Society Review, 39*(1), 83–124. https://doi.org/10.1111/j.0023-9216.2005.00078.x

Matthiesen, S. B., & Einarsen, S. (2004). Psychiatric distress and symptoms of PTSD among victims of bullying at work. *British Journal of Guidance & Counseling, 32*(3), 335–356. https://doi.org/10.1080/03069880410001723558

Mayer, J. D., Caruso, D. R., & Salovey, P. (2016). The ability model of emotional intelligence: Principles and updates. *Emotion Review, 8*(4), 290–300. https://doi.org/10.1177/1754073916639667

Mazutis, D., & Slawinski, N. (2008). Leading organizational learning through authentic dialogue. *Management Learning, 39*(4), 437–456. https://doi.org/10.1177/1350507608093713

McCord, M. A., Joseph, D. L., Dhanani, L. Y., & Beus, J. M. (2018). A meta-analysis of sex and race differences in perceived workplace mistreatment. *Journal of Applied Psychology, 103*(2), 137–163. https://doi.org/10.1037/apl0000250

McDonald, P., Charlesworth, S., & Cerise, S. (2011). Below the "tip of the iceberg": Extra-legal responses to workplace sexual harassment. *Women's Studies International Forum,34*(4), 278–289. https://doi.org/10.1016/j.wsif.2011.03.002

Merkin, R.S., Shah, M.K. (2014). The impact of sexual harassment on job satisfaction, turnover intentions, and absenteeism: Findings from Pakistan compared to the United States. *SpringerPlus 3*, 215. https://doi.org/10.1186/2193-1801-3-215

Meyer, F., Le Fevre, D. M., & Robinson, V. M. (2017). How leaders communicate their vulnerability: Implications for trust building. *International Journal of Educational Management, 31*(2), 221–235. https://doi.org/10.1108/IJEM-11-2015-0150

Miao, C., Humphrey, R. H., & Qian, S. (2018). Emotional intelligence and authentic leadership: A meta-analysis. *Leadership & Organization Development Journal, 39*(5), 679–690. https://doi.org/10.1108/LODJ-02-2018-0066

Mikula, G., & Wenzel, M. (2000). Justice and social conflict. *International Journal of Psychology, 35*(2), 126–135. https://doi.org/10.1080/002075900399420

Misati, E., & Walumbwa, F. O. (2018). Authentic leaders as change Agents. In F. Ovadje & S. Aryee (Eds.), *Routledge handbook of organizational change in Africa* (pp. 138–154). Routledge. https://doi.org/10.4324/9781315630113-8

Morral, A. R., Schell, T. L., Cefalu, M., Hwang, J., Gelman, A., & Assault, S. (2018). *Sexual assault and sexual harassment in the U.S. military, Volume 5. Estimates for installation- and command-level risk of sexual assault and sexual harassment from the 2014 RAND military workplace study*. RAND Corporation. https://www.rand.org/pubs/research_reports/RR870z7.html

Neall, A. M., & Tuckey, M. R. (2014). A methodological review of research on the antecedents and consequences of workplace harassment. *Journal of Occupational and Organizational Psychology, 87*(2), 225–257. https://doi.org/10.1111/joop.12059

Nembhard, I. M., & Edmondson, A. C. (2006). Making it safe: The effects of leader inclusiveness and professional status on psychological safety and improvement efforts in health care teams. *Journal of Organizational Behavior: The International Journal of Industrial, Occupational and Organizational Psychology and Behavior, 27*(7), 941–966. https://doi.org/10.1002/job.413

Ng, T. W., & Feldman, D. C. (2015). Ethical leadership: Meta-analytic evidence of criterion-related and incremental validity. *Journal of Applied Psychology, 100*(3), 948–965. https://doi.org/10.1037/a0038246

Nielsen, M. B., & Einarsen, S. (2012). Outcomes of exposure to workplace bullying A meta-analytic review. *Work & Stress, 26*(4), 309–332. https://doi.org/10.1080/02678373.2012.734709

Okimoto, T. G., & Wenzel, M. (2014). Bridging diverging perspectives and repairing damaged relationships in the aftermath of workplace transgressions. *Business Ethics Quarterly, 24*(3), 443–473. https://doi.org/10.5840/beq201471515

O'Reilly, J., & Banki, S. (2016). Research in work and organizational psychology: social exclusion in the workplace. In P. Riva & J. Eck (Eds.), *Social exclusion: Psychological approaches to understanding reducing its impact* (pp. 133–155). Springer International Publishing. https://doi.org/10.1007/978-3-319-33033-4_7

Parzefall, M. R., & Salin, D. M. (2010). Perceptions of and reactions to workplace bullying: A social exchange perspective. *Human Relations, 63*(6), 761–780. https://doi.org/10.1177/0018726709345043

Peirce, E. R., Rosen, B., & Hiller, T. B. (1997). Breaking the silence: Creating user-friendly sexual harassment policies. *Employee Responsibilities and Rights Journal, 10*(3), 225–242. https://doi.org/10.1023/A:1025643318386

Perry, E. L., Block, C. J., & Noumair, D. A. (2020). Leading in: Inclusive leadership, inclusive climates and sexual harassment. *Equality, Diversity and Inclusion: An International Journal*. https://doi.org/10.1108/EDI-04-2019-0120

Porter, T. H., Day, N., & Meglich, P. (2018). City of discontent? The influence of perceived organizational culture, LMX, and newcomer status on reported bullying in a municipal workplace. *Employee Responsibilities and Rights Journal, 30*(2), 119–141. https://doi.org/10.1007/s10672-017-9310-8

Puente, S., Crous, F., & Venter, A. (2007). The role of a positive trigger event in actioning authentic leadership development. *SA Journal of Human Resource Management, 5*(1), 11–18. https://doi.org/10.4102/sajhrm.v5i1.103

Quick, J. C., & McFadyen, M. (2017). Sexual harassment: Have we made any progress? *Journal of Occupational Health Psychology, 22*(3), 286–298. https://doi.org/10.1037/ocp0000054

Raver, J. L., & Nishii, L. H. (2010). Once, twice, or three times as harmful? Ethnic harassment, gender harassment, and generalized workplace harassment. *Journal of Applied Psychology, 95*(2), 236–254. https://doi.org/10.1037/a0018377

Ribeiro, N., Duarte, A. P., Filipe, R., & de Oliveira, R. T. (2020). How authentic leadership promotes Individual Creativity: The mediating role of affective commitment. *Journal of Leadership & Organizational Studies*, 27(2), 189–202. https://doi.org/10.1177/1548051819842796

Robotham, K., & Cortina, L. (2019). Promoting respect as a solution to workplace harassment. *Equality, Diversity and Inclusion: An International Journal*. https://doi.org/10.1108/EDI-04-2019-0137

Romero, E. J., & Cruthirds, K. W. (2006). The use of humor in the workplace. *Academy of Management Perspectives, 20*(2), 58-69. https://doi.org/10.5465/amp.2006.20591005

Rospenda, K. M., & Richman, J. A. (2004). The factor structure of generalized workplace harassment. *Violence and Victims, 19*(2), 221–238. https://doi.org/10.1891/vivi.19.2.221.64097

Rossiter, L., & Sochos, A. (2018). Workplace bullying and burnout: The moderating effects of social support. *Journal of Aggression, Maltreatment & Trauma, 27*(4), 386–408. https://doi.org/10.1080/10926771.2017.1422840

Rotundo, M., Nguyen, D. H., & Sackett, P. R. (2001). A meta-analytic review of gender differences in perceptions of sexual harassment. *Journal of Applied Psychology, 86*(5), 914–922. https://doi.org/10.1037/0021-9010.86.5.914

Rowe, M. (1996). Dealing with harassment: A systems approach. *Sexual Harassment: Perspectives, Frontiers, and Response Strategies, Women & Work, 5*, 241–271. https://doi.org/10.4135/9781483327280.n12

Shaver, P. R., Mikulincer, M., Lavy, S., & Cassidy, J. (2009). Understanding and altering hurt feelings: An attachment-theoretical perspective on the generation and regulation of emotions. In A. L. Vangelisti (Ed.), *Advances in personal relationships. Feeling hurt in close relationships* (pp. 92–119). Cambridge University Press. https://doi.org/10.1017/cbo9780511770548.007

Shestowsky, D. (2004). Procedural preferences in alternative dispute resolution: A closer, modern look at an old idea. *Psychology, Public Policy, and Law, 10*(3), 211–249. https://doi.org/10.1037/1076-8971.10.3.211

Shore, L. M., Cleveland, J. N., & Sanchez, D. (2018). Inclusive workplaces: A review and model. *Human Resource Management Review, 28*(2), 176–189. https://doi.org/10.1016/j.hrmr.2017.07.003

Sitkin, S. B., & Bies, R. J. (1994). *The legalistic organization*. SAGE.

Sitkin, S. B., & Roth, N. L. (1993). Explaining the limited effectiveness of legalistic "remedies" for trust/distrust. *Organization Science, 4*(3), 367–392. https://doi.org/10.1287/orsc.4.3.367

Snyder, M. L., Stephan, W. G., & Rosenfield, D. (1976). Egotism and attribution. *Journal of Personality and Social Psychology, 33*(4), 435–441. https://doi.org/10.1037/0022-3514.33.4.435

Stockdale, M. S., Bisom-Rapp, S., O'Connor, M., & Gutek, B. A. (2004). Coming to terms with zero tolerance sexual harassment policies. *Journal of Forensic Psychology Practice, 4*(1), 65–78. https://doi.org/10.1300/J158v04n01_05

Stone, A. G., Russell, R. F., & Patterson, K. (2004). Transformational versus servant leadership: A difference in leader focus. *Leadership & Organization Development Journal, 25(4),* 349–361. https://doi.org/10.1108/01437730410538671

Tajfel, H., & Turner, J. C. (1984). Social groups and identities. Routledge.

Tepper, B. J., Simon, L., & Park, H. M. (2017). Abusive supervision. *Annual Review of Organizational Psychology and Organizational Behavior, 4*, 123–152. https://doi.org/10.1146/annurev-orgpsych-041015-062539

Thibaut, J. W., & Walker, L. (1975). *Procedural justice: A psychological analysis*. Erlbaum Associates.

Thomas, K. W., & Kilmann, R. H. (1978). Comparison of four instruments measuring conflict behavior. *Psychological Reports, 42*(3_suppl), 1139–1145. https://doi.org/10.2466/pr0.1978.42.3c.1139

Turner, J. C. (1982). Towards a cognitive redefinition of the social group. *Social Identity and Intergroup Relations*, 15–40.

Valsania, S. E., León, J. A. M., Alonso, F. M., & Cantisano, G. T. (2012). Authentic leadership and its effect on employees' organizational citizenship behaviours. *Psicothema, 24*(4), 561–566. https://www.redalyc.org/pdf/727/72723959009.pdf

van Loon, R., & van Dijk, G. (2015). Dialogical leadership: Dialogue as condition zero. *Journal of Leadership, Accountability & Ethics, 12*(3), 62–75. http://digitalcommons.www.na-businesspress.com/JLAE/vanLoonR_Web12_3_.pdf

Vogelgesang, G. R., Leroy, H., & Avolio, B. J. (2013). The mediating effects of leader integrity with transparency in communication and work engagement/performance. *The Leadership Quarterly, 24*(3), 405–413. https://doi.org/10.1016/j.leaqua.2013.01.004

Wagner, S. H., Parker, C. P., & Christiansen, N. D. (2003). Employees that think and act like owners: Effects of ownership beliefs and behaviors on organizational effectiveness. *Personnel Psychology, 56*(4), 847–871. https://doi.org/10.1111/j.1744-6570.2003.tb00242.x

Walumbwa, F. O., Avolio, B. J., Gardner, W. L., Wernsing, T. S., & Peterson, S. J. (2008). Authentic leadership: Development and validation of a theory-based measure. *Journal of Management, 34*(1), 89–126. https://doi.org/10.1177/0149206307308913

Walumbwa, F. O., & Schaubroeck, J. (2009). Leader personality traits and employee voice behavior: mediating roles of ethical leadership and work group psychological safety. *Journal of Applied Psychology, 94*(5), 1275–1286. https://doi.org/10.1037/a0015848

Wang, D. S., & Hsieh, C. C. (2013). The effect of authentic leadership on employee trust and employee engagement. *Social Behavior and Personality: An International Journal, 41*(4), 613–624. https://doi.org/10.2224/sbp.2013.41.4.613

Warszewska-Makuch, M., Bedyńska, S., & Żołnierczyk-Zreda, D. (2015). Authentic leadership, social support and their role in workplace bullying and its mental health consequences. *International Journal of Occupational Safety and Ergonomics, 21*(2), 128–140. https://doi.org/10.1080/10803548.2015.1028230

Wilkerson, J. M., & Meyer, J. C. (2019). On observers' conjunctive attributions and blame for workplace mistreatment. *Organization Management Journal, 16*(2), 111–122. https://doi.org/10.1080/15416518.2019.1604201

Wilson, F., & Thompson, P. (2001). Sexual harassment as an exercise of power. *Gender, Work & Organization, 8*(1), 61–83. https://doi.org/10.1111/1468-0432.00122

Yammarino, F. J., Dionne, S. D., Schriesheim, C. A., & Dansereau, F. (2008). Authentic leadership and positive organizational behavior: A meso, multilevel perspective. *The Leadership Quarterly, 19*(6), 693–707. https://doi.org/10.1016/j.leaqua.2008.09.004

Zhang, Y., & Bednall, T. C. (2016). Antecedents of abusive supervision: A meta-analytic review. *Journal of Business Ethics, 139*(3), 455–471. https://doi.org/10.1007/s10551-015-2657-6

Zhang, Y., Liu, X., Xu, S., Yang, L. Q., & Bednall, T. C. (2019). Why abusive supervision impacts employee OCB and CWB: A meta-analytic review of competing mediating mechanisms. *Journal of Management, 45*(6), 2474–2497. https://doi.org/10.1177/0149206318823935

Zhou, J., Ma, Y., Cheng, W., & Xia, B. (2014). Mediating role of employee emotions in the relationship between authentic leadership and employee innovation. *Social Behavior and Personality: An International Journal, 42*(8), 1267–1278. https://doi.org/10.2224/sbp.2014.42.8.1267

Zugelder, M. T., Champagne, P. J., & Maurer, S. D. (2006). An affirmative defense to sexual harassment by managers and supervisors: Analyzing employer liability and protecting employee rights in the United States. *Employee Responsibilities and Rights Journal, 18*(2), 111–122. https://doi.org/10.1007/s10672-006-9008-9

CHAPTER 10

DESTRUCTIVE LEADERSHIP EPISODES

Why Can't We Learn From Them?

Laura Gail Lunsford, Art Padilla, and Paul Mulvey

ABSTRACT

The main purposes of our chapter are to foster more thought about destructive leadership as a process rather than a person and about how to prevent or minimize negative impacts of toxic episodes. We focus on destructive leadership using the university as the organizational vehicle through which to examine it. The toxic triangle model frames our analysis of three university scandals: Nassar and Michigan State University; Sandusky and Pennsylvania State University; and the fake ("paper") classes at the University of North Carolina at Chapel Hill. In addition to a destructive leader, susceptible followers and conducive environments must be present for destructive leadership outcomes to occur. Our analysis takes a holistic view of leadership and attempts to integrate the literature with work on leader-member exchange and whistleblowers. The time dimension over which toxic episodes unfold is also examined. We argue that additional interdisciplinary work is needed to integrate relevant literatures. The role of checks and balances need more careful examination to inform a broader analysis of

Leadership:
Leaders, Followers, and Context, pp. 255–288

conducive environments. Organizational leaders should consider how to strengthen internal checks and balances, such as boards of trustees, to limit toxic environmental influences.

> "A board cannot perform much better than its president, although it can be a good deal worse"
>
> —Clark Kerr

> "We learn from history that we learn nothing from history."
>
> —George Bernard Shaw

Leadership has been traditionally studied using exemplary episodes with good or great organizational outcomes (Harrison, 2018; Khan et al., 2016). In addition to this emphasis on positive leadership situations, the historical focus has been mostly on the positional leaders themselves, on their traits and behaviors, and much less on followers and on the environments where leaders and followers interact (Avolio, 2007). Recently, increased attention has been devoted to not-so-exemplary, toxic situations and on broader, more holistic approaches (Dinh et al., 2014; Erickson et al., 2007; Krasikova et al., 2013). We propose that as much may gleaned from negative as from positive leadership events.

We define a negative or toxic leadership *episode* as an event or group of events resulting in poor outcomes for the organization relative to its peers. Toxic or destructive leadership is a general term encompassing such episodes. Some scholars define destructive leadership in terms of bosses' behaviors and traits: a leader who somehow intends to harm the organization (Craig & Kaiser, 2013; Krasikova et al., 2013; Mackey et al., 2019) or, more commonly, a leader who exhibits "bad" traits (Judge et al., 2009). In our view, meaningful analyses of destructive leadership require going beyond intentions, behaviors, or traits of an individual. We also posit that a comprehensive consideration of destructive leadership requires a broader, longer, and more inclusive analysis of the leadership process (Mulvey & Padilla, 2010).

In this chapter we focus on destructive leadership episodes using the university as the organizational vehicle. We first describe the toxic triangle framework (Padilla et al., 2007). Next, we identify three factors that add explanatory power to the toxic triangle: lack of protections for whistleblowers, leader-member exchange theory, and a time dimension. We then examine recent destructive leadership episodes using three university scandals at the Michigan State University (MSU), Pennsylvania State University (Penn State), University of North Carolina at Chapel Hill

(UNC) to show how toxic leadership emerges in organizations. Finally, we discuss how conducive environments may be of greater importance toward damaging organizational outcomes than has been previously recognized by scholars. The chapter concludes with recommendations for scholars and implications for practice.

TOXIC TRIANGLE

The toxic triangle model indicates that destructive leadership results from the interaction of leaders, followers, and environments (Padilla et al., 2007). In this formulation all three elements are required to explain and predict negative leadership episodes that leave an organization worse off relative to its peers or competitors (see Figure 10.1). In an important sense, the toxic triangle framework was proposed as an alternative to the leader-centric focus of much of the leadership literature of the last 50 years.

There have been important calls for broadening approaches to the study of leadership (Avolio, 2007), recognizing the limited perspective of previous leadership studies. And indeed, an increasing number of scholars have embraced more comprehensive approaches to understand toxic leadership (Fosse et al., 2019; Schyns & Schilling, 2013; Thoroughgood et al., 2018).

In the main, however, the behaviors and traits of lousy leaders continue to be equated with destructive leadership writ large. Contrariwise, the toxic triangle approach indicates that bad leaders are centrally important, but that destructive outcomes are also—and perhaps more importantly—about susceptible followers and conducive environments. We next briefly describe the three elements of the toxic triangle to provide theoretical context to our presentation of the three case studies.

Destructive Leaders

Destructive leaders are not necessarily destructive all of the time (Padilla et al., 2007; Thoroughgood et al., 2018). A destructive leader may be viewed as toxic by some followers but not so by other followers (Schyns & Schilling, 2013). We observe that leadership events are seldom as black-white or as definitively clear-cut as much of the literature suggests. Additionally, it may actually be difficult to determine who the specific "leader" of an event may be. In any event, Padilla and colleagues (2007) proposed five factors: charisma, personalized use of power, narcissism, negative life themes, and an ideology of hate. Below we cite some of the evidence scholars have found for some of these factors.

Figure 10.1

Revised Toxic Triangle With Lack of Protections for Whistleblowers, Leader-Member Exchange, and Time

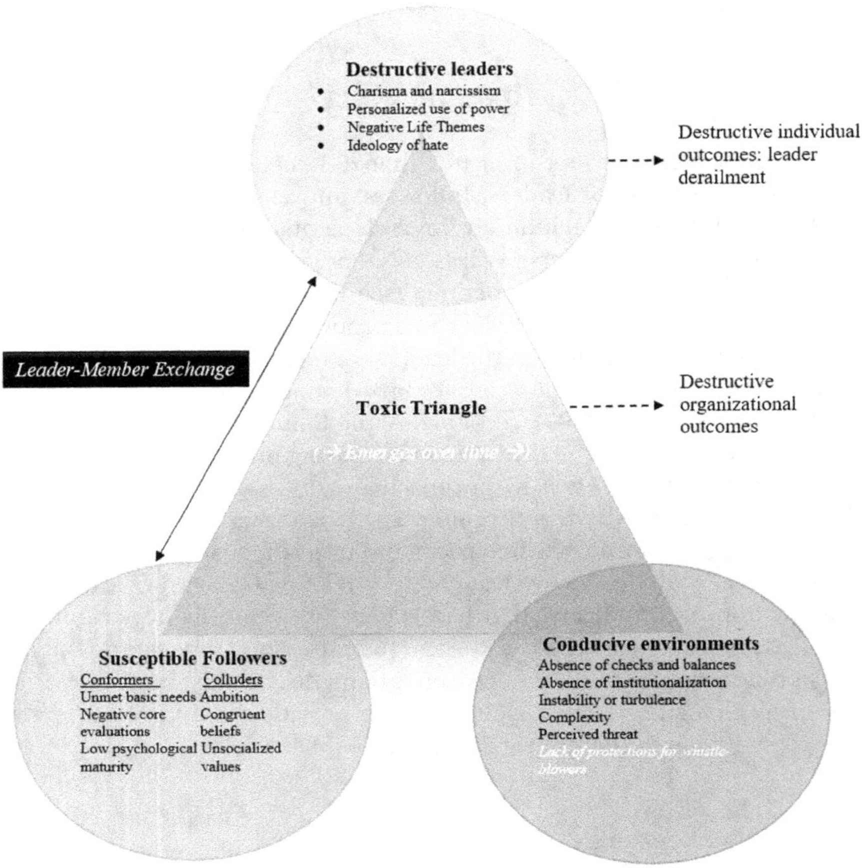

Note. Additions to the model are italicized in white font.

Charisma

Pundt (2014) proposed that leader use of charisma may be an antecedent to abusive leadership. He proposed five pathways by which charisma may lead to destructive leader behavior. For example, followers may perceive a leader as abusive when the leader exaggerates their qualities, which is a leader's use of overdramatized charisma. Lee et al. (2018) investigated the effects of charismatic leadership and abusive supervision. Abusive supervision attenuated the effects of charisma on outcomes such as team processes (i.e., cohesion and communication) and subjective measures of team performance over three months. Padilla et al. (2007) observed not all charismatic leaders are destructive, although many destructive leaders tend to be viewed as charismatic.

Personalized Use of Power

Personalized power is associated with bad leaders. Erickson and colleagues (Erickson et al., 2015) surveyed over 2,000 U.S. workers who reported being receivers of or witnesses to negative leader behaviors. Respondents noted that three specific behaviors were most frequently associated with bad leaders: making significant decisions without information, playing favorites, and being ineffective at coordinating and managing. Results of this study indicated that destructive leadership behaviors, as experienced and observed by targets and witnesses, increased over time if left unchecked (Erickson et al., 2015).

Narcissism

Hansbrough and Jones (2014) posited that leader narcissism influenced their cognitive processes. For example, narcissistic leaders interpreted a follower's facial expressions in ways that led the leader to believe that a follower's mistakes were intentional. As a result, these leaders viewed their abusive behaviors as reasonable responses to followers' supposed willfully-poor actions.

Literature on psychopathy and Machiavellianism, when joined with narcissism, results in the so-called "dark triad." This view adds a contextual element to leader and followers. Abusive supervision has been found to be positively related to leader psychopathy (Wisse & Sleebos, 2016) and to subordinate perceptions of abusive supervision with leader Machiavellianism (Kiazad et al., 2010). However, Wisse and Sleebos (2016) highlighted that these relationships weaken when the organization in question has a stronger culture of ethics. Put in the terminology of the toxic triangle, these relationships weaken when there are stronger followers and environments.

Negative Life Themes

Negative life themes refer to abusive or painful life experiences, usually occurring in childhood. These negative themes result in a worldview that reflects a lack of empathy for others and destructive close relationships (Padilla, 2013, p. 206). Some children are resilient after experiencing adversity but individuals are unlikely to flourish if multiple risk factors are experienced, for example, childhood abuse, poverty, lack of positive adult figures (Evans et al., 2013).

It is important to remember, as we consider the destructive leaders in the case studies below, that the available information about the perpetrators and principal actors is not nearly as detailed as it is for well-known totalitarian rulers like Mussolini or Mao and for other such infamous individuals. It is not unreasonable, even in the absence of detailed biographies and background studies, to believe that Nassar at MSU or Sandusky at Penn State had psychological problems and probably many of the other flaws and characteristics discussed above.

Susceptible Followers

Thoroughgood and colleagues (2012) extended the conceptualization of susceptible followers by placing conformers and colluders into more refined groups. The new taxonomy, based on differing personalities and needs, identified five categories of susceptible followers, three conformer types and two colluder types.

1. *Conformers—lost souls*: Lost souls are attracted to charismatic leaders whom they believe may provide clarity, direction, and increased self-esteem; offer a sense of community and belonging; and instill a clearer sense of self (Fromm, 1941; Howell & Shamir, 2005; Wright & Wright, 1982).
2. *Conformers—authoritarians:* Unlike the "lost souls," whose personal identification with leaders shapes their compliance, the authoritarian feels an obligation to obey based on the leader's status and position, which reflects the legitimacy of his or her power (Raven, 1993).
3. *Conformers—bystanders:* Perhaps the most common type of susceptible follower, bystanders seek to minimize the costs (e.g., loss of position, property, status, or life) of failing to conform by submitting to the leader and allowing destructive leadership to occur (Kellerman, 2004; Padilla et al., 2007).
4. *Colluders—opportunists:* Opportunists carry out destructive orders because they believe there is an instrumental link between their compliance and contingent rewards (Bass, 1985; Kuhnert & Lewis, 1987), suggesting exchanges are triggers at the core of their susceptibility (Barbuto, 2000).

5. *Colluders—acolytes:* Unlike lost souls, acolytes hold a firm sense of self and seek expression of their ideological values and beliefs via the leader's mission (Howell & Shamir, 2005). They are "true believers" not requiring strong inducements from destructive leaders to aid in achieving toxic organizational results (Barbuto, 2000).

There are myriad examples of conformers and colluders in the cases that follow below. We find that bystanders (conformers) are the most common susceptible follower in these cases. Further, positional leaders such as the university athletic directors or presidents may often be best viewed as a type of susceptible follower (e.g., colluder acolytes, colluder bystanders) in these negative leadership episodes, rather than as principal perpetrators of misdeeds.

Conducive Environments

Instability, perceived threat, certain cultural conditions, and/or an absence of checks and balances would be expected to create environments conducive to toxic leadership emergence (Mulvey & Padilla, 2010). Instability refers to less predictable environments and may result from social, political, or economic forces. The environments of public universities that are included in our three case studies have exhibited dramatic decreases in state support even as they face increases in enrollment (Taylor et al., 2020). Presidential tenure among public universities has also decreased sharply, leading to greater organizational instability (Monks, 2012; Padilla & Ghosh, 2000). And of course, the size and economic impact of big-time college sports have risen to unparalleled levels, creating huge pressures to enroll athletes inadequately prepared for rigorous academic work and to generate revenues to build new athletic facilities and pay stunning coach salaries.

Strong and prosperous groups tend to have transparent processes with countervailing centers of power. These organizations check or balance or restrain the power of leaders and elite groups. Weak or ineffective groups, by contrast, shield leaders from outside scrutiny and thereby facilitate toxic leader and follower behaviors specifically and the process of destructive leadership generally (Fukuyama, 2011; Padilla et al., 2007; Padilla, 2013). Managerial discretion in the management literature and the notion of presidentialism from political science concern the degree to which senior managers or executives are insulated from oversight and influence of others (Crossland & Hambrick, 2007; Linz & Valenzuela, 1994). Organizational environments with empowered followers and effective cultures or environments that share authority and power are different from those with more centralized structures in two respects: level of transparency and number and quality of checks and balances. There is an interesting paradox here: the stronger and more autonomous the central authority, the less empowered and influential the followers and the less effective the organizational controls (Argyris, 1998; Finkelstein & Hambrick, 1990).

Checks and balances may be internal or external to an institution. Erickson and colleagues (2015) reported two effective internal checks that may prevent hiring or keeping destructive leaders: a) educating selection committees on destructive leader behaviors and, b) regular performance reviews that solicit employee feedback. Similarly, Sharma (2018) proposed that organizations can organize leader promotions and advancements around cooperative goal accomplishments to allow for greater leader accountability. Financial audits and the print and television media are also important external checks although the power and influence of the media have seriously dissipated over the last three decades. Athletic scandals have generated significant media attention in the past and the three episodes described below all received extraordinary media attention considering the decline of newspapers and massive reductions in staff. In the cases analyzed below many such elements of conducive environments are present. Each university scandal also led to investigative reports by outside individuals that highlighted many of the elements of conducive environments discussed above.

WHISTLEBLOWERS

Whistleblowers may provide important internal checks and balances in organizations and illustrate the interaction between leaders and followers. A fundamental question is: why don't more employees call out bad behaviors? A partial answer is found in the nomenclature of susceptible followers discussed above (Thoroughgood et al., 2012). Whistleblowing research emerged, in part, out of the bystander intervention (Latane & Darley, 1968, 1970), prosocial behavior (Dozier & Miceli, 1985), and diffusion of responsibility (Mathes & Kahn, 1975) literatures. In general, the leadership and whistleblowing literatures have not intersected widely while the destructive leadership and whistleblowing literatures have yet to overlap. It is an area that warrants further exploration. A lack of protection for whistleblowers, in the toxic triangle model, is a factor contributing to a conducive environment (see Figure 10.1).

Whistleblowing is a process involving a whistleblower, the complaint, the receiver of the complaint, and the organization or person against which the complaint is lodged (Near & Miceli, 1985). The process is "the disclosure by organization members (former or current) of illegal, immoral, or illegitimate practices under the control of their employers, to persons or organizations that may be able to effect action" (Near & Miceli, 1985, p. 4). According to Near and Miceli (1985) the whistleblowing process involves two decisions by the whistleblower: "Is the observed activity illegal, immoral or illegitimate? and if yes: Should the activity be reported?" (p. 5). These whistleblower decisions will be affected by their motivation to act, their individual characteristics, the circumstances around the activity, and the power of those involved (Near & Miceli, 1985).

One reason to focus on internal whistleblowers is that large, complex organizations are relatively impenetrable to outsiders (Miethe, 1999). Even so, while the whistle-blowing activity may be on the rise (Miceli et al., 1999) most employees who believe they could blow the whistle do not do so (e.g., Brown, 2008; Miceli & Near, 1992; Miceli et al., 2008), and these numbers are likely lower in high power distance cultures (Treviño & Nelson, 2017).

Some of these factors overlap with the toxic triangle model (Padilla et al., 2007). For example, Near and Miceli (1985) argue that the lower an individual's moral development, the higher their self-esteem, and the higher their internal locus of control (i.e., low maturity and core self-evaluations), the less likely he or she will be to report perceived wrongdoing. The individual would be seen as a conformer (bystander) in the susceptible follower taxonomy described earlier.

Padilla and colleagues (2007) noted that managerial discretion allows managers the freedom from constraints to do their jobs, but that this discretion can lead to an abuse of power. Educational institutions have been bastions of "academic freedom" where leaders are allowed and allow much autonomy to their units (Aberbach & Christensen, 2018). Autonomy and decentralization in large organizations, including universities, may allow the problem to grow to the point where leaders find it difficult to manage without severe repercussions to their tenure and their organizations. In sum, the research on whistleblowing highlights the organizational inertia towards ignoring or covering up malfeasance.

Whistleblowing research may add to our knowledge and explanation of destructive leadership. In the cases we will present the questionable activity was not stopped; the whistleblower's report was essentially ignored, and the whistleblower was punished only when their report became public. Why did their reports, that is, checks and balances, not stop the wrongdoing that ultimately lead to toxic leadership in each of these cases? In fact, the risks of negative effects from being a whistleblower (e.g., loss of position, legal action, criminal charges, public scrutiny, embarrassment, effects on family members, and social stigma) are high and the potential for having the toxic behavior stopped are low (Shine, 2007).

LEADER-MEMBER EXCHANGE

Leaders and followers are two of three elements of the toxic triangle. The principal focus of susceptible follower research has been on the types of followers (Padilla et al., 2007) and the subtypes within those categories (Thoroughgood et al., 2012). However, an exploration of the relationship between leaders and followers may increase our understanding of why destructive episodes occur (Schyns, 2015). Scholars are beginning to examine how abusive supervision (what they refer to as destructive leadership) influences employee workplace behavior (Mackey et al., 2018).

Leader-member exchange (LMX) is framework that adds to our understanding of the leader-follower interaction in destructive leadership episodes. LMX is unique in the pantheon of leadership theories as it focuses on the dyadic relationships between leaders and followers and posits that the relationship quality between leaders and members are the key to understanding leader effects on followers and their organizations (Graen & Uhl-Bien, 1995).

LMX was developed to focus on positive leadership experiences. However, LMX can explain relationships between destructive leaders and susceptible followers. The taxonomies of conformers (including the authoritarians, lost souls, bystanders) and colluders (acolytes and opportunists) is useful here (Padilla et al., 2007; Thoroughgood et al., 2012). Colluders would be expected to have higher quality relationships with their leaders than would conformers.

Followers are the first line of defense against destructive leaders (Thoroughgood et al., 2012), but organizational and cultural norms often socialize followers not to challenge leaders (e.g., Mulvey et al., 1996). The high-quality relationships between destructive leaders and susceptible followers (i.e., colluders) in a strong context or culture that promotes the appearance of excellence may result in their strong motivation to protect each other and the organization rather than report wrongdoing. Those susceptible followers with lower quality relationships with the leader may not know of the issues, or if they do they assume others will take the lead to report illegal or inappropriate behaviors.

Through the lens of LMX theory, flipping the toxic triangle may be helpful. Characteristics of toxic leaders may be applied to followers (e.g., personalized power, narcissistic, negative life themes) and leaders may display some of the characteristics associated with followers (Schyns, 2015). In all three destructive leadership cases discussed below, organizational leaders were, at the best, negligently unaware of the toxic behavior, or at worst, covered the toxic behavior to protect themselves and their organization.

TIME

Destructive leadership episodes invariably occur over significant periods of time whereas most leadership research investigating such episodes does not consider a time dimension. The cases we analyze below unfolded over decades. However, in reviews of the leadership research over the last 50 years little of the leadership research is longitudinal (e.g., Dulebohn et al., 2012; Kozlowski et al., 2016; Schyns & Schilling, 2013). When the research is longitudinal the time frames rarely extend beyond one year (e.g., Bass et al., 2003; Britt et al., 2012; Detert, et al., 2007; Eid et al., 2008; Nahum-Shani et al., 2014; Yammarino et al., 1993). Keller's (2006) study is a rare exception by extending the study to period to five years. Schyns and Schilling (2013) included a consideration of the time dimension by acknowledging that a longer time period is needed for the negative follower behaviors to occur. Thoroughgood et al. (2018) also highlighted the importance of a dynamic time frame. Their perspective emphasized that time is needed for leaders and followers to interact and for negative patterns and behaviors to emerge fully.

Toxic leadership behaviors, such as in the UNC paper classes case, may start with behaviors that are unethical or unfair rather than blatantly illegal. For example, a professor may give student-athletes second chances or grade their work more leniently than that of other students. Once that behavior goes unnoticed and unpunished, other increasingly immoral behavior might be attempted. Gino and Bazerman (2009) found support for this slippery slope when subjects were exposed to gradually increasing misconduct or questionable or unethical behavior. They found that people were less likely to reject "unethical decisions" if those decisions were increasingly more unethical over time rather than if they were abrupt. Or, to use the "boiling frog syndrome" noted by Senge (1994); people would be less likely to note unethical behavior of others if it gradually increased over time.

In summary, the toxic triangle shows that a destructive leader, without susceptible followers and conducive environments, is insufficient for poor organizational outcomes to occur. Bad leaders are derailed and ejected from their organizations. Toxic leadership occurs through the interaction of destructive leaders, susceptible followers, and conducive environments. Our review suggests that three additions to the toxic triangle model provide additional explanatory power. Lack of protections for whistleblowers contributes to creating conducive environments; LMX further explains the leader-follower interactions; and these episodes take a long time to develop. Figure 10.1 presents these additional elements.

PROLOGUE TO DESTRUCTIVE LEADERSHIP CASES

We selected the scandals at MSU, Penn State, and UNC for two principal reasons. First, there was extensive media and scholarly discussion of these events that was helpful in analyzing the outcomes and circumstances of these episodes. Second, our decades-long experience in and familiarity with the university organizational context facilitates our ability to understand and analyze events.

These three cases are not unique. There have been numerous unfortunate incidences in both academic and corporate organizations and their implications and lessons apply broadly to other organizational settings. There have been recent scandals, all involving sexual abuse and misconduct at, for example, the University of Southern California (Medina, 2018), Ohio State (Bauer-Wolf, 2019) and Baylor University (Cash, 2018). The controversies at Volkswagen (Goodman, 2015) involving cheating on emissions controls; at Theranos (Carreyrou, 2015), involving fraudulent blood testing; and at Boeing (Slotnick, 2019), involving faulty airplanes, are illustrative of destructive leadership episodes at for-profit companies. These scandals were not the result of a single bad actor, but instead were destructive precisely because each scandal involved many individuals and situations or environments that left the organization worse off relative to its peers.

Michigan State University and the Nassar Scandal

> "MSU stonewalls the very investigation it pledged to support"
>
> —Forsyth, 2018, p. 2

More than 330 women were sexually abused over a period 22 years by Larry Nassar while he was employed as a professor and physician at MSU and was associated with USA Gymnastics as a physician for Olympic athletes. The story of how he abused so many women for such a long time includes the firing of MSU's leaders; employee whistleblowers who were ignored; payouts of hundreds of millions of dollars in fines, fees, and judgements to survivors, lawyers, and the U.S. Department of Education; and reputational damage to MSU (Denhollander, 2019). Nassar and his immediate boss, William Strampel, dean of MSU's medical school, were sentenced to jail time; the retired women's gymnastics coach Kathie Klages awaits sentencing after a jury found her guilty of two counts of lying to a police officer about Nassar's abuse (Garcia, 2020a); and the Michigan State Attorney's office plans to appeal the dismissal of charges against former President

Lou Anna Simon (Garcia, 2020b) who asserts she did not know that it was Nassar who was the sports medicine doctor abusing women.

Destructive Leaders

Nassar is the central destructive leader in this case. He was a worldwide leader in treating elite gymnasts and other athletes (Mack & Lawler, 2017). The sexual abuse he committed suggests the presence of negative life themes (Vandiver, 2006), but little information is available about his early life.

William Strampel, the dean of the medical school, was Nassar's immediate boss and could also be considered a destructive leader in this episode. During his 15-year tenure as dean, complaints about Strampel's inappropriate and erratic behavior reached the president, three provosts, and the university's lawyer, among others. The negative information in his regular performance reviews, which included 360-degree employee feedback, was ignored, according to the Office of Civil Rights (Stanley, 2019). Strampel was sentenced to jail after being convicted for failing ensure Title IX protocols were followed, which could have stopped Nassar in 2014. Strampel, through his narcissism and personalized use of power, fostered a climate where sexual harassment and misconduct was tolerated.

Susceptible Followers

The MSU President, Lou Anna Simon, spent her 45-year professional career at MSU, rising from the faculty ranks to become provost, vice president, then president in 2005. Having spent her entire career in various positions at MSU, she arguably had a strong incentive to protect the institution's reputation. She was a positional leader but is considered a follower in this negative leadership episode. Her accomplishments had been touted widely up until her handling of the Nassar case. In court, she acknowledged she knew of a doctor's sexual abuse but did not specifically know it was Nassar (Garcia, 2020b). She resigned the day Nassar was convicted. In September 2019, the U.S. Department of Education released the report on their Title IX investigations and fined MSU $4.5 million. The then-provost, June Youatt, is another superior from an organizational point of view but a susceptible follower in this leadership episode as a bystander who allowed Dean Strampel's poor behavior to continue. Youatt resigned the day the Title IX investigation was released.

However, it was not just Nassar's superiors who did nothing. An investigation by the Michigan Attorney General documented 10 employees, from disparate offices, who knew and ignored complaints about Nassar between 1997 and 2015 (Forsyth, 2018). Most survivors were silenced by coaches and trainers (Denhollander, 2019) through various admonitions, excuses, and warnings, noting to victims that no other athletes had complained. Employees who knew about Nassar perhaps did not want to believe the reports, much less "blow the whistle." They conformed while Nassar's egregious behavior continued. Only one employee reported Nassar's abuse to the Title IX office, and that report was essentially ignored.

Conducive Environments

Forsyth (2018) found that MSU had internal checks and balances such as regular 360 employee reviews and Title IX investigations that theoretically should have stopped Nassar. Yet these checks and balances did not prevent the abuse—why not?

First, MSU had a dysfunctional culture that valued protecting the school's reputation at all costs. For example, the dean's poor performance reports were ignored by the provost as were several documented cases where abuse was reported but ignored by the various susceptible followers noted above. Second, the internal checks and balances were not well established. The MSU Board of Trustees (BOT) are publicly elected to oversee the institution and to provide internal checks on behavior. However, the BOT supported the president almost to the end, over the institution (Forsythe, 2018). It took an external body to motivate the BOT into action. The Michigan House of Representatives voted 96–11 for the President to resign or for the Board of Trustees to fire her. Ultimately, the BOT exercised some of their check and balances power by asking the state Attorney General to investigate how this abuse could have happened at MSU. The resulting report (Forsyth, 2018) noted that an important lesson from the MSU episode is that "automatic deference to authority creates presumptions that work against those without authority" (Forsyth, 2018, p. 10). The report continued: MSU leaders failed to provide much of the requested information and the public may never know what really happened. According to Forsyth (2018), MSU had, and continues to have, a culture that hides the truth in favor of protecting its reputation and funding.

Third, the big-time sports environment at MSU created a secretive culture that led to protecting the institution's reputation over calling out any wrongdoing. Nassar had large photographs of Olympian gymnasts in the hallway at the entrance to his offices. His patients were typically awed by them. It may have been Nassar's association with the women's USA Olympic team that led so many people to express disbelief of reports of sexual assault (Denhollander, 2019).

Denhollander, the first survivor to come forward publicly, did so only after reading about the abuse of gymnasts on the USA Team in a news story published in the IndyStar (Crawford & Haneline, 2018). She delayed reporting Nassar for over a decade. Her training as a lawyer almost uniquely prepared her to have the knowledge and the fortitude to publicly name Nassar and describe the unbelievable in precise, legalistic descriptions until it could no longer be ignored (Denhollander, 2019). The state of Michigan has had state-level whistleblower protections since 1980. However, the penalty for violating Michigan's Whistleblowers' Protection Act (n.d.) is relatively minor, a fine of up to $500.

Penn State and Sandusky's Sexual Abuse

> Four of the most powerful people at The Pennsylvania State University—President ... Spanier, Senior Vice President-Finance and Business ... Schultz, Athletic Director ... Curley and Head Football Coach ... Paterno-failed to protect against a child sexual predator harming children for over a decade. These men concealed Sandusky's activities from the Board of Trustees, the University community and authorities. They exhibited a striking lack of empathy for Sandusky's victims by failing to inquire as to their safety and well-being, especially by not attempting to determine the identity of the child who Sandusky assaulted in the Lasch Building in 2001. (Freeh Sporkin & Sullivan, LLC., 2012, p. 14).

Jerry Sandusky's sexual abuse of boys was known to Penn State employees and leaders, including Coach Paterno, as early as 1994, although it had been going on before 1994. The list of negative outcomes of this toxic leadership episode is long (Thoroughgood & Padilla, 2013). In addition to the unimaginable harm caused to the 10 documented survivors, the University paid out over $100 million to survivors, to lawyers, and to cover NCAA penalties. The finances and reputation of the University clearly suffered, although we note, only temporarily as in the cases of the other two universities in this study. The University's credit rating was downgraded by Moody and there was the lost revenue from bowl games for four seasons. Paterno's reputation, closely tied to the University's, was tarnished; his name removed from awards, trophies and his 900-pound brass statue was removed from outside the football stadium.

Destructive Leaders

Jerry Sandusky, the destructive leader in this case, continues to claim his innocence in the 45 counts of child sex abuse that led to his 30- to 60-year prison sentence in 2012 at the age of 68. He founded a charity, the Second Mile, for at-risk youth and was a community leader in addition to holding a position as an assistant coach and defensive coordinator on the Penn State football team. As was the case with Nassar, it is likely he had negative life themes as is common with male, sexual predators. He was also charismatic as demonstrated by his popularity with the young men (and their parents) participating in the Second Mile.

Susceptible Followers

The positional leaders, such as the university president and vice president, were the susceptible followers in this episode. Specifically, they were certainly conformers and, in some ways, colluding and enabling followers as well. Several superiors knew about but ignored Sandusky's actions. A police investigation in 1998 about Sandusky's abuse was known by several Penn State's leaders making Coach Paterno's continued claims that he knew nothing more problematic. Despite his denials, Paterno was fired from the university and passed away soon thereafter from lung cancer.

Graham Spanier, one of the nation's longest serving presidents who was often sought out for other university vacancies, reportedly chose to ignore reports of Sandusky's abuse and to prioritize the University reputation over disclosure of possible criminal behavior. He was convicted for his role in the scandal, but later the conviction was overturned on a legal technicality. According to the Chronicle of Higher Education (Stripling, 2019), the judge agreed that Spanier's prosecutors had "improperly applied a [Pennsylvania] child endangerment law, from 2007, to hold Spanier accountable for his conduct in 2001" (para. 2)

Spanier was not the only colluder. Other employees who both colluded and conformed were the mid-level managers, athletic director Curley and Vice President Schultz, who reportedly sought to protect their own and the University's reputation. Curley and Schutlz were charged with felony perjury and for failing to report Sandusky's abuse. They were eventually convicted of a misdemeanor charge of child endangerment, and each received a few months in jail.

A janitor, James Calhoun, who witnessed Sandusky's sexual abuse, is a classic example of a conformer. He was troubled by what he witnessed and in tears reported it to his coworkers and to their supervisor, Jay Witherite. Nothing was done with this revelation and Calhoun was afraid to pursue it out of fear of losing his job. In the *Freeh Report* he was quoted as saying he was afraid that "they'll get rid of all of us" (Freeh Sporkin & Sullivan, LLC., 2012, p. 22).

Conducive Environments

There were few internal or external checks and balances on the big-time sports culture at Penn State. Faculty governance was relatively weak (Thoroughgood & Padilla, 2013). The BOT was composed of numerous former football players and there was a lack of transparency, accountability, and board independence. It may be tempting to suggest that the publicly-elected trustees at Michigan State were more likely to include prominent former athletes and boosters of the university. Public election of trustees is an exception in American higher education; besides Michigan, only Colorado, Nebraska, and Nevada elect trustee boards by popular vote (Kelchen, 2018). However, it is true that these sorts of individuals are also widely present in public university boards that are not elected by voters but are instead appointed by governors or legislatures.

Finances and the celebrity of sports contributed to an environment where there was an economic motivation to ignore Sandusky's abuse. There was a strong economic incentive not to question decisions when it came to the Nittany Lions football team. Culturally, there was (and still is) student and alumni hero worshipping of Jo Pa (Paterno) and big-time sports. In fact, the alumni and fans argued Paterno had done no wrong. According to ESPN's article "Joe Paterno is Now the Winningest Coach" (2015) his vacated wins were restored in 2017 by the NCAA making him, again, the winningest coach in NCAA history. Within three years of the scandal the Penn State team returned to the ranks of the elite football teams, competing in a minor bowl game in 2014 and in the Rose Bowl in 2016.

The Penn State Board of Trustees, which should have served as a crucial and indispensable internal check and balance, claimed to remedy wrongs and accept the consequences (Strauss, 2012) but then successfully lobbied to reduce the NCAA fine of $100 million. After firing Paterno, the BOT commissioned a former FBI director to investigate; his findings are in what is called the *Freeh Report* (Freeh Sporkin & Sullivan LLC., 2012). Freeh's hard-hitting investigation concluded that Penn State and its senior officials had ignored evidence and had acted improperly on several different and important levels. The report noted that "the most powerful people at The Pennsylvania State University ... failed to protect against a child sexual predator harming children for over a decade" (Freeh Sporkin & Sullivan LLC., 2012, p. 14).

A major whistleblower in this case was Mike McQueary, a former Penn State quarterback, who was a low-level employee (a graduate student) when he reported an incident in 2001 to Paterno. His report was ignored but he also did nothing further while advancing to a full-time position with the Nittany Lions, his dream job. As in the MSU case, it took external influences to provide the needed counterweight for McQueary's complaint to be heard. Investigators contacted McQueary in 2010 to provide corroboration needed for the Pennsylvania Attorney General to pursue the case. McQueary's testimony earned the ire of Penn State and football fans and coaches. His contract was not renewed; he was unable to get another job in college football or sports; and he separated from his wife and child. However, he was eventually awarded $12 million from Penn State in a defamation and whistleblower lawsuit (Boren, 2017), because of a 2011 public statement issued by Penn State where the university president defended the perjury of Curley and Schultz.

University of North Carolina's "Paper Classes" Scandal

> UNC-Chapel Hill escaped NCAA sanctions, in what was one of the longest-running academic scandals in college sports history, in large part by refusing to identify as fraudulent 16 years of classes that had no instruction and were graded by a secretary. (Kane, 2017, para. 1)

Between 1992 until 2009, the University of North Carolina at Chapel Hill (UNC) offered hundreds of "paper" or fake independent study classes thorough its African American Studies department. (They were called "paper" classes because the sole requirement for the three-hour class was a term paper). About half of the students were athletes, including dozens from the football and basketball programs and all the key players in the 2005 men's basketball NCAA championship team. The destructive outcomes from this episode include the departure or separation of numerous university leaders, institutional reputational awkwardness, and considerable resources allocated during a protracted, three-year investigation by the NCAA. Eventually, after several years of indecision and hesitancy, the NCAA averred no jurisdiction to intervene because the fake classes were also taken by some non-athletes (Tracy, 2017). The university's regional accrediting body imposed a one-year probation for the fake courses, a penalty more embarrassing than substantial for a highly regarded university (Korn, 2015).

The list of departures is impressive: the football coach; the athletic director; a chair of the faculty; a department head; several advisors and tutors; one (and possibly two) campus chancellors; and the system-wide president. In addition to resignations and firings, the seemingly interminable episode resulted in an erosion of trust and unsympathetic media attention for a premier university where unfailingly favorable coverage had previously existed. The University spent at least $21 million in lawyers, PR, and investigative costs to defend the institution (Kane, 2018; Smith & Willingham, 2019).

This case illustrates how organizational or positional leaders may be in fact followers in a negative leadership episode. The UNC episode is also extraordinary due to its breadth and duration, highlighting how destructive leadership episodes unfold over decades.

Destructive Leaders

The destructive leaders in the UNC case were the departmental secretary, Deborah Crowder, and the department head, Professor Julius Nyang'oro. Crowder seemingly masterminded the classes that kept many athletes academically eligible, working in part with athletic tutors and coaches (Smith & Willingham, 2019). She reportedly believed she was supporting the athletes. Professor Nyang'oro, chair of the African American Studies department, continued offering the classes for another two years after Crowder's retirement in 2009, receiving significant, "overload" payment for "independent study" classes that normally would be individually approved by a dean on a student-by-student basis.

Susceptible Followers

When allegations about the classes emerged, Chancellor Holden Thorp, who was previously the dean of the college at the time the courses were offered, declared his surprise. Thorp, who rose through the ranks at UNC, claimed neither he nor his associates in the college of arts and sciences were aware of the fake classes. Following additional revelations resulting from tenacious newspaper reporting (Stripling, 2012), Thorp announced his plans to resign his chancellorship and return to the faculty. Within a few months Thorp left Chapel Hill and moved to Washington University in St. Louis as provost (Kiley, 2013).

Carol Folt was named chancellor in 2013 and a few weeks after arriving in Chapel Hill acknowledged that "there was a failure in academic oversight for years ... and it has undermined our integrity and our reputation and created a very unhealthy atmosphere of distrust" (Stancill, 2014). Others saw her as protecting athletics as she "maintained the fiction that all previous investigators had done all they could do" (Smith & Willingham, 2015, p. 264). Folt later became embroiled in a controversy about a Confederate statue ("Silent Sam") on campus and left in 2019 to become president of the University of Southern California (Hamilton & Ryan, 2019).

Numerous people knew about the fake classes, including administrators, coaches, and tutors. An investigative report stated these individuals were "knowingly complicit" in the scandal while maintaining that the scandal was academic and not athletic (Wainstein, 2014, p. 64). One of the innumerably embarrassing revelations that dribbled out over the long span of this scandal involved the chair of the faculty. The chair, an untenured instructor and director of a center on ethics, also served as advisor to the women's basketball team and had guided athletes toward the fake classes with written suggestions about the grades the athletes needed (New, 2014).

Conducive Environments

The main conducive factors were the lack of internal check and balances, no protections for whistleblowers, financial and reputational concerns, an absence of institutionalization, and organizational complexity. The usual institutional processes of approval for independent studies and summer classes involving department chair, dean, and registrar, were absent.

All members of the local trustee board at the Chapel Hill campus were prominent alumni. Several had close connections with the athletic department through its booster group, the Ram's Club. As the scandal grew, UNC, like Michigan State, hired a recognized citizen to investigate allegations—a former Republican Governor of North Carolina and chemistry professor at Davidson College, Jim Martin. Martin released his findings in December, 2012. There was wrongdoing in academics, Martin said, but it was not due to athletic pressures. After additional newspaper reports emerged, Martin reversed field and affirmed it was "an extraordinary athletic scandal" (Hood, 2015).

Internal checks and balances of faculty review and staff reports of bad behavior were largely ignored. For example, a faculty committee (the Faculty Executive Committee) released a report documenting 50 courses of concern but the report was quickly shelved. History professor Jay Smith, the most outspoken UNC faculty member during this episode, later became one of the two whistleblowers and co-author of the book *Cheated* (Smith & Willingham, 2019). Smith maintains few if any systemic changes have been made at UNC. Mary Willingham, a former UNC learning specialist, worked with athletes and was the original whistleblower who confirmed many of the allegations. Named "Whistleblower of the Year" in 2014, she received a settlement from UNC for $350,000 though she did not get her job back as she had wanted.

Continued pressure from national and local publications led the systemwide Board of Governors, which has ultimate statutory responsibility for the 17 UNC campuses, to intervene. They joined the Chapel Hill campus in commissioning Kenneth Wainstein, a former U.S. Justice official, to investigate again. The report reached two conclusions: (1) the courses were a result of a "loose, decentralized approach to management" and, of overarching importance to coaches and senior administrators, (2) there was "no evidence that the higher levels of the University tried in any way to obscure the facts or the magnitude of this situation" (Wainstein, 2014, p. 6).

The initial or triggering episode that started all of it involved sports agents and football players. It led to minor NCAA punishments. The significantly larger scandal of the fake classes that followed was uncovered only after extraordinary reporting but did not lead to any NCAA penalty. It did not result in the draconian "lack of institutional control" NCAA penalty, as would have likely occurred had there been a finding that it was an athletic, and not an academic, scandal.

Throughout the episode, there were major differences in perception about the gravity of the event. The local newspaper, among many others, was convinced that UNC was guilty of a major athletic cover-up designed to protect the popular men's basketball team in particular (Lyall, 2014). National publications derided the university's insistence that there was no athletic scandal (Tracy, 2017). Affected coaches claimed to know nothing. Some campus administrators conceded mistakes were made but that none of them were intentional or related to athletics. Alumni and others suggested that "everyone is doing it."

DISCUSSION

These cases illustrate four points, which we discuss next. First, all three elements of the toxic triangle are needed for destructive leadership events to take place and a conducive environment may arguably be the most critical of the three elements. These cases show that destructive leadership was only possible when a destructive leader acted in concert with susceptible followers and conducive environments.

Divergences among or conflicts between organizational goals (e.g., success in sports vs. integrity in recruiting academically well-prepared athletes) are additional contextual factors contributing to possible unethical behavior and potentially toxic outcomes (Kerr, 1975). However, destructive leaders continue their bad actions only when others allow them to do so, either by conforming or colluding with the leader's actions. Many individuals of authority in their respective communities knew about Nassar, Sandusky, and Nyang'oro but, remarkably, few of them ever reported the destructive leaders. And when reports were made they were almost universally disbelieved, disparaged, or ignored. We suggest here that it was the conducive aspects of environments that made it very difficult for superiors and followers to intervene. These cases demonstrate that environments conducive to toxicity are difficult to overcome in avoiding destructive leadership episodes.

This element of the toxic triangle, the environment, warrants more attention than it has received in understanding destructive leadership episodes. In particular, the celebrity and money in Division I sports appears to exacerbate the factors producing a conducive environment for toxic leadership. College sports are a valuable adjunct to the university experience and many people across America enjoy them. But it is inescapable that big-time sports present huge challenges to the major universities choosing to play at the highest levels of competition. All of the major scandals discussed above involved big-time sports. According to Branch (2011), they appear to have corrupted universities where "educators are in thrall to their athletics departments because of television riches."

But Branch (2011) is not entirely correct about the lure of riches: most of the money in big-time college sports stays within athletic departments. Salaries of university presidents and other top administrators may be "pulled" upwards by the bewilderingly high coaches' salaries but otherwise, there is little spillover into the main academic purposes of the university. The athletic enterprise and its upwardly spiraling funding are now entirely outside and independent of the rest of the campus.

College sports are entertainment activities in which many provosts or deans rising to the office of president, a common route of promotion, have not had any relevant experience. University presidents generally have little familiarity negotiating celebrity salaries for coaches or TV deals or with the financing of "state of the art" facilities for athletics. These issues are not comparable to promotion and tenure discussions or allocation of resources based on teaching loads. Yet universities put presidents in charge of massive athletic departments, usually the largest economic entity on a campus with the possible exception of a very large medical complex, without much preparation and with substantial pressures from "boosters" on their trustee boards. Many presidents at major public universities are hired by influential trustees with deep, personal ties to coaches and athletic departments.

In addition, the principal faculty influence on college sports on a campus comes through its faculty advisory committee and particularly its chair. The chair of the advisory committee represents the university at NCAA and athletic conference meetings and the committee usually oversees athletic recruitment, including exceptions to regular admission standards, and compliance with rules and regulations. Yet, the chairs (unlike other committee members) are often not selected by the faculty at large but rather are hand-picked by presidents or other senior administrators in consultation with athletic interests. Members of athletics advisory committees in the past have received free tickets and preferential seating to sporting events. These appointments and customs vary from university to university, of course, but the usefulness of athletic advisory committees may be compromised by such practices.

The media, an external check and balance, through dogged, tenacious—one is tempted to say extraordinary—journalistic reporting led to the discovery of the three destructive leadership episodes discussed here. In the case of Michigan State, Denhollander saw a story in the IndyNews about Nassar and publicly came forward, thereby encouraging many other survivors to tell their stories. *The New York Times* credits Raleigh reporter Dan Kane's persistent demands for public records month after month for the revelations in the UNC case. At Penn State it was McQueary's public confirmation, after a tip steered the police to contact him, that led to Sandusky's conviction. Yet, in spite of the importance of the media in the exposure of these unethical and corrupt events, these reporters were unusually unique. This is both good news and bad news; good because the episodes came to light, bad because it apparently took phenomenal effort to bring that light.

The newspaper and broadcast TV news industries are in a profound state of decline. Significant areas of the country are now called "news deserts," with no newspaper or TV coverage. The decline of the so called "fourth estate" affects not only university athletic scandals but the in-depth, continuing coverage of corruption and misdeeds in all sorts of organizations at all levels.

Second, for most individuals it is difficult to "blow the whistle" on a colleague, leader, or follower given the risk to the whistleblower (Shine, 2007), the relationships involved, and strong organizational contexts (Miceli et al., 2008). For a variety of reasons, including the dyadic relationships among leaders and followers and forces preventing whistleblowing, it is incredibly hard for followers to report their colleagues and for superiors to want to investigate reports of wrongdoing. Yet, whistleblowers are an indispensable check on bad actors and actions in organizations. Without whistleblowers episodes of destructive leadership could have continued in all three cases. Organizations need to find effective methods to encourage, support, and protect whistleblowers. In addition, receivers of these whistleblowing reports need encouragement, support, and protection so as to not to ignore or bury the information provided by the whistleblowers. At the same time processes to encourage action against wrongdoing should be sensitive to false reports by whistleblowers.

Faculty oversight in college sports has reportedly been declining, even though a strong faculty voice might make the president's job easier. However, there appear to be few incentives for faculty members to get involved or to blow whistles. The very people in charge of the institution, the trustees, are usually among the biggest sports boosters and fans. They in turn put considerable pressure on administrators to have successful athletic programs. In addition, related interests such as the increasingly powerful athletic conferences (e.g., Atlantic Coast Conference, Southeastern

Conference, and Big Ten Conference) as well as television networks and local media profit substantially from popular college sports.

Third, we often look to the overall organizational leader to praise or to blame, when in fact there are leaders throughout the organization who may be responsible for destructive leadership. These cases examine in relevant detail the various leaders, followers, and environments. In some instances, leaders and followers are problematic to define. Is the university president, for example, the "leader" or is the "leader" the chief perpetrator of the misdeeds and the president a colluding or conforming "follower?"

Finally, the cases highlight the need for more attention to a time dimension in studying leadership events. The scandals explain how cross-sectional research fails to identify fully toxic leadership episodes because these events often develop over years and even decades These scandals unfolded over decades: over 15 years at Penn State; 22 years at Michigan State; and 18 years at UNC. In the case of Michigan State and Penn State, there were horrible consequences for the many young people and others who suffered perhaps irreparable harm. The consequences at UNC are harder to pinpoint and define, but they are real nonetheless, in terms of institutional mistrust leading to discord in governance structures and cynicism about phrases such as the "Carolina Way."

The time dimension is also relevant when considering how long destructive outcomes persist. We note that major public universities are huge economic and organizational entities and are obviously capable of continuing their principal missions of education and research more or less unimpeded. None of these universities has disappeared, as did, for example, Enron, after serious destructive leadership episodes. Indeed, all of the universities made nearly complete organizational comebacks. In the case of UNC and Penn State, there also continue to be denials of wrongdoing among significant elements of their communities. These considerations underscore two points about leadership episodes in general and destructive ones in particular: they are not black-or-white in the eyes of everyone concerned and they seem to be always temporary after some period of shock, distress, and setback.

FUTURE RESEARCH

We suggest three areas for future research. First, different approaches, for example, longitudinal and/or case studies are required to accommodate the time dimension over which toxic leadership episodes unfold; cross-sectional studies are useful but incomplete.

Second, additional interdisciplinary work is needed to integrate relevant literatures. Here we attempted to integrate the whistleblower and LMX literatures with the toxic triangle. LMX, for example, offers a potential vehicle to explain the interactions between toxic leaders and susceptible followers. As LMX theory focuses on the quality of the exchange between leaders and followers, the high quality has assumed positive outcomes for the LMX pair and the organization. However, toxic leaders may exploit these high-quality relationships to the detriment of the organization and its constituencies as in the UNC, Penn State, and MSU cases. Unfortunately, much of the LMX work does not look beyond the dyad (Avolio et al., 2009). Combining LMX and the destructive leadership literatures may add value to both in understanding when and how the leader follower relationships may harm the organization.

Another area for future inquiry is trait activation theory (Tett & Burnett, 2003; Tett & Guterman 2000), which might offer an explanation to the interaction of toxic leader traits and environments or situations. Trait activation theory posits that trait-relevant situational cues prompt responses from leaders with those traits (Tett & Burnett 2003). Toxic leaders may express toxic traits, such as narcissism, when presented with trait-relevant situational cues, such as a weak board of trustees. Or, for example, it may explain why Nassar was enabled to behave unethically and illegally because of the climate of the medical school, which insulated and protected him. There are other fruitful areas to explore, especially from political science and management.

Third, the role of checks and balances should be examined more carefully and incorporated into a broader analysis of conducive environments. For example, the collapse of the newspaper industry raises concerns about external oversight of organizations. It was journalistic investigations, over a considerable period of time, that brought to light all three of the destructive leadership episodes discussed here.

RECOMMENDATIONS FOR PRACTICE

The paper title suggests that we do not seem to learn from previous toxic leadership episodes. University athletic scandals are almost painfully formulaic. They seem to replicate a fairly common pattern or formula: a revelation in the media; surprise or denial expressed by the main actors; an investigation; new revelations, surprises, and additional denials; firings and departures; return to normal.

At the same time, we recognize thankfully that there are thousands of private, public, and nonprofit organizations that seem to be doing their jobs well without running afoul of the law or without engaging in unethical or inappropriate behavior. It may be that these illegal or unethical "squeaky" wheels get most of the public attention. However, while these episodes may be few relative to the grand total, there are enough destructive leadership episodes to warrant further scrutiny and attention about their causes and how to prevent or minimize them.

A continued overemphasis on leader behaviors is not enough. In fact, there are few policy implications from studies that focus on leaders alone. Most CEOs do not take batteries of psychological tests that may reveal, a priori, undesirable flaws or abusive behaviors. Past behavior predicts future behavior fairly well, it is said, but organizations do a remarkably poor job in examining past behavior of potential job prospects (Hogan et al., 1994). Mistakes in hiring are to be expected, and it is organizationally prudent to detect those mistakes before they happen or to address them quickly if they do occur.

Internal checks and balances need to be both sufficiently strong and adequately institutionalized to intervene effectively in long-emerging events. These cases suggest organizational leaders should consider three actions: (a) increasing transparency with members of boards of trustees, (b) including independent outsiders on such boards, and (c) strengthening protections for whistleblowers.

First, boards of trustees need to be involved regularly in reports related to athletics, given its out-sized influence on universities. Presidents should be expected to share data on athletic admissions, and exceptions, as well as all Title IX reporting. It is more difficult to neglect uncomfortable or inappropriate behaviors when more individuals are directly involved. Trustees are expected to be both critics and advocates simultaneously for their universities. There is always a fragile balance between advocacy and criticism. Clark Kerr's poignant comment about boards and presidents cited at the start of this paper underscores the primacy of effective communications between board members and presidents, including educating trustees on the intricacies and challenges of universities.

These cases show that it does not seem to matter if trustees are appointed or elected; in most cases they are overwhelmingly alumni or have close connections to the institution. Most trustees are appointed with the knowledge of the presidents and in many instances are carefully selected by them. There is nothing improper or nefarious about this: presidents have observed many of these potential trustees over months and years on alumni boards or some college committee. Many such individuals are economically successful and able to make significant contributions to the university. Other board members and even the state's governors and legislators are often likely to defer to a president's judgement in those appointments. One recent criticism made of university boards is that political trustee appointees, especially at the major public universities, are closely aligned with the politicians who appoint them and tend not to be very independent of those politicians or of their agendas. Working effectively with boards is a skill, and as with any skill, some presidents are more skillful at it than are others. It behooves trustees choosing presidents to find the more skillful ones.

Second, research suggests that having "outsiders" on boards is associated with more independence by those board members; it probably makes sense to have some outsiders on every board. One can be an effective critic while also being a supporter of the institution. There is often a delicate dance between the university president and his or her board regarding college sports. If the chief university administrator is surrounded by "yes" men and women and isn't comfortable with, or at least tolerant of, well meaning, courteous criticism from faculty and others, it should ring warning bells for trustees. At the same time, trustees need to appreciate the difference between policy and operation. Given the frequent turnover of both presidents and trustees, this is not only a delicate dance but also a frustratingly difficult one for many presidents.

Third, a properly functioning, internal whistleblowing procedure with externally monitored checks and balances system may reduce toxic behaviors in organizations. Using data of almost 2 million whistleblowing reports from NAVEX Global, who provide internal whistleblowing systems to thousands of organizations, Stubben and Welch (2019) found that internal whistleblowing volume is negatively related to the number and amount of government fines and material lawsuits filed against the organization.

CONCLUSION

University examples of destructive leadership are, unfortunately, more plentiful than the three cases presented and likely more widespread in all types of organizations. In this chapter we argued that research is largely cross-sectional in contrast to many destructive leadership episodes that unfold over decades. Integration of whistleblower and LMX literatures with the toxic triangle is helpful. Organizational leaders should consider how strengthen internal checks and balances, such as boards of trustees, ombuds, and other resources to limit conducive environments from which toxic leadership emerges.

REFERENCES

Aberbach, J. D., & Christensen, T. (2018). Academic autonomy and freedom under pressure: Severely limited, or alive and kicking? *Public Organization Review, 18*(4), 487–506. https://doi:10.1007/s11115-017-0394-2

Argyris, C. (1998). Empowerment: The emperor's new clothes. *Harvard Business Review, 76*(3), 98–105. https://hbr.org/1998/05/empowerment-the-emperors-new-clothes

Avolio, B. J. (2007). Promoting more integrative strategies for leadership theory-building. *American Psychologist, 62*(1), 25. https://doi.org/10.1037/0003-066X.62.1.25

Avolio, B. J., Walumbwa, F. O., & Weber, T. J. (2009). Leadership: Current theories, research, and future directions. *Annual Review of Psychology, 60*, 421–449. https://doi.org/10.1146/annurev.psych.60.110707.163621

Barbuto, J. E., Jr. (2000). Influence triggers: A framework for understanding follower compliance. *The Leadership Quarterly, 11*(3), 365–387. https://doi.org/10.1016/S1048-9843(00)00045-X

Bass, B. M. (1985). Leadership: Good, better, best. *Organizational Dynamics, 13*, 26–40. https://doi.org/10.1016/0090-2616(85)90028-2

Bass, B. M., Avolio, B. J., Jung, D. I., & Berson, Y. (2003). Predicting unit performance by assessing transformational and transactional leadership. *Journal of Applied Psychology, 88*, 207–218. https://doi.org/10.1037/0021-9010.88.2.207

Bauer-Wolf, J. (2019, May). 2 decades of abuse, 177 victims, no action. *Insider Higher Ed.* https://www.insidehighered.com/news/2019/05/20/former-ohio-state-doctor-abused-nearly-200-young-men-no-consequences-decades.

Boren, C. (2017, November). Mike McQueary ends whistleblower lawsuit against Penn State. *The Washington Post.* https://www.washingtonpost.com/news/early-lead/wp/2017/11/07/mike-mcqueary-ends-whistleblower-lawsuit-against-penn-state/

Branch, T. (2011, October). The shame of college sports. *The Altantic.* https://www.theatlantic.com/magazine/archive/2011/10/the-shame-of-college-sports/308643/

Britt, T. W., Wright, K. M., & Moore, D. (2012). Leadership as a predictor of stigma and practical barriers toward receiving mental health treatment: A multilevel approach. *Psychological Services, 9*, 26–37. https://doi.org/10.1037/a0026412

Brown, A.J. (2008). *Whistleblowing in the Australian public sector: Enhancing the theory and practice of internal witness management in public sector organizations.* ANU E-Press. https://www.jstor.org/stable/j.ctt24h7w1

Carreyrou, J. (2015, October). Hot startup Theranos has struggled with its blood-test technology. *The Wall Street Journal.* https://www.wsj.com/articles/theranos-has-struggled-with-blood-tests-1444881901

Cash, M. (2018, October). NCAA completes investigation into Baylor's sexual assault scandal and cites school for 'lack of institutional control,' one of the most serious charges possible. *Business Insider.* https://www.businessinsider.com/ncaa-completes-investigation-baylor-2018-10

Craig, S. B., & Kaiser, R. B. (2013). Destructive leadership. In M. Rumsey (Ed.) *The Oxford handbook of leadership* (pp. 439–454). Oxford University Press.

Crawford, D. & Haneline, A. (2018, January). IndyStar's Nassar coverage from start to end. *IndyStar.* https://www.indystar.com/story/sports/2018/01/24/indystar-larry-nassar-usa-gymnastics-investigation/1062120001/

Crossland, C., & Hambrick, D. C. (2011). Differences in managerial discretion across countries: how nation-level institutions affect the degree to which CEOs matter. *Strategic Management Journal, 32*(8), 797–819. https://doi.org/10.1002/smj.913

Denhollander, R. (2019). *What is a girl worth? My story of breaking the silence and exposing the truth about Larry Nassar and USA Gymnastics*. Tyndale House.

Detert, J. R., Trevino, L. K., Burris, E. R., & Andiappan, M. 2007. Managerial modes of influence and counterproductivity in organizations: A longitudinal business-unit-level investigation. *Journal of Applied Psychology, 92*(4), 993–1005. https://doi.org/10.1037/0021-9010.92.4.993

Dinh, J. E., Lord, R. G., Gardner, W. L., Meuser, J. D., Liden, R. C., & Hu, J. (2014). Leadership theory and research in the new millennium: Current theoretical trends and changing perspectives. *The Leadership Quarterly, 25*(1), 36–62. https://doi.org/10.1016/j.leaqua.2013.11.005

Dozier J. B., & Miceli M. P. (1985) Potential predictors of whistle-blowing: A prosocial behavior perspective. *Academy of Management Review, 10*(4), 823–836. https://doi.org/10.5465/amr.1985.4279105

Dulebohn, J. H., Bommer, W. H., Liden, R. C., Brouer, R. L., & Ferris, G. R. (2012). A meta-analysis of antecedents and consequences of leader-member exchange: Integrating the past with an eye toward the future. *Journal of Management, 38*(6), 1715–1759.

Eid, J., Johnsen, B. H., Bartone, P. T., & Nissestad, O. A. (2008). Growing transformational leaders: Exploring the role of personality hardiness. *Leadership & Organization Development Journal, 29*, 4–23. https://doi.org/10.1108/01437730810845270

Erickson, A., Shaw, J. B., & Agabe, Z. (2007). An empirical investigation of the antecedents, behaviors, and outcomes of bad leadership. *Journal of Leadership Studies, 1*(3), 26–43. https://doi.org/10.1002/jls.20023

Erickson, A., Shaw, B., Murray, J., & Branch, S. (2015). Destructive leadership. *Organizational Dynamics, 4*(44), 266–272. https://doi.org/10.1016/j.orgdyn.2015.09.003

Evans, G. W., Li, D., & Whipple, S. S. (2013). Cumulative risk and child development. *Psychological Bulletin, 139*(6), 1342. https://doi.org/10.1037/a0031808

Finkelstein, S., & Hambrick, D. C. (1990). Top-management-team tenure and organizational outcomes: The moderating role of managerial discretion. *Administrative Science Quarterly, 35*(3), 484–503. https://doi.org/10.2307/2393314

Freeh Sporkin, & Sullivan, LLC. (2012). *Report of the special investigative counsel regarding the actions of the Pennsylvania State University related to child sexual abuse committed by Gerald A. Sandusky*. https://www.documentcloud.org/documents/396512-report-final-071212.html

Forsyth, W. (2018, December). *Status of the independent special counsel's investigation into Michigan State University's handling of the Larry Nassar matter*. https://www.michigan.gov/documents/ag/MSU_Investigation_Status_Update_final.redacted_JOB_644663_7.pdf

Fosse, T. H., Skogstad, A., Einarsen, S. V., & Martinussen, M. (2019). Active and passive forms of destructive leadership in a military context: a systematic review and meta-analysis. *European Journal of Work and Organizational Psychology, 28*(5), 708–722. https://doi.org/10.1080/1359432X.2019.1634550

Fromm, E. (1941). *Escape from freedom*. Holt Rinehart & Winston.

Fukuyama, F. (2011). *The origins of political order: From prehuman times to the French Revolution*. Farrar, Straus and Giroux.

Garcia, S. (2020a, February 14). Former coach is convicted of lying about knowledge of abuse by Larry Nassar. *The New York Times*. https://www.nytimes.com/2020/02/14/us/kathy-klages-trial-larry-nassar.html

Garcia, S. (2020b, May 13). Charges against former Michigan State President are dismissed. *The New York Times*. https://www.nytimes.com/2020/05/13/us/michigan-state-university-president-charges.html

Gino, F., & Bazerman, M.H (2009). When misconduct goes unnoticed: The acceptability of gradual erosion in others' unethical behavior. *Journal of Experimental Social Psychology, 45*(4), 708–719. https://doi.org/10.1016/j.jesp.2009.03.013

Goodman, L. M. (2015, December 15). Why Volkswagen cheated. *Newsweek*. https://www.newsweek.com/2015/12/25/why-volkswagen-cheated-404891.html

Graen, G. B., & Uhl-Bien, M. (1995). The relationship-based approach to leadership: Development of LMX theory of leadership over 25 years: Applying a multi-level, multi-domain perspective. *Leadership Quarterly, 6(2),* 219–247. https://doi.org/10.1016/1048-9843(95)90036-5.

Hamilton, M., & Ryan, H. (2019, September 20). USC President Carol Folt's daunting task: Fix a university battered by scandal. *Los Angeles Times*. https://www.latimes.com/california/story/2019-09-19/usc-presdent-carol-folt-inaugurated-and-takes-on-the-daunting-task-to-fix-university

Hansbrough, T. K., & Jones, G. E. (2014). Inside the minds of narcissists: How narcissistic leaders' cognitive processes contribute to abusive supervision. *Zeitschrift Für Psychologie, 222*(4), 214–220. https://doi.org/10.1027/2151-2604/a000188

Harrison, C. (2018). Leadership research and theory. In *Leadership Theory and Research* (pp. 15–32). Palgrave Macmillan.

Hogan, R., Curphy, G. J., & Hogan, J. (1994). What we know about leadership: Effectiveness and personality. *American Psychologist, 49*(6), 493. https://doi.org/10.1037/0003-066X.49.6.493

Hood, J. (2015). *Catalyst: Jim Martin and the Rise of North Carolina Republicans*. John F. Blair.

Howell, J. M., & Shamir, B. (2005). The role of followers in the charismatic leadership process: Relationships and their consequences. *Academy of Management Review, 30*, 96–112. https://doi.org/10.5465/amr.2005.15281435

Joe Paterno is the winningest coach. (2015, January 16). *ESPN*. https://www.espn.com/college-football/story/_/id/12179571/joe-paterno-111-wins-were-vacated-restored

Judge, T. A., Piccolo, R. F., & Kosalka, T. (2009). The bright and dark sides of leader traits: A review and theoretical extension of the leader trait paradigm. *The Leadership Quarterly, 20*(6), 855–875. https://doi.org/10.1016/j.leaqua.2009.09.004

Kane, D. (2017, October 13). NCAA faces criticism for UNC decision. *News and Observer*. https://www.newsobserver.com/article178784981.html

Kane, D. (2018, August 10). New legal bills push UNC's tab for academic scandal to $21 million. *News and Observer*. https://www.newsobserver.com/latest-news/article216462745.html

Kelchen, R. (2018). *Higher education accountability*. JHU Press.

Keller, R. T. (2006). Transformational leadership, initiating structure, and substitutes for leadership: A longitudinal study of research and development project team performance. *Journal of Applied Psychology, 91*(1), 202–210. https://doi.org/10.1037/0021-9010.91.1.202

Kellerman, B. (2004). *Bad leadership: What it is, how it happens, why it matters*. Harvard Business Press.

Kerr, S. (1975). On the folly of rewarding A, while hoping for B. *Academy of Management Journal, 18*(4), 769–783. https://doi.org/10.5465/255378

Khan, Z. A., Nawaz, A., & Khan, I. (2016). Leadership theories and styles: A literature review. *Leadership, 16*(1), 1–7.

Kiazad, K., Restubog, S., Zagenczyk, T., Kiewitz, C., & Tang, R. L. (2010). In pursuit of power: The role of authoritarian leadership in the relationship between supervisors' Machiavellianism and subordinates' perceptions of abusive supervisory behavior. *Journal of Research in Personality, 44*, 512–519. https://doi.org/10.1016/j.jrp.2010.06.004

Kiley, K. (2013, February 18). Stepping out of the spotlight. *Insider Higher Ed*. https://www.insidehighered.com/news/2013/02/18/unc-chapel-hill-chancellor-holden-thorp-become-provost-washington-university-st

Korn, M. (2015, June 11). UNC-Chapel Hill put on yearlong probation by accreditor. *The Wall Street Journal*. https://www.wsj.com/articles/unc-chapel-hill-put-on-yearlong-probation-by-accreditor-1434047690

Kozlowski, S. W., Mak, S., & Chao, G. T. (2016). Team-centric leadership: An integrative review. *Annual Review of Organizational Psychology and Organizational Behavior, 3*, 21–54.

Krasikova, D. V., Green, S. G., & LeBreton, J. M. (2013). Destructive leadership: A theoretical review, integration, and future research agenda. *Journal of Management, 39*(5), 1308–1338. https://doi.org/10.1177/0149206312471388

Kuhnert, K. W., & Lewis, P. (1987). Transactional and transformational leadership A constructive-developmental analysis. *Academy of Management Review, 12*, 648–657. https://doi.org/10.5465/amr.1987.4306717

Latane, B., & Darley, J. M. (1968) Group inhibition of bystander intervention in emergencies. *Journal of Personality and Social Psychology, 10*, 215–221. https://doi.org/10.1037/h0026570

Latane, B., & Darley, J. M. (1970). *The unresponsive bystander: Why doesn't he help?* Appleton-Century-Crofts.

Lee, J., Wang, G., & Piccolo, R. F. (2018). Jekyll and Hyde leadership: A multilevel, multisample examination of charisma and abuse on follower and team outcomes. *Journal of Leadership & Organizational Studies, 25*(4), 399–415. https://doi.org/10.1177/1548051818757692

Linz, J. J., & Valenzuela, A. (Eds.). (1994). *The failure of presidential democracy* (Vol. 1). JHU Press.

Lyall, S. (2014, April 27). Reporter digging into scandal hits a university's raw nerve. *New York Times*. https://www.nytimes.com/2014/04/27/sports/reporter-digging-into-scandal-hits-a-universitys-raw-nerve.html

Mack, J., & Lawler, E. (2017, February). MSU doctor's alleged victims talked for 20 years. Was anyone listening? *MLive*. https://www.mlive.com/news/page/msu_doctor_alleged_sexual_assault.html

Mackey, J. D., McAllister, C. P., Maher, L. P., & Wang, G. (2019). Leaders and followers behaving badly: A meta-analytic examination of curvilinear relationships between destructive leadership and followers' workplace behaviors. *Personnel Psychology*, *72*(1), 3–47. https://doi.org/10.1111/peps.12286

Mathes, E. W., & Kahn, A. (1975). Diffusion of responsibility and extreme behaviour. *Journal of Personality and Social Psychology*. *31(5)*, 881–886. https://doi.org/10.1037/h0076695

Medina, J. (2018, October 19). University of Southern California to pay $215 million over sex abuse scandal. *New York Times*. https://www.nytimes.com/2018/10/19/us/usc-sex-abuse-settlement-george-tyndall.html

Miceli, M. P., & Near, J. P. (1992). *Blowing the whistle: The organizational and legal implications for companies and employees*. Lexington Books.

Miceli M. P., Near J. P., & Dworkin T. M. (2008). *Whistle-blowing in organizations*. Routledge.

Miceli, M. P., Rehg, M., Near, J. P., & Ryan, K. C. (1999). Can laws protect whistle-blowers? Results of a naturally occurring field experiment. *Work and Occupations*, *26*(1), 129–151. https://doi.org/10.1177/0730888499026001007

Miethe, T. D. (1999). *Whistleblowing at work: Tough choices in exposing fraud, waste, and abuse on the job*. Westview Press.

Monks, J. (2012). Job turnover among university presidents in the United States of America. *Journal of Higher Education Policy and Management*, *34*(2), 139–152. https://doi.org/10.1080/1360080X.2012.662739

Mulvey, P. W., Veiga, J. F., & Elsass, P. M. (1996). When teammates raise a white flag. *Academy of Management Executive*, *10*(1), 40–49. https://doi.org/10.5465/ame.1996.9603293195

Mulvey, P. W., & Padilla, A. (2010). The environment of destructive leadership. In B. Schyns and T. Hansbrough (Eds.), *When leadership goes wrong: Destructive leadership, mistakes, and ethical failures* (pp. 49–71). Information Age Publishing.

Nahum-Shani, I., Henderson, M. M., Lim, S., & Vinokur, A. D. (2014). Supervisor support: Does supervisor support buffer or exacerbate the adverse effects of supervisor undermining? *Journal of Applied Psychology*, *99*, 484–503. https://doi.org/10.1037/a0035313

Near, J.P. & Miceli, M.P. (1985). Organizational dissidence: The case of whistle-blowing. *Journal of Business Ethics*, *4*(1), 1–16. https://doi.org/10.1007/BF00382668

New, J. (2014, October, 23). Two decades of 'paper classes.' *Inside Higher Ed*. https://www.insidehighered.com/news/2014/10/23/report-finds-academic-fraud-u-north-carolina-lasted-nearly-20-years

Padilla, A. (2013). *Leadership: Leaders, followers, and environments*. Wiley & Sons.

Padilla, A., & Ghosh, S. (2000). Turnover at the top: The revolving door of the academic presidency. *Presidency*, *3*(1), 30–37. https://eric.ed.gov/?id=EJ615002

Padilla, A., Hogan, R., & Kaiser, R. B. (2007). The toxic triangle: Destructive leaders, susceptible followers, and conducive environments. *The Leadership Quarterly*, *18*(3), 176–194. https://doi.org/10.1016/j.leaqua.2007.03.001

Pundt, A. (2014). A multiple pathway model linking charismatic leadership attempts and abusive supervision. *Zeitschrift für Psychologie, 222*(4), 190–202. doi:10.1027/2151-2604/a000186

Raven, B. H. (1993). The bases of power: Origins and recent developments. *Journal of Social Issues, 49,* 227–251. https://doi.org/10.1016/j.leaqua.2007.03.001

Schyns, B. (2015). Leader and follower personality and LMX. In T. N. Bauer & B. Erdogan (Eds.), *The Oxford handbook of leader-member exchange*. Oxford University Press.

Schyns, B., & Schilling, J. (2013). How bad are the effects of bad leaders? A meta-analysis of destructive leadership and its outcomes. *The Leadership Quarterly, 24*(1), 138–158. https://doi.org/10.1016/j.leaqua.2012.09.001

Senge, P. M. (1994). *The fifth discipline: The art and practice of the learning organization*. Currency Doubleday.

Sharma, P. N. (2018). Moving beyond the employee: The role of the organizational context in leader workplace aggression. *The Leadership Quarterly, 29*(1), 203–217. https://doi.org/10.1016/j.leaqua.2017.12.002

Shine, D. B. (2007). Pity the Sox whistleblower; pity the Sox lawyer whistleblower! *Labor Law Journal, 58*(4), 228–241.

Slotnick, D. (2019). Boeing CEO Dennis Muilenburg is out as the 737 Max crisis drags on. Here's the complete history of the plane that's been grounded since 2 crashes killed 346 people 5 months apart. *Business Insider.* Retrieved July 1, 2019. https://www.businessinsider.com/boeing-737-max-timeline-history-full-details-2019-9

Smith, J. M., & Willingham, M. (2019). *Cheated: The UNC scandal, the education of athletes, and the future of big-time college sports*. Potomac Books.

Stancill, J. (2014, January 23). UNC chancellor says university accepts responsibility for academic fraud. *News and Observer.* https://www.newsobserver.com/news/local/education/unc-scandal/article16915172.html

Stanley, S. L. (2019, September). OCR Docket No. 15-18-6901. https://msu.edu/ourcommitment/_assets/documents/OCR-MSU-Agreement-2019.pdf

Strauss, V. (2012, July). Penn State Board of Trustees failed: Sandusky report. *Washington Post.* https://www.washingtonpost.com/blogs/answer-sheet/post/penn-state-trustees-failed-sandusky-report/2012/07/12/gJQALjBTfW_blog.html

Stripling, J. (2012, September 17). Controversies take a toll on Holden Thorp, who will resign at Chapel Hill. *The Chronicle of Higher Education.* https://www.chronicle.com/article/Controversies-Take-a-Toll-on/134506

Stripling, J. (2019, April 30). With last-minute ruling, Graham Spanier evades jumpsuit and 'Hard Cell'. *The Chronicle of Higher Education.* https://www.chronicle.com/article/With-Last-Minute-Ruling/246212

Stubben, S., & Welch, K. (2019). Evidence on the use and efficacy of internal whistleblowing wystems. http://doi.org/10.2139/ssrn.3273589

Taylor, B. J., Cantwell, B., Watts, K., & Wood, O. (2020). Partisanship, white racial resentment, and state support for higher education. *The Journal of Higher Education,* 1–30. https://doi.org/10.1080/00221546.2019.1706016

Tett, R. P., & Burnett, D. D. (2003). A personality trait-based interactionist model of job performance. *Journal of Applied Psychology, 88*(3), 500. https://doi.org/10.1037/0021-9010.88.3.500

Tett, R. P., & Guterman, H. A. (2000). Situation trait relevance, trait expression, and cross-situational consistency: Testing a principle of trait activation. *Journal of Research in Personality, 34*(4), 397–423.

Thoroughgood, C. N., Padilla, A., Hunter, S. T., & Tate, B. W. (2012). The susceptible circle: A taxonomy of followers associated with destructive leadership. *The Leadership Quarterly, 23*(5), 897–917. https://doi.org/10.1016/j.leaqua.2012.05.007

Thoroughgood, C. N., & Padilla, A. (2013). Destructive leadership and the Penn State scandal: A toxic triangle perspective. *Industrial and Organizational Psychology, 6*(2), 144–149. https://doi.org/10.1111/iops.12025

Thoroughgood, C. N., Sawyer, K. B., Padilla, A., & Lunsford, L. (2018). Destructive leadership: A critique of leader-centric perspectives and toward a more holistic definition. *Journal of Business Ethics, 151*(3), 627–649. https://doi.org/10.1007/s10551-016-3257-9

Tracy, M. (2017). N.C.A.A.: North Carolina will not be punished for academic scandal. *New York Times*. https://www.nytimes.com/2017/10/13/sports/unc-north-carolina-ncaa.html

Treviño, L. K., & Nelson, K. A. (2017). *Managing business ethics: Straight talk about how to do it right.* Wiley & Sons.

Vandiver, D. M. (2006). A prospective analysis of juvenile male sex offenders: Characteristics and recidivism rates as adults. *Journal of Interpersonal Violence, 21*(5), 673–688. https://doi.org/10.1177/0886260506287113

Wainstein, K. (2014, October). Investigation of irregular classes in the Department of African and Afro-American Studies at the University of North Carolina at Chapel Hill. http://media2.newsobserver.com/smedia/2014/10/22/13/42/1rQra6.So.156.pdf

The Whistleblowers' Protection Act. (n.d.). https://www.legislature.mi.gov/documents/mcl/pdf/mcl-Act-469-of-1980.pdf

Wisse, B. & Sleebos, E. (2016). When the dark ones gain power: Perceived position power strengthens the effect of supervisor Machiavellianism on abusive supervision in work teams. *Personality and Individual Differences, 99*, 122–126. https://doi.org/10.1016/j.paid.2016.05.019

Wright, F., & Wright, M. S. W. (1982). Violent groups. *Group, 6*, 25–34.

Yammarino, F. J., Spangler, W. D., & Bass, B. M. (1993). Transformational leadership and performance: A longitudinal investigation. *Leadership Quarterly, 4*(1), 81–102. https://doi.org/10.1016/1048-9843(93)90005-E

CHAPTER 11

INTEGRATING LEADERSHIP AND POWER

A Micro Process Model

Nicolas Bastardoz and David V. Day

ABSTRACT

Power and leadership are closely related constructs but tend to be treated independently in the literature. We offer a conceptual framework to integrate their relation. We first review standard operationalizations of leadership and approaches dealing with power (i.e., influence tactics, organizational politics, shared/collective leadership) to highlight important limitations preventing the study of leadership as an influence process toward the achievement of shared goals. Building on these approaches as well as the French and Raven (1959) bases of power, we take a microlens at the interaction episode and offer a process model of leadership. We propose that leadership occurs when an agent activates a power source in a leading attempt that a target ultimately accepts. We offer propositions regarding characteristics of agents and targets—ultimately leaders and followers when influence towards shared goals occurs—to explain the emergence of leadership. Our approach departs from standard operationalization of leadership by studying leadership as a dynamic influence process, not a position of formal power. In a later section,

Leadership:
Leaders, Followers, and Context, pp. 289–330

we discuss how power differences and the stability of the power source can inform the leadership process. We conclude by offering various recommendations to apply our micro process model to the study of leadership.

Power is ubiquitous in organizations (Anderson & Brion, 2014; Pfeffer, 1981). It guides social relationships and affects how individuals think, feel, and behave (Keltner et al., 2003). Power also is crucial for the exercise of effective leadership (Bass & Bass, 2009; Yukl, 2002): Having power distinguishes those who become leaders and wields influence from those who follow and become the recipient of influence (Stogdill, 1950). Some have even argued that "power is the currency of a leader" (Kirkpatrick & Locke, 1991, p. 52) and that leaders are "by definition, wielders of power" (Williams, 2014, p. 1368). Although power and leadership are inextricably linked and support similar influence processes, these two constructs tend to be treated independently and as distinct phenomena in the literature. We argue that power and leadership are closely connected and should be treated concomitantly. The aims of this manuscript are to review and integrate power approaches to leadership and offer a conceptual model positioning power bases as antecedents to leadership.

Despite a long tradition and an extensive research record, the leadership literature is frequently criticized for its ambiguity and lack of conceptual precision (Antonakis, 2017). Scholars have suggested different explanations such as poor methodologies (Antonakis et al., 2010; Podsakoff et al., 2003) or conceptualizations (Banks et al., 2018; Yukl, 1999). We also suggest other shortcomings including a divide between the conceptualization and operationalization of leadership in research, a fixation on static leadership "styles," and a general oversight when it comes to incorporating power into the nomological network of leadership research. We elaborate on these shortcomings below.

The conceptualization and operationalization of leadership diverge, leading to what we call a "leadership divide." Leadership is generally conceptualized as a social influence process towards the achievement of shared goals (Antonakis & Day, 2018; Bass & Stogdill, 1990; Yukl, 2002). However, our objects of study—"leaders"—tend to be mere powerholders (i.e., individual in positions of authority), and not so much wielders of the full range of influence tactics. Leadership studies too rarely focuses on the genuine influence achieved by leaders. This leadership divide creates confusion and ambiguity ultimately preventing the validity of our scientific record.

In addition, the vast majority of studies focuses on endogenous perceptions of retrospective leadership behaviors or styles (Antonakis et al., 2016; Arthur et al., 2017). These studies not only suffer from attributional and categorization issues by relying on perceptual questionnaires (Day, 2012; Lord et al., 1978) but also miss the dynamic and interactional nature of leadership. Following its conceptualization, we contend that leadership scholars should focus on brief instances or moments of leadership whereby leaders influence followers in some goal-direction fashion. This perspective requires to study the emergence of leadership as a dynamic influence process if it aims to be coherent and consequential.

It is also our perspective that leadership theories tend to focus on highly ideological, prescriptive, and positively valenced leadership styles (Alvesson, 2020; Alvesson & Einola, 2019; Collinson & Tourish, 2015). This positivity bias may be explained because the literature on leadership emerged out of the human-relations movement in a shift away from power relations (Shamir & Eilam-Shamir, 2017). We believe that such a one-sided perspective on leadership is not practical because it produces unrealistic expectations for anyone willing to lead in an organizational context (Alvesson, 2019). At another extreme, power and authority tend to be portrayed as something inherently negative with undesirable consequences (Pfeffer, 1981). There is a vast literature in social psychology investigating the negative effects of power and authority on individuals' affects, cognitions, and behaviors (see Sturm & Antonakis, 2015, for a review). These differences may explain why the two different literatures have evolved in parallel. We thus argue that if leadership research aims to be valid, consequential, and practical, power has to be explicitly considered in our leadership models.

With this overarching goal in mind, our manuscript makes three critical contributions to the study of leadership. Our first contribution is in providing a review of leadership and power approaches. Starting with their conceptualization, we show that these constructs are tightly interrelated and thus offer conceptual clarity by clearly highlighting similarities and discrepancies between both constructs. For instance, leadership emerges when influence in directions of shared or common goals is achieved. In contrast, authority relations emerge when agents can impose their goals on targets (who do not share these goals). Reviewing then the leadership literature, we identify a leadership divide as well as important limitations in current leadership approaches dealing with power. For instance, these approaches focus either on influence without common goals (i.e., influence tactics, organizational politics) or on the emergence of informal leaders (i.e., shared/collective leadership). These limitations are important stepping stones for a comprehensive model of leadership looking at the origin of leadership from designated or nondesignated individuals (designated individuals hold formally appointed roles as opposed to nondesignated individuals; see Ashford & Sitkin, 2019, pp. 457–458).

Another contribution lies in offering a conceptual model of the leadership process. Building on French and Raven (1959) bases of social power, we take a micro, event-based lens on the leadership process. This perspective locates the emergence of leadership at the interaction episode, a micro timeframe. Our conceptual model indicates that leadership emerges when agents activate power sources and when targets are influenced—agents and targets thus becoming respectively leaders and followers. The different bases of power can be categorized in two broad clusters—formal power and personal power—which are associated with different mechanisms and distal outcomes. We also offer valuable propositions around the characteristics of agents, targets, and situations moderating the likeliness and effectiveness of a leading attempt. This approach provides a novel angle to the study of leadership, departing from the common outcomes-based leadership styles (Antonakis et al., 2016; Van Knippenberg & Sitkin, 2013). Specifically, we differentiate power bases (the "what") from styles (the "how") because these are two separate mechanisms ultimately interacting to predict leadership. Approaching leadership from this new standpoint raises crucial aspects currently unexplored in the leadership literature.

Our final contribution lies in the integration of research findings stemming from the sociopsychological power literature (e.g., Galinsky et al., 2003; Magee & Galinsky, 2008). Despite an extensive literature and its similarity with leadership, few sociopsychological ideas about power have made inroads into the leadership literature (Ashford & Sitkin, 2019). By discussing power dynamics and forging new constructs into the leadership nomological network, we aim to generate novel insights for leadership researchers. We discuss how the dispersion of power within groups and organizations is a double-edge sword in that it is both a necessary condition for leadership to emerge, yet it may alienate and disengage potential followers. We also discuss the stability of the power hierarchy. Because unstable powerholders tend to protect their power and act in more individualistic ways, a focus on the stability of the power hierarchy offers new insights to leadership researchers. In this endeavor, we pay particular attention to the changing world of work affecting power dynamics.

CONCEPTUALIZATIONS OF LEADERSHIP AND POWER

Although it has been said (and often repeated) that "there are almost as many different definitions of leadership as there are persons who have attempted to define the concept" (Bass & Stogdill, 1990, p. 11), leadership is generally defined as *social influence towards the achievement of shared goals* (Antonakis & Day, 2018; Bass & Stogdill, 1990; Yukl, 2002). One component of this definition proposes that leadership occurs when *followers are influenced in some way*. Leadership is thus understood as an outcome of some influential process (Drath et al., 2008; Salancik et al., 1975). To become a leader, an agent needs to influence a target who, by being influenced, becomes a follower. This process is dynamic such that who is influencing and who is being influenced can change instantaneously. Thus, who is a leader and who is a follower is equally dynamic. Leadership thus occurs in social interactions, not by having a certain trait or holding a position in a hierarchy. The leadership process more generally aims at understanding how this social influence process unfolds. By definition, leadership also requires *shared (or common) goals and outcomes* (Pfeffer, 1977). For some leading to happen, agents and targets need to collaborate in some goal-directed activities where both parties implicitly or explicitly share ex-post some goal. Individuals may either have common goals ex-ante or come to agree ex-post on some common goals. In the former case, a leading attempt could target the direction and level of effort individuals exert to achieve these shared goals. In the latter case, a leading attempt would target the production of shared goals ex-post (e.g., through readying people behind a vision) which may then result in increased coordination and cooperation.

Power has also been defined in various ways (e.g., Emerson, 1962; Galinsky et al., 2003; Weber, 1924/1947). One way in which power has been defined is as asymmetric control over valued resources (Emerson, 1962; Keltner et al., 2003; Magee & Galinsky, 2008), with a recent definition suggesting that power is "having the discretion and the means to asymmetrically enforce one's will over others" (Sturm & Antonakis, 2015, p. 139). This latter definition focuses on power as having some *discretion*, or latitude, about one's actions. Powerful individuals differ from the powerless in that they can more likely determine their own fate. It also stipulates that power requires possessing some *means*, or sources of power. Power so defined is thus an antecedent to a social process. Powerful individuals can finally *enforce their will* by imposing their preferences and needs. Whether powerful and powerless individuals share common goals or not is irrelevant due to the asymmetrical nature of the relationship.

These definitions highlight two main distinctions between power and leadership. Although having some kind of power may be necessary for leadership, the sheer possession or application of power does not constitute leadership. In other words, power and leadership are not interchangeable constructs. Power can be an antecedent of leadership only to the extent that leaders and followers ultimately share common goals. A supervisor who convinces a subordinate to engage in a behavior for his/her personal advantage (often referred to as pseudo-transformational; Christie et al., 2011) would not exhibit leadership. The self-serving use of power does not produce leaders and followers but rather dominance and command. Even so, the line between authority and leadership is however thin. Whether a relationship is categorized as authority or leadership may only be determined ex-post, once the social influence process has ended and outcomes have materialized. For instance, a target may realize only after much effort and cooperation that an agent was deceptive. Importantly (but also disturbingly), leadership studies rarely discuss and reflect on whether leaders and followers share implicitly or explicitly some kind of goal. This crucial dimension is always assumed or left in the background. Because there can be no leadership without shared goals, we argue that leadership scholars should more explicitly investigate and discuss the existence of shared goals (rather than consider them as a given) whenever subordinates and supervisors are studied in the field.

Another distinction concerns the degree of freedom available to agents and targets in the process. Powerholders have full latitude to enforce their will so that the powerless can be coerced to engage in certain actions (within the powerholder's sphere of influence). A typical example would be the dominance-based hierarchies observed in various animal species whereby alpha-males coerce low-dominant animals into powerless roles. Conversely, leadership tends to be freely—although not necessarily explicitly—granted so that following cannot be coerced (Blom & Lundgren, 2020; Collinson, 2006). Recent discussions on followership highlight the critical role played by followers in the emergence of leadership, because it is their openness to being swayed that allows for leadership to occur (Bastardoz & Van Vugt, 2019; Shamir, 2007; Uhl-Bien et al., 2014). Without followers, there is no leadership.

It is worth noting an important question that has stirred up and divided leadership theorists (cf. Vroom & Jago, 2007): Does the exercise or formal power or authority constitute leadership? Certain prominent scholars have argued that leadership consists of the incremental influence over and above mechanical compliance to routine directives by formal organizational authority (Hermalin, 1998; Katz & Kahn, 1978). From this viewpoint, influence emerging from formal power and authority should not be classified as leadership. This idea is implicit in mainstream theories depicting leadership styles as inherently free of the exercise of formal power or authority (Alvesson & Einola, 2019; Shamir & Eilam-Shamir, 2017). Although this approach is ideologically appealing, it is also reductionist and lacks external validity (Hannah et al., 2014). In line with its definition, we consider that leadership may emerge from the use of formal power and authority if individuals in the process have some goals in common. We do not aim to have the final word on the matter; this discussion nonetheless emphasizes that our understanding of leadership would be improved if we explicitly recognize that both formal and informal sources of power can act as antecedents of leadership.

LEADERSHIP DIVIDE

Following the commonly agreed definitions, the terms "leaders" and "followers" refer to individuals genuinely leading (influencing) or following (being influenced). This may sound obvious but considering the published literature shows why this should not be taken for granted. We performed a search in 10 of the most important journals publishing empirical leadership research (i.e., *Academy of Management Journal, Administrative Science Quarterly, Journal of Applied Psychology, Journal of Organizational Behavior, Journal of Management, Journal of Personality and Social Psychology, Leadership Quarterly, Organizational Behavior and Human Decision Processes, Organization Science*, and *Personnel Psychology*). We gathered all articles containing a declination of "lead" in the title or abstract for the years 2017 and 2018 and which had a sample of "leaders" and "followers." Across the 97 relevant papers containing 136 studies, 115 studies (85%) sampled individuals in positions of formal authority (i.e., managers, supervisor) as leaders and subordinates as followers (similar to the 84% Ancona & Backman, 2008, reported for the period 2003–2008; cited in DeRue, 2011). This finding suggests that leadership research tends to sample indiscriminately supervisors and managers as leaders, without much discussion regarding their actual influence and leadership.

Considering managers as "leaders" and subordinates as "followers" leads to what we call a "*leadership divide*"—a discrepancy between how leadership is conceptualized and operationalized. As our review indicates, the leadership literature is replete with studies sampling managers or supervisors who are implicitly assumed to be leaders without much discussion regarding their influence.[1] In an exchange of theoretical letters some 15 years ago, Art Bedeian (Bedeian & Hunt, 2006) complained that the bulk of leadership studies in management research is about supervisors and argued that an operationalization so inconsistent with definitions of leadership would threaten the validity of the resulting body of scientific knowledge. Many leadership scholars have echoed these criticisms over the years (e.g., see Ashford & Sitkin, 2019; DeRue, 2011; Shamir & Eilam-Shamir, 2017 for recent examples), without any significant impact on this practice. We argue that the loose application of the terms leader, follower, and leadership has rendered these construct meaningless and generated cynicism among nonleadership scholars. Because leaders do not necessarily lead followers, the term leadership has lost any precise scientific meaning.

Leading happens when at least one target is influenced, not by holding a position in a hierarchy. Having a formal role in a hierarchy may spur someone to emerge as a leader; yet authority and formal power do not de facto make someone a leader (Hunter et al., 2007). Leadership researchers should clearly justify how their study truly is about "leaders" or "leadership," providing evidence that leading occurred. In the absence of leadership evidence (i.e., influence and common goals), the term "leader" and "follower" should simply be avoided. It is no longer appropriate to enable and perpetuate this leadership divide. Given the current state of the leadership field, we propose in a later section a conceptual model easily operationalizable that centers on the emergence of leadership influence. We first review approaches that explicitly deal with power in the leadership process.

REVIEW OF LEADERSHIP APPROACHES DEALING WITH POWER

Influential reviews of the leadership landscape have identified power as an important subfield (e.g., Dinh et al., 2014; Zhao & Li, 2019). These reviews have identified political theory and influence tactics as major approaches in this subfield. Another important sub-field connecting leadership and power includes the shared/collective leadership approaches because they deal explicitly with informal leaders. We briefly introduce each approach, emphasize major findings and insights, but also identify key limitations that will serve as a basis for our conceptual model.

Influence Tactics

Influence tactics are ways in which power sources can be used to get something done. This line of research started after Kipnis and colleagues (1980) developed a preliminary taxonomy of tactics organizational members use to convince other members. Yukl and colleagues (e.g., Yukl & Falbe, 1990; Yukl et al., 1996; Yukl et al., 2008) were instrumental in extending this line of research and developed survey items measuring 11 proactive influence tactics. A recent meta-analysis found that certain influence tactics (e.g., rational persuasion, inspirational appeal, apprising) are positively related with task- and relation-oriented outcomes whereas other tactics (e.g., pressure) are negatively related to these outcomes (Lee et al., 2017). In addition, various contextual factors moderate the effectiveness of influence tactics such as the directional use of tactics (e.g., Yukl & Tracey, 1992) or whether tactics have been used alone or in combination (e.g., Kipnis & Schmidt, 1988). This line of research specifies how organizational members can and should persuade targets in a top-down, bottom-up, or lateral direction. As long as this influence process is targeted towards achieving shared goals, it can be considered as leadership.

We believe this latter point to be a crucial limiting factor with respect to the study of leadership. Certain influence tactics do not necessarily require common goals such that their use results in authority relations, that is, in relations characterized by goal asymmetry. For instance, the use of an ingratiation tactic could hardly produce leadership. Another important limitation is that most of the research on influence tactics has been done at the dyadic level; research at the group or team level is almost nonexistent. Given that work teams are ever more important, this dyadic focus is a crucial limitation. Adding to this, research on influence tactics is not very popular lately. A majority of research findings relies on outdated research designs, especially single-source data. Finally, research on the combination of tactics is very limited (Yukl & Gardner, 2020) indicating that much research still needs to be done to understand how influence tactics interact when used together.

Political Theories

Political theories in organizations flourished after Jeffrey Pfeffer (1981) and Henry Mintzberg (1983) offered extensive examinations of power and politics in organizations. These two books sparked the research on the political nature inherent to organizations, leading to theories explaining how power can and should be used for political reasons. In the leadership field, Ferris and colleagues developed this line of research and especially the political skill construct (Ferris et al., 2019; Ferris et al., 2000; Munyon et al., 2015). Defined as the "ability to effectively understand others at work, and to use such knowledge to influence others to act in ways that enhance one's personal and/or organizational objectives" (Ferris et al., 2005, p. 127), the political skill construct is a mix of affective, behavioral, and cognitive characteristics. Important work outcomes are linked with politically skilled individuals such as work productivity, OCB, and job satisfaction (Munyon et al., 2015). This knowledge is important as it indicates how certain skills help individuals navigate the inherent complexity of organization more efficiently, eventually allowing them to get their way and seize more resources.

Despite its practical value, the literature on organizational power and politics offers only limited insights to understand the leadership process. First, politically skilled individuals can use their talent for organizational goals but also for personal goals, generally not sanctioned by an organization (Ferris et al., 2000). Individuals who use politics for self-serving ends, no matter how influential, do not produce any kind of leadership (there is no shared goal). Along this line, political behaviors within organizations tend to be negatively perceived because they more often than not lead to the personal appropriation of organizational resources rather than the pursuit of shared goals. Another critical issue is the tautological and outcomes-based nature of the political skill construct (Antonakis et al., 2016). Given its conceptualization as "the ability to effectively understand," political skill is by definition expected to correlate with other desirable characteristics and outcomes. These important shortcomings limit our understanding of how political behaviors can be used to produce leadership.

Shared/Collective Leadership

Due to the changing nature of works towards a knowledge-oriented economy, theories of shared and collective leadership[2] emerged to incorporate the increase in functional and empowered teams within organizations (Contractor et al., 2012; Yammarino et al., 2012). The general idea behind these approaches is that leadership emerges not only from formally appointed individuals (Gronn, 2002) but also from team members stepping up as informal leaders when the task or context match their expertise (Friedrich et al., 2009). These approaches allow for the study of multiple forms of leadership (e.g., leading up, leading horizontally), exerted at numerous places in organizations and through various means. Meta-analyses have shown that shared or collective approaches to leadership relate positively with effectiveness and attitudinal outcomes at the team level (D'Innocenzo et al., 2016; Wang et al., 2014).

Although providing many critical insights into the leadership phenomenon, these approaches are limited in their scope. They are especially relevant for self-managed work teams but rarely focus on groups with individuals holding formal power (see Ensley et al., 2006 for a notable exception). Not considering the influence and leadership of individuals in formal or authority roles reduces the external validity and applicability of research findings to a broader range of organizational structures. Shared or collective leadership should thus ideally be studied together with "vertical leadership" (Carson et al., 2007). The operationalization of shared leadership using network studies is also problematic. Such operationalization provides static or retrospective snapshots of leadership, but it does not allow to capture the origin of their influence, such as how and why individuals in a network emerge as leaders.

To conclude this selective review, we acknowledge that much relevant work has been done to integrate power and leadership. Literature on influence tactics provide important insights regarding how an agent can affect a target. The organizational politics literature offers practical knowledge, away from idealistic leadership styles. Shared/collective approaches explain the emergence of informal leaders in teams or networks. Building on all three approaches, our conceptual model focuses on power sources as antecedents to the emergence of leadership. Our model extends current approaches because it can be applied to all individuals within the organization, including individuals holding nondesignated roles in a hierarchy.

Also, our model focuses at its core on the leadership influence process to study leadership how and when it happens.

A MICRO PROCESS MODEL OF LEADERSHIP

Leadership is a specific influence process. To understand how this process unfolds, we argue that it needs to be conceptualized and studied at a micro level. We follow recent developments in the team and leadership literatures advocating for taking an event-based lens (Eberly et al., 2013; Hoffman & Lord, 2013; Morgeson et al., 2015). Our assertion is that leadership requires to be studied whenever influence happens, at the level of an interaction episode (see Ammeter et al., 2002, for a similar argument). An interaction episode is an interpersonal encounter between two or more individuals who interact together. Interaction episodes in our conceptual leadership model are similar to "role episodes" concerning the taking of organizational roles discussed in Katz and Kahn (1978, see pp. 194–195 and Figure 7.1, p. 196). Studying the emergence of leadership at the interaction episode considers the dynamism and flexibility of agents and targets' behaviors (McClean et al., 2019).

This lens considers the importance of time in the emergence of leadership, albeit at a more microlevel than previously discussed (Day & Dragoni, 2015). Leadership is a dynamic phenomenon that can happen frequently and instantaneously, what Gronn (2002) calls "brief bursts of synergy" (p. 430) and Ashford and Sitkin (2019) label "acts of leadership" (p. 458). We argue that these "bursts" or "acts," what we would refer to as "successful leading attempts," must be studied when they happen. Given that interaction episodes are frequent and can be short lived, leading attempts will fade, be reinforced, or replaced as new leading attempts are made in future interaction episodes.

To understand how leadership materializes, we get back to the origin of the influence. We argue that agents have at their disposal "power bases" they can activate to persuade targets. Power bases become antecedents of leadership whenever two conditions are realized: (a) the target is influenced; and (b) the leader and follower share, implicitly or explicitly, some common goal (see Figure 11.1). Under such precise conditions can agents be labeled as "leaders" and targets as "followers." Should these two conditions not be realized, the power bases would not be antecedent to leadership. For instance, an agent may fail to sway a target despite activating a power basis (i.e., a failed attempt at leading). In another scenario, the target may be persuaded but not share any goals ex-post with the agent and although some influence is being observed, what emerges from such interaction is not leadership (i.e., an authority relation emerges). We now introduce and discuss our conceptual model.

Figure 11.1

Power and Leadership

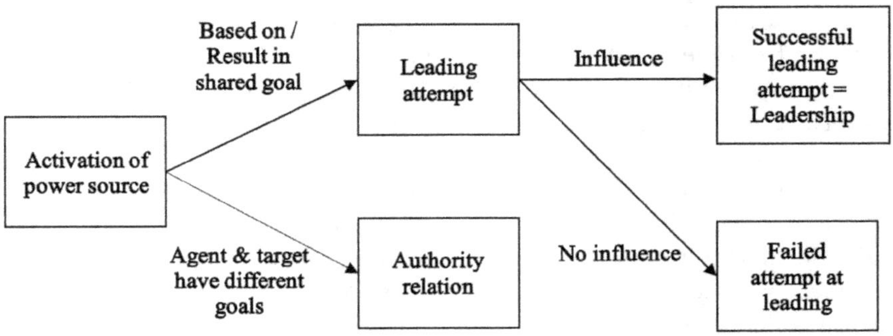

At the beginning of an interaction episode, individuals aiming to lead need to activate one or more power bases in a leading attempt. In their foundational paper, French and Raven (1959) identified five different bases (or sources) of social power: (a) reward; (b) coercive; (c) legitimate; (d) referent; and (e) expert. Reward and coercive bases rely on the promise or threat of exchanges. Agents are powerful because they have control over valued resources or have the capacity to sanction targets. Examples of reward power include the potential to offer a pay increase, a promotion, or an interesting job opportunity to the target. Examples of coercive power include the capacity to assign boring tasks or fire the target. Legitimate power stems from the agent's holding some organizational roles or titles (Weber, 1968). This power basis resides in the target holding an organizationally sanctioned position in a formal structure. Taken together, coercive, reward, and legitimate bases of power are referred collectively as formal bases of power.

Referent power emanates from the target's identification with the agent. Targets identify with the agent because they identify with, admire, or affectively like the agent. An expert basis relates to the possession of some relevant knowledge or skills necessary to execute a task or a function. In addition to the five original bases of social power, another basis of power called informational power originated from the sociological literature on network (Etzioni, 1961; Pettigrew, 1972) and has been added later to the taxonomy of power bases (Raven, 1993). Informational power refers to having information others value and can derive from an individual's position in an informal advice network such as being central, bridging unconnected others, or holding a boundary role position (Anderson & Brion, 2014; Brass, 1985; Krackhardt, 1990). Considered together, referent, expert, and informational bases of power are referred collectively as personal or informal bases of power.

> **Proposition 1:** Leading attempts are based on the activation of a power source, either formal (e.g., reward, sanction, legitimate) or personal (e.g., referent, expertise, informational).

Once an agent has made a leading attempt, a target's response validates or invalidates the emergence of leadership. If the agent is convinced, we observe a successful leading attempt and thus leadership. An agent then becomes a "leader" and a target becomes a "follower." If a leading attempt fails to influence the agent, we are in the presence of a failed attempt at leading and the interaction episode ends. The process is somewhat similar to leaders claiming and followers granting a leader identity (DeRue & Ashford, 2010). Our perspective differs because in our model, leadership is instantiated when followers are influenced and not when followers cognitively grant the identity to the leader. Successful leading attempts leads to leadership outcomes such as cooperation, coordination, and/or increased effort. These proximal outcomes instantiate the emergence of leadership.

> **Proposition 2:** Successful leading attempts lead to proximal outcomes such as cooperation, coordination, and increased efforts.

These proximal outcomes over time and multiple interaction episodes lead to distal outcomes (although one interaction episode could theoretically suffice). An important aspect is that the kind of proximal and distal outcomes the agent desires should drive the use of a specific power basis. Stated differently, the outcome wanted affects how appropriate the use of certain power bases is because different sources of power predict different kinds of outcomes (Kelman, 1958; Podsakoff & Schriescheim, 1985).

Formal bases of power predict compliance, conformity, and task performance. The reliance on formal power in hierarchies tends to create passive, dependent, and alienated employees (Argyris, 1957). The use of coercion tends to lead to fear and submission (Katz & Kahn, 1978), and also resentment. Forcing compliance may backfire and result in the opposite outcome that the influencing agent originally intended (reactance theory; Brehm & Brehm, 1981). In comparison to coercion and sanctions, the promise and use of rewards is linked with more positive perceptions and attitudes towards the powerholder (Podsakoff et al., 2006). Reward power can be a prominent way to increase effort, coordinate group activities, and enhance task performance when used appropriately (Pink, 2011; Zehnder et al., 2017). Finally, legitimate power works particularly well to induce a target's compliance although without special enthusiasm or commitment (Yukl & Falbe, 1991). Altogether, activating formal bases of power produce compliance and/or conformity through their reliance on extrinsic motivation.

> **Proposition 3a:** Leading attempts based on formal sources of power lead to distal outcomes such as compliance, conformity, and in-role behaviors.

The use of personal power tends to be associated with outcomes such as targets' commitment, engagement, and satisfaction. Personal power differs significantly from formal sources of power in that individuals who have personal power cannot enforce their will but rather rely on the target's recognition of their informal power. Targets have more latitude to accept or reject the influence attempt based on personal bases of power. Informational and expert power generally lead to better performing and satisfied employees because powerholders can remove the obstacles to perform the task (House, 1996) and offer the necessary guidance (Antonakis & House, 2014). Referent power is an antecedent of engagement and extra-effort because targets identify with the agent's values and vision (Shamir et al., 1993).

> **Proposition 3b:** Leading attempts based on personal sources of power lead to distal outcomes such as commitment, engagement, satisfaction, and extra-role behaviors.

All agents are not as likely to activate a power source and be successful in their leading attempts. Although the leadership literature is replete with studies investigating individual differences as antecedents of the emergence as leaders and followers (see Bastardoz & Van Vugt, 2019; Zaccaro et al., 2018, for reviews), our micro lens suggests a more granular approach. Based on identified capitals (Bastardoz & Van Vugt, 2019) and attributes (Zaccaro et al., 2018), we propose that agents are more likely to activate a power source if they have strong motives, beliefs, or an extroverted personality. Motives include constructs such as the motivation to lead (Badura et al., 2020), leader identity (Miscenko et al., 2017), or need for achievement. Individuals with high levels of these constructs have an interest or need to influence and lead and thus are more likely to seek to lead by activating a power basis. Beliefs include constructs such as self-confidence, self-efficacy, or low risk perceptions (Zhang et al., 2020). Individuals high on these constructs feel more upbeat and self-assured in activating a power basis.

Finally, an extroverted personality expresses itself in outgoing behaviors which reduces the cost of signaling one's intentions to lead.

> **Proposition 4a:** Agents with (a) strong motives; (b) strong beliefs; and/or (c) high levels of extroversion will be more likely to activate their power source and attempt to lead.

The context should also be propitious to the activation of power sources: Agents may not activate their power source unless they see a benefit to lead. In certain cases, the costs associated with successful leading attempts (e.g., coordinating large groups) may simply be higher than the expected gains so there are no benefits associated with leading (Zehnder et al., 2017). In other contexts, the proximal outcomes associated with leadership (e.g., collaboration, cooperation, extra-effort) may be obtained without leadership. Such context prevents the activation of power sources because it would simply not be required and could potentially backfire at the agent (Bastardoz & Van Vugt, 2019; Hooper et al., 2010). Finally, the characteristics of other agents within the dyad, group, or organization would also moderate the activation of power sources. The presence of individuals with organizationally prescribed roles or particular traits or states (especially those identified under Proposition 4a) may create a constraining context and inhibit the activation of power sources because agents may perceive such individuals as less amenable to be persuaded and more likely to deny their leading attempt.

> **Proposition 4b:** Agents will be more likely to activate their power source in contexts where (a) it is beneficial to lead; (b) leadership is needed; and (c) targets are open to influence.

Once an agent has made a leading attempt, targets have to decide whether to accept or reject it. To inform their response, we propose that targets rely on characteristics of the agents. An important characteristic is the reputation or credibility of the agent (Cialdini, 2007; Cialdini & Goldstein, 2004). Having a good reputation or high credibility generates trust which increases the likelihood that agents accept leading attempts because targets are less likely to be abused or deceived (Ammeter et al., 2002; Choo, 1964; Hambrick & Lovelace, 2018). Agents with reputation or credibility have idiosyncratic credits (Hollander, 1958) such that targets believe the agent's leading attempt will be beneficial for them, the group, and/or the organization. Another important characteristic deals with the prototypicality of the agent with an in-group. Social identity theory of leadership predicts that targets are more likely to follow and endorse agents who are representative of the in-group prototype (Haslam et al., 2010; Hogg, 2001). Individuals prototypical of the values, behaviors, and attitudes shared by in-group members are thus more likely to see their leading attempts be successful.

> **Proposition 5a:** Leading attempts will be more successful (and thus produce leadership) if the agent (a) has a good reputation; (b) is credible; and/or (c) is prototypical of the social entity.

Agents do not all respond similarly to leading attempt. For instance, certain individuals are less open or susceptible to influence (Bearden et al., 1989). This trait-like characteristic explains why certain attempts at leading may fall flat with certain followers. For instance, Barbuto Jr (2000) suggested that followers have different degrees of anticipated resistance to persuasion depending on whether a request is (a) consistent with their intentions, (b) within the degree of what they would consider acceptable because they are indifferent, willing, or consider the request legitimate, or (c) outside their influence zone and thus refused under any circumstances. This anticipated resistance shows both some individual difference characteristics—in that certain individuals are more likely to be convinced by others—but also show some inter-situational variability—in that different leading attempts may be responded to with different anticipated resistance by the same individual. On the one hand, certain individuals may be highly reluctant to accept a leading attempt based on formal sources of power; targets may for instance counter the leading attempt or the interaction may turn into an authority relation (e.g., by having the target not internalize the goal). On the other hand, certain targets (especially individuals holding formal roles) may reject leading attempts from nondesignated agents because they consider that only designated agents should lead. Another target's characteristic is the need to belong or affiliate with others (Baumeister & Leary, 1995; McClelland, 1961). Individuals high on these needs will be more amenable to influence to ensure a satisfying relationship with other members and agents especially. Finally, social identity theory (Haslam et al., 2010; Hogg, 2001) also predicts that leading attempts are more likely to be successful when targets identify with the social entity (i.e., the dyad, group, or organization). A target who does not identify with the social identity salient in the leading attempt is unlikely to respond positively to a leading attempt.

> **Proposition 5b:** Leading attempts will be more successful if target individuals are (a) open to influence; (b) high on belongingness or affiliation needs; and/or (c) identified with the social entity.

This micro process model of leadership allows to distinguish the "what" from the "how" in the generation of leadership. Distinguishing the bases of power (i.e., the "what") from how the leading attempt is implemented and executed (i.e., the "how" or power activation approach) is critical to understand more precisely the origin of leadership. The power activation approach is a state-like characteristic that show some within-individual variability across different interaction episodes. It refers to how a power basis is activated, how a leading attempt is behaviorally enacted. For instance, an agent can draw on any basis of power in different ways such as being nice, bossy, polite, caring, overbearing, and/or individually considerate.

Note that the construct of power activation approach differs from the "leadership style." A leadership style is defined as "the manner in which specific behaviors are expressed" (House & Aditya, 1997, p. 451) and is usually considered as a general or dispositional tendency. For instance, Gandhi is referred as a more passive charismatic leader compared to the more active Mandela or Martin Luther King. Overall, the power activation approach or style should match or complement power bases to enhance the likelihood that a leading attempt becomes successful. How a power source is activated affects thus the emergence of leadership, beyond the effect of the power source itself.

> **Proposition 6:** The power activation approach moderates the effectiveness of a leading attempt.

Once an interaction episode is complete, successful, and unsuccessful leading attempts as well as their associated outcomes feed back into the model to inform future interaction episodes (or leadership events). Proximal and distal outcomes of leadership serve as important reference points and indicators to update the power sources and characteristics of the target (Ammeter et al., 2002). For instance, a leader who successfully exerted leadership and obtained positive distal outcomes may see her expert power increases because followers saw her as an individual with the skills and knowledge required for such task. This change may then encourage her to activate her (increased) perceived expert power in a subsequent event or interaction episode (P1). The successful outcome may also boost her self-confidence or leader identity, which may increase the likelihood of future leading attempt (P3a). Also, targets may now perceive her as someone with a high reputation for success and credibility to walk the talk increasing the future success of leading attempt (P5a). Power sources and characteristics of individuals are thus not stable but rather tend to be informed by previous leadership events (see Figure 11.2 for our full conceptual model).

> **Proposition 7:** The outcome of successful leading attempt feed back into the process by increasing the target's (a) personal power sources (e.g., expert power, referent power); and/or (b) characteristics (e.g., beliefs, reputation).

Figure 11.2

A Micro Process Model of Leadership

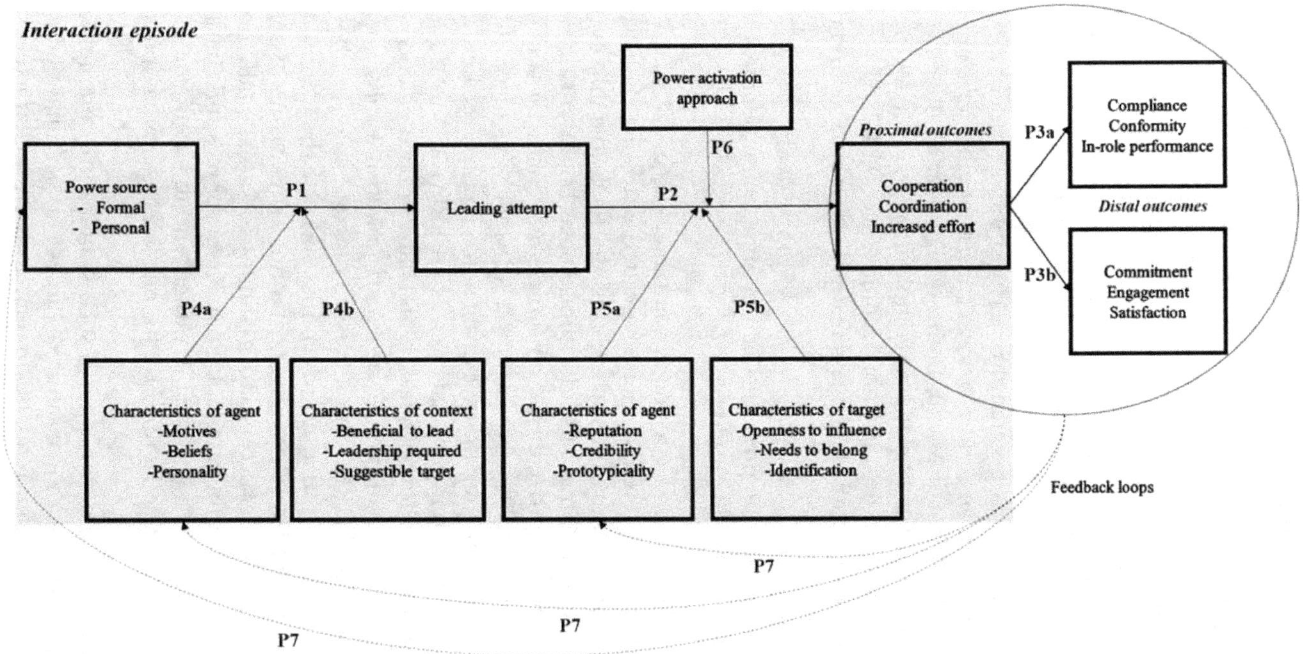

Note. The part in grey happens at the interaction episode (very microlevel). Multiple interaction episodes may be required until distal outcomes materialize.

Implications for Leadership Research and Theory

Integrating the power bases as antecedents of leadership offers intriguing challenges for the study of leadership. We discuss three issues such an integration raises, regarding the importance of context to leadership, how the power bases are thought to interact to produce leadership, and various leadership types that emerge from activating different power sources.

The Importance of Context

This process model at the level of interaction episode suggests that leadership is tied to the context and task. This dynamic and fluid perspective, underpinned by evolutionary psychology (Van Vugt, 2006) and microrole transitions (Ashforth et al., 2000), paints a more pragmatic and contemporary picture of leadership in which who leads and follows evolves based on situational demands. It indicates that individuals willing to lead should seek situations or tasks where they have power bases they can activate. Individuals may have some capacity for leadership because a situation offers them a power basis, but slightly changing the task, team, or context may eliminate that potential source of influence and leadership.

To reflect the dynamic and shifting nature of power, Aime et al. (2014) introduced the construct of power heterarchy defined as "a relational system in which the relative power among team members shifts over time as the resources of specific team members become more relevant (and the resources of other members become less relevant) because of changes in the situation or task" (p. 328). Aime and colleagues found that power heterarchies increase the variability of individuals expressing power as long as the expression of power is perceived as legitimate. Applying the power heterarchy construct to leadership reveals the contextual nature of leadership. Today, work is often performed in functional groups whose membership fluctuates and participation varies. Group members tend to rely less and less on authority to guide their interactions and teamwork. Who leads is not fixed or in stable hands. Rather, it oscillates based on situational demands (Barley, 1986; Davis & Eisenhardt, 2011). If and when the context and its leadership requirement changes, power bases, and the potential to exert leadership shift from one individual to another.

This approach also highlights that the emergence of leadership cannot be understood in a static, decontextualized, and single-shot way. The sequence in which interaction episodes unfold suggests that similar leading attempts result in different outcomes. An important factor concerns how the repeated use of the same power bases may lead to diminishing returns. For instance, agents repeatedly activating their referent power by signaling charisma may involve their targets on a too intense emotional level, ultimately burning them out (Bastardoz, 2020). As an another example, a manager relying mainly on personal power may benefit from using formal bases of power just once to reinforce her credibility or legitimacy. Managers should also consider the long-term consequences of using certain tactics in the short-term because agents who become alienated (e.g., through the inappropriate use of formal bases of power) may not be open to future leading attempts.

Another aspect refers to the presence and quality of alternative individuals leading in the environment. As social comparison (Festinger, 1954) and equity (Adams, 1965) theories would predict, the kind of power basis an agent uses will moderate the effect of the power basis and leading attempt on other members. For example, if a target sees another supervisor use personal bases of power to lead, it may reduce the effectiveness of the target's supervisor leading attempts based on formal bases of power due to potential fairness or equity concerns (e.g., "why should I be treated as such?"). Other targets and agents become part of the context that moderate the effectiveness of power bases.

Interaction Between Power Bases

It is noteworthy to underline that different fields of research have focused on one specific power basis at a time without concurrently considering the possibility that other power bases might be activated concurrently. Broadly categorized, (a) the power literature has centered primarily on the effect of formal sources of power; (b) team and instrumental leadership approaches have widely concentrated on expertise; (c) new genre leadership theories (e.g., transformational or charismatic leadership) have extensively aimed attention at referent power; and (d) the sociology literature has mainly focused on informational power through their focus on networks. This compartmentalization is damaging because the joint effect of different power bases may be nonadditive and nonlinear.

Combining different power bases may produce synergies, offset each other, or even backfire. Agents relying on different power bases should thus ensure that their combined effect produce synergies. For instance, expert or informational power produce leadership in an relatively effortless manner when combined with legitimate power (Pfeffer, 1981). Expert and informational power require relatively more effort to sway targets when the agent does not possess legitimate power. As another example, a manager possessing referent power and activating a formal basis of power may potentially crowd out the intrinsic motivation associated with the identification of would-be targets. Likewise, jointly activating referent and coercive power may send contradicting signals and induce the target to react more negatively than if each tactic was used separately. Unfortunately, the different literatures provide only limited guidance as to how different power bases interact to produce leadership (see Yukl & Gardner, 2020 for a similar argument regarding influence tactics).

Possessing formal power necessarily affects how the activation of personal power is perceived. In formal organizations, leadership still emerges mainly from individuals in legitimate or authority roles (Shamir & Eilam-Shamir, 2017). Targets however react to a variety of cues and reasons when a leading attempt is made by an agent holding formal power over them. As Shamir and Eilam-Shamir (2017) nicely puts it: "Formal authority is always in the background in managers-subordinates relationships ... formal authority is seldom the only basis of a leader's appeal, request, or demand. Neither is it the only basis of subordinates' or followers' response to the leader's appeal" (p. 380). Thus, we believe that explicitly recognizing the effect of different bases of power—especially formal power interacting with another personal source of power—will provide important insights to our understanding of leadership happening within organizations.

Finally, agents possess different power bases signal important aspects of their character when they activate a particular source of power. It is indeed costly for agents to explain or justify the values, information, or expertise behind their leading attempts when they could more easily rely on their formal power to get things done. In fact, we argue that activating personal sources of power show a commitment to a certain type of leading (see next section). For example, when a supervisor argues that a task should be done because it is the right thing to do (even though she could threaten to reward or punish her subordinate to perform the task), she signals in a costly way how her subordinate is valued and/or the task is important. To the contrary, activating formal sources of power is a relatively easy and quick path to influence others. The activation of "cheap" power bases indicates to the target that he is not valued and/or the task is not important. Targets who believe that the agent could have used personal bases of power to influence them would very likely react negatively to a leading attempt based on sanctions or rewards. We argue that those perceived and recognized as great leaders refrain from using their formal power unless it is necessary to do so (e.g., to establish their credibility).

Different "Types" of Leadership

Building on the two broad categories of power (formal vs. personal) as well as on the distinction regarding designated or nondesignated roles (Ashford & Sitkin, 2019; DeRue, 2011) within organizations allows to uncover three different types of leadership: "Formal," "traditional," and "pure." *Formal leadership* refers to the kind of leadership that emerges when a designated individual persuades followers by activating a formal source of power. *Traditional leadership* concerns a type of leadership that originates from a designated individual who successfully activates a personal basis of power. *Pure leadership* pertains to yet another sort of leadership emanating from nondesignated individuals influencing other organizational members (designated and nondesignated individuals alike) through the activation of personal sources of power.

Importantly, these leadership types are not fixed within individuals. They are fluid and bound to each interaction episode. For instance, a supervisor may at a certain time use "formal" leadership by influencing through rewards and only a moment later use "traditional" leadership by successfully activating some expert power. Similarly, supervisors may use "traditional" leadership with their subordinates and in a later meeting with their hierarchy use "pure" leadership. Furthermore, an individual may use one leadership type in an interaction episode and only a moment later (in a different interaction episode) be a target of a leading attempt so that the individual is then a follower. That being said, we may observe certain individual difference in the frequency of use of each different leadership type.

Having different leadership types illustrates how leadership may emerge from designated individuals in a top-down way ("formal" or "traditional" leadership) or from nondesignated individuals in lateral or bottom-up ways ("pure" leadership). Due to the extent focus on managers and supervisors in leadership research, formal and traditional leadership types have been extensively studied whereas pure leadership has received considerably less attention. Organizations encouraging pure leadership signal that leadership is desired and encouraged from everyone. Organizations with cultures supporting the emergence of leadership from all its constituents, no matter their position in the organizational hierarchy, are likely to have high employees' commitment, morale, and ultimately performance. An important caveat is that perceiving, assessing, and rewarding pure leaders is not an easy task for organizations.

Pure leadership relies on personal bases of power, which are inherently subjective and relatively unstable. In comparison to individuals holding an organizationally sanctioned role with an objective and stable basis of power (Magee & Galinsky, 2008; Wellman et al., 2020), personal bases of power are intangible and can vanish rapidly when the task, context, or individuals present change (Bastardoz & Van Vugt, 2019). For instance, individuals possessing informational power may see their power vanish if the task changes or if new individuals having similar or better information join the team. Pure leadership is also precarious because followers can easily exit the relationship and deny the target's influence without being formally penalized. Given such premises, pure leadership will vary extensively in its application from formal or traditional leadership. Individuals using pure leadership will tend to be more attentive of followers' need and desires. They also need to ensure their power basis remains recognized, and are thus likely to regularly make their power bases salient in order to reinforce and legitimize future leading attempts.

These leadership types inform the study of leadership at different organizational levels because it highlights that first-level employees cannot rely on formal or traditional leadership. First-level employees can only become pure leaders. To encourage pure leadership, organizations should ensure that conditions are favorable and should avoid making the formal hierarchy too prevalent in their culture. Another consequence is that high-level managers cannot be pure leaders unless they attempt to convince someone outside of the organizational hierarchy. Legitimacy and role expectations always lurk in the background to taint their relationships with organizational members (Katz & Kahn, 1978; Shamir & Eilam-Shamir, 2017). Furthermore, certain managers may believe that their influence stems from traditional leadership ("their vision") when in fact their influence originate from the implicit formal power lurking in the background.

Finally, pure leadership is theoretically not limited in the number of followers it could affect compared to formal and traditional leadership (see also Bastardoz & Van Vugt, 2019, p. 91). It is particularly relevant when considering the application of our conceptual model to nonorganizational contexts. YouTube influencers posting videos and swaying large crowds of followers online through pure leadership sees relatively no limit to their influence. In comparison, formal and traditional leadership are always limited by organizational constraints. That is not to say all follower groups of formal or traditional leadership are inherently small. Leaders relying on legitimate power (e.g., elected presidents) may indeed rely on large enough crowds of followers.

INTEGRATING SOCIOPSYCHOLOGICAL POWER WITH LEADERSHIP

In the following section, we aim to enhance the leadership literature by integrating two important constructs from the sociopsychological literature. This integration informs our conceptual model of leadership and poses an interesting conundrum for leadership researchers. We give a particular attention to the future world of work because we believe that the changing nature of work will crucially impact how leadership emerge in a volatile and uncertain future.

Power Distribution

The question of how power should be distributed within groups has received considerable attention without clear, conclusive findings (Anderson & Brown, 2010). Two major theories can explain these contradictory predictions. On the one hand, the functionalist theory suggests that power differences lead to better group performance due to enhanced interactions, improved coordination, and clarity in how resources are allocated (Halevy et al., 2011). On the other hand, conflict theory argues that power imbalances lead to heightened interpersonal conflict, higher competition and individualism, and enhanced engagement in political behaviors (Greer et al., 2017). In a recent meta-analysis, Greer et al. (2018) found that the overall net effect of power dispersion in groups is on average negative, indicating that more equal distributions of power led to less conflict and better performance. Another recent meta-analysis shows that empowered individuals report being more satisfied, committed, and engaged than those reporting low levels of empowerment (Kim et al., 2018). In this regard, the shift towards more shared leadership, empowered subordinates, or holacracy structures in organizations seems to have merit.

Although we fully concur that minimizing formal power differences produces positive outcomes, we also believe that certain power imbalances may be desirable. It is unrealistic to expect that all power differences in organizations be eliminated so that organizational hierarchies become flat. Proponents of shared leadership, empowerment, and new organizational structures have not yet properly addressed how individuals remain accountable of their actions and decisions when power is equally distributed. Many organizations still consider supervisors and managers as accountable for individuals under their span of control. These individuals may simply not delegate tasks or projects and empower their subordinates if they remain accountable for those outcomes. Accountability and responsibility are crucial in organizations (Pitesa & Thau, 2013; Rus et al., 2012), and it may become a problem when power is too widely distributed.

Power differences and hierarchies based on personal sources of power may also not be so detrimental. For example, Tarakci et al. (2016) found that power differences based on expert power did not hurt the performance of the group compared to when power differences were misaligned with expertise levels of group members. Current findings and meta-analyses rely mostly on formal power differences, which have been a major focus in the social-psychological literature. We thus argue that differences on personal sources of power may still favor the emergence of leadership because followers can always exit the relationship if the leader starts abusing his/her power. As we indicated earlier, because personal power lies in the eye of the beholder, it is inherently unstable and can less easily be abused.

This discussion indicates that organizations should keep a fine balance between (a) empowering their powerless employees, and (b) ensuring that certain employees remain accountable and responsible of their decision so that organizational goals are pursued. Organizations should also ensure that their formal leaders are open to being influenced by employees with no formal power in a culture whereby their position of power does not come under too much pressure of being eliminated.

We believe that new forms of work—including gig or temporary workers—create strong power imbalances in favor of organizations that may inhibit the emergence of leadership. Dependency theory (Emerson, 1962) predicts that power originates from possessing un-substitutable, scarce, and important resources. Temporary workers tend to be highly replaceable and are thus likely to be dependent on the organization for work and money. They are thus very likely to accept formal sources of power (Bass & Bass, 2009; Katz & Kahn, 1978), and the activation of referent power is extremely complicated. For instance, how could a CEO vision activate and integrate a temporary worker's self-concept if the worker does not belong in the organization or identify with it? This reliance on formal sources of power is magnified considering that outsourced contractors are hired on a market basis which makes the transactional aspect of their relationship with the organization even more salient. Because personal sources of power will rarely guide the leadership interactions between organizations and contracted workers, this situation will very likely generate authority relations or compliance, rather than leadership and commitment. This prediction of dependency theory is also valid for employees who lack alternative options (e.g., in regions with primarily one main employer), are nonunionized, lack language skills, or are heavily invested in their organizations (Bastardoz & Van Vugt, 2019).

Power Stability

The stability of a power source also affects the leadership process. Mutable power hierarchies increase the susceptibility of group conflicts (Hays & Bendersky, 2015). Unstable or changing power hierarchies generate stress for powerholders (Sapolsky, 2005) who then engage in more risky behaviors (Jordan et al., 2011), appropriate more resources for their personal interests (Pettit et al., 2010), and keep powerless individuals under tight control (Feenstra et al., 2020; Mead & Maner, 2012). Unstable powerholders are unlikely to encourage others to lead and shine because in doing so, their authority position may become even more unstable and ultimately lead to their removal. Certain individuals holding formal power may discriminate others to ensure that their power remains secure (Maner

& Mead, 2010). For instance, managers may attempt to suppress leading attempts by pure leaders to keep hold on their power. Such behaviors are critical impediments for organizational effectiveness.

This discussion has important ramifications in a constantly changing world of work. With the advent of digitization and new technologies replacing or changing human work, many individuals will see their expert or informational power disappear or at risk of being replaced. Employees who used to be powerful individuals through their possession of unsubstitutable knowledge and skills are now being replaced by robots, machines, or a younger workforce proficient with the use of information technologies. Technological disruptions create unstable conditions whereby individuals see their power bases erode, and with it, their potential for leadership. These conditions inevitably create frictions and conflicts considering how powerholders tend to cling to power. More research will be required to understand how technological changes affect the exercise of leadership within organizations.

DISCUSSION AND AVENUES FOR FUTURE RESEARCH

Power and leadership are inextricably linked. Leadership emerges when power bases are activated and lead to a certain kind of influence targeted at a common goal. We have first provided conceptual clarity in distinguishing the two constructs as well as discussing their interrelationship. In our review of the literature, we have identified a leadership divide that threatens the validity of empirical findings as well as important limitations in power approaches to leadership. Taking a microlevel lens, we offer a conceptual model that links the emergence of leadership to the activation of different power sources. We have made various propositions regarding agents, targets, and contextual characteristics moderating the activation of power bases as well as the effectiveness of a leading attempt. This conceptual model raises intriguing and consequential questions for the study of leadership. Finally, we have discussed how the distribution and stability of power, constructs which have originated in the social psychology literature, can affect the leadership process. We discuss now avenues for future research this conceptual integration uncovers and offer suggestions for methodologies to appropriately test our conceptual model.

Applying such a fine-grained and dynamic lens offers new insights on the leadership phenomenon. Leadership can emerge anytime and from anyone part of a dyad, group, or organization. The act of leading is thus not tied solely to individuals holding designated roles. Leadership can occur multiple times during an event or group meeting across different interaction episodes, either from the same individual (e.g., CEO during a townhall presentation) or from different individuals (e.g., team members in a group meeting). Leadership can also be absent if no individuals attempt to lead or if the leading attempt is thwarted. Focusing on the moment or instances of leadership allows a more precise understanding of leadership as a social influence process.

Our conceptual model shows that someone does not need to be labeled as a leader to actually lead. Leadership does not rest on followers' assessment of someone as a leader; rather, leaders are individuals who have influence in the realization of shared goals, and it does not matter for the occurrence of leadership whether leaders or followers explicitly recognize this reality. We depart in that regard from conventional wisdom suggesting that leadership emerges when one or more followers recognize and label someone as a leader. Naturally, it is very likely that leadership occurred when someone is recognized as a leader. But it may also be that leadership did not occur and the reported perceptions were merely a social construction (Meindl, 1995). Followers may also, voluntarily or involuntarily, not recognize that they are being led and thus fail to grant the "leader" label to an individual who genuinely leads (Ashford & Sitkin, 2019). In lieu of leadership lying in the eye of the follower, we contend that leadership lies in leading. Future research may inquire why some individuals may lead but are not perceived as leaders. Conversely, understanding why and how some individuals are perceived as leaders without having any influence towards shared goals could also inform about laypeople conceptions of leadership (see in that regard Kniffin et al., 2020; Zaar et al., 2020).

Our approach places power bases as resources individuals can draw from to exercise influence and leadership. As the feedback loop in our conceptual model indicates (see Figure 11.2), certain power bases may emerge from previous successful leading attempts. For instance, an individual may have referent power because targets associate positive emotions from earlier leadership episodes. To avoid omitted variable bias and endogeneity problems in future empirical investigations, the underlying cause of referent power needs to be appropriately modeled (see Sajons, 2020). Potent sources of referent power may include (a) values-based and emotionally-laden signaling (i.e., charisma; Antonakis et al., 2016), which has been extensively linked as an antecedent or correlate of referent power (Conger & Kanungo, 1998; Shamir et al., 1993); (b) a high reputation of trustworthiness and consistency achieved through successful leadership interactions (Ocasio et al., 2020), self-sacrificial behaviors, or by consistently walking the talk (Bastardoz, 2020); (c) performing in an ethical or authentic manner showing the agent's commitment to a certain set of desirable values (Brown & Treviño, 2006); (d) being prototypical of a group or organization identity (Haslam et al., 2010; Hogg, 2001); or (e) liking that can be based on physical attractiveness, friendship ties, humor, or similarity in interests (among others). Indeed, a long list of reasons—of which a majority has been discussed as a specific leadership style—may act as the source of referent power. Because of this, simply measuring referent power through perceptual questionnaires would miss the point and lead to spurious correlations. Informational power is also endogenous when reported through network data because the network positions that individuals occupy are not randomly or exogenously allocated. Future studies investigating referent and informational bases of power as antecedents of leadership in the field should precisely model how such power emerged.

The origins of legitimate power also matter for its effectiveness. Individuals holding legitimate positions of power within organizations can obtain such positions either through appointment or through election. Elected individuals tend to be more effective in producing change than randomly selected or appointed individuals (Brandts et al., 2014). Hollander (1992) suggested that elected individuals lead to heightened psychological identification. Similarly, Bastardoz and Van Vugt (2019) propose that bottom-up emergence and election of supervisors lead to higher subordinates' engagement because subordinates had a say on the decision and were more likely to select someone who had their best interests at heart. Despite its positive ramifications for targets' engagement, individuals are rarely elected in for-profit organizations. Our contention would be that organizations may increase the occurrence of leadership (as opposed to authority relations; see Figure 11.1) if they were to select more frequently their leaders in a bottom-up rather than top-down fashion (see also De Cremer & Van Dijk, 2008).

Our process model gives contextual factors a central role in the understanding of leadership. Given the multidimensional nature of context, Oc (2018) distinguished between the discrete and omnibus contexts. Our discussion of context in this chapter has mainly focused on characteristics pertaining to the discrete context such as the individuals present in the interaction episode (e.g., social context). We also believe that the distal context would provide important information regarding our conceptual model. For instance, pure leadership may be expected and desired in certain national cultures (e.g., low power distance, individualism) or types of organizations (e.g., start-ups, NGOs, or social movements such as the current Black Lives Matter). On the contrary, formal, or traditional leadership may be better tolerated and attempts at pure leadership rejected in certain national cultures (e.g., high power distance, collectivist) or types of organization (e.g., prison, army, state-owned). Crises or difficult economic conditions may also call for more formal or traditional leadership.

Beyond the stability and general distribution of power differences, the sociopsychological literature offers interesting insights related to outcomes associated with being or feeling powerful. Major theories such as the approach-inhibition (Keltner et al., 2003) and situated focus (Guinote,

2007) contend that powerful individuals seek to satisfy their own preferences and goals. Powerholders are freed from conformity whereas powerless individuals generally follow the prescribed situational norms to guide their behaviors. For instance, research findings indicate that the suffering of others affected powerful individuals to a lesser extent (Van Kleef et al., 2008) and high-power individuals tend to be immune to others' emotions (Van Kleef et al., 2006). These findings suggest that designated individuals may incorrectly read a situation and so fail to appropriately tailor their behaviors, ultimately encouraging authority relations instead of leadership. Such individuals may have a particularly hard time being individually considerate or emotionally attuned. These predictions stand in stark contrast to standard leadership theories.

In our attempt to integrate leadership and power, we also recognize that our conceptual model is mainly cognitive and may miss important emotional bases of power as antecedents of leadership. Our approach assumes that individuals make reasoned (but not necessarily explicit) decisions when it comes to following a leader. This assumption is overly restrictive considering how emotions can make and break leaders. Shared feelings, rather than shared goals, may be a necessary and sufficient condition for the emergence of leadership. Take the case of a politician who, during a political rally or a televised speech, creates a community of feeling common to multiple individuals who had different emotions prior to the address. Future work investigating power bases as antecedents of leadership may target more emotional aspects as preconditions for the existence of leadership.

Methodologies for Future Research

Our conceptual model requires a shift in how leadership is studied. Rather than conveniently focusing on managers or supervisors who hold formal power, it requires researchers to explore and scrutinize meticulously instances of leadership. Ashford and Sitkin (2019) summarizes the challenges associated with such an undertaking:

> Once we move beyond the study of formally appointed supervisors, we immediately face questions of, for example: Who do we study? How do we find a sample of "leaders?" What will we study about them? We don't even really have a language for talking about these issues. (p. 457)

Furthermore, the use of questionnaires in field studies should appropriately consider how memory biases and cognitive classifications may affect findings (Day, 2014; Lord et al., 1978), preventing a retrospective measurement of individuals' power sources. Although there is no silver bullet, we believe that researchers still have the possibility to produce findings with clear causal policy implications.

First, we encourage investigations of natural interactions. Objective raters could code in situ or through recorded video for successful and unsuccessful leading attempts based on the activation of different bases of power (Bass, 1954; Gerpott et al., 2019). Researchers could complement with interviews of organizational members regarding their perception of the leading attempt and the bases of power underlying these attempts. Content coding of successful and failed leading attempts via e-mails or intraorganizational chats may also provide additional insights into the behavioral activation of power bases. Indeed, understanding how individuals who have experienced one or multiple failed leading attempts react and how it affects their future leading attempts may offer critical new knowledge. Artificial intelligence techniques such as machine learning provide significant opportunities to analyze archival or big data. As a rare example of such approach, Zhu et al. (2011) studied the dynamic emergence of shared leadership at Wikipedia using machine learning models. All these approaches would focus on what individuals do, rather than what supervisors and subordinates perceive or recall.

Field researchers may also focus on how organizational members (try to) sway others to pursue common goals. Participants may report the frequency, origin, and form of their different leading attempts. These same organizational members may report how often they were the target of leading attempts, who were the agents, and whether leading attempts were successful. Such studies may build on Yukl's influence tactics research (Yukl & Falbe, 1990; Yukl & Tracey, 1992) although important adjustments would be in order. These studies should be done under shorter time frames (ideally at the interaction episode) or even as a daily diary study to reduce the bias inherent due to cognitive classification and partial memory. Also, new questionnaires have to be developed with a clear behavioral (rather than attributional or perceptual) focus. For instance, researchers should develop items measuring to what extent others "use knowledge or expertise," "make use of private information," or "build on the legitimacy of their organizational role." Generally, it would be interesting to explore how power bases vary within-individuals across tasks, contexts, or organizations.

Experimental work may be conducted to identify causal relations. The different power bases are easily amenable to experimental manipulation, and their interaction can be studied in a controlled environment. Studying configurations of power bases could probably best be studied experimentally and replicated cross-sectionally in the field. Individual characteristics may also be manipulated or measured (if exogenous) to study the moderation propositions laid out in this manuscript. Simulations using agent-based modeling may also be interesting to study the emergence of leadership by modeling various individuals and combinations of power bases across multiple interactions episodes. Finally, neuroscientific experiments may offer important evidence for the comprehension of the leadership proces. For instance, it may be that different leadership types are linked with different neural pathways within followers such that pure leadership provokes a different neural activity in followers compared to formal or traditional leadership.

CONCLUSION

We have attempted to integrate power and leadership beyond existing frameworks to offer a timely process model of leadership. We have argued that leadership—defined as the successful application of social influence to achieving shared goals—results from a leader activating relevant and available power bases during short-lived interaction episodes. These power bases interact with agents and target characteristics to produce leadership. The manuscript offers conceptual clarity regarding the process of leadership. This approach shows that leading is dynamic and context-based, and operates at a microlevel. We hope that the conceptual model and its associated implications will empower leadership scholars to lead and enrich the study of contemporary leadership.

REFERENCES

Adams, J. S. (1965). Inequity in social exchange. In L. Berkowitz (Ed.), *Advances in experimental social psychology* (Vol. 2, pp. 267–299). Elsevier. https://doi.org/10.1016/S0065-2601(08)60108-2

Aime, F., Humphrey, S., DeRue, D. S., & Paul, J. B. (2014). The riddle of heterarchy: Power transitions in cross-functional teams. *Academy of Management Journal, 57*(2), 327–352. https://doi.org/10.5465/amj.2011.0756

Alvesson, M. (2019). Waiting for Godot: Eight major problems in the odd field of leadership studies. *Leadership, 15*(1), 27–43. https://doi.org/10.1177/1742715017736707

Alvesson, M. (2020). Upbeat leadership: A recipe for–or against–"successful" leadership theory. *The Leadership Quarterly*. Advance online publication. https://doi.org/10.1016/j.leaqua.2020.101439

Alvesson, M., & Einola, K. (2019). Warning for excessive positivity: Authentic leadership and other traps in leadership studies. *The Leadership Quarterly, 30*(4), 383–395. https://doi.org/10.1016/j.leaqua.2019.04.001

Ammeter, A. P., Douglas, C., Gardner, W. L., Hochwarter, W. A., & Ferris, G. R. (2002). Toward a political theory of leadership. *The Leadership Quarterly, 13*(6), 751–796. https://doi.org/10.1016/S1048-9843(02)00157-1

Ancona, D., & Backman, E. (2008). *Distributed, shared or collective leadership: A new leadership model for the collaborative era.* Annual Meeting of the Academy of Management, Anaheim, CA.

Anderson, C., & Brion, S. (2014). Perspectives on power in organizations. *Annual Review of Organizational Psychology and Organizational Behavior, 1*(1), 67–97. https://doi.org/10.1146/annurev-orgpsych-031413-091259

Anderson, C., & Brown, C. E. (2010). The functions and dysfunctions of hierarchy. *Research in Organizational Behavior, 30*, 55–89. https://doi.org/10.1016/j.riob.2010.08.002

Antonakis, J. (2017). On doing better science: From thrill of discovery to policy implications. *The Leadership Quarterly, 28*(1), 5–21. https://doi.org/10.1016/j.leaqua.2017.01.006

Antonakis, J., Bastardoz, N., Jacquart, P., & Shamir, B. (2016). Charisma: An ill-defined and ill-measured gift. *Annual Review of Organizational Psychology and Organizational Behavior, 3*(1), 293–319. https://doi.org/10.1146/annurev-orgpsych-041015-062305

Antonakis, J., Bendahan, S., Jacquart, P., & Lalive, R. (2010). On making causal claims: A review and recommendations. *The Leadership Quarterly, 21*(6), 1086–1120. https://doi.org/10.1016/j.leaqua.2010.10.010

Antonakis, J., & Day, D. V. (2018). *The Nature of Leadership* (2nd ed.). Sage publications.

Antonakis, J., & House, R. J. (2014). Instrumental leadership: Measurement and extension of transformational–transactional leadership theory. *The Leadership Quarterly, 25*(4), 746–771. https://doi.org/10.1016/j.leaqua.2014.04.005

Argyris, C. (1957). *Personality and organization: The conflict between system and the individual.* Harper & Brothers.

Arthur, C. A., Bastardoz, N., & Eklund, R. (2017). Transformational leadership in sport: Current status and future directions. *Current Opinion in Psychology, 16*, 78–83. https://doi.org/10.1016/j.copsyc.2017.04.001

Ashford, S. J., & Sitkin, S. B. (2019). From problems to progress: A dialogue on prevailing issues in leadership research. *The Leadership Quarterly, 30*(4), 454–460. https://doi.org/10.1016/j.leaqua.2019.01.003

Ashforth, B. E., Kreiner, G. E., & Fugate, M. (2000). All in a day's work: Boundaries and micro role transitions. *Academy of Management Review, 25*(3), 472–491. https://doi.org/10.5465/amr.2000.3363315

Badura, K. L., Grijalva, E., Galvin, B. M., Owens, B. P., & Joseph, D. L. (2020). Motivation to lead: A meta-analysis and distal-proximal model of motivation and leadership. *Journal of Applied Psychology, 105*(4), 331–354. https://doi.org/10.1037/apl0000439

Banks, G. C., Gooty, J., Ross, R. L., Williams, C. E., & Harrington, N. T. (2018). Construct redundancy in leader behaviors: A review and agenda for the future. *The Leadership Quarterly, 29*(1), 236–251. https://doi.org/10.1016/j.leaqua.2017.12.005

Barbuto, J. E., Jr. (2000). Influence triggers: A framework for understanding follower compliance. *The Leadership Quarterly, 11*(3), 365–387. https://doi.org/10.1016/S1048-9843(00)00045-X

Barley, S. R. (1986). Technology as an occasion for structuring: Evidence from observations of CT scanners and the social order of radiology departments. *Administrative Science Quarterly, 31*(1), 78–108. https://doi.org/10.2307/2392767

Bass, B. M. (1954). The leaderless group discussion. *Psychological Bulletin, 51*(5), 465–492. https://doi.org/10.1037/h0056881

Bass, B. M., & Bass, R. (2009). *The Bass Handbook of Leadership: Theory, research, and managerial applications* (4th ed.). Free Press.

Bass, B. M., & Stogdill, R. M. (1990). *Handbook of leadership* (3rd ed.). Free Press.

Bastardoz, N. (2020). Signaling Charisma. In J. P. Zuquete (Ed.), *Routledge International Handbook of Charisma* (1st ed., pp 313–323). Routledge. https://www.taylorfrancis.com/chapters/edit/10.4324/9780429263224-33/signaling-charisma-nicolas-bastardoz

Bastardoz, N., & Van Vugt, M. (2019). The nature of followership: Evolutionary analysis and review. *The Leadership Quarterly, 30*(1), 81–95. https://doi.org/10.1016/j.leaqua.2018.09.004

Baumeister, R. F., & Leary, M. R. (1995). The need to belong: Desire for interpersonal attachments as a fundamental human motivation. *Psychological Bulletin, 117*(3), 497–529. https://doi.org/10.1037/0033-2909.117.3.497

Bearden, W. O., Netemeyer, R. G., & Teel, J. E. (1989). Measurement of consumer susceptibility to interpersonal influence. *Journal of Consumer Research, 15*(4), 473–481. https://doi.org/10.1086/209186

Bedeian, A. G., & Hunt, J. G. (2006). Academic amnesia and vestigial assumptions of our forefathers. *The Leadership Quarterly, 17*(2), 190–205. https://doi.org/10.1016/j.leaqua.2005.12.006

Blom, M., & Lundgren, M. (2020). The (In)voluntary follower. *Leadership, 16*(2), 163–179. https://doi.org/10.1177/1742715019888078

Brandts, J., Cooper, D. J., & Weber, R. A. (2014). Legitimacy, communication, and leadership in the turnaround game. *Management Science, 61*(11), 2627–2645. https://doi.org/10.1287/mnsc.2014.2021

Brass, D. J. (1985). Men's and women's networks: A study of interaction patterns and influence in an organization. *Academy of Management Journal, 28*(2), 327–343. https://doi.org/10.5465/256204

Brehm, S. S., & Brehm, J. W. (1981). *Psychological reactance: A theory of freedom and control*. Academic Press.

Brown, M. E., & Treviño, L. K. (2006). Ethical leadership: A review and future directions. *The Leadership Quarterly, 17*(6), 595–616. https://doi.org/10.1016/j.leaqua.2006.10.004

Carson, J. B., Tesluk, P. E., & Marrone, J. A. (2007). Shared leadership in teams: An investigation of antecedent conditions and performance. *Academy of Management Journal, 50*(5), 1217–1234. https://doi.org/10.5465/amj.2007.20159921

Choo, T.-H. (1964). Communicator credibility and communication discrepancy as determinants of opinion change. *The Journal of Social Psychology, 64*(1), 65–76.

Christie, A., Barling, J., & Turner, N. (2011). Pseudo-transformational leadership: Model specification and outcomes. *Journal of Applied Social Psychology, 41*(12), 2943–2984. https://doi.org/10.1111/j.1559-1816.2011.00858.x

Cialdini, R. B. (2007). *Influence: The psychology of persuasion*. HarperCollins.

Cialdini, R. B., & Goldstein, N. J. (2004). Social influence: Compliance and conformity. *Annual Review of Psychology, 55*, 591–621. https://doi.org/10.1146/annurev.psych.55.090902.142015

Collinson, D. (2006). Rethinking followership: A post-structuralist analysis of follower identities. *The Leadership Quarterly, 17*(2), 179–189. https://doi.org/10.1016/j.leaqua.2005.12.005

Collinson, D., & Tourish, D. (2015). Teaching leadership critically: New directions for leadership pedagogy. *Academy of Management Learning & Education, 14*(4), 576–594. https://doi.org/10.5465/amle.2014.0079

Conger, J. A., & Kanungo, R. N. (1998). *Charismatic leadership in organizations*. SAGE.

Contractor, N. S., DeChurch, L. A., Carson, J., Carter, D. R., & Keegan, B. (2012). The topology of collective leadership. *The Leadership Quarterly, 23*(6), 994–1011. https://doi.org/10.1016/j.leaqua.2012.10.010

D'Innocenzo, L., Mathieu, J. E., & Kukenberger, M. R. (2016). A meta-analysis of different forms of shared leadership–team performance relations. *Journal of Management, 42*(7), 1964–1991. https://doi.org/10.1177/0149206314525205

Davis, J. P., & Eisenhardt, K. M. (2011). Rotating leadership and collaborative innovation: Recombination processes in symbiotic relationships. *Administrative Science Quarterly, 56*(2), 159–201. https://doi.org/10.1177/0001839211428131

Day, D. V. (2012). Leadership. In S. W. Kozlowski (Ed.), *The Oxford handbook of organizational psychology* (Vol. 1, pp. 696–729). Oxford University Press.

Day, D. V. (2014). The future of leadership: Challenges and prospects. In D. V. Day (Ed.), *The Oxford handbook of leadership and organizations* (pp. 859–867). Oxford University Press.

Day, D. V., & Dragoni, L. (2015). Leadership development: An outcome-oriented review based on time and levels of analyses. *Annual Review of Organizational Psychology and Organizational Behavior, 2*(1), 133–156. https://doi.org/10.1146/annurev-orgpsych-032414-111328

De Cremer, D., & Van Dijk, E. (2008). Leader-follower effects in resource dilemmas: The roles of leadership selection and social responsibility. *Group Processes & Intergroup Relations, 11*(3), 355–369. https://doi.org/10.1177/1368430208090647

DeRue, D. S. (2011). Adaptive leadership theory: Leading and following as a complex adaptive process. *Research in Organizational Behavior, 31*, 125–150. https://doi.org/10.1016/j.riob.2011.09.007

DeRue, D. S., & Ashford, S. J. (2010). Who will lead and who will follow? A social process of leadership identity construction in organizations. *Academy of Management Review, 35*(4), 627–647. https://doi.org/10.5465/amr.35.4.zok627

Dinh, J. E., Lord, R. G., Gardner, W. L., Meuser, J. D., Liden, R. C., & Hu, J. (2014). Leadership theory and research in the new millennium: Current theoretical trends and changing perspectives. *The Leadership Quarterly, 25*(1), 36–62. https://doi.org/10.1016/j.leaqua.2013.11.005

Drath, W. H., McCauley, C. D., Palus, C. J., Van Velsor, E., O'Connor, P. M., & McGuire, J. B. (2008). Direction, alignment, commitment: Toward a more integrative ontology of leadership. *The Leadership Quarterly, 19*(6), 635–653. https://doi.org/10.1016/j.leaqua.2008.09.003

Eberly, M. B., Johnson, M. D., Hernandez, M., & Avolio, B. J. (2013). An integrative process model of leadership: Examining loci, mechanisms, and event cycles. *American Psychologist*, *68*(6), 427–443. https://doi.org/10.1037/a0032244

Emerson, R. M. (1962). Power-dependence relations. *American Sociological Review*, *27*(1), 31–41. https://doi.org/10.2307/2089716

Ensley, M. D., Hmieleski, K. M., & Pearce, C. L. (2006). The importance of vertical and shared leadership within new venture top management teams: Implications for the performance of startups. *The Leadership Quarterly*, *17*(3), 217–231. https://doi.org/10.1016/j.leaqua.2006.02.002

Etzioni, A. (1961). *A comparative analysis of complex organizations*. The Free Press.

Feenstra, S., Jordan, J., Walter, F., & Stoker, J. I. (2020). Antecedents of leaders' power sharing: The roles of power instability and distrust. *Organizational Behavior and Human Decision Processes*, *157*, 115–128. https://doi.org/10.1016/j.obhdp.2020.01.005

Ferris, G. R., Ellen III, B. P., McAllister, C. P., & Maher, L. P. (2019). Reorganizing organizational politics research: A review of the literature and identification of future research directions. *Annual Review of Organizational Psychology and Organizational Behavior*, *6*, 299–323. https://doi.org/10.1146/annurev-orgpsych-012218-015221

Ferris, G. R., Harrell-Cook, G., & Dulebohn, J. H. (2000). Organizational politics: The nature of the relationship between politics perceptions and political behavior. In *Research in the Sociology of Organizations* (Vol. 17, pp. 89–130). https://doi.org/10.1016/S0733-558X(00)17004-1

Ferris, G. R., Treadway, D. C., Kolodinsky, R. W., Hochwarter, W. A., Kacmar, C. J., Douglas, C., & Frink, D. D. (2005). Development and validation of the political skill inventory. *Journal of Management*, *31*(1), 126–152. https://doi.org/10.1177/0149206304271386

Festinger, L. (1954). A theory of social comparison processes. *Human Relations*, *7*(2), 117–140. https://doi.org/10.1177/001872675400700202

French, J. R., & Raven, B. (1959). The bases of social power. In D. P. Cartwright (Ed.), *Classics of Organization Theory* (pp. 150–167). Institute for Social Research, University of Michigan.

Friedrich, T. L., Vessey, W. B., Schuelke, M. J., Ruark, G. A., & Mumford, M. D. (2009). A framework for understanding collective leadership: The selective utilization of leader and team expertise within networks. *The Leadership Quarterly*, *20*(6), 933–958. https://doi.org/10.1016/j.leaqua.2009.09.008

Galinsky, A. D., Gruenfeld, D. H., & Magee, J. C. (2003). From power to action. *Journal of Personality and Social Psychology*, *85*(3), 453–466. https://doi.org/10.1037/0022-3514.85.3.453

Gerpott, F. H., Lehmann-Willenbrock, N., Voelpel, S. C., & van Vugt, M. (2019). It's not just what is said, but when it's said: A temporal account of verbal behaviors and emergent leadership in self-managed teams. *Academy of Management Journal*, *62*(3), 717–738. https://doi.org/10.5465/amj.2017.0149

Greer, L. L., de Jong, B. A., Schouten, M. E., & Dannals, J. E. (2018). Why and when hierarchy impacts team effectiveness: A meta-analytic integration. *Journal of Applied Psychology*, *103*(6), 591–613. https://doi.org/10.1037/apl0000291

Greer, L. L., Van Bunderen, L., & Yu, S. (2017). The dysfunctions of power in teams: A review and emergent conflict perspective. *Research in Organizational Behavior, 37*, 103–124. https://doi.org/10.1016/j.riob.2017.10.005

Gronn, P. (2002). Distributed leadership as a unit of analysis. *The Leadership Quarterly, 13*(4), 423–451. https://doi.org/10.1016/S1048-9843(02)00120-0

Guinote, A. (2007). Behaviour variability and the situated focus theory of power. *European Review of Social Psychology, 18*(1), 256–295. https://doi.org/10.1080/10463280701692813

Halevy, N., Chou, E. Y., & Galinsky, A. D. (2011). A functional model of hierarchy: Why, how, and when vertical differentiation enhances group performance. *Organizational Psychology Review, 1*(1), 32–52. https://doi.org/10.1177/2041386610380991

Hambrick, D. C., & Lovelace, J. B. (2018). The role of executive symbolism in advancing new strategic themes in organizations: A social influence perspective. *Academy of Management Review, 43*(1), 110–131. https://doi.org/10.5465/amr.2015.0190

Hannah, S. T., Sumanth, J. J., Lester, P., & Cavarretta, F. (2014). Debunking the false dichotomy of leadership idealism and pragmatism: Critical evaluation and support of newer genre leadership theories. *Journal of Organizational Behavior, 35*(5), 598–621. https://doi.org/10.1002/job.1931

Haslam, S. A., Reicher, S. D., & Platow, M. J. (2010). *The new psychology of leadership: Identity, influence and power*. Psychology Press.

Hays, N. A., & Bendersky, C. (2015). Not all inequality is created equal: Effects of status versus power hierarchies on competition for upward mobility. *Journal of Personality and Social Psychology, 108*(6), 867–882. https://doi.org/10.1037/pspi0000017

Hermalin, B. E. (1998). Toward an economic theory of leadership: Leading by example. *American Economic Review, 88*(5), 1188–1206. http://www.jstor.org/stable/116866

Hoffman, E. L., & Lord, R. G. (2013). A taxonomy of event-level dimensions: Implications for understanding leadership processes, behavior, and performance. *The Leadership Quarterly, 24*(4), 558–571. https://doi.org/10.1016/j.leaqua.2013.03.009

Hogg, M. A. (2001). A social identity theory of leadership. *Personality and Social Psychology Review, 5*(3), 184–200. https://doi.org/10.1207/S15327957PSPR0503_1

Hollander, E. P. (1958). Conformity, status, and idiosyncrasy credit. *Psychological Review, 65*(2), 117–127. https://doi.org/10.1037/h0042501

Hollander, E. P. (1992). Leadership, followership, self, and others. *The Leadership Quarterly, 3*(1), 43–54. https://doi.org/10.1016/1048-9843(92)90005-Z

Hooper, P. L., Kaplan, H. S., & Boone, J. L. (2010). A theory of leadership in human cooperative groups. *Journal of Theoretical Biology, 265*(4), 633–646. https://doi.org/10.1016/j.jtbi.2010.05.034

House, R. J. (1996). Path-goal theory of leadership: Lessons, legacy, and a reformulated theory. *The Leadership Quarterly, 7*(3), 323–352. https://doi.org/10.1016/S1048-9843(96)90024-7

House, R. J., & Aditya, R. N. (1997). The social scientific study of leadership: Quo vadis? *Journal of Management*, *23*(3), 409–473. https://doi.org/10.1016/S0149-2063(97)90037-4

Hunter, S. T., Bedell-Avers, K. E., & Mumford, M. D. (2007). The typical leadership study: Assumptions, implications, and potential remedies. *The Leadership Quarterly*, *18*(5), 435–446. https://doi.org/10.1016/j.leaqua.2007.07.001

Jordan, J., Sivanathan, N., & Galinsky, A. D. (2011). Something to lose and nothing to gain: The role of stress in the interactive effect of power and stability on risk taking. *Administrative Science Quarterly*, *56*(4), 530–558. https://doi.org/10.1177/0001839212441928

Katz, D., & Kahn, R. L. (1978). *The social psychology of organizations* (Vol. 2). Wiley.

Kelman, H. C. (1958). Compliance, identification, and internalization three processes of attitude change. *Journal of Conflict Resolution*, *2*(1), 51–60. https://www.jstor.org/stable/172844

Keltner, D., Gruenfeld, D. H., & Anderson, C. (2003). Power, approach, and inhibition. *Psychological Review*, *110*(2), 265–284. https://doi.org/10.1037/0033-295X.110.2.265

Kim, M., Beehr, T. A., & Prewett, M. S. (2018). Employee responses to empowering leadership: A meta-analysis. *Journal of Leadership & Organizational Studies*, *25*(3), 257–276. https://doi.org/10.1177/1548051817750538

Kipnis, D., & Schmidt, S. M. (1988). Upward-influence styles: Relationship with performance evaluations, salary, and stress. *Administrative Science Quarterly*, *33*(4), 528–542. https://doi.org/10.2307/2392642

Kipnis, D., Schmidt, S. M., & Wilkinson, I. (1980). Intraorganizational influence tactics: Explorations in getting one's way. *Journal of Applied Psychology*, *65*(4), 440–452. https://doi.org/10.1037/0021-9010.65.4.440

Kirkpatrick, S. A., & Locke, E. A. (1991). Leadership: Do traits matter? *Academy of Management Executive*, *5*(2), 48–60. https://doi.org/10.5465/ame.1991.4274679

Kniffin, K. M., Detert, J. R., & Leroy, H. L. (2020). On leading and managing: Synonyms or separate (and unequal)? *Academy of Management Discoveries*. Advance online publication. https://doi.org/10.5465/amd.2018.0227

Krackhardt, D. (1990). Assessing the political landscape: Structure, cognition, and power in organizations. *Administrative Science Quarterly*, *35*(2), 342–369. https://doi.org/10.2307/2393394

Lee, S., Han, S., Cheong, M., Kim, S. L., & Yun, S. (2017). How do I get my way? A meta-analytic review of research on influence tactics. *The Leadership Quarterly*, *28*(1), 210–228. https://doi.org/10.1016/j.leaqua.2016.11.001

Lord, R. G., Binning, J. F., Rush, M. C., & Thomas, J. C. (1978). The effect of performance cues and leader behavior on questionnaire ratings of leadership behavior. *Organizational Behavior and Human Performance*, *21*(1), 27–39. https://doi.org/10.1016/0030-5073(78)90036-3

Magee, J. C., & Galinsky, A. D. (2008). Social hierarchy: The self-reinforcing nature of power and status. *Academy of Management Annals*, *2*(1), 351–398. https://doi.org/10.5465/19416520802211628

Maner, J. K., & Mead, N. L. (2010). The essential tension between leadership and power: When leaders sacrifice group goals for the sake of self-interest. *Journal of Personality and Social Psychology, 99*(3), 482–497. https://doi.org/10.1037/a0018559

McClean, S. T., Barnes, C. M., Courtright, S. H., & Johnson, R. E. (2019). Resetting the clock on dynamic leader behaviors: A conceptual integration and agenda for future research. *Academy of Management Annals, 13*(2), 479–508. https://doi.org/10.5465/annals.2017.0081

McClelland, D. C. (1961). *The achieving society*. https://doi.org/10.1037/14359-000

Mead, N. L., & Maner, J. K. (2012). On keeping your enemies close: Powerful leaders seek proximity to ingroup power threats. *Journal of Personality and Social Psychology, 102*(3), 576–591. https://doi.org/10.1037/a0025755

Meindl, J. R. (1995). The romance of leadership as a follower-centric theory: A social constructionist approach. *The Leadership Quarterly, 6*(3), 329–341. https://doi.org/10.1016/1048-9843(95)90012-8

Mintzberg, H. (1983). *Power in and around organizations*. Prentice Hall.

Miscenko, D., Guenter, H., & Day, D. V. (2017). Am I a leader? Examining leader identity development over time. *The Leadership Quarterly, 28*(5), 605–620. https://doi.org/10.1016/j.leaqua.2017.01.004

Morgeson, F. P., Mitchell, T. R., & Liu, D. (2015). Event system theory: An event-oriented approach to the organizational sciences. *Academy of Management Review, 40*(4), 515–537. https://doi.org/10.5465/amr.2012.0099

Munyon, T. P., Summers, J. K., Thompson, K. M., & Ferris, G. R. (2015). Political skill and work outcomes: A theoretical extension, meta-analytic investigation, and agenda for the future. *Personnel Psychology, 68*(1), 143–184. https://doi.org/10.1111/peps.12066

Oc, B. (2018). Contextual leadership: A systematic review of how contextual factors shape leadership and its outcomes. *The Leadership Quarterly, 29*(1), 218–235. https://doi.org/10.1016/j.leaqua.2017.12.004

Ocasio, W., Pozner, J.-E., & Milner, D. (2020). Varieties of political capital and power in organizations: A review and integrative framework. *Academy of Management Annals, 14*(1), 303–338. https://doi.org/10.5465/annals.2018.0062

Pearce, C. L., & Conger, J. A. (2002). *Shared leadership: Reframing the hows and whys of leadership*. SAGE.

Pettigrew, A. M. (1972). Information control as a power resource. *Sociology, 6*(2), 187–204. https://doi.org/10.1177/003803857200600202

Pettit, N. C., Yong, K., & Spataro, S. E. (2010). Holding your place: Reactions to the prospect of status gains and losses. *Journal of Experimental Social Psychology, 46*(2), 396–401. https://doi.org/10.1016/j.jesp.2009.12.007

Pfeffer, J. (1977). The ambiguity of leadership. *Academy of Management Review, 2*(1), 104–112. https://doi.org/10.5465/amr.1977.4409175

Pfeffer, J. (1981). *Power in organizations*. Ballinger.

Pink, D. H. (2011). *Drive: The surprising truth about what motivates us*. Penguin.

Pitesa, M., & Thau, S. (2013). Masters of the universe: How power and accountability influence self-serving decisions under moral hazard. *Journal of Applied Psychology, 98*(3), 550–558. https://doi.org/0.1037/a0031697

Podsakoff, P. M., Bommer, W. H., Podsakoff, N. P., & MacKenzie, S. B. (2006). Relationships between leader reward and punishment behavior and subordinate attitudes, perceptions, and behaviors: A meta-analytic review of existing and new research. *Organizational Behavior and Human Decision Processes, 99*(2), 113–142. https://doi.org/10.1016/j.obhdp.2005.09.002

Podsakoff, P. M., MacKenzie, S. B., Lee, J.-Y., & Podsakoff, N. P. (2003). Common method biases in behavioral research: A critical review of the literature and recommended remedies. *Journal of Applied Psychology, 88*(5), 879–903. https://doi.org/10.1037/0021-9010.88.5.879

Podsakoff, P. M., & Schriescheim, C. A. (1985). Field studies of French and Raven's bases of power: Critique, reanalysis, and suggestions for future research. *Psychological Bulletin, 97*(3), 387–411. https://doi.org/10.1037/0033-2909.97.3.387

Raven, B. H. (1993). The bases of power: Origins and recent developments. *Journal of Social Issues, 49*(4), 227–251. https://doi.org/10.1111/j.1540-4560.1993.tb01191.x

Rus, D., van Knippenberg, D., & Wisse, B. (2012). Leader power and self-serving behavior: The moderating role of accountability. *The Leadership Quarterly, 23*(1), 13–26. https://doi.org/10.1016/j.leaqua.2011.11.002

Sajons, G. B. (2020). Estimating the causal effect of measured endogenous variables: A tutorial on experimentally randomized instrumental variables. *The Leadership Quarterly*. Advance online publication. https://doi.org/10.1016/j.leaqua.2019.101348

Salancik, G., Calder, B., Rowland, D., Leblebici, H., & Conway, M. (1975). Leadership as an outcome of social structure and process: A multidimensional analysis. In J. G. Hunt & L. L. Larson (Eds.), *Leadership frontiers* (pp. 81–101). Kent State University Press.

Sapolsky, R. M. (2005). The influence of social hierarchy on primate health. *Science, 308*(5722), 648–652. https://doi.org/10.1126/science.1106477

Shamir, B. (2007). From passive recipients to active co-producers: The roles of followers in the leadership process. In B. Shamir, R. Pillai, M. Bligh, & M. Uhl-Bien (Eds.), *Follower-centered perspectives on leadership: A tribute to the memory of James R. Meindl* (pp. 9–39). Information Age Publishing.

Shamir, B., & Eilam-Shamir, G. (2017). Reflections on leadership, authority, and lessons learned. *The Leadership Quarterly, 28*(4), 578–583. https://doi.org/10.1016/j.leaqua.2017.06.004

Shamir, B., House, R. J., & Arthur, M. B. (1993). The motivational effects of charismatic leadership: A self-concept based theory. *Organization Science, 4*(4), 577–594. https://doi.org/10.1287/orsc.4.4.577

Stogdill, R. M. (1950). Leadership, membership and organization. *Psychological Bulletin, 47*(1), 1–14. https://doi.org/10.1037/h0053857

Sturm, R. E., & Antonakis, J. (2015). Interpersonal power: A review, critique, and research agenda. *Journal of Management, 41*(1), 136–163. https://doi.org/10.1177/0149206314555769

Tarakci, M., Greer, L. L., & Groenen, P. J. (2016). When does power disparity help or hurt group performance? *Journal of Applied Psychology, 101*(3), 415–429. https://doi.org/10.1037/apl0000056

Uhl-Bien, M., Riggio, R. E., Lowe, K. B., & Carsten, M. K. (2014). Followership theory: A review and research agenda. *The Leadership Quarterly, 25*(1), 83–104. https://doi.org/10.1016/j.leaqua.2013.11.007

Van Kleef, G. A., De Dreu, C. K., Pietroni, D., & Manstead, A. S. (2006). Power and emotion in negotiation: Power moderates the interpersonal effects of anger and happiness on concession making. *European Journal of Social Psychology, 36*(4), 557–581. https://doi.org/10.1002/ejsp.320

Van Kleef, G. A., Oveis, C., Van Der Löwe, I., LuoKogan, A., Goetz, J., & Keltner, D. (2008). Power, distress, and compassion: Turning a blind eye to the suffering of others. *Psychological Science, 19*(12), 1315–1322. https://doi.org/10.1111/j.1467-9280.2008.02241.x

Van Knippenberg, D., & Sitkin, S. B. (2013). A critical assessment of charismatic-transformational leadership research: Back to the drawing board? *Academy of Management Annals, 7*(1), 1–60. https://doi.org/10.5465/19416520.2013.759433

Van Vugt, M. (2006). Evolutionary origins of leadership and followership. *Personality and Social Psychology Review, 10*(4), 354–371. https://doi.org/10.1207/s15327957pspr1004_5

Vroom, V. H., & Jago, A. G. (2007). The role of the situation in leadership. *American Psychologist, 62*(1), 17–24. https://doi.org/10.1037/0003-066X.62.1.17

Wang, D., Waldman, D. A., & Zhang, Z. (2014). A meta-analysis of shared leadership and team effectiveness. *Journal of Applied Psychology, 99*(2), 181–198. https://doi.org/10.1037/a0034531

Weber, M. (1947). *The theory of economic and social organization* (T. Parsons, Trans.). The Free Press. (Original work published 1924)

Weber, M. (1968). *On charisma and institution building*. The University of Chicago Press.

Wellman, N., Applegate, J. M., Harlow, J., & Johnston, E. W. (2020). Beyond the pyramid: Alternative formal hierarchical structures and team performance. *Academy of Management Journal, 63*(4), 997–1027. https://doi.org/10.5465/amj.2017.1475

Williams, M. J. (2014). Serving the self from the seat of power: Goals and threats predict leaders' self-interested behavior. *Journal of Management, 40*(5), 1365–1395. https://doi.org/10.1177/0149206314525203

Yammarino, F. J., Salas, E., Serban, A., Shirreffs, K., & Shuffler, M. L. (2012). Collectivistic leadership approaches: Putting the "we" in leadership science and practice. *Industrial and Organizational Psychology, 5*(4), 382–402. https://doi.org/10.1111/j.1754-9434.2012.01467.x

Yukl, G. (1999). An evaluation of conceptual weaknesses in transformational and charismatic leadership theories. *The Leadership Quarterly, 10*(2), 285–305. https://doi.org/10.1016/S1048-9843(99)00013-2

Yukl, G. (2002). *Leadership in organizations* (5th ed.). Prentice Hall.

Yukl, G., & Falbe, C. M. (1990). Influence tactics and objectives in upward, downward, and lateral influence attempts. *Journal of Applied Psychology, 75*(2), 132–140. https://doi.org/10.1037/0021-9010.75.2.132

Yukl, G., & Falbe, C. M. (1991). Importance of different power sources in downward and lateral relations. *Journal of Applied Psychology, 76*(3), 416–423. https://doi.org/10.1037/0021-9010.76.3.416

Yukl, G., & Gardner, W. L. (2020). Power and influence tactics. In G. Yukl & W. L. Gardner (Eds.), *Leadership in Organizations* (9th ed.). Pearson.

Yukl, G., Kim, H., & Falbe, C. M. (1996). Antecedents of influence outcomes. *Journal of Applied Psychology, 81*(3), 309–317. https://doi.org/10.1037/0021-9010.81.3.309

Yukl, G., Seifert, C. F., & Chavez, C. (2008). Validation of the extended influence behavior questionnaire. *The Leadership Quarterly, 19*(5), 609–621. https://doi.org/10.1016/j.leaqua.2008.07.006

Yukl, G., & Tracey, J. B. (1992). Consequences of influence tactics used with subordinates, peers, and the boss. *Journal of Applied Psychology, 77*(4), 525–535. https://doi.org/10.1037/0021-9010.77.4.525

Zaar, S., Van den Bossche, P., & Gijselaers, W. (2020). How business students think about leadership: A qualitative study on leader identity and meaning-making. *Academy of Management Learning & Education, 19*(2), 168–191. https://doi.org/10.5465/amle.2017.0290

Zaccaro, S. J., Green, J. P., Dubrow, S., & Kolze, M. (2018). Leader individual differences, situational parameters, and leadership outcomes: A comprehensive review and integration. *The Leadership Quarterly, 29*(1), 2–43. https://doi.org/10.1016/j.leaqua.2017.10.003

Zaccaro, S. J., Rittman, A. L., & Marks, M. A. (2001). Team leadership. *The Leadership Quarterly, 12*(4), 451–483. https://doi.org/10.1016/S1048-9843(01)00093-5

Zehnder, C., Herz, H., & Bonardi, J.-P. (2017). A productive clash of cultures: Injecting economics into leadership research. *The Leadership Quarterly, 28*(1), 65–85. https://doi.org/10.1016/j.leaqua.2016.10.004

Zhang, C., Nahrgang, J. D., Ashford, S. J., & DeRue, D. S. (2020). The risky side of leadership: Conceptualizing risk perceptions in informal leadership and investigating the effects of their over-time changes in teams. *Organization Science*. Advance online publication. https://doi.org/10.1287/orsc.2019.1350

Zhao, H., & Li, C. (2019). A computerized approach to understanding leadership research. *The Leadership Quarterly, 30*(4), 396–416. https://doi.org/10.1016/j.leaqua.2019.06.001

Zhu, H., Kraut, R. E., Wang, Y.-C., & Kittur, A. (2011). Identifying shared leadership in Wikipedia. *Proceedings of the SIGCHI Conference on Human Factors in Computing Systems*. https://doi.org/10.1145/1978942.1979453

NOTES

1. As a cautionary note, we recognize that not all leadership research falls prey to this inconsistent operationalization. Research on the emergence of leaders (Gerpott et al., 2019) or collective approaches to leadership such as team (Zaccaro et al., 2001), shared (Pearce & Conger, 2002), or distributed (Gronn, 2002) leadership focus on informal leadership. These approaches remain a minority in the field.

2. We also include other approaches in this stream of research such as distributed leadership or power sharing approaches.

CHAPTER 12

A UNIFYING FRAMEWORK FOR SYSTEMS AND CONFIGURATIONAL MODELS OF LEADERSHIP AND SUBSTITUTES

J. Lee Whittington, Brian Murray, and R. Greg Bell

ABSTRACT

There is an emerging convergence in the broader leadership literature that leadership must be understood as a dynamic system that involves the leader, the follower, the context, and the relationships among these components. Each component of this system is important and may contribute directly to a variety of outcomes. However, each component cannot be examined in isolation of the others because each factor may interact with the others. Despite the recognition of the need to examine the leadership process holistically, advances in this direction have been limited by reliance on symmetric linear hypotheses and methods that primarily focus on direct and mediated relationships. Our study begins with an examination of three perspectives on leadership as a configural system. From these perspectives we develop a framework for the configurational and systems study of leadership and

Leadership:
Leaders, Followers, and Context, pp. 331–367

derive five core propositions fundamental to this perspective: individual insufficiency, combinatorial effects, equifinality, asymmetry, and time relativity. We close with a consideration of the implications of this perspective and opportunities for leadership research.

The body of scholarship broadly labeled as leadership is diverse, complex, and characterized by themes that ebb and flow cyclically (Bommer et al., this volume; Dinh et al., 2014), but lacks a central or unifying framework (Avolio, 2007; Meuser et al., 2016). In their review of leadership literature reviews, Zhao and Li (2019) identified eight comprehensive reviews published from 2000 to 2018 that categorized leadership studies into as few as eight categories or themes and up to as many as 29 approaches to leadership and over four dozen theories. They further showed how interest in topics and the dominance of particular researchers has shifted over time. Zhao and Li (2019) applied artificial intelligence (AI) to their review of the leadership literature from 1990 to 2017 and formed a network of five interconnected clusters of leadership topics (e.g., transformational, leader-member exchange, personality) among 56 widely studied topics related to leadership (e.g., satisfaction, turnover, organization change). Although their network and trend analyses demonstrated the connectedness of leadership topics relative to a variety of correlates and interests, it also showed that there is no enduring, unifying perspective central to the five major topic areas they identified.

Zhao and Li's (2019) review and analysis illustrated at least three additional issues endemic to the field. Published research in leadership is leader focused without equal regard to the follower. For example, though followership was a related topic in the network, it was not central among the five leader topic clusters, nor was it a relatively highly studied topic. Research emanating from the leader-member exchange (LMX) sector of the network showed the greatest attention to the follower, follower perceptions, relationship, or outcomes, but it was proportionally a smaller part of the network than leader characteristics, styles, and development. Finally, leadership is often studied without regard to its context (see also Osborn et al., 2002; Porter & McLaughlin, 2006; cf. Dinh et al., 2014). From the AI review, cross-cultural, organizational culture, entrepreneurship, and public leadership were among the few contextual elements within the network of topic clusters (Zhao & Li, 2019).

In contrast to the larger body of leadership research, there is a growing appreciation of leadership as a system that recognizes the interconnectedness of leader, follower, and context (e.g., Avolio, 2007; Thoroughgood et al., 2018). This tripartite perspective has developed independently as systems in public arenas (Kellerman, 2014, 2018), explanations of follower attraction and responsiveness to leaders (e.g.,

Klein & House, 1995; Padilla et al., 2007), recognition of substitutes for leadership (Kerr & Jermier, 1978), and configurational modeling of equifinality for bundles of leader, follower, and contextual elements as well as asymmetric relationships of bundles to individual and organizational outcomes (Whittington & Bell, 2013, 2016; Whittington et al., 2013). Even though they are distinctive in their presentations of leadership systems, the perspectives offer a set of underlying assertions for understanding leadership systems as configurations: (a) leaders, followers, and context are each necessary but none is individually sufficient for explaining leadership and its outcomes, (b) leadership is a summative and compensatory phenomenon, (c) multiple combinations or substitutions among leader, follower, and contextual elements may lead to the same outcome and specific combinations may be necessary to realize a particular outcome, (d) different combinations may lead to positive outcomes than lead to negative outcomes for an individual construct, and (e) leadership systems are time sensitive in that they develop over time and may have different configurations and effects at different times. These five underlying assertions to date have not been examined together among the configurational systems perspectives on leadership.

The purpose of the present chaptet is: (a) to introduce and review the core elements of each of the listed perspectives, (b) develop a unifying framework across their shared assumptions and evidence, (c) contrast the evidence produced by the current linear and symmetric perspective on leadership to a nonlinear, multidimensional, and asymmetric configurational approach, and (d) show the development of the propositions uniting the configurational systems perspectives. The benefits of this exposition are that it offers a unifying framework in which to order the extensive and disparate approaches to studying leadership, it transforms thought on leadership from the leader (characteristics, behaviors, style, outcomes) to a holistic view of the leader in relation to the follower within the context (e.g., Avolio, 2007). It also provides an analytic perspective that allows for contradictory relationships between leader and outcome variables when different variable combinations are present as well as asymmetric relationships between leader measures and positive versus negative levels of outcomes.

Our exposition is structured in four parts. First, we provide an introduction and overview of three configurational and systems perspectives. Second, we integrate the perspectives into a tripartite framework and derive five propositions that we regard as core and common among them. Third, we contrast the evidence from traditional leadership research to configural-systems analysis. We close with a consideration of the implications of adopting a configural-systems perspective as a unifying framework within leadership research.

THREE PERSPECTIVES ON LEADERSHIP SYSTEMS AND CONFIGURATIONS

The study of leadership as a system requires a pivot from the isolated study of paired variable relationships, such as leader and outcome or leader and follower characteristics and behaviors, to configurations of leader-follower-context joint characteristics relative to outcomes or simultaneous cocreation or influence among leader-follower-context to form configurations. Systems are composed of interconnected components that act upon one another or are responsive to changes in one another, bound the actions or outcomes from one another, and may enhance, neutralize, or substitute for one another in the system's influence on relevant outcomes or correlates. In the study of systems, questions regarding intra- and intersystem dynamics are both relevant. For the present study of leadership, the components interacting within the system are defined to include the leader, follower, and context. Configurations are discrete combinations or permutations of the system's components that jointly influence or correlate with external theoretically relevant variables.

For the development and exposition of a system and configurational framework, we draw on three perspectives. First, leadership scholars have recognized that there are three interactive components that are needed to fully define leadership phenomena that include the leader, follower, and context in a tripartite system (e.g., Kellerman, 2016; Klein & House, 1995; Padilla, 2012; Padilla et al., 2007). Second, a set of leadership scholars have defined leadership systems according to combinations of leader, follower, and context characteristics that may substitute, enhance, or negate the effects of other components of the system, and more than one configuration of the components may yield similar positive or negative outcomes (e.g., Kerr & Jermier, 1978; Podsakoff et al., 1993, 1996; Whittington et al., 2013). Finally, several examinations of leadership have described the system of relationships and their outcomes to be time dependent such that the outcomes may be different depending on the maturity or evolution of particular combinations of leader, follower, and context (e.g., cumulative effect of multiple episodes, Bastardoz & Day, this volume; phases of leadership making, Graen & Uhl-Bien, 1995; emergence of a toxic triangle, Thoroughgood et al., 2018). We discuss each perspective in turn.

The Tripartite System of Leader, Follower, and Context

Putting the Leader and Follower in Context

For over a decade Barbara Kellerman consistently criticized the leader-centric approach to both academic leadership studies and the leadership "industry" that has emerged with bold claims to develop leaders (e.g., Kellerman, 2012). According to her arguments, this approach does not reflect the complexity of the leadership process. In place of this leader-centric approach, Kellerman (2004, 2014, 2016) called for viewing leadership as a dynamic system consisting of three moving parts: the leader, the follower, and the context.

Kellerman's (2016) system viewpoint reflects the fact that leadership does not exist in a vacuum. Rather, it involves the leader and the follower as individuals who each have a set of motives and resources, and the relationship between these individuals (Burns, 1978). Each member of a leader-follower dyad brings a full set of individual differences and personal cognitions to the relationship. These individual differences include personality traits, motives, values, and unique developmental experiences (Bennis & Thomas, 2002), as well as a variety of broader cultural influences. Leaders and followers also bring a complex set of cognitive processes to their individual roles and the relationship with one another. These cognitions include the implicit leadership theories (ILT) that inform a leader's behaviors (Wofford et al., 1998). ILTs also have a strong influence on how followers interpret those behaviors (Rush et al., 1977; Lord & Maher, 1993). In a parallel process, implicit followership theories influence followers' attitudes and behaviors and the leader's interpretation and evaluation of those attitudes and behaviors (Sy, 2010; Epitropaki et al., 2013).

Relevant to Kellerman's perspective, in a recent review of contextual, contingency, and situational approaches to leadership, Ayman and Lauritsen (2018) identified two sets of proximate contextual factors that may moderate the relationship between the leader's characteristics, style or behavior and individual and group level outcomes. The first set of moderating factors was the interpersonal context that consists of culture, organizational setting, nature of the tasks, diversity of group composition, follower characteristics, and communication medium. The second set of factors was intrapersonal factors. These included the interaction of the traits, personality, and gender roles of both the leader and the follower. These intrapersonal factors also included impression management tactics.

Clearly the leader-follower relationship is itself complex; however, these relationships are made even more complicated because they are embedded in a set of "concentric circles of contexts" (Kellerman, 2018, p. 134). As such, leadership is never "contextually neutral" (Avolio, 1999, p. 178). Kellerman (2018) positions these contexts as proximate and distal. The proximate context is of immediate interest and importance to the leader. The distal context is more general and is not specific to any single individual, group, or institution.

Historically, contingency and situational approaches to leadership have focused on a full set of factors in the proximal context. Kellerman (2018) did not discount the importance of those approaches; the consideration of the proximate context of the leader-follower relationship is necessary. Kellerman (2014) however questioned whether that emphasis is sufficient. In response to her concern, she identified six sets of distal contexts: foundations, evolutions, revolutions, populations, futures, and inversions. We agree with Kellerman's observation that leaders and followers, and the relationships among them, are "located not just in a single context, but in several different ones, simultaneously" (Kellerman, 2018, p. 134); however, in this chapter we are focusing on the promixal context of the leadership system.

Given this complexity, Kellerman (2016) argued that the study of leadership must entail each component of the leadership system: the leader, the follower, the contexts and the relationships among these components. Each component of this system is important and may contribute to a variety of outcomes. However, these three factors cannot be examined in isolation of the others because each of these factors also impinges on the other two. Thus, there are a variety of possible main effects, interactive effects, and indirect effects among these factors and a variety of attitudinal and behavioral outcomes. When viewed as a system, each combination of these elements forms an interactive web of reciprocal determinism (Bandura, 1986).

Triangle Models of the Leadership System

Kellerman's call for considering leadership as a system is not new. Klein and House (1995) used a similar approach to understand charismatic leadership. Padilla et al. (2007) likewise developed an interactional perspective in their description of the toxic triangle that leads to the emergence of destructive leaders (see also Padilla, 2012, for a more general exposition of the leadership triangle). Each of these models illustrates how viewing leadership as a system of interactions among the leader, follower, and proximal context may be applied.

Klein and House (1995): The Charismatic Leadership System. Each of the triangle models include the three components of leader, follower, and context to elicit a specific organizational outcome. Klein and House (1995) used fire as a metaphor to describe the leadership system that produces charisma. In order to start and maintain a fire there must be flammable material, oxygen, and some spark that ignites the fire. Extending this metaphor to leadership, they identified susceptible followers as the flammable material, the challenges or crises in immediate context as the oxygen that creates a conducive environment, and the charismatic leader as the spark ignites the fire. Each of these components is necessary for the creation of a charismatic "fire," yet none is sufficient in isolation of the other factors.

The charismatic leader has a set of personal characteristics that provides the spark to start the fire (Klein & House, 1995). These personal traits and behaviors include prosocial assertiveness, self-confidence, need for social influence, moral conviction, and concern for the moral exercise of power. These leaders are also effective communicators who can articulate inspiring distal visons that challenge the status quo, and also express high expectations and confidence in their followers.

Followers are the necessary flammable material and their susceptibility to the effects of the leader's characteristics and behaviors is based on at least three factors (Klein & House, 1995). First, there are some followers who are vulnerable and or looking for direction or psychological meaning in life. These followers may lack self-confidence or have heightened anxiety due to a strong sense of uncertainty about their present or future condition. These meaning-seekers may appear dependent and submissive and the leader's power over them is based on need deficiencies and a hope for a better future. Other followers are susceptible to a leader's influence based on their comfort and compatibility with the leader's vision and style. For these followers there is a congruence between their personal values and those of the leader. These followers identify with the leader, and the leader's power in these circumstances is due, at least in part, because followers agree with them. Finally, Klein and House alternatively posit that the impact of a potentially charismatic leader may have little to do with characteristics of followers. Rather, leaders with charismatic qualities are so compelling and persuasive that all followers regardless of their personal characteristics readily fall under these leaders' influence.

A fire requires oxygen. In order for charisma to emerge there must be a conducive environment. The ambiguity associated with a crisis is the most favorable context for the emergence of charisma (Klein & House, 1995). In crises individuals are uncertain and distressed, which makes them vulnerable to the influence of persuasive leaders who offer a hopeful and inspiring vision that resolves the crisis. In the workplace context, the emergence of charismatic relationships also is facilitated in ambiguous situations, such as when performance goals cannot be clearly defined and measured (Shamir et al., 1993). This lack of clarity around performance expectations makes it difficult to link extrinsic rewards with individual performance. When there are few situational cues, constraints, and reinforcers to guide behavior and provide incentives for specific performance, people have a need for the leader to provide the comfort of sense-making that the crisis situation requires.

In summary, charisma is the interaction of elements within a system. The charismatic relationship is the product of a leader with charismatic qualities (the spark) influencing one or more followers who are open to charisma (the flammable material), within a charisma-conducive environment (the oxygen). Each component of the system is necessary, but no single component is sufficient.

Padilla, Hogan, and Kaiser (2007): The Toxic Leadership System. Padilla and colleagues developed a similar system approach to leadership in their description of the toxic triangle that leads to the emergence of destructive leaders. The "fire" of destructive leadership is a "confluence of the characteristics of destructive leaders, the motives and needs of vulnerable followers, and a set of contextual conditions" that provides the favorable conditions necessary for the emergence of a dark and destructive leader (Padilla et al., 2007, p. 179)

Destructive leaders share many of the characteristics of charismatic leaders identified by Klein and House (1995). Both charismatic leaders and destructive leaders are effective communicators with "exceptional rhetorical skills" (Padilla et al., 2007, p. 181). However, destructive leaders are differentiated from charismatic leaders by "an ideology of hate, unsocialized needs for power, energy, unusual perseverance, and physical and psychological stamina" (Padilla et al., 2007, p. 180). The destructive leader's selfish need for power reflects the egotistic motive pattern that drives unethical leaders (Kanungo & Mendonca, 1996).

These destructive leaders also may exhibit the "dark triad" of personality traits: narcissism, psychopathy, and Machiavellianism (Jonason & Webster, 2010). These destructive leaders seek attention and admiration, and believe they deserve special treatment. They tend to be callous and insensitive to the needs of others, and they manipulate others to achieve their personal agenda. This combination of traits results in a "short-term, agentic, exploitative social strategy" (Jonason & Webster, 2010, p. 420).

The presence of these dark and destructive traits in a leader is not enough to create a toxic situation. Followers have similar needs for status, reassurance and stability, security, and belonging. When the basic needs for belonging, meaningfulness, and a desire for status are unmet, followers may be particularly vulnerable to these toxic leaders. These psychological deficiencies are exacerbated by low core self-evaluations (Judge & Bono, 2001), low needs for autonomy, and sense that their current situation could not get any worse. These factors combine with anxiety and fear to make these individuals particularly susceptible to a dark leader who meets the unmet needs and offers "hope" for an improved condition. Destructive leaders are aware of their followers' dependence on them and exploit these vulnerabilities.

The characteristics of destructive leaders and the motives of followers interact in a set of contextual factors that provide the conditions necessary for the emergence of a dark and destructive leader. Padilla et al. (2007)

identified several contextual factors that contribute to an environment that is conducive to toxic leadership: institutionalization, structural stability, environmental upheaval, centralized leadership, cultural homogeneity, social conditions, and domination by rivals. As with Kellerman's (2018) concentric circles of context, these factors are not mutually exclusive and may be operating simultaneously.

Institutionalization refers to the efficacy of established systems of checks and balances that create restraints on the unilateral use of power (Padilla et al., 2007). Where institutionalized processes are in place, the potentially destructive individuals may be "neutralized" or limited. However, the absence of these constraints and balances of power creates opportunities for those with destructive tendencies to take unfair advantage of others (Padilla et al., 2007).

The same crisis conditions that provide the oxygen for charismatic leadership to emerge may contribute to destructive leadership. Crises and structural ambiguity create a sense of desperation and a search for meaningfulness. When faced with crises, followers are more likely to yield to the rapid responses and decisive decision making of self-assured leaders whose actions may provide at least a temporary calm amid the perceived storm (Bass, 1985; Conger & Kanungo, 1987; Thoroughgood et al., 2018). Confident charismatic leaders with a malevolent bent may seize the opportunity to exploit the need for sense-making to gain personal power and influence (Padilla et al., 2007).

Distal contexts also contribute to the emergence of destructive leaders. These distal contexts include culture, homogeneity of the population, and socioeconomic conditions. Cultural factors may also exacerbate the emergence of destructive leadership. Where there is a tradition of centralized leadership, there may also be a culture of dependency and inaction among followers who defer to those in leadership roles (Hofstede, 1991; Luthans et al., 1998). The acceptance and docility of these followers is a particularly important contributor to the emergence of destructive leaders where there is also a high level of cultural homogeneity. These conditions make it easier to bring a similar group together even though a diverse constituency is less likely to defer to one vision (Padilla et al., 2007; Thoroughgood et al., 2018).

Desperate economic and social conditions, such as poverty, unequal distribution of wealth, and racism, facilitate a climate of discontent. In these situations, people often feel marginalized and inferior. Toxic leaders leverage these conditions to rally support through the use of divisive themes that separate rather than unite people. Destructive leaders intentionally aggravate these situations by perpetuating a focus on perceived threats and focusing on "enemies" and rivals in order to strengthen their power and keep followers motivated (Padilla et al., 2007)

Beyond illustrative cases from history, there has been limited research conducted to investigate the toxic triangle. The scarcity of advances through empirical investigations notwithstanding, the appeal of the model continues to draw interest and refinement. Pundt (2014) developed a theoretical model identifying charismatic leadership as the antecedent of destructive leadership. Exploring the link between charismatic and destructive leadership, Pundt identified five distinct pathways through which charismatic leadership could lead to abusive and toxic situations. More recently, Thoroughgood et al. (2018) criticized approaches to the destructive leaders phenomenon as being too narrowly focused on the behaviors of a "bad" leader at the exclusion of the followers and the contexts in which these destructive leaders and toxic environments emerge. They argued for a more balanced understanding of destructive leadership that explicitly recognizes that leadership is a dynamic, cocreational process among flawed leaders, susceptible followers, and conducive environments.

Interactions and Configurations Among the Tripartite System's Elements

The Substitutes for Leadership Model

The need to include context as a factor in understanding the leadership process is not new. Contingency and situational leadership models have been a dominant aspect of the leadership research landscape since they first emerged in the late 1960s and early 1970s. These approaches have focused primarily on the proximate factors that have an immediate impact on the relationship between the leader's behaviors or characteristics and a variety of follower attitudinal and behavioral outcomes.

An extensive list of contextual factors is present in the "substitutes-for-leadership" framework developed by Kerr and Jermier (1978). This model was developed to place leadership in the context of a dynamic organizational and social setting. In their original taxonomy, Kerr and Jermier identified fourteen situational contingencies that were divided into three broad categories: (1) characteristics of followers, (2) the nature of the follower's task, and (3) organizational characteristics. According to Podsakoff et al. (1993) the substitutes model has at least three advantages over earlier contingency situational approaches to leadership. First, the model represents the most comprehensive attempt to identify the potential factors that may moderate the relationship between leader behavior and subordinate attitudes and behaviors. Second, the model focuses more attention on organizational factors that may moderate the effectiveness of a leader's behavior on follower behavior. Finally, the substitutes model provides some guidance for leaders who may want to create substitutes in their environment to supplement or enhance their effectiveness (Howell et al., 1986; Podsakoff et al., 1993).

Several subordinate characteristics may function as neutralizers for leadership. These include ability, experience, training, knowledge, need for independence, "professional" orientation, and indifference toward organizational goals (Kerr & Jermier, 1978). There are also a variety of task characteristics that may function as substitutes for leadership. These include tasks that are unambiguous and routine, methodologically invariant, provide feedback concerning accomplishment, and intrinsically satisfying (Kerr & Jermier, 1978). The characteristics of the organization that may substitute or neutralize leadership behaviors include formalization in the form of explicit plans, goals, and areas of responsibility, inflexibility, highly specified and active advisory and staff functions, cohesive work groups, organizational rewards not within the leader's control, and spatial distance between the superior and the subordinates (Kerr & Jermier, 1978).

Contextual factors potentially moderate the relationship between a leader's behavior and various follower outcomes (Kerr & Jermier, 1978). In an extension of the early conceptualization of the substitutes for leadership model, Howell et al. (1986) developed a typology of moderators based on the mechanisms by which these contextual factors may operate. According to Howell et al. (1986), the contextual factors may act as neutralizers, substitutes, or enhancers of the relationship between leader behavior and associated outcomes. Neutralizers are those characteristics that inhibit or diminish the leader's behavioral influence on the follower's outcomes, thus making it effectively impossible for leadership behavior to make a difference. Substitutes are contextual factors that render leadership behavior unnecessary. Accordingly, substitutes replace the relationship between the leader behavior and the follower outcome. Enhancers are contextual factors which strengthen the relationship between the leadership behavior and the follower outcome.

Podsakoff and his associates have examined a variety of leadership behaviors in conjunction with the substitutes for leadership model. Podsakoff et al. (1993) examined the relationships between substitutes for leadership and supportive leadership and contingent reward leadership behaviors. Their results provided partial support for the substitutes for leadership model. They found that many of the 13 subordinate, task, and organizational characteristics identified by Kerr and Jermier (1978) contributed significantly to the variance accounted for in subordinate performance, attitudes, and role perceptions. Furthermore, by including the substitutes variables with the leadership behaviors, Podsakoff et al. (1993) "were able to account for substantially greater portions of the variance in the criterion variables than traditionally reported in the leadership literature" (p. 39).

The study of the substitutes for leadership model also includes the full-range of transformational and contingent reward behaviors. Podsakoff et al. (1996) observed that both transformational leader behaviors and substitutes for leadership had unique effects on a wide variety of follower outcomes. They also found that the total proportion of variance accounted for by the substitutes for leadership and the transformational leader behaviors was substantially greater than previously had been reported for either alone. Furthermore, they identified that many of the transformational leader behaviors were significantly related to several of the substitutes for leadership variables. In contrast to these positive relationships, when the 858 possible interaction effects were tested, only 69 (8% of a possible 858) were statistically significant, and only 18 (or approximately 2.1% of the total) of these interactions behaved in a manner consistent with that specified by Howell et al. (1986).

Despite the limited support for the substitutes model, Podsakoff et al. (1996) did not suggest that research on the interplay between transformational leadership and the various substitutes should cease; instead, they encouraged continued research in this area for at least two reasons. First, they expressed concern that previous models that did not include these contextual variables were mis-specified and may have led to biased estimates of relationships found for transformational leaders. By omitting these substitutes variables, research obscures the importance of these "contextual" variables. Second, these observations suggested that leaders can influence the substitutes variables. If so, managers may have a stronger impact than previously suggested because they can influence subordinates both directly through their behavior and indirectly by shaping the context in which the subordinates work. Therefore, Podsakoff et al. (1996, p. 295) suggested that "some substitutes that may be particularly good candidates" for additional research in the context of transformational leadership. Their recommendations included intrinsically satisfying tasks and organizational formalization in the form of explicit goals.

In a responsive subsequent field study of the substitutes model relative to transformational leadership, Whittington et al. (2004) tested the moderating effects of job enrichment and goal difficulty on the relationship between transformational leadership and three follower outcomes: performance, affective organizational commitment, and organizational citizenship behavior. Their results indicated that both transformational leadership and job enrichment had significant main effects on in-role performance, organizational citizenship behaviors, and the affective commitment of employees. In addition, they found that job enrichment substituted for the effects of transformational leadership on affective commitment. Although difficult goals did not have a significant main effect on any of the outcomes, goal setting was shown to enhance the relationships between transformational leadership and both affective commitment and performance.

Leadership Systems as Configurations

The argument for the need to examine leadership as a dynamic system of interaction among leaders, followers, and context within which they operate is consistent with a growing recognition among organizational researchers that many factors contribute to performance. As such they should not be evaluated in isolation from each other; instead, they should be examined as configurations that may mutually enhance the ability of each to achieve important organizational outcomes (Fiss et al., 2013). Configurational perspectives allow for the study of "multi-dimensional constellations of conceptually distinct characteristics that commonly occur together" (Fiss, 2007, p. 1180). Employing a configurational approach enables examinations into how multiple factors can combine together along different paths to achieve similar outcomes (Aguilera et al., 2008; Hoskisson et al., 2009; Ward et al., 2009). Configurational approaches assume more complex and nonlinear causality where variables found to be causally related in one configuration may be unrelated in other configurations (Fiss, 2007).

Previous research in this area has been limited to evaluating how certain individual task and motivational factors affect employee attitudes and behaviors. Methodological constraints have hampered the ability of researchers to approach leadership substitutes in a more fully interactive manner. Consequently, these factors often have been examined in isolation of each other (Villa et al., 2003). Scholars have yet to consider how different combinations of task and motivational factors could combine in dissimilar ways to produce comparably high levels of employee attitudes and behaviors. By taking a configuration approach, researchers can address the notion of equifinality, which assumes that a variety of paths can lead to a similar outcome (Katz & Kahn, 1966). The configurational approach allows scholars to more thoroughly evaluate an integrative approach to leadership (Avolio, 2007). Additionally, configurational logic enables researchers to examine the bundles of factors that lead to low levels of employee performance and attitudes which may be different from the bundles that lead to high levels.

Despite its growing application in organizational research, scholars point out that "use of configurational logic is noticeably absent in leadership research to date" (Short et al., 2008, p. 1070). In response to this call, Whittington and colleagues (Whittington & Bell, 2013, 2016; Whittington et al., 2013) adopted a configurational approach in a series of comparative reanalysis with extension studies to examine critical deficiencies in leadership substitutes research. Across these studies, they sequentially reexamined an existing data set extending the findings with the addition of variables and examination of different configurational questions.

Whittington et al. (2013) initially applied configurational analysis to reexamine previous analyses of enriched jobs and difficult goals as potential substitutes for transformational leadership. They also examined the role of the quality of the leader-follower relationship (LMX) as a potential substitute for the effect of transformational leadership on employee in-role performance, extra-role performance (OCB), and affective commitment. Of nine configuration solutions associated with high levels of outcome variables, only three included the presence of high transformational leadership behavior, while two included the absence of transformational leadership behavior. The dominant predictor in these solutions was the presence of an enriched job, which appeared in seven high outcome configurations. LMX and a combination of LMX and enriched jobs each appeared in four of solutions. Goal difficulty appeared in only one solution where it combined with LMX to produce high performance.

Together, these results supported the idea of equifinality for the outcomes of levels high performance, organizational citizenship behaviors, and affective commitment. Even though transformational leadership was associated with these outcomes, the findings suggested there are many roads that will lead to positive employee attitudes and behaviors. In the absence of a transformational leader, LMX, enriched jobs, and challenging goals were shown to work in conjunction with each other to attain results equivalent to those associated with transformational leadership configurations. The prominence of both LMX and enriched jobs provided support for the claim that "the task that a person performs and the person to whom the individual is responsible are probably the two most basic points of contact that employees have in the organization" (Griffin, 1982, pp. 153–154).

An advantage of the configurational perspective is that it facilitates an examination of "causal asymmetry" (Ragin, 2008). Causal asymmetry logic suggests that sets of conditions leading to the presence of the outcome can often be different from the set of conditions leading to the absence of the outcome (Ragin, 2008). Also, the concept of causal asymmetry suggests that equifinality may change depending on outcome levels; as one moves across outcome *levels*, different *sets* of equally effective configurations may arise (Fiss, 2008, 2011). For instance, even though the presence of a particular combination of causes may lead to high levels of outcomes, a completely different set of factors may lead to low levels of those same outcomes.

Scholars tend to avoid research that examines poor outcomes (Hirak et al., 2012). Although there is some evaluation of poor leadership outcomes

(Kellerman, 2004), the majority of leadership research tends to share a normative bias favoring research that evaluates factors that promote positive employee and organizational outcomes (Bass & Bass, 2009; Shamir et al., 1993; Sosik et al., 1997; Yukl, 2012). However, examining the conditions that lead to low levels of employee outcomes may have important implications for diagnosing performance deficiencies and attitudinal problems. The reliance upon traditional methodologies based on correlational methods by leadership substitutes researchers has reinforced this normative bias in that they assume a causal symmetry, which implies that low levels of independent variables will be associated with low levels of the dependent variables of interest. According to the logic of symmetry, the outcome of modeling low performance outcomes would be the same as high performance outcomes. Shifting away from the traditional correlational, symmetric bias to a causal configuration-based approach unlocks considerable opportunities to advance our understanding of leadership as a system.

Whittington and Bell (2016) conducted a set of post hoc analyses to examine the causal asymmetry among leader-follower relationships, goal difficulty, and enriched jobs and low rather than high levels of performance, OCB, and affective commitment. The results of their analysis supported the idea of causal asymmetry: the solutions that led to low in-role performance, citizenship behaviors, and affective commitment were not simply the inverse of high-level solutions. Low performance was associated with the absence of a high-quality relationship between the leader and the follower. Low citizenship behaviors can be achieved in two different ways, with low levels of MPS, LMX, and less difficult goals, or with a configuration of high MPS and difficult goals together with low levels of LMX. Three configurations were associated with low levels of affective commitment. Two of these configurations indicated an absence of a high-quality leader-follower relationship. The third low affective commitment outcome was associated with the absence of an enriched job.

The results of these studies demonstrated that a configurational perspective and its associated methodology are helpful for understanding and investigating the interdependencies and causal complexity associated with the leadership system. The evaluation of leadership bundles yielded novel findings primarily because a configurational perspective and methodology enabled the researchers to consider variables simultaneously. Additionally, extending leadership research to consider causal asymmetry identified configurations that led to the presence of high in-role performance, citizenship behaviors, and affective commitment that were different from those conditions that led to low levels of these important outcomes among employees.

Configural Leadership Systems Are Time Relative

Time is an important consideration in understanding organizational phenomena and systems (George & Jones, 2000). In the study of leadership systems, researchers have recognized the role time can play as phases of leader-follower relationship development (Graen & Uhl-Bien, 1995), the cross-level emergence of leadership systems and outcomes that arise from the interaction of leaders and environments (Lichtenstein & Plowman, 2009), the cumulative effect of multiple episodes (Bastardoz & Day, this volume), or the interplay between the timing of organizational processes and leadership behaviors, decisions, and effectiveness (Dinh et al., 2014). Thoroughgood et al. (2018) incorporated time in the tripartite leadership system to recognize that toxic systems of leader, follower, and environment develop over time and that destructive leadership is emergent and may be transient (see also Lunsford et al., this volume).

The role of time is particularly important to the configural-systems study of leadership for three reasons. First, a system is evolutionary in its form. The characteristics of a system develop over time as the elements interact, and those interactions may change the individual elements' characteristics, the nature of their interaction, and the outcomes that they affect (Lichtenstein & Plowman, 2009). Second, a configuration of substitutes may emerge as a system of relationships matures. For example, if a transformational leader is effective in developing followers' knowledge, skills, and abilities as well as their ability to self-manage, lead, or work autonomously, the contextual elements and leader behaviors that were necessary and effective early in the relationship later may no longer be functional and other contextual elements and follower characteristics may substitute or take their place in the configuration that drives individual and organizational outcomes. Third, leadership forms and effectiveness may vary in relation to time-bound events (Dinh et al., 2014).

A UNIFYING FRAMEWORK FOR STUDYING LEADERSHIP SYSTEMS AND CONFIGURATIONS

The implied framework underlying the reviewed perspectives is a tripartite model anchored by the leader, follower, and context. This framework is illustrated in Figure 12.1. It is an adaptation and generalization of the revised Toxic Triangle model (Lunsford et al., this volume). There are seven framework elements that define the internal system components which may be studied in discrete configurations. The elements include: leader, follower, context, relationship between the leader and follower, interaction between the follower and context, bilateral influence of the leader on context and context on leader, and time. External to the framework are the antecedents, correlates, and outcomes of the combinations and permutations of the configurations.

Framework Elements

The leader element encompasses characteristics, behaviors, and leadership styles of individuals acting in formal or informal leadership roles. For example, Lunsford et al. (this volume) within the perspective of toxic leadership defined this element to include characteristics such as charisma and narcissism and behaviors including the personalized use of power. From the studies of leadership substitutes and configurations, researchers have

Figure 12.1

A Unifying Framework for Systems and Configurational Models

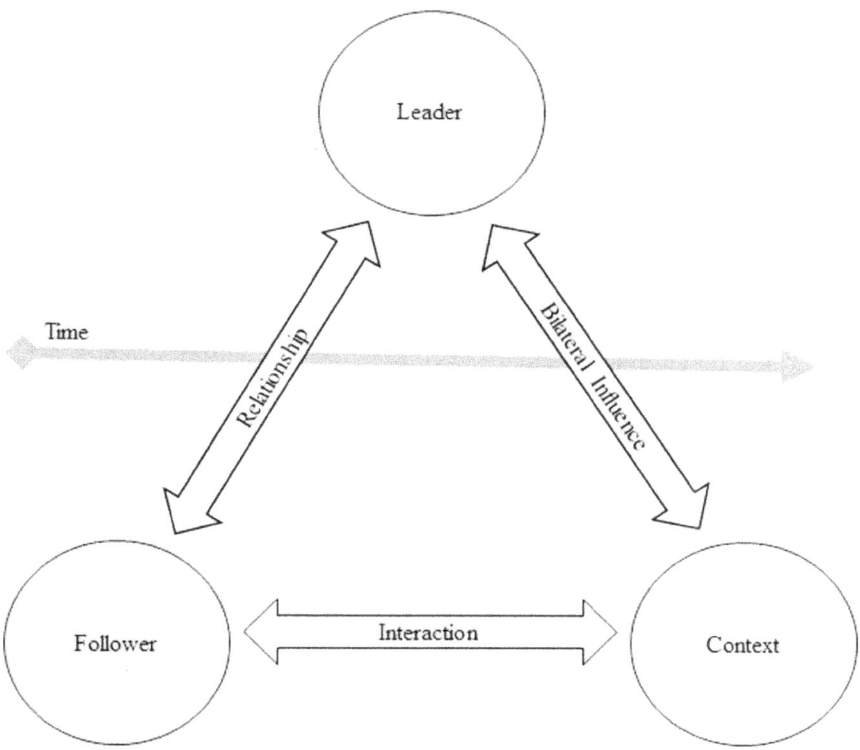

Note. Adapted from Lunsford et al. (this volume).

defined this element to include full-range leadership's transformational and transactional components.

The follower element encompasses characteristics and behaviors of followers. For example, Lunsford et al. (this volume; see also Padilla et al., 2007; Thorougood et al., 2018) characterized followers as susceptible conformers and colluders. Several leadership studies have included propensity to trust as an important follower attribute (Dirks & Ferrin, 2002).

The context element includes the contextual characteristics in which the follower and leader are operating. In their exposition of the revised Toxic Triangle, Lunsford et al. (this volume) characterized a "conducive" environment that included an absence of checks and balances, instability, and the presence of a perceived threat. In studies of leadership substitutes and configurations, Whittington and colleagues included contextual elements such as job enrichment and goal difficulty (Whittington & Bell, 2016; Whittington et al., 2004).

The relationship between the leader and follower composes an element of the framework that recognizes the quality or form of the relationship as well as the dynamic nature of the creation of it. For example, DeRue and Ashford (2010) defined a claiming-granting process for the formation of identities as follower and leader. Lunsford et al. (this volume) incorporated the influence of LMX connecting the leader and the follower in their revised Toxic Triangle. Whittington and Bell (2016) incorporated LMX in their configurational analysis of leadership bundles as drivers of job performance, OCB, and affective commitment.

A second connective element within the framework is the interaction between the follower and context. On the one hand, interaction recognizes the multiple ways in which an individual experiences and reacts to the job, work environment, and organization such as attention, cognitive availability, psychological presence, and coupling of self to the work role or organization that might be experienced as engagement (Saks, 2006), which Robinson et al. (2004) also positioned as an interplay between the follower and the work environment. On the other hand, the climate in which leadership operates may be a function of individuals and group members' characteristics and interactions (Dinh et al., 2014).

The third connective element in the framework is the bilateral influence of the leader on context and context on leader (Porter & McLaughlin, 2006). The influence may be characterized as the quality of the fit between the two elements (e.g., a situational contingency), the active management of one toward the other (e.g., performance management programming from leader to context or leadership development from context to leader), or the interchangeable equivalence between them (e.g., contextual substitutes for leadership attributes or behaviors).

The final element of the framework is time. Time for a leadership system is multidimensional and has both intra- and intersystem implications for variable relationships. Time relative to a system may be conceived as a linear evolution, life cycle, accumulated episodes, or series of discrete developmental phases (see McClean et al., 2019 for review of leadership time models). Time relative to the form and effectiveness of a configuration of system elements may define it as event or context bound, enduring or stable, or cyclically transient.

Core Propositions

The fundamental propositions of a system and configurational framework for leadership express the foundational ideas of individual insufficiency, combinatorial effects, equifinality, causal asymmetry, and time relativity. These propositions are derived from the shared characteristics of the systems and configurational perspectives we reviewed, and in our view are core and necessary for a unified understanding of leadership as the leader and follower acting, reacting, and coacting within and in response to their environment.

Individual Insufficiency

Some effects rely on particular configurations of the leadership system, and individual attributes of the configuration cannot alone trigger a particular effect. Both the Toxic Triangle and the charismatic leader triangle are predicated on the existence and form of all three elements (leader, follower, and context) occurring simultaneously. The elements are each necessary but not sufficient. Likewise, configurational bundles act as a whole in their effect on leadership outcomes. Individual elements of the bundles do not achieve the same level or type of outcome as the full configuration. Accordingly, each element of a leadership configuration is necessary, but not sufficient to achieving a particular outcome at a specified level.

Leadership as a system construct requires that the relevant attributes of the leader, follower, and context be included in examinations of leadership antecedents, correlates, and outcomes to produce valid analytic results. Undoubtedly, any one attribute within a leadership system element will correlate with external variables and outcomes. One need only look to any of the reviews of leadership studies to get a sense of the magnitude of possible bivariate correlations between measures of the leader and external variables (e.g., Dirks & Ferrin, 2002; Zhao & Li, 2019). However, in explaining leadership effects on external variables, the amount of variance explanation, reliability of relationship identification, and susceptibility to accepting a spurious correlation as a true effect is impacted by a specification deficiency when the system is examined as isolated elements.

> **Proposition 1.** Isolated examinations of leadership elements belonging to a configuration of leader, follower, and context are insufficient to validly model leadership system effects.

Combinatorial Effects

A system is defined both by its elements and the interdependencies among those elements. A change in one element impacts the balance among the system of elements and may influence changes in other elements as well as the resultant impacts on external variables. For the leadership system, evidence from studies of leadership substitutes and configurations demonstrate a balancing or tradeoff among characteristics and levels of attributes within the elements in their relationship to external variables. Substitution studies differed in the effects they showed relative to outcomes with statistical interactions manifesting for some substitutes and outcomes (i.e., a multiplicative form) or additive multiple independent variable linear models describing other combinations of the elements and their outcomes (i.e., a summative form). Configurational studies showed different numbers of element members within a combination and multiple potential combinations of elements in their relationship to outcome measures (i.e., a compensatory form).

> **Proposition 2.** A leadership system's effects are a function of the combination and interaction among its elements, and the form of the combination may be summative, multiplicative, or compensatory.

Equifinality

Research regarding configurations and substitutions for leadership demonstrate that multiple configurations of leadership system elements exist simultaneously to which employees can respond in the same manner. Subsets of combinations of leader traits and job elements may be interchangeable in determining employees' satisfaction, performance, or commitment. Tradeoffs among the elements may yield similar attitudinal and behavioral responses due to the presence of one attribute compensating for the absence of another attribute within the system. For example, in the prediction of outcomes normally attributed to transformational leadership, substitutes for leadership interaction tests have yielded results supporting the neutralizing, enhancing, and substituting roles that job design elements can play (Podsakoff et al., 1996; Whittington et al., 2004). The evidence from configurations for transformational and transactional leadership combined with multiple job design elements and LMX support the argument that multiple combinations exist and that specific combinations exist for different outcomes (Whittington & Bell, 2016).

Proposition 3. Multiple configurations or substitutions among leadership system elements may lead to the same outcome.

Asymmetry

The principle of asymmetry suggests that the configurations of leadership elements that determine positive levels of follower responses for an outcome may be different from the leadership elements that drive negative levels of responses for the same outcome. Because a leader trait in a particular context evokes a high level of an outcome does not mean that the lack of the trait in the same context drives a low response on the outcome. Other elements of the context may substitute for the lack of the leader trait and nullify a negative impact. Alternatively, the leader trait may serve only as a single direction attitude stimulus, but its absence does not likewise stimulate an inverse attitudinal response. For example, abusive supervision as an element of a leadership configuration might be expected to drive lower than average or negative attitudinal responses, but there is no theoretical basis for its absence having an inverse symmetric effect of driving higher than average attitudinal responses. The effect of its absence is more likely truncated at the mean attitudinal response. Empirical evidence supports the asymmetry of leadership element configurations in determining follower outcomes (Whittington & Bell, 2016).

Proposition 4. Different configurations of leadership system elements may lead to positive outcomes than lead to negative outcomes for an individual outcome construct.

Time Relativity

Time is an important element in leadership research including its necessity or relationship to the ordering and duration of leadership processes, the longitudinal unfolding of processes, the interaction of leadership and time in optimizing outcomes, and the interaction of time and levels (Dinh et al., 2014; McClean et al., 2019; Porter & McLaughlin, 2006). Time was explicitly introduced to the Toxic Triangle system's perspective by Thoroughgood et al. (2018) to acknowledge that a toxic relationship between destructive leaders and susceptible followers emerges over time in a conducive environment or may be cyclically transient. Likewise, substitutes for leadership may emerge as a leader-follower relationship matures that would not have been viable for nascent or developing relationships. Bastardoz and Day (this volume) qualified their model of power and leadership as potentially dependent on the accumulation of multiple episodes. Asymmetry also may be reflected in combinations over time, such that the configurations of leadership elements that predict outcomes from mature systems may be absent during early system development. The time element allows for different configurations of elements that may influence high and low levels of outcome variables at different stages of the leader-follower relationship.

> **Proposition 5.** Leadership system configurations' effects on external variables at early stages of system maturity may be different than at later stages of maturity, may be relative to different time bound events or accumulated episodes, or may be cyclically transient.

ANALYTIC IMPLICATIONS OF THE FRAMEWORK

In leadership research, articles incorporating quantitative methods such as regression, structural equation modeling (SEM), and meta-analysis are among the most highly cited studies (Antonakis et al., 2014). These methods are particularly useful for modeling and testing both direct and mediated relationships. As such, they are indicative of theory and analysis in contemporary leadership studies that relate and test individual predictors or sets of independent variables to one or more mediators and dependent variables. Outcomes are stated as direct and indirect functions of leader and follower attributes and contextual measures. These analyses are often grounded in a leader centric focus that assumes that the leader's attributes or behavior has a direct main effect on the followers' outcomes.

Where leader, follower, and contextual variables are hypothesized for a joint or interactive effect incremental to their individual effects, moderation is tested using bivariate interaction variables. These tests are common to substitutes for leadership studies or studies of moderating contextual effects. It is rare that more than two variables are included in an interaction due to the analytic complexity, issues such as collinearity, and the difficulty to interpret interactions incorporating three or more variables.

An alternative to regression-based analysis has emerged in the form of fuzzy set/qualitative comparison analysis (fs/QCA). This method allows for the analysis of multiple factors simultaneously rather than considering a set of independent variables that have main or interaction effects on the dependent variables; consequently, it allows researchers to empirically derive configurations or bundles of elements that lead to equivalent levels of the outcome variable. Configurational comparative methods are particularly appropriate when researchers argue that a combination, or bundle, of factors work in concert with one another to be a sufficient cause for an outcome (Mahoney & Goertz 2006). The number of scholars investigating economic and organizational phenomena with set-theoretic methods has risen considerably in the last few years (Fiss, 2007, 2008, 2011; Grandori & Furnari, 2008; Greckhamer et al., 2008; Jackson, 2005; Kogut et al., 2004; Pajunen, 2008; Schneider et al., 2010).

A key advantage of configurational methods is the possibility of addressing multiple conjunctural causation (Ragin, 2009), which has three important implications. First, an outcome can be produced by multiple conditions. Second, fs/QCA recognizes there can be more than one combination of conditions leading to the outcome under investigation (i.e., equifinality). This ability is particularly important when it is likely or theorized that there are more ways than one to bring about the outcome or that the causal conditions combine in complex ways. The form of fs/QCA results also call attention to a multimodal form of causality that differs from unimodal determinism underlying a traditional quantitative approach. Third, fs/QCA allows for outcomes to occur as a result of the presence or the absence of a condition. Conjunctural causation is particularly useful when it is likely that there can be multiple reasons to bring about an outcome, and when causal conditions could combine in multiple ways to bring about an outcome.

Configurational comparative methods also offer a number of advantages over regression analysis (Ragin, 2009). First, evaluating how multiple factors interact to produce an outcome can be challenging with regression (Braumoeller, 2004). There is a limit to the number of interaction effects that can be included in one regression analysis. This limitation means that complex theoretical arguments might be hard to test or be even untestable. Further, if an outcome (dependent variable) occurs and the given cause (independent variable) does not, it counts as negative evidence for the strength of that causal relationship (Epstein et al., 2008, p. 68). This result means that if a factor does influence an outcome in only a handful of cases, it can become masked or invisible because of the overlap in variance explained by two or more variables.

Fs/QCA helps overcome issues associated with regression analysis by ignoring variation and distribution in variables and by not isolating the net independent effect of each variable on an outcome (Ragin, 2006). In contrast to regression analysis, configurational comparative methods can identify the causal patterns that differ across subsets of cases, allowing more complex causal narratives to be found. This distinction arises because the configurational methodology is not centered on variable distributions and the search for patterns of covariation, difference, or frequency clustering. Further, fs/QCA relaxes some of the assumptions often associated with quantitative techniques, such as permanent causality, additivity, and causal symmetry (Ragin, 2006). Instead, the technique is quite helpful in evaluating both the number and complexity of alternative paths leading to a desired outcome. However, despite all of the advantages of configurational comparative methods, an important strength of regression analysis is that it allows for assessing the average effect of a variable. This possibility is particularly relevant if the scholar's theory is centered on a particular factor and the scholar is interested in estimating how large the net impact of this singular variable on the dependent variable is.

Traditional linear models, such as regression and SEM, stand in stark contrast to emerging fs/QCA approaches both in their purpose and the information they provide. As such, they are complements rather than substitutes for the study of leadership systems and configurations. Consistent with its empirical, exploratory, and qualitative roots, configurational analysis is inductive and derives its results empirically. Consequently, theory or configural themes and explanations for patterns of relationships to outcomes are derived from the analysis. Conversely, linear models are constructed from theory to deductively test relationships. Used in tandem as mixed methods, they offer the potential to advance leadership theory and research in our understanding of multicausality (i.e., equifinality) and asymmetric causality (i.e., different configurations of cause for high levels than for low levels of a dependent variable).

A Comparative Review of Linear and Fs/QCA Analyses

An often studied variable as a correlate, mediator, or outcome to leadership is trust (e.g., Dirks & Ferrin, 2002; Dulebohn et al., 2012; Goodwin et al., 2011). As such, trust is an important opportunity to differentiate between the type of information that may be derived from a system or configurational assessment of leadership and traditional linear analyses common to the leadership literature. In this section, we provide a comparison of published research on the leadership-trust relationship and comparative re-analyses of data subjected to both linear and fs/QCA configuration assessment (Goodwin et al., 2011; Whittington & Bell, 2013, 2016; Whittington et al., 2013).

Trust's importance for sustaining individual and organizational effectiveness is well-established (McAllister, 1995; Robinson, 1996). The leader-follower relationship is no exception. When subordinates trust a leader, they are willing to be exposed to the leader's actions and are certain that their interests will not be abused (Mayer et al., 1995). When followers trust their leaders, they may exhibit more organizational citizenship behaviors and thus better equip the leader to accomplish the goals of the organization (Colquitt et al., 2007; Goodwin et al., 2011; McAllister, 1995). Trusting followers also perform better and exhibit less counterproductive behavior that may come from their intentions to quit (Colquitt et al., 2007).

Using Goodwin et al.'s (2011) data, Whittington and colleagues (Whittington & Bell, 2013, 2016; Whittington et al., 2013) subjected it to re-analysis using the fs/QCA methodology to examine the forms of configurations related to OCB, job performance, and affective commitment as well as questions of asymmetry of configurations between high and low levels of the employee outcomes. Whittington and Bell (2013) examined trust as a target or outcome variable for leadership configurations, and Whittington and Bell (2016) conducted post hoc analyses beyond their reporting that positioned trust within the leadership configuration (n.b., analysis and results detail for post hoc analyses are available from the first author). From their assessment of the Goodwin et al. data, we can examine how the approaches compared.

In the linear analysis (Goodwin et al., 2011), trust was positioned according to theory and prior research as a mediator between transformational leadership and employee outcomes. The authors reported that there was a significant, positive effect of leadership on trust and that there were positive relationships between transformational leadership and OCB, job performance, and affective commitment that were fully mediated by trust.

In the fs/QCA re-analysis of the data with trust as an outcome of the leadership system (Whittington & Bell, 2013), the authors established a leadership system of transactional leadership, transformational leadership, LMX, goal setting, and enriched job design, which reflected leader style, leader-follower relationship, and job context elements. The authors reported four bundles or configurations of leadership system elements that were related to high levels of trust. Of the four configurations, only one bundle included high levels of transformational leadership (combined with high levels of LMX). In contradiction to the linear analysis relating transformational leadership positively to trust, two of the bundles did not include transformational leadership (instead showing LMX with other elements in each), and the remaining bundle was composed of a low level of transformational leadership when combined with high levels of transactional leadership and enriched job design with low goal setting. In the examination of asymmetry, two system configurations were related to low levels of trust. Consistent with the linear analysis expectation that lower transformational leadership should be associated with lower trust, both bundles included a low level of transformational leadership as a member element, which was alternately combined with low LMX and low goal setting and with low LMX, low enriched job, and high transactional leadership.

In post hoc analysis beyond their reporting in Whittington and Bell (2016), the authors examined trust as a member of the previously defined leadership system elements (trust as an attribute of the follower) related to the outcomes of OCB, job performance, and affective commitment. Just as with the linear model assessment in which trust fully mediated the relationship between leadership and employee outcomes, trust plays a prominent role in the configurations that the authors found. For OCB as a high outcome, there were four identified configurations, of which high trust level was a member of three, and the absence (low level) of trust was a member of the fourth. Contrary to the linear assessment, high transformational leadership was a member of only one configuration, and a low level of transformational leadership was a member of two configurations. In the examination of asymmetry, two configuration bundles were associated with low OCB. Trust alternated such that it was present in both, but low in one that included low levels of all other system elements, and high in the other solution which was composed of a split among the elements at high and low levels. As expected relative to the linear analysis, transformational leadership was a member of both configurations such that its absence (low level) was associated with low levels of OCB.

For the job performance outcome, there was inconsistency and asymmetry evident in the results relative to the linear analysis. In relation to high job performance, trust acted as expected, and transformational leadership acted in contradiction. There were two configurations of which a high level of trust was a member of each; conversely, transformational leadership was neutral for one configuration and was a low level for the other. For the low-level job performance outcome, trust was inconsistent relative to the linear models findings. There were two configurations, of which trust was a member of only one, but was at a low level as expected. Transformational leadership acted as expected relative to the linear analysis in that it was a member of both configurations such that low transformational leadership was related to low job performance; however, it contrasted with the linear fully-mediated findings, because it was present even when low trust was not present.

For the affective commitment outcome, trust's membership in configurations was relatively consistent with the linear analysis and demonstrated characteristics of symmetry. Transformational leadership's membership in configurations was inconsistent and at times contrary to the findings of the linear analysis. For high affective commitment, there were five solution configurations. Trust was a member of four of the five configurations at the expected level of high trust; however, one configuration included low trust (as well as low levels for all other included leadership elements). For low affective commitment, there were four associated configurations, of which low level of trust was a member of each. Transformational leadership, on the other hand, was a member of only one configuration for high affective commitment, was absent (neutral) for two, and was at a low level for the remaining two. For low affective commitment, transformational leadership was present in all four configurations. As expected, it was at a low level in three of them, but at a high level in the fourth.

In this comparison of the linear and fs/QCA configuration analyses conducted by Whittington and colleagues, we demonstrated three important points. First, in alignment with our first proposition, whereas a linear test of a mediated model provided evidence of a single, positive indirect relationship for transformational leadership through trust to employee outcome variables, a configuration assessment showed multiple configurations for the leadership system, of which transformational leadership was not always an element in the relationship to the mediator or outcome variables.

Second, as preliminary evidence for our second and third propositions, the inclusion and direction of the transformational leadership element in configurations varied when trust was external to the system (outcome variable) versus when it was internal to the system. When trust was included in the system, it acted in a manner consistent, though not perfectly, with the expectations from the linear model. Transformational leadership, on the other hand, appeared inconsistently in configurations and in multiple cases in contradiction to the linear model predictions. As with the linear model for which trust took on a fully mediating role, in the configurational analysis, its inclusion with transformational leadership introduced a complexity in the way that they combined in the formation of leadership system bundles.

Third, consistent with our fourth proposition, the configuration analyses showed that there were asymmetries in the relationship between transformational leadership, trust, and the employee outcome variables. These asymmetries were not possible to see from the linear analysis and were in contrast to its findings such that there were instances of both the absence of a positive association and of the presence of a negative association between transformational leadership and each of the other variables.

Despite the strong support for the positive outcomes associated with transformational leadership, the results obtained through configurational analyses raise questions about the role of transformational leadership for obtaining positive employee outcomes reported in linear analyses. Transformational leadership alone was never a sufficient condition in Whittington and Bell's (2013) analyses. These analyses provided a way to evaluate a proposed system of leadership that involves the leader, the follower, and the context in which they operate as depicted in Figure 12.1.

DISCUSSION

There is a growing recognition among organizational researchers that many factors contribute to performance and that they should not be evaluated in isolation from each other. The need for this kind of research has become particularly acute in the area of leadership studies as more scholars are calling for a shift away from leader-centric approaches and encouraging the investigation of leadership as a system consisting of the leader, the follower, the context, and the relationships among each of these system components (Avolio, 1999, 2007, 2011; Kellerman, 2016; Klein & House, 1995; Padilla et al., 2007). In this chapter, we embraced this system perspective by examining configurations of leader behaviors, leader-follower relationships, and job context that may mutually enhance the ability of each to achieve important organizational outcomes (Fiss et al., 2013).

Employing a configurational approach enables examinations into how multiple factors can combine together along different paths to achieve similar outcomes (Aguilera et al., 2008; Hoskisson et al., 2009; Ward et al., 2009). Configurational approaches assume more complex and nonlinear causality where variables found to be causally related in one configuration may be unrelated in other configurations (Fiss, 2007). By using a configurational approach, we were also able to demonstrate how "multi-dimensional constellations of conceptually distinct characteristics that commonly occur together" (Fiss, 2007, p. 1180) may be asymmetrically related to important outcomes.

We examined transformational leadership paradigm within a configurational analysis. Transformational leadership is "the single most dominant leadership paradigm and also holds the top spot in terms of published articles in all the premier journals" (Antonakis & Day, 2018, p.13). Several individual studies and meta-analyses have identified strong empirical support for the linkages between transformational leadership and trust, employee performance, job satisfaction, commitment to the organization, and organizational citizenship behaviors (Banks et al., 2016; Bycio et al., 1995; Dumdum et al., 2013; Goodwin et al., 2011; Hoch et al., 2018, Howell & Avolio, 1993; Judge & Piccolo, 2004; Lowe et al., 1996; Whittington et al., 2004). These results have been impressive, yet a review of the leadership and motivation literature suggests that task and motivational factors such as enriched job design, challenging goals, transactional leadership, and quality leader-follower relationships (LMX) may be potential substitutes for transformational leadership (Kerr & Jermier, 1978; Podsakoff et al., 1996). There has been limited attention paid to examining these in conjunction with one another as components of a leadership system in a fully interactive manner. This lack of research attention may stem from methodological constraints and the difficulty of attempting to explain interactions among more than three variables with standard linear statistical techniques.

The results of the incorporation of causal asymmetry to the unified systems and configurational framework has important implications for both theory and practice. Whittington and Bell's (2013, 2016) findings suggested that low levels of employee attitudes and behaviors are not attributable to a single source, but are due to a combination of leadership and contextual factors, and those configurations of elements were different than combinations associated with high levels of employee outcomes.

Taken as a whole, our framework illustrates that leadership substitute configurations can combine in multiple ways to influence employee attitudes and behaviors. Our review of linear and configuration analysis results lent further support to the idea that leadership is best understood as an interactive system that includes leader behaviors, task characteristics, and the interpersonal aspects of the leader-follower relationship. The review and comparison of results reinforced our contention that evaluating leadership substitutes from a configurational perspective holds considerable promise as a field of inquiry for future studies. Among the many opportunities is the need for future research into explanations of why certain leader substitute combinations occur, their durability, and the contextual factors beyond those we explored here that may alter their formation.

The present study makes several important contributions to the leadership literature. First, we have addressed the criticisms of previous substitutes for leadership-based research. For instance, Villa et al. (2003) argued that many of the factors examined in earlier substitutes for leadership research were supported by a strong theoretical rationale. In response, our chapter develops and provides a framework for the major substitutes for leadership advanced in leadership literature. Furthermore, by adopting a configural-systems approach, our framework answers calls for more sophisticated research of leadership substitutes (e.g., Avolio et al., 2009).

Second, our exposition of the framework positioned the fs/QCA methodology as a complement to traditional linear analysis and provided a way to derive more complex and integrated models of leadership (Avolio 2007; Podsakoff et al., 1996). This method offers a way to conduct research that explores the possible conditions that link leadership behavior, outcomes associated with that behavior, and the situational variables (e.g., substitutes) that may impact the relationships between leader behavior and employee outcomes. These conditions include (a) a leadership main effects model, (b) a substitute's main effect model, and (c) an interactive effects model (Villa et al., 2003). The fs/QCA method provides a robust approach to exploratory data analysis and should be used in conjunction with other data analysis methods to gain a fuller understanding of the leadership system.

Third, by leveraging the fs/QCA methodology, our framework allowed us to extend the understanding of cause-effect relationships in leadership by exploring causal asymmetry. Our review of Whittington and Bell's (2013, 2016) results illustrated the presence of causal asymmetry in that the bundles of leadership system elements that lead to high levels of performance, organizational citizenship behavior, and affective commitment are in fact different from those that lead to low levels of these important outcomes. Combinations of leader substitutes that lead to high levels of one outcome can actually lead to low levels of another performance measure.

Fs/QCA methodology as a way to implement the analysis supporting the proposed framework is not without limitations. As the method currently stands, only one outcome variable or factor and roughly ten potential "causes" may be considered in a single analysis. In addition, interpreting the output from fs/QCA is not necessarily straightforward and results are subject to criticism because they are sensitive to the calibrations researchers employ. However, despite the limitations, fs/QCA is valuable in identifying and investigating interdependencies and causal complexity among factors that researchers may otherwise overlook. It necessarily must be considered as a complement to the deductive linear forms of analysis that characterize contemporary leadership research to transition it to a leadership systems perspective.

CONCLUSION

Leadership does not take place in a vacuum—it is never contextually neutral (Avolio, 1999). Our framework incorporated several related perspectives to identify seven elements of a leadership system that may combine in configurations that relate to outcomes with equifinality and asymmetry. Our comparative review of studies reporting results of alternate analysis methods applied to a common data set provided evidence to illustrate our framework's three core propositions. Our framework's fundamental message for future leadership research is that the leader, follower, and context matter interdependently, and when one element is isolated from the system, the comparison to an outcome is potentially deficient in what it can report about the true nature of the relationship.

REFERENCES

Aguilera, R. A., Filatotchev, I., Gospel, H., & Jackson, G. (2008). An organizational approach to comparative corporate governance: Costs, contingencies, and complementarities. *Organization Science, 19*, 475–492. https://doi.org/10.1287/orsc.1070.0322

Antonakis, J., Bastardoz, N., Liu, Y., & Schriesheim, C. A. (2014). What makes articles highly cited? *The Leadership Quarterly, 25*(1), 152–179. https://doi.org/10.1016/j.leaqua.2013.10.014

Antonakis, J., & Day, D. V. (2018). Leadership: Past, present, and future. In J. Antonakis & D. V. Day (Eds.), *The nature of leadership* (3rd ed., pp. 3–26). SAGE.

Avolio, B. (1999). *Full leadership development: Building the vital forces in organizations* SAGE.

Avolio, B. (2007). Promoting more integrative strategies for leadership theory-building. *American Psychologist, 62*, 25–33. https://doi.org/10.1037/0003-066X.62.1.25

Avolio, B. (2011). *Full range leadership development*. SAGE.

Avolio, B., Walumbwa, F. O., & Weber (2009). Leadership: Current theories, research, and future directions. *Annual Review of Psychology, 60*, 421–449. https://doi.org/10.1146/annurev.psych.60.110707.163621

Ayman, R., & Lauritsen, M. (2018). Contingencies, context, situation, and leadership. In J. Antonakis & D. V. Day (Eds.), *The nature of leadership* (3rd ed., pp. 138–166). SAGE.

Banks, G. C., McCauley, K. D., Gardner, W. L., & Guler, C. E. (2016). A meta-analytic review of authentic and transformational leadership: A test for redundancy. *The Leadership Quarterly, 27*(4), 634–652. https://doi.org/10.1016/j.leaqua.2016.02.006

Bass, B. M. (1985). *Leadership and performance beyond expectations*. Free Press.

Bass, B. M., & Bass, R. (2009). *The Bass handbook of leadership: Theory, research, and managerial applications*. Simon and Schuster.

Bandura, A. (1986). *Social foundations of thought and action*. Prentice Hall.

Bastardoz, N., & Day, D. V. (2022). Integrating leadership and power: A micro process model. In J. H. Dulebohn, B. Murray, & D. L. Stone (Eds.). *Leadership: Leaders, followers, and context* (Chapter 11). Information Age Publishing.

Bennis, W. G., & Thomas, R. J. (2002). *Geeks and geezers: How era, values, and defining moments shape leaders-how tough times shape good leaders*. Harvard Business School Press.

Bommer, W. H., Milevoj, E., & Biggane, J. (2022). 21st century leadership research in elite general management journals: Where the first 20 years have taken us and where we may be going. In J. H. Dulebohn, B. Murray, & D. L. Stone (Eds.), *Leadership: Leaders, followers, and context* (Chapter 3). Information Age Publishing.

Braumoeller, B. F. (2004). Hypothesis testing and multiplicative interaction terms. *International Organization, 58*, 807–820. https://www.jstor.org/stable/3877804

Burns, J. M. (1978). *Leadership*. Harper & Row.

Bycio, P., Hackett, R., & Allen, J. (1995). Further assessments of Bass's (1985) conceptualization of transactional and transformational leadership. *Journal of Applied Psychology, 80*, 468-478. https://psycnet.apa.org/doi/10.1037/0021-9010.80.4.468

Colquitt, J. A., Scott, B. A., & LePine, J. A. (2007). Trust, trustworthiness, and trust propensity: A meta-analytic test of their unique relationships with risk taking and job performance. *Journal of Applied Psychology, 92*(4), 909. https://psycnet.apa.org/doi/10.1037/0021-9010.92.4.909

Conger, J. A., & Kanungo, R. N. (1987). Toward a behavioral theory of charismatic leadership in organizational settings. *Academy of Management Review, 12*(4), 637–647. https://doi.org/10.5465/amr.1987.4306715

DeRue, D. S., & Ashford, S. J. (2010). Who will lead and who will follow? A social process of leadership identity construction in organizations. *Academy of Management Review, 35*(4), 627–647. https://doi.org/10.5465/amr.35.4.zok627

Dinh, J. E., Lord, R. G., Gardner, W. L., Meuser, J. D., Liden, R. C., & Hu, J. (2014). Leadership theory and research in the new millennium: Current theoretical trends and changing perspectives. *The Leadership Quarterly, 25*(1), 36–62. https://doi.org/10.1016/j.leaqua.2013.11.005

Dirks, K. T., & Ferrin, D. L. (2002). Trust in leadership: Meta-analytic findings and implications for research and practice. *Journal of Applied Psychology, 87*(4), 611–628. http://dx.doi.org/10.1037/0021-9010.87.4.611

Dulebohn, J. H., Bommer, W. H., Liden, R. C., Brouer, R. L., & Ferris, G. R. (2012). A meta-analysis of antecedents and consequences of leader-member exchange: Integrating the past with an eye toward the future. *Journal of Management, 38*(6), 1715–1759. https://doi.org/10.1177%2F0149206311415280

Dumdum, U. R., Lowe, K. B., & Avolio, B. J. (2013). A meta-analysis of transformational and transactional leadership correlates of effectiveness and satisfaction: An update and extension. In B Avolio & F. Yamarrino (Eds.), *Transformational and charismatic leadership: The road ahead 10th anniversary edition* (pp. 39–70). Bingley. https://doi.org/10.1108/S1479-357120130000005008

Epitropaki, O., Sy, T., Martin, R., Tram-Quon, S., & Topakas, A. (2013). Implicit leadership and followership theories "in the wild": Taking stock of information-processing approaches to leadership and followership in organizational settings. *The Leadership Quarterly, 24*(6), 858–881. https://doi.org/10.1016/j.leaqua.2013.10.005

Epstein J., Duerr D., Kenworthy L., & Ragin C. (2008). Comparative employment performance: A fuzzy-set analysis. In L. Kenworthy & A. Hicks (Eds.), *Method and substance in macrocomparative analysis* (pp. 67–90). Palgrave Macmillan. https://doi.org/10.1057/9780230594081_3

Fiss, P.C. (2007). A set-theoretic approach to organizational configurations. *Academy of Management Review, 32*, 1180–1198. https://doi.org/10.5465/amr.2007.26586092

Fiss, P. C. (2008). Case studies and the configurational analysis of organizational phenomena. D. Byrne & C. C. Ragin (Eds.), *The SAGE handbook of case-based methods* (pp. 424–440). SAGE.

Fiss, P. (2011). Building better causal theories: A fuzzy set approach to typologies in organization research. *Academy of Management Journal, 54*(2), 393–420. https://doi.org/10.5465/amj.2011.60263120

Fiss, P., Cambre, B., & Marx, A. (2013). *Research in sociology of organizations (RSO): Configurational theory and methods in organizational research*. Emerald Group. https://doi.org/10.1108/S0733-558X(2013)0000038005

George, J. M., & Jones, G. R. (2000). The role of time in theory and theory building. *Journal of Management, 26*(4), 657–684. https://doi.org/10.1016/S0149-2063(00)00051-9

Goodwin, V. L., Whittington, J. L., Murray, B., & Nichols, T. (2011). Moderator or mediator? Examining the role of trust in the transformational leadership paradigm. *Journal of Managerial Issues, 23*(4), 409–425. https://www.jstor.org/stable/23209107

Graen, G. B., & Uhl-Bien, M. (1995). Relationship-based approach to leadership: Development of leader-member exchange (LMX) theory of leadership over 25 years: Applying a multi-level multi-domain perspective. *The Leadership Quarterly, 6*(2), 219–247. https://doi.org/10.1016/1048-9843(95)90036-5

Grandori, A., & Furnari, S. (2008). A chemistry of organization: Combinatory analysis and design. *Organization Studies, 29*(3), 459–485. https://doi.org/10.1177%2F0170840607088023

Greckhamer, T., Misangyi, V. F., Elms, H., & Lacey, R. (2008). Using qualitative comparative analysis in strategic management research: An examination of combinations of industry, corporate, and business-unit effects. *Organizational Research Methods, 11*(4), 695–726. https://doi.org/10.1177%2F1094428107302907

Griffin, R. (1982). *Task design: An integrative approach*, Scott, Foresman and Company.

Hirak, R., Peng, A., Carmeli, A., & Schaubroeck, J. (2012). Linking leader inclusiveness to work unit performance: The importance of psychological safety and learning from failures. *The Leadership Quarterly, 23*(1), 107–117. https://doi.org/10.1016/j.leaqua.2011.11.009

Hoch, J. E., Bommer, W. H., Dulebohn, J. H., & Wu, D. (2018). Do ethical, authentic, and servant leadership explain variance above and beyond transformational leadership? A meta-analysis. *Journal of Management, 44*(2), 501–529. https://doi.org/10.1177%2F0149206316665461

Hoskisson, R. E., Castleton, M. W., & Withers, M. C. (2009). Complementarity in monitoring and bonding: More intense monitoring leads to higher executive compensation. *Academy of Management Perspectives, 23*(2), 57–74. https://doi.org/10.5465/amp.2009.39985541

Hostede, G. (1991). *Cultures and organizations: Software of the mind*. McGraw-Hill.

Howell, J. & Avolio, B. (1993). Transformational leadership, transactional leadership, locus of control, and support for innovation: Key predictors of consolidated-business-unit performance. *Journal of Applied Psychology*, 78, 891–902. https://doi.org/10.1037/0021-9010.78.6.891

Howell, J., Dorfman, P. & Kerr, S. (1986). Moderator variables in leadership research. *Academy of Management Review, 11*, 88–102. https://doi.org/10.5465/AMR.1986.4282632

Jackson, G. (2005). Employee representation in the board compared: A fuzzy sets analysis of corporate governance, unionism and political institutions. *Industrielle Beziehungen, 12*(3), 252–279. https://www.jstor.org/stable/23277235

Jonason, P. K., & Webster, G. D. (2010). The dirty dozen: A concise measure of the dark triad. *Psychological Assessment, 22*(2), 420–432. https://doi.org/10.1037/a0019265

Judge, T. A., & Bono, J. E. (2001). Relationship of core self-evaluations traits—self-esteem, generalized self-efficacy, locus of control, and emotional stability—with job satisfaction and job performance: A meta-analysis. *Journal of Applied Psychology*, *86*(1), 80. https://doi.org/10.1037//0021-9010.86.1.80

Judge, T. A., & Piccolo, R. F. (2004). Transformational and transactional leadership: a meta-analytic test of their relative validity. *Journal of Applied Psychology*, *89*(5), 755–768. https://doi.org/10.1037/0021-9010.89.5.755

Kanungo, R. N., & Mendonca, M. (1996). *Ethical dimensions of leadership*. SAGE.

Katz, D. & Kahn, R. L. (1966). *The social psychology of organizations*. Wiley.

Kellerman, B. (2004). *Bad leadership: What it is, how it happens, why it matters*. Harvard Business Review Press.

Kellerman, B. (2012). *The end of leadership*. Harper Business.

Kellerman, B. (2014). *Hard times: Leadership in America*. Stanford University Press.

Kellerman, B. (2016). Leadership—It's a system, not a person! *Daedalus*, *145*(3), 83–94. https://doi.org/10.1162/DAED_a_00399

Kellerman, B. (2018). *Professionalizing leadership*. Oxford University Press.

Kerr, S., & Jermier, J. (1978). Substitutes for leadership: Their meaning and measurement. *Organizational Behavior and Human Performance*, *22*, 375-403. https://doi.org/10.1016/S1048-9843(97)90011-4

Klein, K. J., & House, R. J. (1995). On fire: Charismatic leadership and levels of analysis. *The Leadership Quarterly*, *6*(2), 183–198. https://doi.org/10.1016/1048-9843(95)90034-9

Kogut, B., MacDuffie, J. P., & Ragin, C. (2004). Prototypes and strategy: Assigning causal credit using fuzzy sets. *European Management Review*, *1*(2), 114–131. https://doi.org/10.1057/palgrave.emr.1500020

Lichtenstein, B. B., & Plowman, D. A. (2009). The leadership of emergence: A complex systems leadership theory of emergence at successive organizational levels. *The Leadership Quarterly*, *20*(4), 617–630. https://doi.org/10.1016/j.leaqua.2009.04.006

Lord, R. G., & Maher, K. J. (2002). *Leadership and information processing: Linking perceptions and performance*. Routledge.

Lowe, K. B., Kroeck, K. G., & Sivasubramaniam, N. (1996). Effectiveness correlates of transformational and transactional leadership: A meta-analytic review of the MLQ literature. *The Leadership Quarterly*, *7*(3), 385–425. https://psycnet.apa.org/doi/10.1037/0021-9010.89.5.755

Lunsford, L. G., Padilla, A., & Mulvey, P. (2022). Destructive leadership episodes: Why can't we learn from them? In J. H. Dulebohn, B. Murray, & D. L. Stone (Eds.) *Leadership: Leaders, followers, and context* (Chapter 10). Information Age Publishing.

Luthans, F., Peterson, S. J., & Ibrayeva, E. (1998). The potential for the "dark side" of leadership in post–communist countries. *Journal of World Business*, *33*(2), 185–201. https://doi.org/10.1016/S1090-9516(98)90005-0

Mahoney, J., & Goertz, G. (2006). A tale of two cultures: Contrasting quantitative and qualitative research. *Political Analysis*, *14*(3), 227–249. doi:10.1093/pan/mpj017

Mayer, R. C., Davis, J. H., & Schoorman, F. D. (1995). An integrative model of organizational trust. *Academy of Management Review, 20*(3), 709–734. https://doi.org/10.5465/amr.1995.9508080335

McAllister, D. J. (1995). Affect-and cognition-based trust as foundations for interpersonal cooperation in organizations. *Academy of Management Journal, 38*(1), 24–59. https://doi.org/10.5465/256727

McClean, S. T., Barnes, C. M., Courtright, S. H., & Johnson, R. E. (2019). Resetting the clock on dynamic leader behaviors: A conceptual integration and agenda for future research. *Academy of Management Annals, 13*(2), 479–508. https://doi.org/10.5465/annals.2017.0081.

Meuser, J. D., Gardner, W. L., Dinh, J. E., Hu, J., Liden, R. C., & Lord, R. G. (2016). A network analysis of leadership theory: The infancy of integration. *Journal of Management, 42*(5), 1374–1403. https://doi.org/10.1177/0149206316647099

Osborn, R. N., Hunt, J. G., & Jauch, L. R. (2002). Toward a contextual theory of leadership. *The Leadership Quarterly, 13*, 797–837. https://doi.org/10.1016/S1048-9843(02)00154-6

Padilla, A. (2012). *Leadership: Leaders, followers, and environments*. Wiley.

Padilla, A., Hogan, R., & Kaiser, R. B. (2007). The toxic triangle: Destructive leaders, susceptible followers, and conducive environments. *The Leadership Quarterly, 18*(3), 176–194. https://doi.org/10.1016/j.leaqua.2007.03.001

Pajunen, K. (2008). Institutions and inflows of foreign direct investment: A fuzzy-set analysis. *Journal of International Business Studies, 39*(4), 652–669. https://doi.org/10.1057/palgrave.jibs.8400371

Podsakoff, P., MacKenzie, R., & Bommer, W. (1996). Transformational leader behaviors and substitutes for leadership as determinants of employee satisfaction, commitment, trust, and organizational citizenship behaviors. *Journal of Management, 22*, 259–298. https://doi.org/10.1016/s0149-2063(96)90049-5

Podsakoff, P. M., Niehoff, B. P., MacKenzie, S. B., & Williams, M. L. (1993). Do substitutes for leadership really substitute for leadership? An empirical examination of Kerr and Jermier's situational leadership model. *Organizational Behavior and Human Decision Processes, 54*(1), 1–44. https://doi.org/10.1006/obhd.1993.1001

Porter, L. W., & McLaughlin, G. B. (2006). Leadership and the organizational context: Like the weather? *The Leadership Quarterly, 17*, 559–576. https://10.1016/j.leaqua.2006.10.002

Pundt, A. (2014). A multiple pathway model linking charismatic leadership attempts and abusive supervision. *Zeitschrift für Psychologie, 222*(4), 190–202. https://doi.org/10.1027/2151-2604/a000186

Ragin, C. C. (2006). Set relations in social research: Evaluating their consistency and courage. *Political Analysis, 14*, 291–310. doi:10.1093/pan/mpj019

Ragin, C. C. (2008). *Redesigning social inquiry: Fuzzy sets and beyond.* University of Chicago Press.

Ragin, C. C. (2009). Qualitative comparative analysis using fuzzy sets (fsQCA). *Configurational comparative methods: Qualitative comparative analysis (QCA) and related techniques, 51*, 87–121. https://dx.doi.org/10.4135/9781452226569.n5

Robinson, S. L. (1996). Trust and breach of the psychological contract. *Administrative Science Quarterly*, 574–599. https://www.jstor.org/stable/2393868

Robinson, D., Perryman, S., & Hayday, S. (2004), *The drivers of employee engagement.* Institute for Employment Studies, Brighton.

Rush, M. C., Thomas, J. C., & Lord, R. G. (1977). Implicit leadership theory: A potential threat to the internal validity of leader behavior questionnaires. *Organizational Behavior and Human Performance, 20*(1), 93–110. https://doi.org/10.1016/0030-5073(77)90046-0

Saks, A M. (2006). Antecedents and consequences of employee engagement, *Journal of Managerial Psychology, 21*(7), 600–619. https://doi.org/10.1108/02683940610690169

Schneider, M. R., Schulze-Bentrop, C., & Paunescu, M. (2010). Mapping the institutional capital of high-tech firms: A fuzzy-set analysis of capitalist variety and export performance. *Journal of International Business Studies, 41*(2), 246–266. https://doi.org/10.1057/jibs.2009.36

Shamir, B., House, R.J., & Arthur, M.B. (1993). The motivational effects of charismatic leadership: A self-concept based theory. *Organization Science, 4,* 1–17. https://doi.org/10.1287/orsc.4.4.577

Short, J.C., Payne, G.T., & Ketchen, D.J. (2008). Research on organizational configurations: Past accomplishments and future challenges. *Journal of Management, 34,* 1053–1079. https://doi.org/10.1177/0149206308324324

Sosik, J. J., Avolio, B. J., & Kahai, S. S. (1997). The impact of leadership style and anonymity on group potency and effectiveness in a GDSS environment. *Journal of Applied Psychology, 82,* 89–103. https://doi.org/10.1037/0021-9010.82.1.89

Sy, T. (2010). What do you think of followers? Examining the content, structure, and consequences of implicit followership theories. *Organizational Behavior and Human Decision Processes, 113*(2), 73–84. https://doi.org/10.1016/j.obhdp.2010.06.001

Thoroughgood, C. N., Sawyer, K. B., Padilla, A., & Lunsford, L. (2018). Destructive leadership: A critique of leader-centric perspectives and toward a more holistic definition. *Journal of Business Ethics, 151,* 627–649. https://doi.org/10.1007/s10551-016-3257-9

Villa, J. R., Howell, J. P., Dorfman, P. W., & Daniel, D. L. (2003). Problems with detecting moderators in leadership research using moderated multiple regression. *The Leadership Quarterly, 14*(1), 3–23. https://doi.org/10.1016/S1048-9843(02)00184-4

Ward, A., Brown, J., & Rodriguez, D. (2009). Governance bundles, firm performance and the substitutability and complementarity of governance mechanisms. *Corporate Governance, An International Review, 17*(5), 646–660 doi:10.1111/j.1467-8683.2009.00766.x

Whittington, J. L., & Bell, R. G. (2013). Evaluating substitutes for transformational leadership: A configurational perspective. *Academy of Management Annual Meeting Proceedings.* https://doi.org/10.5465/ambpp.2013.11523abstract

Whittington, J. L., & Bell, R. G. (2016). Leader–member exchange, enriched jobs, and goal-setting: Applying fuzzy set methodology. *Journal of Business Research, 69*(4), 1401–1406. https://doi.org/10.1016/j.jbusres.2015.10.115

Whittington, J. L., Goodwin, V. L., & Murray, B. (2004). Transformational leadership, goal difficulty, and task design: Independent and interactive effects on employee outcomes. *The Leadership Quarterly, 15*(5), 593–606. https://doi.org/10.1016/j.leaqua.2004.07.001

Whittington, J. L., McKee, V., Goodwin, V. L., & Bell, R. G. (2013). Applying fuzzy set methodology to evaluate substitutes for leadership. In P. C. Fiss, B. Cambré, & A. Marx (Eds.), *Research in sociology of organizations (RSO): Configurational theory and methods in organizational research, 38* (pp. 279–302). https://doi.org/10.1108/S0733-558X(2013)0000038016

Wofford, J. C., Goodwin, V. L., & Whittington, J. L. (1998). A field study of a cognitive approach to understanding transformational and transactional leadership. *The Leadership Quarterly, 9*(1), 55–84. https://doi.org/10.1016/S1048-9843(98)90042-X

Yukl, G. (2012). *Leadership in organizations* (8th ed.). Prentice-Hall.

Zhao, H. & Li, C. (2019). A computerized approach to understanding leadership research. *The Leadership Quarterly, 30*(4), 396–416. https://doi.org/10.1016/j.leaqua.2019.06.001

ABOUT THE AUTHORS

Nicolas Bastardoz is a Senior Research Associate and chair of Human Resource Management and Leadership of the University of Zurich, Switzerland. He holds a PhD thesis from the Faculty of Business and Economics at the University of Lausanne. He is currently acting as Associate Editor and Methods Advisor of *The Leadership Quarterly*. His research has been published in *Leadership Quarterly*, *Annual Review of Organizational Psychology and Organizational Behavior*, *Organizational Research Methods*, among other journals. His research interests span two broad domains: Leadership (and particularly charisma) and Quantitative methods.

R. Greg Bell, PhD, is Professor of Management and Associate Dean of Faculty Affairs at the University of Dallas Gupta College of Business. His areas of research include corporate governance, international entrepreneurship, and corporate sustainability. His work has been published in journals including the *Academy of Management Journal*, *Journal of International Business Studies*, *Strategic Management Journal*, and *Entrepreneurship Theory and Practice* among others.

Jonathan Biggane is an Associate Professor in the department of management at California State University, Fresno. He holds a PhD from the University of Memphis in Organizational Behavior and an MBA from the University of North Carolina Wilmington. His work has been published in leading journals such as *Human Resource Management Review* and the *Journal of Business and Psychology*. He also serves as a reviewer and subject matter expert for prominent journals in the fields of Human Resources and Organizational Behavior.

Isabel Bilotta, MA, is a PhD student in Industrial-Organizational Psychology at Rice University. Her research centers on achieving equity and inclusion for individuals with varied identities, backgrounds, and perspectives in the workplace. She also examines the roles that leaders play in effectively managing diverse employees and creating inclusive organizational cultures. As a consultant with NASA's behavioral performance group, she provides the astronaut selection committee with critical information related to the equitable assessment and selection of astronaut candidates.

William H. (Bill) Bommer is currently a professor of organizational behavior and leadership at California State University, Fresno. At CSU Fresno, he is also the Director of the Craig International Program. He holds a PhD in Organizational Behavior from Indiana University and a master's degree in Organizational Development from Bowling Green State University. He has published over 60 research articles and three books. His research has been published in a number of leading academic journals including *Journal of Applied Psychology, Academy of Management Journal, Academy of Management Learning & Education, Journal of Organizational Behavior, Organization Science, Organizational Behavior and Human Decision Processes, Personnel Psychology, Journal of Vocational Behavior, Journal of Business Ethics, Leadership Quarterly*, and the *Journal of Management.* His current research focuses on leadership in the organizational setting with a primary focus on positive forms of leadership and leadership development. In addition to his publication record, Dr. Bommer has presented more than 75 research papers at national or international professional meetings.

Julio C. Canedo is an associate professor of management at the Marilyn Davies College of Business of the University of Houston Downtown. He earned a PhD degree in Organization and Management Studies from the University of Texas at San Antonio. He is certified in coaching, human resource management (HRM), and ethics. An HRM practitioner for 10 years and consultant in organizational performance for over 15 years. He also served in student affairs for six years and was a computer systems developer for one year. His research interests include strategic HRM, leadership, HRM, e-HRM, organizational behavior, and cross-cultural issues at work. He has published in *Organizational Dynamics, Research in Human Resource Management,* the *Journal of Managerial Psychology, AIS Transactions on Human-Computer Interaction,* the *Journal of Business and Entrepreneurship, Oxford University Press, TIP The Industrial-Organizational Psychologist,* and the *Business Journal of Hispanic Research.* He has presented his work at national and regional conferences of the *Academy of Management* and in sponsored corporate events in Latin America. He founded Results Alignment (http://www.resultsalignment.com), a consulting company focused on enhancing organizational performance through the strategic alignment of individual contributions.

James Carlson received his bachelor's degree from Brigham Young University and his master's degree from Texas Tech University. His academic research interests have spanned business ethics, creativity, leadership, and stakeholder theory. His research has been published in a variety of outlets, including *Academy of Management Review.* He has worked as a consultant and developed software for academics and the private sector, most recently for startups in the "Silicon Slopes" of Utah. He is currently a software engineer at Lendio, a leading provider of small business financing solutions.

Shannon K. Cheng, MA, is a PhD student in Industrial-Organizational Psychology at Rice University. Her research interests focus on diversity, inclusion, and well-being from a multilevel perspective—working to understand the individual-level and what challenges marginalized individuals are experiencing at work, the interpersonal-level and how people from different backgrounds can better serve as allies for each other, and the organization-level and how organizations can create more inclusive cultures and policies that support employee performance and well-being.

Claudia C. Cogliser is professor of management and Area Coordinator for the Area of Management at Texas Tech University. Cogliser earned her doctorate in business administration with a concentration in organizational behavior from the University of Miami in 1997. She has won numerous research and teaching awards and contributed chapters to several books. Her scholarly work focuses on leadership, sexual harassment, and research methods and has been cited over 7,000 times in scholarly outlets. Her research has been published in peer-reviewed journals including the *Journal of Management, The Leadership Quarterly, Journal of Organizational Behavior*, and *Group & Organization Management*

Trevor Cox is an Assistant Professor of Organizational Leadership at the University of Central Oklahoma (UCO) and the Assistant Chair for the Department of Adult Education and Safety Sciences. His main research areas are Inclusive Leadership, leadership development, and Transformative Learning. He has presented at the Academy of Management, International Leadership Association, and International Transformative Learning conferences on these topics and continues to write and teach in the area. As a practitioner he is an active member of the Diversity Committee at UCO working on strategic DEI initiatives and does consulting with individuals and organizations on diversity, inclusion, equity, and adult education.

David V. Day is Professor of Psychology and Academic Director of the Kravis Leadership Institute at Claremont McKenna College (USA). He also holds the titles of Steven L. Eggert '82 P'15 Professor of Leadership and George R. Roberts Research Fellow at the College. He has held previous professorial appointments at the University of Western Australia, Singapore Management University, Penn State University, and Louisiana State University. He is a Fellow of the American Psychological Association, American Psychological Society, International Association of Applied Psychology, and the Society for Industrial and Organizational Psychology. Dr. Day has published more than 100 peer-reviewed journal articles, books, and book chapters, many pertaining to the core topics of leadership and leadership development. His research has been published in the *Journal of Applied Psychology*, *Personnel Psychology*, *Academy of Management Journal*, *Journal of Management*, *Leadership Quarterly*, among other journals. He serves on numerous editorial boards and as the Editor of *The Leadership Quarterly Yearly Review*. In 2010, he was awarded the Walter F. Ulmer Research Award from the Center for Creative Leadership for outstanding, career-long contributions to applied leadership research.

James H. Dulebohn, PhD, is professor of human resources and organizational behavior at Michigan State University. His research interests include leadership, virtual teams and team-centric organizations, organizational justice, eHRM, and employee compensation and benefits. His work has been published in journals including *Academy of Management Journal*, *Personnel Psychology*, *Journal of Management*, and *Journal of Applied Psychology* among others. He also has served as coeditor and author for the research volumes in the IAP series on Research in Human Resource Management including *The Only Constant in HRM Today is Change*, *The Brave New World of eHRM 2.0*, and *Human Resource Management Theory and Research on the New Employment Relationships*. He earned his doctorate from the University of Illinois.

William L. (Bill) Gardner is the Paul Whitfield Horn Distinguished Professor, the Jerry S. Rawls Chair in Leadership. and the Director of the Institute for Leadership Research in the Rawls College of Business at Texas Tech University. Additionally, he serves as an Associate Editor for *The Leadership Quarterly*. He received both his doctorate and MBA degrees from Florida State University. He is a dedicated teacher whose courses include leadership, business ethics, organizational behavior, research methods, group dynamics, and management history within the undergraduate, masters, working professionals, and doctoral programs. His research focuses on authentic and charismatic leadership, leadership development, business ethics, and social influence processes within organizations. He has published extensively in peer-reviewed journals such as the *Academy of Management Review, Academy of Management Journal, Group & Organization Management, The Leadership Quarterly, Journal of Management, Journal of Management Studies,* and the *Journal of Organizational Behavior.*

Miriam Grace is a Technical Fellow and Senior Systems Architect responsible for Business/Technology Strategy for the Boeing Company Enterprise Sales and Marketing technology portfolio. Miriam is a Certified Business Architect, focusing on value delivery across the extended Boeing global enterprise. She is a frequent contributor to scholarly journals and publications addressing professional design opportunities and challenges and their relationship to leadership directions for the 21st century. She has a master's degree in Whole Systems Design and PhD in Design Leadership.

George B. Graen is a Chief Scientist at the LMXLOTUS specializing in "no fear" alliance through collaboration training of executive team coaches. He was a faculty member of the University of Illinois at CU, the University of Cincinnati, Keio University, Tokyo, Japan, Nagoya University, Nagoya, Japan, University of Science and Technology, Hong Kong. George is the father of the dominant scientific structural equation model of the development of team excellence through learning about and practicing unique strategic alliance (USA) in professional teams. He has published over 150 professional papers and books. George has concentrated his international research on Eastern organizations especially Nippon and Peoples Republic of China. George believes that the future of business lies with organizations that provide psychologically safe and socially meaningful new work experience (NWX).

Daniel P. Gullifor is an assistant professor in the College of Business at the University of Wisconsin–Eau Claire. He received his PhD from Texas Tech University, and his Bachelor of Science and Master of Business Administration from Bradley University. His research focuses on leadership, the impostor phenomenon, and core self-evaluations and has been published in such scholarly outlets as the *Journal of Management, The Leadership Quarterly, Journal of Social Psychology,* and *Research in Personnel and Human Resources Management.* In both 2017 and 2018, the Rawls College of Business recognized his research contributions with the Outstanding Contributions to Research as a Doctoral Student Award.

Andrew Johnson is an associate professor of management at Texas A&M University–Corpus Christi. He earned a PhD degree in Organization and Management Studies from the University of Texas at San Antonio with a concentration in Strategic Management. His primary areas of research are the impact of social change on organizations, political ideology in the workplace, and corporate political activity. He has prior experience in state and local government. His research is published in *Journal of Management*, *Journal of Organizational Behavior*, *Human Resource Management Review*, and *Business & Society*.

Eden B. King, PhD, is the Lynette S. Autrey Professor of Industrial-Organizational Psychology at Rice University. Dr. King is pursuing a program of research that aims to make work better for everyone. This research—which has yielded over 100 scholarly products and has been featured in outlets such as the *New York Times*, *Good Morning America*, and *Harvard Business Review*—addresses three primary themes: (1) current manifestations of discrimination and barriers to work-life balance in organizations, (2) consequences of such challenges for its targets and their workplaces, and (3) individual and organizational strategies for reducing discrimination and increasing support for families. In addition to her scholarship, Dr. King has partnered with organizations to improve diversity climate, increase fairness in selection systems, and to design and implement diversity training programs. She is currently coeditor of the *Journal of Business and Psychology* and the immediate past-President of the Society for I-O Psychology.

Gary P. Latham is the Secretary of State Professor of Organizational Effectiveness in the Rotman School of Management, University of Toronto. He has cross appointments in the Department of Psychology, Industrial Relations, and School of Nursing. He is a Fellow of the Academy of Management (AoM), Association for Psychological Science (APS), the American Psychological Association (APA), Fellow and Past President of the Canadian Psychological Association, Division 1 (Work and Organizational Psychology) of the International Association of Applied Psychology, and the Society for Industrial-Organizational Psychology (SIOP). He is also a Fellow of the National Academy of Human Resources, and the Royal Society of Canada. He is the recipient of such awards as: Distinguished Contributions to Psychology both as a Science and a Profession (SIOP), Life- time Achievement awards from both the Human Resources Division and Organizational Behavior (AoM), Scholar-Practitioner award (AoM), the James McKeen Cattell Award (APS), and the Losey award for life-time achievement of scientific research to human resource problems from the Society for Human Resource Management (SHRM). He has served on the boards of the Center for Creative Leadership, SHRM, and currently the SHRM Foundation. He is the current editor of *Organizational Dynamics*.

Edwin A. Locke is Dean's Professor of Leadership and Motivation Emeritus at the R.H. Smith School of Business, University of Maryland. He is a Fellow of the Association for Psychological Science (APS), the American Psychological Association, the Society for Industrial & Organizational Behavior, and the Academy of Management. He is the recipient of the Distinguished Scientific Contribution Award (Society for I/O Psychology), the Lifetime Achievement Award from the Academy of Management (OB Division), the J. M. Cattell Award (APS) and the Distinguished Scientific Contribution Award from the Academy of Management. He, with Gary Latham, has spent over 50 years developing goal setting theory, ranked No. 1 in importance among 73 management theories. The full theory building process for goal theory is reported (w. Latham) in *Organizational Psychology Review*, 2020, pp. 1–17. He has published over 320 chapters, articles, reviews, and notes, and has authored, coauthored or edited 16 books including (w. Latham) *A Theory of Goal Setting and Task Performance* and *New Directions in Goal Setting and Task Performance*; *The Prime Movers: Traits of the Great Wealth Creators*; and (w. Kenner) *The Selfish Path to Romance*. He is internationally known for his research on motivation, job satisfaction, leadership, and the philosophy of science. His work has been influenced by Ayn Rand's philosophy of Objectivism.

Brook Lu, BA in psychology, graduated from Rice University in 2020. She is currently pursuing M.Ed. in Mental Health Counseling at University of Pennsylvania. Her undergraduate research focuses on work self-efficacy in working mothers, and gender and racial discrimination in the workplace.

Laura Lunsford earned her PhD at NC State University in social and community psychology. She wrote the *Handbook for Managing Mentoring Programs*, coedited the *SAGE Handbook of Mentoring*, and coauthored *Faculty Development in Liberal Arts Colleges*. She has written over 40 peer-reviewed articles, case studies and chapters on leadership and mentoring. She coauthored one of National Academies of Sciences most downloaded reports *The Science of Effective Mentorship in STEMM*. Her work has appeared in journals such as *Mentoring & Tutoring*, *Journal of Higher Education Policy and Management*, and *To Improve the Academy*. Lunsford has presented on mentoring and leadership at conferences hosted by scholarly associations including the Association for Psychological Science, American Educational Research Association, European Mentoring and Coaching Council, and International Positive Psychology Association. The Department of Education, National Science Foundation, and the LUCE Foundation has funded her work. She was honored with the 2009 International Mentoring Association's Dissertation Award. She has held numerous academic leadership position at NC State University, University of Arizona, Duke

University's Fuqua School of Business, and at the Cameron School of Business at UNC Wilmington. She is an assistant dean and professor of psychology at Campbell University; she was previously a tenured faculty member at the University of Arizona. She consults with organizations on effective mentoring and coaching.

Emil Milevoj, DBA, is the Executive Director of the Lyles Center for Innovation and Entrepreneurship at Fresno State and an assistant professor in the Department of Management at the Craig School of Business. Before joining Fresno State, he worked for several start-up companies. In his previous role, he also served as the Director of the University Business Center at Fresno State where he launched numerous professional development and degree completion programs. He earned his Doctor of Business Administration from Henley Business School, University of Reading, United Kingdom in international business. Dr. Milevoj also earned an MBA from California State University, Fresno. He has received numerous grants and contracts from the U.S. Department of Education, Small Business Administration, Office of Traffic Safety, U.S. Department of Agriculture, U.S. Department of Commerce, and numerous other organizations and foundations. His research interests include innovation, global leadership, gender, international and social entrepreneurship. Dr. Milevoj has also published articles on the success of study-abroad programs and SMEs' internationalization. He has also presented at numerous national and international academic and professional conferences.

Paul Mulvey earned a PhD in Labor and Human Resources from The Ohio State University and a bachelor's degree in Psychology from Lehigh University. His research focuses on toxic leadership, employee reward systems, work teams, recruitment, and organizational culture. He has written two books on reward systems, published book chapters and research articles in journals such as *Academy of Management Journal*, *Industrial Relations*, *Journal of Social Psychology*, *Small Group Research* and *Organizational Behavior and Human Decision Processes*. His research has been funded by the Sustainability Initiative, WorldatWork, TIAA-CREF, Sibson & Company, IBM, and the Council of Labor Research. Mulvey has conducted research, delivered executive education, and consulted with over 60 organizations and has won numerous teaching awards. He has served as an expert witness human resources issues and is a member of WorldatWork, the Association for Talent Development (ATD), the Society for Industrial and Organizational Psychology (SIOP), and the Academy of Management. Mulvey is an Alumni Distinguished Professor in the Department of Management, Innovation, & Entrepreneurship at the Poole College of Management at North Carolina State University in Raleigh, North Carolina.

Brian Murray, PhD, is associate professor of management in the Satish & Yasmin Gupta College of Business at the University of Dallas. He was formerly the university's vice president and CFO and was board president for CARES, a multiple employer self-funded healthcare benefits association. His research includes studies of employee benefits, retirement savings behavior, skill-based pay, leadership and performance management, and work implications for employees who are family caregivers for individuals with special needs. His work has been published in journals including the *Academy of Management Journal*, *Personnel Psychology*, *The Leadership Quarterly*, *Decision Sciences*, and *Human Resource Management Review* among others. He earned his PhD from Cornell University.

Art Padilla. Professor Art Padilla earned his bachelor's degree at NC State University in Raleigh and his PhD at UNC-Chapel Hill. Dr. Padilla served as professor and head of the Management department at NC State before moving to Tucson, AZ where he taught at the Eller College of Management of the University of Arizona. Previously, Dr. Padilla taught at UNC-Chapel Hill and served as academic vice president in the 17-campus University of North Carolina, administering the review and establishment of scores of graduate and undergraduate academic programs across the 17 UNC campuses. He has written about leadership and management, both in professional journals and in the *Washington Post*, *New York Times*, and *Chronicle of Higher Education*. Presidential search committees use his 2005 book, *Portraits in Leadership*. He published *Leadership: Leaders, Followers, and Environments* in 2016. In 2006, he was awarded the Holladay Medal, the highest faculty honor at NC State University. He has won two Fulbright Scholarships, one to Argentina and one to the Dominican Republic, where he also served as economic advisor to the President of the Dominican Republic. During 1980–81 he was a Brookings Institution fellow in Washington, DC, and worked with the transition teams between presidents Carter and Reagan.

Terri A. Scandura is the Warren C. Johnson Endowed Chair and Professor of Management in the Miami Herbert Business School at the University of Miami. From 2007 to 2012, she served as Dean of the Graduate School at the University of Miami. Her fields of interest include leadership, mentorship, and applied research methods. She has been a visiting scholar in Japan, Australia, Hong Kong, China and the United Arab Emirates. Dr. Scandura has authored and co-authored hundreds of presentations, articles, and book chapters. Her research has been published in the *Academy of Management Journal*, the *Journal of Applied Psychology*, the *Journal of International Business Studies*, *Organizational Research Methods*, the *Journal of Management*, *The Leadership Quarterly*, and others. Her book, *Organizational*

Behavior: An Evidence-Based Approach, 3rd edition is published by SAGE Publications. She is a Fellow of the Society for Industrial & Organizational Psychology, the American Psychological Association, and the Southern Management Association. She has received a number of prestigious awards including the Research Methods Division Distinguished Career Award, Academy of Management, the J.G. Hunt Sustained Outstanding Service Award, Southern Management Association, and the Senior Research Award, Miami Herbert Business School,

James M. Schmidtke (PhD, University of Illinois at Urbana-Champaign) is a professor at California State University Fresno Craig School of Business and the Chairperson for the Department of Management. His research focuses on sexual harassment, workplace discrimination, organizational deviance, diversity, and virtual teams. He has published in a variety of journals in human resources, management, and psychology.

Monica M. Sharif is an Assistant Professor of Management in the College of Business & Economics at California State University, Los Angeles. Prior to this position, she spent time as an Assistant Professor at San Francisco State University and Morgan State University. Monica received her PhD in Business Administration, Management from University of Miami, Herbert Business School and her Bachelor of Science from University of California, Irvine. Monica's research focuses on leadership, ethics, cross-cultural diversity and justice. Her work has been published in top journals including *The Leadership Quarterly* and *Journal of Business Ethics*. Monica has received multiple research grants including from CIBER (Center for International Business Education), Center for Blockchain and Financial Technology sponsored by Ripple and the Arsht Center for Ethics.

Dianna L. Stone received her PhD from Purdue University, and is now a Research Professor at the University of New Mexico, a visiting professor at the University at Albany, and an affiliate professor at Virginia Tech. Her research focuses on diversity and cross-cultural issues in organizations, reactions to selection techniques, privacy in organizations, and the use of electronic human resource management and artificial intelligence in human resource management. She has published over 100 articles, books, and book chapters, and results of her research have been published in the *Journal of Applied Psychology, Personnel Psychology, The Academy of Management Review, Journal of Management*, and *Human Resource Management Review*. She is the Editor of *Research in Human Resource Management* (with James Dulebohn), and is a former Editor of the *Journal of Managerial Psychology* and the Associate Editor of *Human Resource Management Review*. She received the Scholarly Achievement Award and the Janet Chusmir Sage

Service Award from the Gender and Diversity Division of the Academy of Management, and received the Trailblazer Award from the PhD Project. She is also a Fellow of the Society for Industrial and Organizational Psychology, the Association for Psychological Science, and the American Psychological Association.

Fred O. Walumbwa (PhD, University of Illinois at Urbana-Champaign) is the Knight-Ridder Byron Harless Endowed Eminent Scholar Chair and a professor at the Florida International University College of Business, Department of International Business, United States. His research focuses on leadership, positive organizational behavior and scholarship, organizational climate and justice, strategic human resource management, and cross-cultural issues in management. He has published widely in a variety of journals in business, management, and psychology.

J. Lee Whittington, PhD, is Professor of Management at the University of Dallas. He focuses his teaching, research, and consulting in the areas of Leadership, Organizational Behavior, and Spiritual Leadership. His research has been published in *The Leadership Quarterly, Academy of Management Review, Journal of Management, Journal of Organizational Behavior, Research in the Sociology of Organizations, Journal of Management, Spirituality, and Religion, Journal of Business Strategy, Journal of Applied Social Psychology, Journal of Managerial Issues,* and the *Journal of Business Research.* He is the author of *Biblical Perspectives on Leadership and Organizations, Enhancing Employee Engagement: An Evidence-Based Approach* (with Simone Meskelis, Enoch Asare, and Sri Beldona) and *Leading the Sustainable Organization* (with Tim Galpin and Greg Bell). While serving as the Dean, J. Lee led the effort for initial accreditation of the University of Dallas College of Business by the *Association to Advance Collegiate Schools of Business (AACSB International)*. He has received multiple awards including the *Haggerty Teaching Excellence Award, Gupta College of Business Award for Innovation, and Gupta College of Business Outstanding Faculty Member.* He has extensive consulting, executive coaching, and leadership development experience with organizations including Life.Church, Nokia, Siemens, FedEx Kinko's, and several government and not-for-profit organizations.

Margaret L. Williams, PhD, is dean of the Jerry S. Rawls College of Business Administration at Texas Tech University. She served as dean at two prior institutions before joining Texas Tech in 2017. Prior to her service in academic administration, Williams was a management faculty member teaching human resources, organizational behavior, and research methods at undergraduate, masters, and doctoral levels at Purdue University, Virginia Commonwealth University, and Wayne State University.

Her research, published in top management and psychology journals, has focused on employee motivation and leadership, diversity and inclusion, and compensation and benefits.

www.ingramcontent.com/pod-product-compliance
Lightning Source LLC
LaVergne TN
LVHW052223200926
848481LV00001B/201